MANAGERIAL ECONOMICS FOR THE SERVICE INDUSTRIES

MANAGERIAL ECONOMICS FOR THE SERVICE INDUSTRIES

Philip H. Bowers

Department of Business Studies
University of Edinburgh, UK.

CHAPMAN & HALL

University and Professional Division

London · Glasgow · Weinheim · New York · Tokyo · Melbourne · Madras

Published by Chapman & Hall, 2–6 Boundary Row, London SE1 8HN, UK

Chapman & Hall, 2–6 Boundary Row, London SE1 8HN, UK

Blackie Academic & Professional, Wester Cleddens Road, Bishopbriggs, Glasgow G64 2NZ, UK

Chapman & Hall GmbH, Pappelallee 3, 69469 Weinheim, Germany

Chapman & Hall USA, One Penn Plaza, 41st Floor, New York NY 10119, USA

Chapman & Hall Japan, ITP-Japan, Kyowa Building, 3F, 2–2–1 Hirakawa-cho, Chiyoda-ku, Tokyo 102, Japan

Chapman & Hall Australia, Thomas Nelson Australia, 102 Dodds Street, South Melbourne, Victoria 3205, Australia

Chapman & Hall India, R. Seshadri, 32 Second Main Road, CIT East, Madras 600 035, India

First edition 1994

© 1994 Philip H. Bowers

Typeset in Times by Florencetype Ltd, Kewstoke, Avon

Printed in Great Britain by Alden Press, Osney Mead, Oxford

ISBN 0 412 57790 9

A catalogue record for this book is available from the British Library

Library of Congress Catalog Card Number: 94-072018

∞ Printed on permanent acid-free text paper, manufactured in accordance with ANSI/NISO Z39.48–1992 and ANSI/NISO Z39.48–1984 (Permanence of Paper).

Contents

Preface

This book was written during a year's sabbatical – for which my hearty thanks to the University of Edinburgh and the Department of Business Studies. It represents my attempt to devise an appropriate framework for managerial economics applicable to the service industries. As with any change in emphasis, the first offering is potentially contentious and I hope it will attract sufficient attention to promote debate on the subject. In writing it, I have had in mind my discussions with the highly intelligent managers whom I meet regularly in the course of the MBA programmes at the Edinburgh University Management School, as well as undergraduates and colleagues. I hope any debate will be widely based and will include practitioners as well as economists. In pursuit of this goal every attempt has been made to avoid unnecessary technicalities, and this itself could be contentious.

Acknowledgements

My thanks go to colleagues at the Department of Business Studies, notably to Professors John Dawson, Lyn Thomas and Andrew McGosh, and to Ian Sams and Jonathan Crook for helpful discussions and support.

Particular thanks are due to my wife, Alison, who not only bore the brunt of the self-absorption that this sort of work involves, and supported me throughout, but also provided help by taking down some of the material directly on the keyboard, and did a considerable amount of copy editing of the final draft. It still amazes me that someone without detailed knowledge of economics could provide such helpful and penetrating comments. As she did not manage to read the whole work, any infelicities of language, as well as errors of fact or theory, remain entirely my responsibility.

Introduction

The incentive for attempting to look at managerial economics in the context of service industries rather than manufacturing stemmed from the experience of living and working in an environment, in Edinburgh, dominated by the service industries. Much of the economic theory which seemed relevant to me remains inaccessible to those I meet, because although it is available in separate sources, no attempt seems to have been made to unify the ideas conceptually or to provide a reader which pulls together the very disparate bibliographic resources. Not only were the sources often difficult to obtain in the libraries but they were often uncompromisingly addressed to the economics profession: for example, while the *Journal of Industrial Economics* is reasonably widely obtainable, Christopher Bliss's work on the rules for profit maximizing in retailing is cast in a form that most students of management would find difficult to absorb, much less apply. Similarly, discussions of profit maximizing which assume fully divisible output, rather than the two-stage optimization process suggested in Chapter 9, cause at the very least difficulties of communication and many real difficulties of application, although Straszheim provided a suitable model in 1974.

Conventional managerial economics seems inappropriate in a second area: it ignores the often variable quality, and in many cases the inherent information asymmetry, in services. This results, at least in part, from the very nature of services – they are unstorable, so they often require the presence of both seller and purchaser in order for 'production' to take place; this means that they involve elements of human interaction with all its potential for pleasure or pain, depending at least in part on the quality of communication. Thus, in this book, information availability in general and information asymmetry in particular form part of the discussion in many chapters.

The presence of the human element in so many services has two other major consequences. Firstly, location and the partially related aspect of time become very important, in ways different from manufacturing. Thus we have to emphasize both, particularly in Chapter 4 (Demand) and in the chapters relating to market structure, since spatial competition becomes important. Secondly, the 'solipsistic and unboundedly rational consumer' with fixed tastes is so far from reality that alternative views at least need to be discussed, particularly where interpersonal relations are an intrinsic part of the production process. Thus, Chapters 3 and 4 both consider the nature of interpersonal relationships within the economic system – in Chapter 3 in relation to the different modes of behaviour implied by personal, political and market relationships, and in the later sections of Chapter 4 in relation to more 'psychological' approaches to consumer demand.

It will be noticed that ordinal utility theory as applied to consumption decisions is barely touched upon in this book, in contrast to the normal practice. This is no accident; it seemed to yield no insights beyond those implicit in the demand curve, and hence to be a burden rather than a help to managers – and one of the only certainties about human beings is that they are social animals. Thus, the usual assumption of independent utility functions is 'heroic'; in other words, it is implausible but makes the theory easier to develop. It is probably dangerous in the managerial context, since many decisions both about products and about employment will in fact be lifestyle decisions, as discussed in Chapter 4 in relation to Earl's work, and therefore heavily related to what other people think, and, finally, since we are interested in managerial decisions and not public policy except in so far as it affects these, this theoretical simplification is unlikely to be needed.

The use of utility theory is justified by the 'derivation' of individual demand curves and hence market demand curves. However, we need not abandon the use of demand curves or functions; nor do we need to go as far along the reductionist road as Becker, whose minimalist approach shows that it is likely that consumers will reduce consumption of a product that has become more expensive in relation to others. This, and the insight that the extent of reduction would depend on substitutability, can be derived from the directions implied by the basic psychological insights of cardinal utility theory and the most general notions of utility maximization and rationality. The problem with ordinal utility theory is the overelaboration of these insights, which only takes us further forward at the cost of losing relevance and insight.

For most of the existing books on managerial economics, the New Institutional Economics, with its emphasis on transactions costs and the limits of the firm, is at best a peripheral consideration. Since at least some of the growth of the service industries is due to the separation of previously internal services into independent organizations, this approach is given more emphasis here. It also provides a basis for deciding what should be contracted out to franchises and what the firm needs to retain as its core activities. This is an issue in modern manufacturing as well as in services, but has particular pertinence in the context of the contracting out of previously public-sector functions. Thus Chapter 5 discusses the Markets and Hierarchies paradigm, and tries to apply it in the context of consultancy services.

The chapters on costs follow a very different path from the discussions usual in managerial economics texts. I believe that many services have short-run marginal costs which are zero, or include only the costs of purchased inputs. This completely alters the basis of discussion. For the analysis of costs in the longer run, methods using isoquants belong with utility theory. The continuous curves are not the way in which the problem presents itself to the manager, and have implicit in them the unwarrantable assumption that technology is constant. The manager faces a choice of schemes, and these require the application of project appraisal techniques. These are briefly discussed in Chapter 7. This chapter has been written on the assumption that anyone serious about this topic should be taking courses on project evaluation and/or corporate finance. Thus, the details of project evaluation are left to those courses, and only an outline is presented here. This is true with the exception of the sections on risk, particularly in relation to the theory of subjective utility; more emphasis is given to this since it is often omitted from project appraisal texts and courses.

The discussion of economies of scale, and the impacts of costs on industrial structure, in Chapter 8 seems relevant to the service sector but it had to be derived entirely from studies based on manufacturing industry because of the lack of data on service industries. Additional emphasis is given to the issues of network economies and what are called in this book 'economies of connectivity'; this term is not drawn from the literature, but the concept seems useful to me.

Chapter 9 (Monopoly and Monopolistic Competition) differs from the usual in its emphasis firstly on the use of the optimal markup as the basis for decisions rather than the purely hypothetical – though theoretically invaluable – demand curve. This approach is extended to operationalize the ideas of Bliss on the setting of retail prices by the use of the optimal markup as modified for use in profit maximization under average price regulation.

Secondly, profit maximization in most services is seen as a two-stage operation. The first stage is to maximize revenue in the case of zero marginal costs for the individual consumer; the second is to optimize the level of service to be provided, which is where the marginal costs of service provision enter the equation. The twin ideas of marginal revenue as normally conceived and of the marginal revenue of service are thus necessary in the analysis of situations in which the units of production differ from the units of consumption. For example, a bus with a capacity of 80 seats has to be put on for a complete route, whereas the passenger only wants a single seat for part of the way. Discussions of this often use the concept of a load factor, but since that is an average measure it has only limited economic significance.

Thirdly, this chapter takes issue with the idea of monopolistic competition and follows the 'Address Branch', which generally suggests spatial oligopoly. It certainly raises questions about the use of the 'representative consumer' in any spatial context. Indeed, the difficult work of this school of monopolistic competition may be as fecund in papers and as limited in potential managerial application as utility theory and the theory of long run production functions.

These themes are taken up and extended in Chapter 10 (Oligopoly). This chapter forms, it is hoped, a basis for the discussion which follows on competition policy and regulation. The emphasis on policy as a managerial variable, which can be influenced by the appropriate application of funds or political leverage, again provides a contrast to normal treatments.

The last two chapters, on transport and health services, provide topical examples of some of the ideas presented in the rest of the book.

Size and importance of the service industries

2

2.1 INTRODUCTION

This chapter aims to set out some of the broad facts relating to the development of the service industries, and some of the theories that have been advanced to explain their development. One might properly ask why this is included in a text devoted to managerial economics. The manager in the modern context needs not only to be master of the technical details of management, but also of the political implications of his position. It is important to be able to take a view of the desirability of service industries, and to be able to combat such government initiatives as the now long abandoned Selective Employment Tax (SET), which provided a tax on services since these were seen as parasitical. While SET is a thing of the past, its modern equivalents live on in programmes for the encouragement of manufacturing, rural assistance and so on.

The first view we shall consider is the Clark–Fisher hypothesis. This essentially states that services represent a development in the industrial structure of nations which is likely to absorb a larger and larger proportion of the workforce because of the combined effects of (i) the income-elastic nature of the demand for services, and (ii) their limited potential for technical progress. They are therefore liable to strangle the very growth that gives rise to the increase in demand. This view appears to gain support from the data of Kuznets (1966), and is incorporated into a formal model by Baumol (1977). The difficulty of relying on services as an engine of growth is taken up by Mayes (1987) on the basis of the problems of exporting services. The continued decline of manufacturing would provide an ever-increasing constraint to national economic growth due to balance of payment problems.

In section 2.3, we shall consider some of the different types of services within the sector to look at their development and potential, and with a view to pointing out the major areas of applicability of different themes of the book.

2.2 SERVICES AND MANUFACTURING: THE CRUCIAL DIFFERENCE

The size of service industries in national employment and income terms would appear to be reason enough to justify the writing of a book about them. However, this is not the basis on which this book was written since there might nevertheless be no difference in the economic theory applicable to the service and manufacturing sectors. If that were the case, the mere window dressing involved in applying the theory to firms and replacing the word 'goods' with the word 'services' would be a waste of time. Thus, it is crucial that there should be differences in the characteristics of the two sectors that make it worthwhile to consider the services separately.

The crucial difference between manufacturing and services is that all services are unstorable, although their consequences may last for a long time. Thus electricity at present cannot be stored, except at heavy relative cost in batteries, or pumped storage schemes. But, in general, the actual process of service production is either immediately taken up by the consumer, e.g. the electric power is used, or it is useless and must be dumped as heat. In the context of garage services or education, if there is no customer, there is no service, only the potential to provide a service. The consumer is thus necessary for production to take place: consumption and production are generally simultaneous and inseparable, most obviously so in the cases of restaurants, education and sport.

The fact that services are unstorable makes it more important to manage their consumption and production through time. Thus, various forms of price discrimination are practised to encourage consumers to purchase during the periods of spare capacity. Increases in the flexibility of employment conditions have also been a major gain for such service industries as supermarkets, where people can now be employed to cope with peak periods and do not need to be employed for the whole day. Technical progress may also be designed to bypass the capacity bottleneck, with beneficial implications for the profits of those who get there first or operate the new technology most effectively. An example of the use both of flexible labour and the new technology of computers and telecommunications is the phenomenal growth and success of the First National Bank, with its complete substitution of these means of communication for the labour and space intensive branch offices of traditional banks.

Given the property of unstorability, decisions to provide a service are more in the nature of capital investment decisions (including such investments as publicity and training) than the short-run production decisions that feature heavily in economics text books. Like the investment decision, the producer's decision is almost always in different units to the consumer's decision; in manufacturing the producer must decide on a complete production facility, for example a production line, whereas the consumer is only interested in single units of output, such as a car or a washing machine. This problem is more acute in the services, where even the short-run decisions, such as whether to put on an extra bus or open another checkout counter, come in units that are not of interest to the consumer, who is interested in only one seat for part of the route, or putting a basket of shopping through the checkout. This means that even short-run decisions are of a different type in service industries. This is discussed particularly in Chapter 6 on short-run costs, and in most of the subsequent chapters.

The service that provides the apparent exception to the unstorability rule and which therefore 'proves' it (in its proper sense in this context of 'testing' the rule) would seem to be insurance, where policies are taken out in much the same way as items are bought in a shop. The enrolment and the provision of the policy document itself is serviced largely at the insurance company's leisure (at least in my experience) and therefore seems like a manufactured item with a production time, relatively speaking, under the manufacturer's control. However, this is not so: firstly, cover is usually established from the moment an application form is handed in and the premium paid, and, secondly, the service comes from the provision of that cover, and the servicing of it has to follow the requirements of claims under the insurance. It is no accident that complaints against insurance companies follow largely from tardy service, as well as from attempts by the insurance company to avoid what the insured consider to be their rights; this is an example of a second major difference between manufactured goods and services: the level of uncertainty and the intangible nature of the service. This is, however, not such a clear difference, and it is certainly not a necessary one.

In contrast to the property of 'unstorability', intangibility is not a necessary condition for being a service, but it is a frequent one. For example, the purchase of electricity is neither uncertain nor intangible; however, most other services do have strong intangible attributes. This does not, of course, distinguish them from many industrialized products: a car or any other 'experience good' has many attributes that only emerge after considerable experience of the use of the good. The difference is often that services are not reproducible in the same way as a manufactured item, since they involve elements of human communication. Almost all of the personal services or business-to-business advisory services are of this type. Individuals go away changed in some way, for example by medical treatment, which may or may not have the desired effect, and where one can often not detect whether it is the treatment or the body's own functions that determine the outcome. In business services, the advice may be 'hard' in the form of a report containing clear information only available to the consultant or someone of different training and experience to the client, or it may involve little more than reassurance or some token of effort made towards solving the problem. The 'outcome' depends crucially on the aptness of the advice – in other words, both the quality of the advice and the ability of the recipient to use and absorb it. This may be vitiated by inability to comprehend, because although the advice is good, it is too far from the recipient's experience to be useful, or because the environment within which the recipient works will not allow the particular solution, because of power play by other members of the organization, or because the consultant has misunderstood the context.

A further example is provided by restaurant meals, which have a tangible element but also strong intangible ones in the form of the atmosphere and the taste given to the particular dish. This leads to an element of uncertainty, which it may pay the producer to try to reduce as much as possible by 'industrializing the service' as is done in many fast food chains, where much effort is devoted to gaining consistency in taste, texture and presentation, and even in the decor of the outlets. The automation of bank transactions by cash machines, and of insurance policy applications by pre-prepared application forms which the client fills in relatively unaided are likely to be driven by the need to reduce labour costs, but have the advantage of standardizing the service.

The intangible and often individual nature of many services makes many of the normal measures of output, and hence productivity, problematic. Perhaps the most extreme case is in government and professional services, where one cannot measure output in any meaningful way. This has led to suggestions that services are not subject to productivity growth and – in the more extreme views – to the suggestion that they are parasitic activities. The rest of this chapter is devoted to material on the growth of services and the debates about this issue.

2.3 SIZE AND GROWTH

The Clark–Fisher hypothesis suggests that economies will go through certain stages in the course of growth. At low levels of income, an economy will be predominantly agricultural; as income increases, because of technical developments and consequently increased productivity in agriculture, surpluses of both agricultural produce and agricultural labour will be created, which can then move to manufacturing. As progress is made in manufacturing – and historically this supported agricultural progress by improved machinery and in more recent times by the development of fertilizers – manufacturing will take over as the largest employer. Manufacturing is subject to the same process as agriculture, with technical changes leading to ever greater productivity, and hence creating more and more income per capita, and freeing labour for the service industries. These are seen as both recipients of labour, which implies lower productivity, and as the source of desirable 'products', which means that they are income-elastic, and hence proportionately more is demanded as incomes increase. This pattern fits for the European countries, but not for either North America or any of the Asian countries, all of which moved directly from agricultural dominance to service dominance in terms of employment (Elfring, 1988, p. 29).

Kuznets (1966) illustrates this pattern in the UK and the USA as shown in Table 2.1. It will be noticed that the share of output is consistently well above that of employment, which implies that value added per employee is higher in services than elsewhere in the economy. This seems surprising if one is thinking of services as domestic service and restaurants; however, much of the income will come from the highly skilled professional services of medicine, law, banking and accountancy, and some from property companies and the major trading companies. Generally speaking, labour markets should work to keep incomes approximately the same across different sectors, since there would otherwise be a strong tendency to switch from the more poorly paid to the better paid; this not only controls the workers in times of excess labour, since their wages will be bid down by the 'reserve army of the unemployed', but also the employers, since they must pay the going wage. This tendency to equal wages could be expected not to happen in the cases of both professional services, as a consequence of long training and the historic grip of associations such as the BMA on entry into their professions, and manufacturing where there was strong unionization. There was no such unionization in most of the periods listed in Table 2.1.

Table 2.1 Service industry shares in employment and output in the UK and USA

	Year				
UK	*1841*	*1901*		*1921*	*1951*
Labour force (%)	34	37		38	38
Output (%)	44	48		44	39
USA	*1870*	*1910*	*1918–1928*	*1950*	*1961–1963*
Labour force (%)	19	27		43	
Output (%)	47		50		53

Source: Kuznets, *Modern Economic Growth: Rate, Structure and Spread*; published by Yale University Press, 1966.

The growth of service sector employment is common to all of the countries surveyed – Sweden, Norway, Australia and Japan as well as the two mentioned in the table. The pattern of growth in the share of total output is much less clear. Growth of share was recorded for all periods examined in the USA from a high initial level, and in Japan from a very low one; decline of share was recorded throughout in Germany and Australia to 1956 and 1939, respectively; in the UK there was a period of increasing share between 1841 and 1901, but a decline otherwise until 1955; in France there was mainly an increase in share; in Norway share increased up to 1910 and declined from then until 1956. We can see, therefore, that the domination of services is not a foregone conclusion if one considers output rather than employment.

Kuznets sees increasing shares of output coming from the shift to distribution implied by the increasing scale, and hence local concentration, of manufacturing industry. The classic paper showing this interrelationship is by D.G. Janelle (1969), in which he demonstrates the balance that is continually being revised between transport and distribution costs and the gains from centralization of production. According to Kuznets, 'The role of trade, and finance to some extent, in bridging the gap between centralized and steady production and dispersed and variable demand, has obviously increased, while the higher per capita consumer income has added to the demand for labour-consuming services, particularly in retail trade' (1966, p. 150). Secondly, he sees the increase in

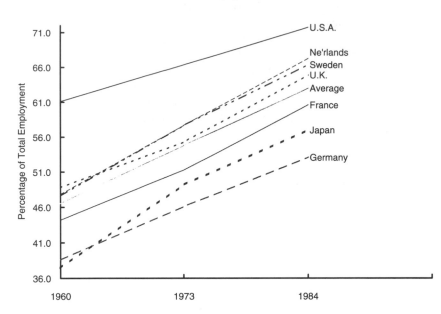

Figure 2.1 Total employment in services as a percentage of total employment.

urbanization as requiring both increased sanitation, health and policing, and hence increased local government. The increased complexity of trade and production necessitated increased national government, even before the two world wars increased the need for soldiery. We have noted, as he does, the income elasticity of recreation, health, education and other professional services; he adds the increased need for repair facilities to match the increase in consumer durables: 'The two latter trends probably more than outweigh the decline in the supply and use of paid domestic service'.

Before considering the implications of this pattern of development in more detail it is worth noting that an analysis based on a huge cross-section of countries in the post-war period by Hollis Chenery (1979) supported the generality of the Clark–Fisher hypothesis. Chapter 1 gives the main supporting material. Elfring's (1988) major study of service industry employment provides data and discussion of the trends and their causes for the period 1960–1984 for seven advanced nations. This is essential reading for those wishing to know more of the pattern of service sector employment. The continued growth of the sector is vividly shown in Figure 2.1.

2.4 SERVICE SECTOR PRODUCTIVITY

The major policy debate has concentrated on the presumed low rate of increase in productivity in the service sector. It is often assumed that because of the personal interaction required in many services increases in productivity will be low, and that therefore the 'service economy' will be one where growth rates will slow down, and the whole economy will eventually stagnate. The neatest analysis of this approach is provided by Baumol (1977). Using four simple assumptions, he shows how costs will increase in the service sector relative to the manufacturing sector; the assumptions are:

1. He divides economic activities into two sectors:
   1: those where there is zero productivity increase;
   2: a technologically progressive sector.
   The difference between the two is defined largely by the role played by labour. In sector 1 labour is an intrinsic part of the process of production; as this is one of the key factors in our definition of the service industries, it is not surprising that sector 1 can be seen as the service sector. Baumol cites the fact that in education teachers cannot be substituted by machines, and that you cannot speed up the production of a string quartet. (Whether in the twentieth century or Mozart's time, four players still have to learn the score and practise together to achieve a satisfactory performance. The process cannot be speeded up significantly.) In critique of Baumol, however, we should point out that you can provide considerable support for teachers by machines, whether through computers or such things as audio-visual equipment. These can, one hopes, speed up the learning process, and thus the amount of output is increased. However, this will not result in any measured increase in productivity if the same number of teachers is required per pupil. Thus we come again to the problem of measuring output. In the case of the string quartet, the use of broadcasting or recording can greatly increase the output, if we measure it by the number of people who can listen to that performance. For sector 2, however, labour is a cooperant factor with capital, and hence is subject to improvements in technology embodied in the capital, as well as those involved in the organization of production.

2. For ease of exposition, all costs other than labour are ignored. Thus the price of a good is its labour input multiplied by the wage.

3. Wage rates will be common to both sectors, since otherwise there would be transfers of labour to the more highly paid work.

4. Again for ease of exposition, he assumes that wages will rise at the rate of output per worker in the technologically progressive industry. (This is essentially the doctrine put out by Mrs Thatcher, and one can see from this model that it causes cost inflation or that pay in the progressive sectors will move smartly ahead of the others and hence should attract extra labour to those sectors. This could be desirable if there are skill requirements for those sectors such that people have to decide in advance what skills to train for, and if there are initially shortages of those skills. If there are no shortages, however, it will merely cause wastage in training and disappointment.) For a constant

price level, pay rates would have to move in line with average productivity of the economy as a whole. The actual level of wage increases will be determined by the labour market; the important point in this model is however *not* the price level, but the relative prices of the output of the two sectors.

With these four assumptions, Baumol shows that the price of output of sector 1 (relative to sector 2) goes up by the rate of growth of productivity in sector 2. (Wages go up in both sectors, but the amount of output per unit of labour is increasing by the rate of growth of productivity in the sector. This is zero in sector 1, and positive in sector 2. Thus the price of sector ii output would remain constant.)

What happens to demand for sector 1's output? Clearly, if it is sensitive to price it will decline relative to the demand for sector 2's output. This will therefore offset the decline in demand for labour, which would otherwise take place in sector 2. This provides a possible explanation for the decline in demand for domestic servants; Baumol is very concerned about the possible declines in demand for such things as high class restaurants, theatre and the arts, and for the problems of financing education and so on – hence his subtitle, 'the anatomy of urban crisis'.

He further asks about the effects on the national growth rate, particularly if the share of output in the two sectors remains constant. Clearly, if the two remain constant less and less labour will be required to produce the output of sector 2, since the amount each worker can produce is increasing continually. Thus with ever declining amounts of labour employed in sector 2, and a larger and larger proportion of the labour employed in sector 1, where there is no growth of output per person, the overall growth rate will decline; it will be the weighted average of that of the two sectors. A numerical example may help to explain:

Assume that each sector has a 50% share of output and of workers, and that productivity increases at the sensational rate of 20% per period in sector 2.

At the end of the first period, the output of sector 1 would be 50 but the output of sector 2 would be $50 + 0.2 \times 50 = 60$.

That is no longer equal shares, and so half of the extra output would need to have been produced by sector 1, thus 5 extra workers would have transferred to sector 1, leaving 45 in sector 2, who are still producing 50% of the output. Unfortunately this simple arithmetic only holds in the first period, and not completely accurately there. Thereafter, the basis for comparison of the productivity of the two sectors has shifted; the manufacturing sector starts the next year with an output per worker of 1.2 units, and so it is no longer sufficient to transfer surplus workers to services; one must actually take extra workers to maintain the service sector's output at 50% of the total. The mathematics for doing this are set out in Appendix 2.A. The effect of this is, however, to reduce the growth of output, as more and more highly productive manufacturing workers are needed to prop up the output of the service industries to maintain the equal share.

This makes the point very clearly that it is dangerous to have an excessive share of output in unprogressive industries. However, is it of policy significance? Baumol points out that unless propped up by state intervention or very high income elasticities of demand, or extreme insensitivity to price, demand for the unprogressive sector's output will decline as it becomes relatively more expensive. Thus if the output is still demanded in spite of its price, it must be highly desirable, and as such should be produced in a free market economy.

If the government is causing the rise in demand, there are two possible poles. Firstly, it is appropriate for the government to produce the service, and it is a desirable service in the sense that people would choose to have it in spite of its cost. In this case, while it may cause difficulties of financing and politics, it should be produced. The opposite pole is the use of resources in undesirable ways for political ends. For example, in the period 1959 to 1981, the numbers employed in health and education, both overwhelmingly public sector activities, very nearly doubled (Allen, 1988, p. 99, table 3.1). Few would doubt the desirability of a healthier and better educated workforce, and some of the increase – at least in education – will be the direct result of the baby boom of the mid-1960s and failure to find a way out of the limits on the productivity of teachers. However, the present educational reforms indicate doubt about the quality of the education, and hence its value for money, particularly in view of the continual decline in our manufacturing competitiveness in those years. In the field of health, the issues again turn on value for money, though this is a much more difficult debate, and we will return to it in the final chapter. It was these concerns that prompted Bacon and Eltis (1976) to suggest that the government was the cause of the decline in manufacturing, by crowding out manufacturing through absorption of labour into services. This has been heavily contested, since during the period in which they were writing, unemployment had been increasing, whereas their hypothesis would suggest constraints from labour shortage (see, for example, Allen, 1988).

The second concern about the policy relevance of the Baumol model is the question of whether in fact the service sector is necessarily 'unprogressive'. Elfring (1988, p. 65) shows the annual average growth rate of 'joint factor productivity' in the USA over the period 1960–1984 to have been almost the same for services in general and for industry; the average annual growth rate for industry was 0.76% and that of the service sector 0.73%. Total factor productivity measures the growth of value added from the sector divided by the total expenditure on inputs of both labour and capital. The usual measure of productivity is labour productivity, which includes only the output per worker. Thus if, as in the USA, the increase in capital stock is lower in the services than in manufacturing, the labour productivity measure overstates the gain in manufacturing. Thus the 1.57% annual rate of labour productivity growth in manufacturing compares with a 1.08% rate in services. This level of growth represents a 25% increase in output per person over 20 years for services as against a 36.6% increase in manufacturing. Thus, while not as fast as manufacturing, the rate of growth is still impressive in services, even in a country with relatively low rates of productivity growth.

Mayes (1987, p. 54, table 5) quotes the UK figures for the growth of output per full-time equivalent worker for manufacturing and various services that were developed by Murfin. These are reproduced in Table 2.2. He also points out that the shift from coal production to oil for energy provision has produced enormous gains in that sector. More generally, we should expect some growth in productivity in most sectors, and spurts of growth as major new techniques are exploited in very particular areas. A good example is provided by the growth of productivity in retailing reported by Amin Rajan (1987, pp. 43–46), where he quotes productivity increases of 3% p.a. in the period 1955–1965, 3.7% in the following decade, and 5% in the decade from 1975 to 1985. Both of the decades from 1965 were characterized by actual falls in employment and a shift towards both female and part-time employment. It seems unlikely that it will be possible to keep up this rate of growth of productivity, unless a new technology as powerful as the combination of self-service and electronic point of sale (EPOS)/electronic funds transfer at point of sale (EFTPOS) becomes available.

Table 2.2 Trend growth rate for output per worker

	Index of output per full-time worker (%)	
Sector	*1971–1985*	*1979–1985*
All industries and services	1.79	2.38
Manufacturing	2.19	4.73
Distribution, hotels, repairs and catering	−0.03	0.82
Transport	1.72	3.05
Communications	3.47	3.44
Banking, finance and insurance	2.57	2.81

Source: Mayes, 'Does manufacturing matter?' *National Institute Economic Review*, November 1987.

Not only is the case against the service industries as 'technologically unprogressive' not proven, therefore, but even within this set of arguments there is some reason to believe that there is considerable bias against the service industries as the result of the way in which the figures are calculated. Firstly, as we have seen, some bias is introduced by the omission of the capital element in the calculation of productivity; there is reason for calculating joint rather than merely labour productivity. This is not normally done, because most countries do not even have an estimate of the capital stock of each sector, and there is a long history of controversy as to what such a stock would mean. Secondly, in many of the figures we have to rely on 'jobs' or 'persons employed' as the denominator in the calculation of output per person. In a sector with a higher share of part-time employees, this can be seriously misleading, particularly if there is a trend towards increased use of part-time workers. Thirdly, many of the services provide the necessary infrastructure for manufacturing, and, indeed, there is a lot of anecdotal evidence (Elfring, 1988; Rajan, 1987) of the shift towards subcontracting of service activities by manufacturing firms. This allows greater freedom of operation and the development of economies of scale, and, in the UK at least, the application of different norms of employment contract for the service sector workers than would have been possible within the relatively unionized manufacturing sector. This shift thus represents a move from manufacturing to services of workers in the lower paid functions such as cleaning and catering and a resulting improvement in the output per manufacturing worker, and potentially a worsening of the output per service sector worker. In recent times in the UK this trend has been exacerbated by the cutting of wages and conditions to many of these workers. Fourthly, some of the service industries provide direct inputs into the improvements in manufacturing technology; this is clearest in the software development and consulting industries, and in the transport and communications sector. It has long been realized that improvements in manufacturing usually imply greater localization of production, and must therefore be complemented with transport and communications to move the output to dispersed consumers.

In summary, this debate about the 'progressiveness' of the service sector is in this author's view wholly sterile. There is always a real issue about government sponsored overproduction, whether it be in the field of armaments, bought from the private manufacturing sector, or created by government corporations, or in the field of social and educational services of whatever variety. There is also always an issue about productivity in any sector, since technological improvements in efficiency are the basis for real growth, and are required to enable an economy to adapt to changes in the environment, whether these are the need to combat the greenhouse effect, urban congestion or threats from new sources of production in lower wage or higher technology countries. However, careful investigation is needed into whether government intervention is desirable or likely to be effective; it can all too often be the result of either firms or social groups lobbying for special treatment. In the case of the service sector, or any such wide general group, any sort of blanket prejudice, positive or negative, is dangerous since there are major interactions between the sectors. These interactions are dominated by market forces, which mostly push towards greater efficiency provided a reasonable degree of competition reigns. Thus constraining them is always liable to produce perverse results. The recent rush into the financial sector following deregulation in the UK, with its very high salaries and apparent overstaffing, seems now to be returning to a more normal level of activity and remuneration. The market does not guarantee against such aberrations, indeed it seems to be strongly disposed towards them, but they are a reflection of the speed of adaptation to new situations, and it seems we still have no better means of economic governance.

2.5 EXPORTS OF SERVICES

More recent concerns have been related to the problems of exports. Services now provide about one-third of total exports, and are still in surplus, although that surplus is narrowing. This however, still leaves manufacturing with two-thirds, and it is difficult to see a rapid transformation to further increases in service sector exports to compensate for manufacturing export declines. This argument is put forward by Mayes (1987).

The structure of UK imports and exports of services can be found from the Pink Book (Central Statistical Office, 1992, table 1.3 current account, pp. 16–17). The data for 1991 are given in Table 2.3.

Table 2.3 UK international trade in services, 1991 (£ million)

Services	Credits (£m)	Debits (£m)	Balances (£m)
General government	412	2808	−2396
Private sector and public corporations			
Sea transport	3658	3643	15
Civil aviation	3927	4397	−470
Travel	7165	9825	−2660
Financial and other services	16540	6039	10501
Interest, profits and dividends			
General government	1763	1897	−134
Private sector and public corporations	75906	75443	463
Transfers			
General government	4894	5943	−1049
Private sector and public corporations	1900	2200	−300
Total invisibles	116164	112195	3969
Of which private sector and public corporations			7849
Total credits (including visible trade)	219577	225898	−6321

Source: Central Statistical Office, *The Pink Book 1992: United Kingdom Balance of Payments*; published by HMSO, 1992.

It can be seen that the UK has benefited considerably from the liberalization of trade in financial services. It is interesting to note that despite British Airways' success in returning to profit and its aggressive expansion, UK citizens still spend more on overseas air transport than is received from abroad. Travel now also accounts for a substantial loss to the UK; this follows a long period from 1968 to 1981 when it was in credit.

The tourism industry poses one of the most interesting examples of public service dilemmas. It is almost impossible to conceive of any tourist who relies entirely on an experience provided solely by a single private firm. There may be an island somewhere wholly owned and run by a company which provides such an all inclusive package, but in almost all other cases it is the combination of private facilities in hotels and other accommodation, and the environment of the place that forms the overall experience. This is made up of the attractions which may be the focus of the visit, but it also includes the impact of the pleasantness and friendliness of the local restaurants and cafes, the quality of public and private transport, and the cleanliness and beauty of the urban environment. Since this is such a diffuse network of contributors and beneficiaries, it is a moot point whether public agencies have a role in promoting and facilitating tourism. The problems of incentives in such a potentially ill-focused agency, the issues relating to public goods, externalities and regulation in Chapter 3, and agency theory in Chapter 5, are all challenging. Equally, without the deliberate use of such assets, and hence advertising and, potentially, filling in of the missing elements of the network, it is likely that they will not be used to their full potential, and that no one individual or even group of individuals will (i) gain enough and (ii) be able to stop others 'free-riding' on their efforts – in other words, benefiting from their expenditures. To put it concretely, if local firms get together to advertise their area, how can they stop the tourists going to those who have refused to participate? It is possible to blame our shift from credit to debit in international travel on the lack of promotion by our tourist authorities (economics of advertising), our declining urban environment (externalities and public goods), the strength of the pound (price effects on demand), the fear of travel induced by terrorism (changes in tastes in demand), international competition in the form of improved facilities elsewhere (cross-elasticities in demand), or the desire for foreign travel by UK citizens due to increased income (income elasticities of demand) and the desire for stimulation (Scitovski's theory of demand; see Chapter 4).

2.6 DISTRIBUTION OF EMPLOYMENT WITHIN THE SERVICE SECTOR

The distribution of employment between the various major categories of services is discussed in Elfring (1988). The varieties of proportion are interesting in this context but some generalizations are in order before discussing the differences between countries. Firstly, it is the producer services and social services, which includes government, that have provided the major growth in service sector employment (Figure 2.2). On average, producer services provided 25% of the growth in service sector employment, and social services provided 50% (see Elfring, 1988, table V.4, p. 112). As can be seen, both distributive services and personal services show little or no growth in most countries. We will consider each category in turn.

2.6.1 Producer services

The producer category in Elfring's definition includes the following services: business and professional, financial, insurance, and real estate. In

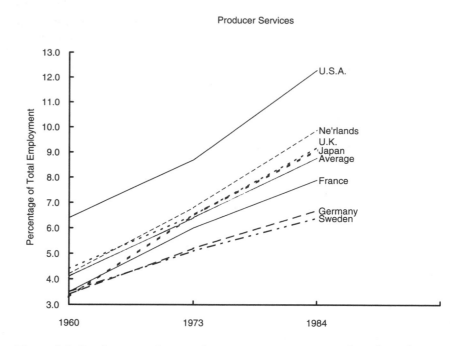

Figure 2.2 Producer services employment as a percentage of total employment.

all countries except Germany over half of the total are in the business and professional services.

The relatively low percentage of such professionals in Germany may well be the result of the very heavy restrictions both on entry into such professions and on practice, as shown by the Deregulation Commission (1991, pp. 281–320). The restrictions lead German businesses to use foreign law and accountancy firms, partly because the localization rules – that each firm may not have branches outside its town of origin – lead to excessively small local firms, which do not have the expertise to verify international dealings, and partly because the entry restrictions make them excessively expensive. According to Elfring (1988, p. 113) it is also attributable to the in-house production of software by industrial firms, rather than the use of software houses.

2.6.2 Distributive services

Distributive services include the areas of retail trade, wholesale trade, transport services and communications. With the exception of France and Japan, these have been relatively static as a proportion of the total (Figure 2.3). Japan's rapid growth in the distributive sector is accounted for at least in part by the deliberately restrictive approach to retailing practised in that country. There were over twice the number of shops per person in Japan as compared with the other countries, and Japanese shopkeepers have rights of protest against the construction of supermarkets which effectively allow them to veto such developments. With this form of

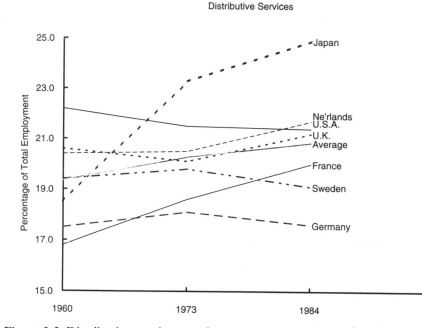

Figure 2.3 Distributive services employment as a percentage of total employment.

protection, retail employment grows roughly in line with consumer spending. In France all subdivisions grew steadily until 1982, and have declined somewhat since then with the exception of continued small growth in communications.

Table 2.4 Employment changes in the distribution services in Great Britain, 1921–1971

Service	Number of jobs (thousands)
Distribution (wholesale and retail)	+800
Transport total	−209.4
Road passenger	+156
Road haulage	+ 63
Other transport	+110
Air transport	+ 73
Railways	−397.4
Sea transport	−125
Port and inland water transport	− 89
Communications	+202

Source: Law, *British Regional Development since World War I*; published by David & Charles, 1980.

In the UK this sector has shown a very substantial growth over the longer term, as shown by Law (1980), whose data for the period 1921 to 1971 is summarized in Table 2.4.

The approximate stability of distributive services in the UK for the period covered by Elfring has now been replaced by a downturn, largely as a result of the recession. Nearly 900 000 jobs were lost in this sector between 1984 and 1992, and the percentage of total employment has declined modestly to 20%. The vast majority of these losses have been in retail trade (593 000) (Department of Employment, 1993, table 1.4, pp. S12–S13). This probably represents the combination of the effect of the recession, which pushes weak shops into bankruptcy, and the progress of automation taking place through the introduction of EPOS. This, it must be remembered, involves much more than speeding through checkouts; it involves integration of sales and ordering, and hence control by central office of the progress of branches.

2.6.3 Social services

Elfring's definition of social services includes all those produced by government. It is therefore far from the usual usage, meaning social work and other welfare services, although these would be included as long as they were provided by government, whether central or local. Elfring's definition also includes 'government proper', central and local government civil service, the military services, health and educational services.

There are two extreme cases in Figure 2.4: Sweden, with 35% of total employment, and Japan, with only 12.9%. As Sweden's welfare state is very well known, its leading position is perhaps not surprising. With over one-third of its workers involved in the non-market sector, the risk of overconsumption through the lack of rationing by price is clear, and appears to be the cause of some of Sweden's severe economic difficulties. That Japan has such a markedly lower figure, approximately half of the average level, results from various causes (Elfring, 1988, pp. 129–131): the international rules against its re-arming mean that it has almost no military forces; the provision of social services by the larger companies means that these services are recorded under the industrial category of the parent company, not the function. This provides one of the clearest examples of the spurious nature of panic about overgrowth of the service sector. Reclassification of workers according to job and not according to the firm's product would cause an immediate massive growth here. Low employment in the educational system in Japan is more difficult to explain since enrolment levels are comparable; however, it seems that expenditures on ancillary aspects such as student lodging and welfare services are much lower. Expenditure on health in Japan as a proportion of GDP was also well below the average, at least in the mid-1970s (Elfring, 1988, p. 130), at 4% in Japan as opposed to an average of 6.4% in the other seven countries. The clearly, though less dramatically, lower level in Germany is due to the smaller expenditure on education due to demographic factors, and the smaller numbers employed in the health services, due to higher pay but similar total expenditure.

Over the longer period (1921–1971) in the UK, this sector showed the gains listed in Table 2.5 (Law, 1980). As in the case of distributive services, there has been a modest decline of approximately 12 000 jobs

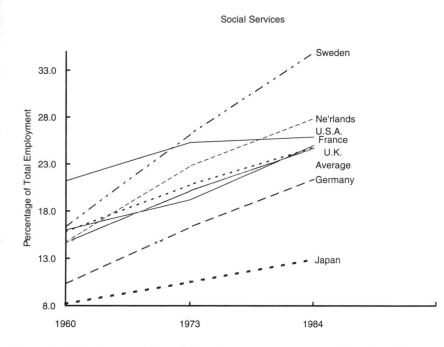

Figure 2.4 Employment in social services as a percentage of total employment.

Table 2.5 Employment changes in the social services in Great Britain, 1921–1971

Service	Number of jobs (thousands)
Central and local government	+ 624
Health	+ 777
Education	+1001

Source: Law, *British Regional Development since World War I*; published by David & Charles, 1980.

between 1991 and 1992, although it is not the recession but rather government policy that has caused this. The only exception is in the health sector, where there has been an increase of 44 600 jobs (Department of Employment, 1993, table 1.4, p. S13). Because of classification problems, it is more difficult to discern whether there has been an overall decline in these jobs since 1984.

2.6.4 Personal services

Elfring's definition of personal services includes hotels, bars and restaurants; recreation and amusements; domestic services; repair services; barber and beauty services; laundry and cleaning services; and miscellaneous personal services (Figure 2.5). The one country far out of line with

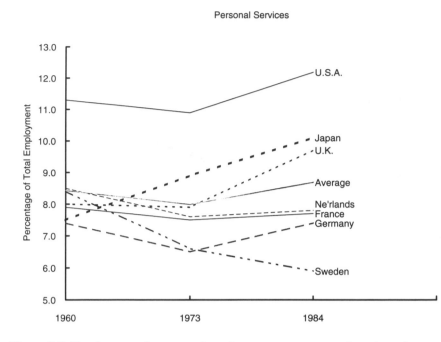

Figure 2.5 Employment in personal services as a percentage of total employment.

the rest is the USA, with 12.2% of total employment as opposed to an average level of about 8.7%. These high levels seem to be fairly consistent across the board. It is interesting to note that the level of domestic service in the USA is proportionately much higher than in all other countries except France. Since we would expect many of these services to be used as the result of shortage of time for domestic work due to high female labour force participation rates (see section 4.4.3), their relative stability in most countries in this period is interesting, and perhaps unexpected. The case of Sweden is interesting; it reflects very low levels in almost all subcategories, and particularly in the dominant employment group in all countries, 'hotels, bars and restaurants'.

The longer term figures of Law (1980) show the huge loss of jobs in domestic service – some 1 151 600 – a loss which Elfring notes continued until 1984. On the other hand, both catering and hotels, and hairdressing gained just over 100 000 jobs each; more importantly in the long run, motor repair gained at least 234 000.

2.7 SUMMARY

The growth in the service sector has been very large over the period since the Industrial Revolution. Much of it has been in services paid for by government, and as such there is a risk that there will be overprovision, but there is also a risk of the opposite. The remainder of the service sector is firmly within the market, and if we believe that there is no better way of organizing economic life, then this is likely to be a self-regulating sector. The enormous changes in distribution of jobs, over the period from 1921 to the present in the UK, and over longer time scales as recorded by Kuznets, support this view. The view that services are inherently low-productivity is, however, to be contested. Various studies show that they are capable of productivity growth, and the rationale of the Baumol model indicates that if they are not, the forces of demand will control their development, since their costs will rise.

APPENDIX 2.A

2.A.1   A mathematical formulation of the Baumol Model

The outputs of the two sectors are given by the following equations:

$$Y_{1t} = a L_{1t} \tag{2.A.1}$$

In words, output of sector 1 at time $t = a$, output per unit labour in sector 1 multiplied by L_{1t} labour employed in sector 1 in time t.

$$Y_{2t} = b e^{rt} L_{2t} \tag{2.A.2}$$

In words, output of sector 2 at time $t = b$, the output per unit labour in sector 2 at time 0, multiplied by e^{rt} the growth factor, for which r = rate of growth of productivity per period, and t = the number of periods elapsed, multiplied by labour employment in sector 2 in time t.

Unit costs of each sector are given by the labour input divided by the output (assumed the only cost; adding other costs merely complicates the model without changing its fundamental message). Hence, relative costs can be derived:

$$C_1 = \frac{L_{1t}}{Y_{1t}} = \frac{L_{1t}}{a L_{1t}} = \frac{1}{a}$$

In words, unit cost in sector 1 (the service sector) = labour employed in sector 1 at time t (the costs of production) divided by the output of sector 1 at time t (substituting Equation 2.A.1 for Y_{1t}).

$$C_2 = \frac{L_{2t}}{Y_{2t}} = \frac{L_{2t}}{b e^{rt} L_{2t}} = \frac{1}{b e^{rt}}$$

In words, unit cost in sector 2 (the progressive sector) = labour employed in sector 1 at time t (the costs of production) divided by the output of sector 1 at time t (substituting Equation 2.A.2 for Y_{2t}).

Thus, substituting the terms obtained in the final columns above:

$$\frac{C_1}{C_2} = \frac{b e^{rt}}{a} \tag{2.A.3}$$

In words, the relative costs of the unprogressive sector increase at the rate of growth of productivity of the progressive sector. Taken over many periods, this would lead to very much higher unit costs in the unprogressive sector, with potential effects on demand for sector 1 output if it is price elastic.

The rate of growth of the labour force employed in sector 1 if output of the two sectors remains equal is:

$$Y_{1t} = Y_{2t}$$

Thus

$$a\,L_{1t} = b\,e^{rt}\,L_2\,t$$

Therefore

$$\frac{L_{1t}}{L_{2t}} = \frac{b}{a}\,e^{rt}$$

i.e. L_1 grows at a rate of e^{rt} compared with L_2.

FURTHER READING

Elfring, T. (1988) *Service Sector Employment in Advanced Economies*, Aldershot, Avebury (Gower Publishing).

The functions and limitations of the market

3

3.1 INTRODUCTION

The virtues of the market as a means of social organization have been extensively advocated under the Conservative regime in the United Kingdom, the Republican presidencies in the USA, and the Christian Democrat regimes in Germany. The European Community legislation and constitution is largely devoted to the furthering of free market ideals. In view of market pervasiveness, it seems advisable to consider its strengths and limitations at a very general level, particularly in the context of 'service' industries, since 'service' and 'market' might be thought to be antitheses.

The utopian abstraction of the 'perfect market' will be examined to establish the signals it would transmit to workers, managers and consumers. Even within this paradigm, there are market failures caused by natural monopoly, public goods and externalities such as pollution. As the market cannot function perfectly, there are arguments for taking certain services out of private market production. We do this because the set of linked signals that provides the self-correcting nature of the perfect market is absent; unfortunately there is no way of replacing it.

The market can naturally break down if this is absent. We will examine how **information asymmetry** could lead to such market breakdown. The breakdown of insurance markets suggests a rationale for the public provision of health care.

Finally we discuss whether 'service' and 'market' really are antithetical. The argument will follow Elizabeth Anderson's excellent article, which suggests three types of exchange relationships: personal, market and political. These non-market economic relationships are particularly important for services, since service often implies a personal relationship, and many of the political relationships are related to public services. Her idealistic view of political relationships is supplemented by the critical views of government as a self-seeking economic agent based on the work of Stigler.

3.2 THE PERFECT MARKET: CASH IS BEST

The classical welfare economics paradigm holds that a competitive cash economy yields the optimum distribution of resources between productive uses, and hence the maximum value to consumers consistent with the existing knowledge, and physical and human resource base. The aim is to satisfy the maximum feasible level of consumer desires. This is subject to the constraint on physical resources, including human labour, and the available technology. The market system is supposed to do this, and to provide a complete set of stimuli so that the individual's pursuit of self-interest actually leads to the socially optimal result. In such a system any distortion by subsidies or taxes will reduce welfare, but cash subsidies are better than subsidies on particular goods, or their free provision. This model also supplies a basis for thinking about the motivation of workers and managers, and about pricing, and is therefore worth outlining. The detail that is gone into here is no substitute for a full treatment of the subject by economics texts designed for this purpose, but should provide the basis for further discussion of the service industries.

The paradigm is centred on the question of how society, in the form of the market economy, achieves the near miracle of organizing the production and distribution of the huge range of goods to vast numbers of people, and the continuous adaptation that this process involves. It therefore examines how consumers might be expected to choose between products, how producers choose whether to produce and how much, and how they choose the means of production, in particular, the balance between capital, labour and other inputs.

Texts rarely stress that such a market relies on the rule of law and a social consensus which prevents fraud and theft from dominating exchange. It is assumed to be present, and we shall make the same assumption.

3.2.1 Consumer choice

Consumers are held to be perfectly informed about prices and the goods available and to have a set of preferences within which they try to maximize their satisfaction. Every good or service is characterized by 'diminishing marginal utility', that is to say that each successive (i.e. marginal) unit of consumption yields lower utility (i.e. satisfaction, a bit of economists' jargon which suggests that people have the most peculiarly functional approach to emotional life). This premise may also be expressed somewhat less restrictively, that consumers prefer a variety of goods in consumption, such that if they trade one good off for another, the rate of exchange of the two goods will shift such that more and more of the more plentiful good will be required to replace each unit of the less plentiful good that has to be given up. This gets over the problem of defining some sort of cardinal measure of 'utility' for each item, and concentrates on the relative value of the items. Given these assumptions, the consumer can increase overall satisfaction by switching from goods with lower satisfaction-to-price ratios at the margin, to those with higher satisfaction-to-price.

From these relationships, it is evident that the consumer will purchase less of a good whose price goes up relative to all other goods, and that we could therefore construct a demand curve for the individual consumer, by presenting choices at all possible prices of the good, with other prices and the consumer's income remaining fixed. These curves for the individual consumer could be summed to get a market demand curve.

Anything that distorts either consumer choice, such as quotas or rationing, or the relative prices, such as taxation or subsidies on some goods but not others, will upset this search for equilibrium. Goods will be consumed where the satisfaction-per-unit price is less than it would be on some other items, and so total satisfaction (assumed to be a simple sum of the satisfaction gained from the consumption of all items) is less than it could be in the absence of the distortions. Because all choices are relative to other items, a single rate of indirect tax on all goods does not distort choice; it is different rates of tax that do.

3.2.2 Producers' choice: How much to produce

The producer is also held to be omniscient about the available production technologies and the costs of inputs; this theoretical device ensures that reactions to changes in prices or technology are not delayed by lack of information. For perfect competition to work, the technology of production has to conform to a set of rules that may hold for agriculture, but does so for almost no other industry or service. The rules are that in the short run, when the amount of capital equipment cannot be varied, the law of diminishing returns holds; that is to say, that the unit costs of production increase progressively as more output is produced. In the long run, when the amount of capital available can be changed, the economic size of firms is limited by the increasing costs of management. We will explore these by looking at the case of a farm.

We might divide the inputs required by a farm along the following broad lines:

- Capital: fixed in the short run
  - Land
  - Buildings
  - Machinery and tools
  - Stock (cattle, sheep, fruit trees etc.)
  - Farm manager(s)
- Direct inputs: variable in the short run
  - Labour
  - Fertilizer
  - Seeds
  - Pesticides

The length of time required to change the stock of capital items will vary, but however long or short, it is defined as the **long run**. The key difference is that all such items usually last longer than a single year, and that capital equipment does not enter into the output in a simple one-for-one relationship; with a given stock of capital you could produce nothing without the addition of the direct inputs. The amount of output that you get from a given stock of capital will vary according to how much of the direct inputs are used.

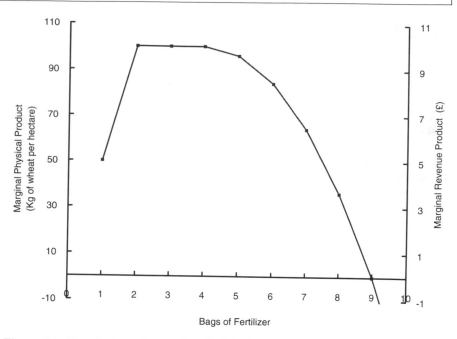

Figure 3.1 Marginal product under diminishing returns: fertilizer use.

Let us consider the **short run** decisions – the short run being the period over which you cannot significantly alter the stock of capital. The farm manager has to decide how much labour, fertilizer, seed and pesticide to apply. Let us take the case of fertilizer. After some very low level, at which results are uncertain, there is a range of fertilizer application over which the relationship is relatively simple, and linear: another bag per hectare increases yield by a given amount. This increase in yield is called the **marginal physical product** (MPP); 'marginal' because it refers to the increase due to the last unit of input; 'physical product' because it is output being measured in physical units, in this case kilograms of wheat.

However, there comes a time when this linear increase no longer holds and each extra bag yields a diminishing MPP, and this gives way to a situation where output actually declines if more fertilizer is added, i.e. the MPP is negative. (In fact, of course, this will depend on the amounts of rainfall and sunshine, and on the type of seed, but in farm management programmes, these are input along with a basic relationship of the type outlined.) This type of relationship is said to follow the law of **diminishing returns**. Figure 3.1 shows such a relationship with the equivalent **marginal revenue product** (MRP), that is, the value of the MPP, obtained by multiplying the MPP by the expected sale price per kilogram. In this case I have assumed 10 pence per kilogram.

The farmer will increase his profits by hiring or buying extra inputs – fertilizer here – up to the point where the MRP is equal to the costs of purchasing the input. In Figure 3.1, if the cost of a bag of fertilizer were £6.40, seven bags would be bought. The same logic can be applied to all of the other inputs, as long as the price is expected to remain constant

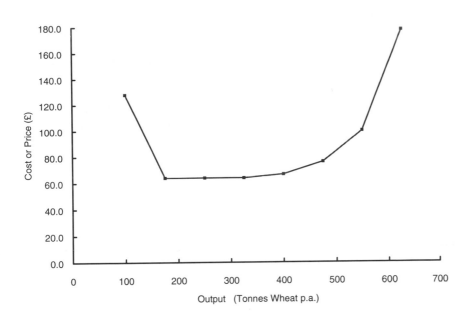

Figure 3.2 Marginal cost under diminishing returns.

however much the firm supplies, and this is basic to perfect competition and a reasonable assumption for agricultural output sold to the national or international markets.

Given this relationship, the cost of the final units of output can easily be calculated; the marginal unit of output will be the unit that is made by the last unit of input. We have just defined the MPP as the number of units of output (and that might be a fraction of a unit) produced by the final unit of variable input that is worth purchasing. That final unit of input has a cost; divide that cost by the number of units of output that it produces and you have the cost per unit of output due to the marginal unit of input; this is the **marginal cost**. This can be more generally defined as the increase in total cost required to produce the last (= marginal) unit of output. As the amount produced by each extra unit of input is declining, the marginal cost is rising. The result of dividing the MPP into the price per bag of fertilizer, £6.40, is given in Figure 3.2. This is difficult to recognize, as to make this useful we need to put it into the context of the output of the farm as a whole; this has been done, in order to give us the marginal cost at various levels of output.

The law of diminishing returns also applies to the relationship between the input of fuel and the output of power from an engine; however, it does not seem to apply to most production lines, where once the factory is working at a normal level the marginal cost remains approximately constant. We shall see in Chapter 6 that the marginal cost is quite likely to be zero in many service industries, or equal to the cost of inputs that are being sold on in the case of retailing.

For the farmer, up to the point where marginal cost equals price, each unit is costing less to produce than it will gain in revenue, and profits must be increasing (or losses decreasing), and so it pays to produce up to that point. This therefore sets the amount each firm is willing to supply, at any given price; it is therefore the **supply curve for the firm**. These supply curves for the firm can be summed to make an industry supply curve, which can be compared to the industry demand curve to get the market price. This is the price at which no consumer would be willing to increase his or her demand, and no firm would be willing to increase output.

3.2.3 Incentives for labour

The classical view of market signals always seems most at variance with reality in the implicit treatment of hire and fire decisions and relations with workers. In its pure form, it assumes that workers are the same sort of commodity as fertilizers or seeds and that they come ready graded by skill, to be hired or fired by the owner–manager as the market dictates. The worker can also switch jobs easily, there being a perfect market in labour, and so, if there are higher wages to be had elsewhere, the worker will switch to those higher wage locations; hence the firm would have to match those higher wages or lose its workforce. The incentive structure is thus seen entirely as a matter of a trade-off between the unpleasantness of a job and the wages it offers. According to this theory, the reason why dustmen are low paid is that there is little skill involved and so although it may be an unpleasant job, competition from many unskilled workers keeps the pay low. The low pay of nurses or university lecturers compared to the skill and responsibility they exercise is attributed to the desirable nature of the job. (It could also be explained by the power of the government as the only effective purchaser of their labour.) The problems of the specificity of skills, whereby a coal miner may have very substantial skills in coal mining, but little for work outside that industry, tend to be ignored in the models of the labour market based on this competitive structure, in the interest of showing how the perfect market should work. The acquisition of further skills by the worker is seen as a purely commercial transaction, a response to the higher wages expected from such higher skills.

3.2.4 How much should firms invest?

The same principles apply, and there is no real problem of information since it is assumed that firms can predict the future! To produce any output – goods or services – will involve a certain amount of capital goods and other items like management, which have to be decided before any production can take place, and which are therefore fixed in the short run. They are thus called 'fixed costs'. The inputs which go directly into production, the variable costs as discussed above, then have to be added to make any output. The manager can forecast the optimum level at which to operate, given perfect information, and so the question of whether to invest more is simply: can one gain enough profits to repay the capital and cover the interest charges?

If this is possible, the capital should be invested. The rate of interest is fixed by the supply and demand for capital. The demand is the amount required for investment; in other words, the sum of the amounts of capital required as the result of the decisions to invest of all of the firms, and those required by consumers who wish to borrow for consumption. The supply of capital is the amount consumers would wish to set aside for future consumption, and firms for future investment or as reserves. In this traditional model, firms will be able to justify less investment if capital becomes more expensive, that is to say if the interest rate rises, and consumers will tend to borrow less. Firms and consumers wishing to set aside capital will see an opportunity to make more money for future consumption, because of the higher interest rate; they will set aside more capital and so increase the supply. There will thus be an equilibrium in the capital market between the supply and the demand for capital. Like any other market in this model, it reflects the consumption pattern, the tastes of consumers (in this case their preference for consumption now rather than later) and the demand for capital. Like the demand for any other factor of production – labour, energy, land or raw materials – demand for capital depends on the opportunities available for its profitable use, which reflect the workings of the product market, with supply being related to the costs as defined by the known technology and costs of inputs, and demand again being defined by consumer tastes and their incomes.

This discussion of investment implies that it is entirely the expansion of output by existing firms that will go to satisfying increased demand. This is by no means exclusively the case. New firms will also come in to take advantage of profitable opportunities. In general they will enter the market if 'supernormal' profits are being made. These are such an important concept, not only within this perfect market paradigm but also in the more recent work that we shall be looking at later, that we will examine them in more detail.

3.2.5 Profits and new firms

If consumer demand increases, firms will produce more even though their marginal costs are increasing, since they will produce up to the point where price is just equal to the marginal cost. Will they make a profit? That depends on their average costs, and these have not been discussed. This section shows how these interact with demand to make profits or losses, and how this will encourage firms to leave the industry or new firms to enter.

The average costs will by definition be the total costs incurred to produce a given quantity, divided by the number of units produced. Total costs, as defined in section 3.2.2 in relation to farming, have two major elements: variable and fixed costs. The **variable costs** are the sum of all the marginal costs incurred to produce the level of output concerned. The **fixed costs** are those resulting from the costs relating to past investment and such things as the management costs of the firm; these do not vary with changes in output in the short run. The investment costs can be expressed as an annual equivalent, as can management salaries, and so we can calculate a total fixed cost for the firm over the appropriate time period. If we divide this total by the number of units produced per year we will get an average of these fixed costs. The more that we can produce, the lower these will be per unit.

The total variable costs are the total of all the marginal costs from the very first unit produced to the last. To find the average, simply divide the total by the number of units produced. If marginal costs decline over the first units produced, the average variable costs will also. As the marginal costs start to increase because of the law of diminishing returns, the average variable costs will continue to decline as long as the marginal costs are below the average variable costs. The average variable costs will increase but much more slowly than the marginal costs once the marginal costs have become greater.

Adding fixed and variable costs together gives us total costs, and so we can also add their averages to give us average total costs. These will fall sharply at first, with the fall in fixed costs per unit, and the falling marginal costs; like the average variable costs, they will continue falling until marginal costs become greater than the average total cost, and will then rise in just the same way. The minimum level at which a firm can produce and cover all of its costs is thus the point at which marginal costs equal average total costs. At this point all the costs are covered, but no more than covered.

What do we mean by profit, and will the firm make one? The definition of profit for accounting and tax purposes is different from that used in economics. **Accounting profits** are the surplus of revenues less the costs actually incurred, but including depreciation, which may simply be a book-keeping figure in that no payment by the firm may be made. **Economic profits** are defined in relation to a surplus *above the level of remuneration that the various factors employed could earn elsewhere*. Thus if the capital invested earns a 15% rate of return, and the market only demands 10% for that type of project, economic profits of 5% are being earned. If the owner–manager is extracting annual profits of £70 000, but could only earn £25 000 in the next best alternative job, he is making economic profits of £45 000. The level of remuneration obtainable elsewhere is considered the 'normal' level, and so economic profits may be called **supernormal profits**. They are also called 'economic rents', because a rent is the amount that land earns precisely because it can produce supernormal profit.

The 'normal' profits are considered part of costs, and thus come into the calculation of fixed costs. For example, the manager above should be allocated an income of £25 000 in the accounts, and the capital should be achieving a rate of return of 10% and this should also be part of the costs. If the site is particularly good, and thus any firm can make a supernormal profit on it, firms would be willing to bid a sum that represented the value of those profits to them for that site, or pay an annual rent equivalent to those supernormal profits and the rent payable at other sites. This explains why supernormal profits are also called 'economic rents'.

In a competitive economy, a firm will make a profit if the price rises above the average costs. If no one expects this to continue, the firm makes a windfall gain, but other firms will not enter the market. If, however, it looks as though profits will continue, other firms will naturally enter to take advantage of this. This might lead to a nice smooth transition so that output from the existing firms and the new ones gradually increases, causing the price to fall, thus eliminating excess profits, or it might happen as a headlong rush; too many firms enter, supply increases by so much that a glut is created; prices fall so that all firms make a loss. The opposite process occurs as firms leave the industry and supply again declines, price rises and normal profits are again established.

3.2.6 Summary of the perfect market

This then completes the circle. Consumers have tastes which they express through the purchase of goods in the market; the relative prices of these goods both enable the consumers to decide how much of each item to purchase, and the producers how much to produce. How much to produce of any item depends not only on the price but also on the costs of inputs, including labour, which the firm demands up to the point where additional units are no longer profitable. Just as the particular goods or services for sale will fall in price if there is a fall in the quantity that consumers demand, so the prices of inputs will fall if there is a fall in demand by producers for that input. Thus if labour is too highly priced, the quantity demanded will fall, and the price of labour – the wage – will also fall. If demand increases, either because of some change in consumption patterns or because costs for that product have fallen and hence prices fall, firms will seek to expand output, and this is likely to generate excess profits. Seeing the opportunity, other firms will enter the industry, and supply will increase further, and so prices will probably fall again.

The system is thus one in which equilibrium may continually be shifting, but with perfect information and speedily adjusting prices, equilibrium will be reached to the maximum satisfaction of all, given the pre-existing distribution of resources.

3.2.7 Market failures: Monopoly, public goods and externalities

Within the traditions of the 'perfect market' as a basis for analysis, certain market failures are recognized. These are situations where the market cannot work in the way specified above. The signals that the market gives are inappropriate.

Monopoly

The first of these situations is where, often for reasons of ownership of natural resources, or for reasons related to the technology available, monopoly results. Wherever this is the case, the private interest of the monopolist would lead to manipulation of the market and prices that are well above marginal costs to be charged. Thus the link between the costs of provision (as determined by the technology available and the cost of the relevant inputs) and the price of the products available to the consumer is broken.

Public goods

This is a much more serious breakdown, in that if goods cannot be provided by the market, but are necessary to the functioning of society, other methods of provision must be found. The two characteristics that define pure public goods are:

1. Non-exclusivity: that is to say, that ownership of the good or service cannot be established, and thus it cannot be sold. The fine views of a city or the light of lighthouses or street lamps, as well as a system of justice and policing, all provide goods to all those in the area, whether they have paid or not.
2. Non-rivalness: in the above examples, not only can one not exclude people in the area from consumption, but there is also no extra cost involved in the provision of the good for an extra person: one person's use of the light from the street lamp does not reduce the light available for others. Consumers are therefore not rivals in consumption, and so marginal cost (the cost of extra provision for the final consumer) is zero and price should therefore be zero.

Since no market can be established, it is normal for such goods to be provided publicly. Various economists have pointed out that this does not need to be by central or local government; it could be done by groups of interested people, such as the local port users' associations who put up many of the Victorian lighthouses. Residents' Associations might put up street lighting and contribute to the paving and maintenance of their local streets. In some places this is also happening with respect to providing private policing by the hiring of security guards.

Externalities

These are the unintended consequences of consumption or production where a public good is created. For example, the use of the private motor car creates both noise and atmospheric pollution. In general, drivers would prefer to be without either, but this is not possible with the present technologies. Almost all forms of pollution fall into this category. But externalities need not be bad; the creation of a beautiful building will enhance the area around it. The growing of fields of flowers for sale may be a source of pleasure to passers by. In all cases an effect is created which has some cost or benefit to those not directly concerned in the transaction, hence the term **external effect**.

It is worth noting that many externalities are related to congestion: up to non-congested levels of use, there may be no significant external effect;

once congestion sets in, there may be a rapid rise in the effect and in its severity. Urban traffic congestion costs are typical of this problem. The key element is that once congestion sets in, the extra time caused by the increase in traffic (at the limit by the final vehicle) affects all of the vehicles in the system. Thus the small increase in cost, by affecting many other people, leads to the large effects observed; recent estimates put the annual costs of traffic congestion to industry in the UK at £15 billion.

The effects of congestion may be such as to produce perverse signals. For individual motorists, traffic congestion is a nuisance which slows down their trip. They bear the costs of delay, but only the delay to themselves. Bus passengers, on the other hand, are delayed by the congestion, often more severely than the motorist since congestion impedes the bus joining the queue of traffic at each stop, and face higher costs because it is not only their time that is wasted but also the driver's time, for which they have to pay by increased fares. Thus the relatively space-inefficient and congestion causing car is relatively favoured by congestion costs.

These externalities are to be distinguished from the effects that any transaction creates in the form of changes to prices. These effects are indeed external to the transaction but they are the means by which the market signals the development of scarcity or relative plenty. They are sometimes called **pecuniary externalities**, but this is now relatively rare, and it is now usually *only those external effects that cause market breakdown that are known as externalities*.

3.2.8 Price signals in the public sector

Once production of a good or service is taken out of the market, or cannot be produced by the market, the interacting set of signals on how to produce, how much to produce and what to produce disappear. Firstly and most obviously the demand side signals cannot exist if an effective command economy is present. Even if, as in the case of health care, the items are potentially **private goods**, i.e. they are both exclusive and rival, if they are provided 'free at the point of sale', there can be no knowledge of the market demand. For example, we have no idea how many hip operations would be requested if each one had to be paid for by the individual patient. Insurance schemes also obscure demand in much the same way; once the patient is insured, the actual operation costs him or her nothing.

On the cost side, if (and it is a big if) inputs need to be purchased which are traded in the competitive market, the price signal remains valid, and we cannot blame inefficiencies on distortions in input prices. However, it is all too often the case that the public sector does not just purchase in the market as if it were a small private sector buyer. This may be because its requirements so dominate the market that it in fact sets the market price, or that it uses its monopsony power to depress market prices, or to ensure that there is no 'market' as such, by acting as a price discriminating monopsonist.

A perfect example of such discrimination occurred recently in Glasgow.

A Health Authority set up a contract with a private agency to provide NHS nursing home beds at £440 per week, when its normal level of payment was £230! If the new organization of the NHS gives budgets to fundholding GPs, Trust hospitals and other district health authorities, so that all of them are competing as purchasers of nursing home beds in the same market, they will not be able to split the market in the way that a monopsonist can, with the result that everyone will have to pay the going price – and if the market is expanding, that price will be the cost of new facilities. Assuming that £440 is the proper price for nursing home places, based on the real cost of producing a place with all new capital, all such places would cost £440. There would no doubt be a considerable expansion of supply, but at the cost of a large rise in the price paid. Under the present system, only the few extra beds needed over the present stock have to be paid for at the marginal cost of all beds, because the Health Authority can discriminate between suppliers since it is a monopsonist. If the combination of expansion of supply and rise in price led to excess bed spaces, the price would probably fall as the various purchasers refused to accept the combination of high price and spare bed spaces.

The public sector generally lacks effective signals on either output or production methods, since for the first there is no price, and thus no means of telling whether consumers would buy more at the existing price or not, and for the second, although it would be possible to institute a system of monitoring and rewards for reducing the costs of production, and then the necessary training and dissemination of these methods, this is in general not practised at present. The competitive pressure that would ensure declining profits if the unit was a high cost producer is not present. It is the aim of many of the 'privatization' exercises, particularly in the National Health Service, to provide this control on costs, but as will be seen in the final chapter, this has been instituted on the basis of belief rather than knowledge since the accounting procedures that would disentangle the enormously complex cost structures of a modern health service were not – and still have not been – developed. Indeed, it is clear that they will be to some extent arbitrary because of the problem of joint costs. Thus uncertainty will remain as to whether a particular unit is a high cost operator on, say, cataract operations, or whether it happens that the accounting for the joint cost elements – the hospital cleaning, laboratories, administration, doctors' time on other eye operations, etc. – makes it appear to be high cost.

We shall, however, see in Chapter 9 that it cannot be assumed that the private market would solve these problems, even where there is competition. Some models suggest that they would not provide the requisite variety, and would follow each other in a copy-cat fashion. It seems likely that in many places hospitals would be monopolies anyway, and that the intermediation by medical insurance might itself cause such distortions that no good solution would emerge. Much of the problem in this case comes from the difficulty of defining the output. This is also true in the case of the police, the efficiency of the judicial system, or (to provide a private sector example) in assessing the value for money that accountants offer their clients. It is even true in a much less obvious way of public transport, whether publicly or privately provided. Public transport contributes to the reduction of congestion, and hence air and noise pollution, but exactly how much is very difficult to measure; it is even more difficult to provide a direct stimulus to the public transport operator that reflects the social benefit of carrying each individual passenger. Thus we may be confident that although the public sector loses certain market stimuli, we shall see that it is in the nature of markets for many services, not a feature of public as opposed to private provision. This is because there is no way of guaranteeing that an optimal solution will emerge because of market failure.

3.3 LACK OF INFORMATION AND MARKET FAILURE

While market failure causes lack of information as shown above, lack of information can cause market failure in a number of ways. Firstly, it is intuitively obvious that if consumers fail to discover alternative sources of supply a monopoly is created by lack of information. This might be overcome by advertising, but we shall see in Chapters 9 and 10 that this is not a sure remedy. It is also clear that labour markets are particularly prone to this type of market failure. We will examine this in Chapter 5 in relation to the question of information asymmetry and the existence of the firm, since this is one of the principal reasons why labour markets are not by any means perfect, and also why the firm is a better means of organizing production and service delivery than subcontracting every aspect of the job.

As we are discussing the major failures of markets, it seems appropriate to discuss the way in which information losses can actually lead to a market going missing – not existing at all. This can happen in insurance markets, and potentially in second-hand markets.

3.3.1 Insurance and information asymmetry

In all insurance contracts there are two major problems relating to information asymmetry: **moral hazard** and **adverse selection**. The first refers to the situation in which the insured person fails to take the normal care so that the risks of a claim are increased. Or we might seek a more general definition: *moral hazard occurs where the terms of a contract cause an opportunistic alteration in the behaviour of one of the parties*. At the limit, this might involve fraud such as dropping a hammer into a basin to claim a new bathroom suite from household insurance, or leaving the car unlocked with the keys in place so that it can get stolen, or less sensationally failing to take care in the form of not buying the security devices to deter burglary. It has been suggested that continuing smoking may be the result of moral hazard; in this view, the individual continues to smoke because he or she does not have to bear the costs of treatment. Considering its normally dire results on health and well-being, it would seem to be more simply a case of addiction, and as such beyond rational behaviour.

In the context of health insurance, adverse selection is probably more important. *Adverse selection occurs when one of the parties is able to select a course of action on the basis of knowledge unavailable to the other party.* The key factor in adverse selection is that the agent has information relevant to the selection of the action not available to the principal. The insured, or the applicant for insurance, can be expected to have better information about his or her risks than the insurer, who can only use general criteria. For a health insurance policy to be viable for the company the premiums must cover three items: the payments to be made for those who fall ill, the administrative costs and the normal profits of the company. Assuming the first to be the determining factor, it is necessary to set the premiums so that the actuarially predicted risk is fully covered. Given that a range of health risks is being insured, the policy has at least to cover the average risk. However, since there is a range of risks, it may be so expensive to insure oneself that it is only worthwhile to do so *if one is at the top end of the risk group.* Furthermore, this will be better known to the insured than to the insurer, who cannot tell which end of the spectrum the insured falls into. (Otherwise, the insurer could set up different conditions which would allow for this information and hence narrow the group.) But if the insured only contract in, i.e. select themselves, if they are in the high risk group, they will involve higher than average payouts. Thus the insurer will be forced to raise the premiums. But if the premium goes up, the less risky will drop out, and so the payouts will increase. If for social-democratic reasons we are unwilling to see large sections of the population without health cover, particularly as health is a classic insurable item (there is a relatively small risk of incurring very high costs), we might like to avoid the expense of administering an insurance based scheme, and provide health care as a public service, as we do, and as President Clinton wishes the Americans to do.

3.3.2 Second-hand markets and information asymmetry

This problem is not confined to insurance. Akerlof (1970) develops a model for the second-hand car market in which the market collapses as the result of a similar process. If owners of cars only sell if their valuation of their car is that it is worth less than the second-hand market price, in other words it is a 'lemon', i.e. one that is of poor quality compared to the criteria on which price can be set for a particular model (age, mileage and visible condition), then the buyers will find that second-hand cars are always poor value. If, however, they are of poor value, the price should be still lower. But if the price is still lower, the better quality cars will be kept by their owners, and so the market will still provide only poor value. And so on until the market disappears.

Any local paper or drive around the town will show that it does not disappear. What is wrong with the model? Jae-Cheol Kim (1985) provides a plausible explanation. The Akerlof model assumes that all people have the same valuation of quality; Kim points out that perhaps for reasons of income, and perhaps because of their jobs, which may depend on the reliability of their cars, or simply for reasons of personal taste, some people may value reliability (the main component of quality in this context) much more highly than others do. Thus some people will wish to buy the most reliable cars, which would be the new ones, and others will be happy to pick up bargains of 'good' older cars. Furthermore, reliability is largely dependent on the level of maintenance, which in turn is determined by the owner. Thus people for whom reliability is very important will both maintain their cars very well and will sell them early, and hence will provide a flow of high quality used cars. A second group may prefer to buy new cars but maintain them well and keep them. The quality of used cars for sale may or may not be higher than those retained by people who keep their cars and maintain them rather than buying new and selling them on. This depends on the distribution of tastes for quality. Research quoted by Kim showed no difference in quality in the light vans and pickups that were kept and that were sold second-hand, thus supporting this argument for the distribution of tastes.

3.3.3 Summary of information asymmetry and missing markets

The key factor in information asymmetry is that one party to a deal has information not available to the other. As we have seen, this can lead to severe difficulties in setting up markets for insurance, and is present in second-hand car markets. The process is one whereby the asymmetry of information makes one party able to benefit at the expense of the other, potentially to the point where it becomes impossible to serve the market demand profitably. These problems are particularly likely in service industries, since the information element in the service and the interaction between supplier and customer both mean that the service will be non-standard. In consumer goods manufacturing the standardization allows information to be gathered by consumer associations or by the press, even where the relevant item will only be purchased once by each household (such as washing machines), or by trying the item out, as in food or other goods where there are repeat purchases.

3.4 PERSONAL, MARKET AND SOCIAL-DEMOCRATIC RELATIONSHIPS

The purpose of this chapter is to show that many of the service industries will not, as their name implies, fit easily into the pure market paradigm. The sections above have operated within the market paradigm. This section considers two alternative paradigms based on the work of Elizabeth Anderson; she shows that the nature of interpersonal relationships and political relationships implies different rules of engagement from market relations. Because many services involve inevitable aspects of either personal or social-democratic relationships or both, we need to examine the social structures that condition these two types of relationship. We may expect them to be different from the pure market structures relating to the purchase of ordinary goods. For example, any person-to-person service – in other words, anything from psychotherapy to accountancy and business advice – has elements of personal trust and mutual care which influence the way in which such a service is actually performed and the regulations and laws that affect it. Analogously, there is no simple decision rule for the extent or for the measure of efficiency of a police service; the rules in this case will not reflect the values implicit in either the sector of personal interactions or that of pure market transactions, but those of 'social democracy'.

Firstly, we will consider the rules of engagement implicit in market relationships.

3.4.1 Market relationships

Market relations, of the type discussed under the perfect market, are characterized by Anderson (1990, p. 182) as having five major characteristics:

1.   Relations are impersonal. It is not the personality of the vendor or the buyer that matters; the exchange of goods or services for money is free and fair, and leads to greater satisfaction on both sides. This means that both parties are fully mobile, and can change trading partners at any time. This impersonality also gives freedom of access; there is no need to be of a particular class or group to obtain the good or service.
2.   Personal advantage may be pursued within the framework of law 'unrestrained by any consideration for the advantage of others'. This implies that each party is expected to take care of himself, and not to depend on the other to look after his interests. It is thus a quintessentially egotistical mode of transaction.
3.   Goods are exclusive and rival. By 'exclusive' we mean that the good can be appropriated fully by the purchaser; others can be excluded from its consumption (and implicitly are so excluded, and do not suffer either benefit or detriment because of market failures). A good is 'rival' when its consumption by one individual precludes the consumption of that item by others; if I eat a Mars Bar, no one else can have it. 'Goods' which need to be shared to be enjoyed, such as a joke, are neither exclusive nor rival.
4.   The market is purely want-regarding; the only value recognized is personal taste. No distinction can be made between the need for shelter of the homeless and the desire for a more luxurious house of the relatively rich. This may be offensive in some contexts but at the same time it guarantees freedom from the intrusion of the prejudices of others in relation to private consumption. Respect is shown to a consumer by the vendor by not prying further into the circumstances of consumption than is needed to establish the type of product required.

5. Dissatisfaction is expressed by 'exit' and not by 'voice'. The consumer in a market transaction has no right to ask for modifications to the product, but has no obligation to purchase. (The interest of marketing persons in modifying the product to suit the customer is simply the expression of the impersonal and irresponsible aspects of market transactions outlined in items 1 and 2 above.) Anderson (p. 190) has an interesting discussion of the use of the characteristics of 'personal' transactions by salesmen to gain advantage in purely market transactions.

The combination of these characteristics means that the good or service has no intrinsic value: 'A thing is an economic good if its production, distribution, and enjoyment is properly governed by these five norms, and its value can be fully realized through use'.

3.4.2 Personal relationships

The key ideals relating to personal relationships are the polar opposite of those relating to market relations. Anderson (1990) suggests that there are two of them:

1. Intimacy
2. Commitment

'Living on intimate terms with another person involves a mutual revelation of private concerns and sharing of cherished emotions that are responsive to the other's personal characteristics' (p. 185). This romantic aspect of personal relations is complemented by the ideal of long-term commitment to the other person, such that the ideal of self is extended to include the other person. This is a complete contrast to the market relationship, which is essentially transitory, or if it is long lasting, is so out of mutual self-interest, not out of devotion or loyalty. The exchange of goods in a personal context is of value principally for the appreciation and cherishing that this exchange demonstrates, rather than the usefulness of the item, as implied in market transactions. The difference is exemplified by the difference in nature of Othello's gift of the handkerchief to Desdemona, from one easily purchased in a Venetian market.

Anderson's paper is full of excellent examples of such relationships – practical jokes between friends who will appreciate them, the abnegation of friendship implied by settling up with a friend for a meal immediately and to the last penny, which implies the lack of long-term trust and the absence of a deferred and possibly unequal return based on caring rather than cash (for amplification of these relationships, see Sahlins, 1974, pp. 149–185.) The example of prostitution can be seen as the use of market norms perverting the intimacy of personal relationships, and as such debasing them. The interesting hybrid case arising out of this discussion is found in professional services: because these often require a sort of intimacy, there is an uneasy relationship between the professional ethics that govern them, and the market nature of the transaction. The professional ethics involve care for the customer's interest; the market nature of the transaction allows the supplier to switch to more profitable opportunities or the client to switch to preferred suppliers (Anderson, 1990, pp. 188–189, footnote 6). In her view the undesirability of lending money between friends is founded on the twin facts that any such loan alters the relationship to one of dependency instead of mutuality, particularly if no interest is charged. But if interest is charged the impersonal norms of the market are brought into the relationship and disaster for one of the parties may be introduced through the changes in the market rate of interest, and for the other party by a default on the loan. Thus guardedness is introduced where openness should be the norm.

3.4.3 Social-democratic relationships

The realm of social-democratic relationships is characterized by the sense of solidarity between members of society, which Anderson calls 'fraternity', and the ideal of 'democratic freedom'. Anderson also calls these 'political' relationships, although this could be seen as an extension of the term 'political' to a particular form of political organization, namely social democracy.

Fraternity is characterized by the willingness of members of society to forgo their claims on certain goods because these would be purchased at the expense of less prosperous members of society. Rationing of foodstuffs in time of crisis seems to provide a good example of a fraternal action, although it is not mentioned. Fraternal action is therefore specifically concerned with the results of any action on income distribution. Almost all models of 'efficient regulatory systems' – e.g. Vickers and Yarrow (1988, chapters 1–4) ignore this. The article by Posner (1971) on 'Taxation by regulation' is one of the few sources to deal with this specifically. This aspect spills over into the requirements of democracy, since as pointed out (Anderson, 1990, p. 193), a member of a democracy can only participate in the joint self-government that this system implies, if that (and thus each) member has the necessary goods to enable participation; sufficient education is the example given. This seems to provide a rationale for **merit goods**, which are defined as goods that individuals who are subject only to market forces will underconsume – i.e. they will consume insufficient quantities as compared to some social norm. This could be because of external effects; for example, inoculation against disease is both a private good – it reduces the inoculated individual's chance of contracting the disease – and a public good: it has the beneficial external effect of reducing the probability of transmission to others. In this case one might conceivably estimate the magnitude of this benefit to society, and reduce the cost of inoculation by that amount, and retain free market choice of consumption. In other cases this external benefit is not clear but there may be consequences for income distribution, as we are seeing in the heated discussions about the imposition of VAT on fuel and its impact on old age pensioners. Under the new higher prices, such groups may not consume 'enough', although this is contrary to the free market paradigm. There is often considerable difficulty in deciding who defines the 'insufficiency' of consumption, as it clearly conflicts with the basic premise that individuals are the best judges of their own welfare.

Democratic action is taken by using 'voice', i.e. by participating in debate at least to the extent of voting, unlike the market solution of 'exit'. Action is taken to distribute the goods provided in common 'in accordance with shared principles (including a shared understanding of citizens' needs), not in accordance with unexamined wants' (Anderson, 1990, p. 193). These goods are distributed on a non-exclusive basis, i.e. all have access to them, not just those who can pay.

Anderson develops these ideas to show how the 'privatization' of goods provided publicly often (always?) loses some of their intrinsic value. The shopping mall, because it is private, is likely to exclude demonstrations, street theatre etc., thereby robbing people of the liveliness of the older public space in the town, which the private mall may have driven out of business because of its superior private provision. A similar argument is made in relation to private gardens rather than public parks. The argument of Titmuss (1971) in relation to the provision of blood as a social good rather than as a private market good is quoted with approval. Essentially public provision avoids the onerous conditions for the recipients, who would otherwise be forced to pay very large sums or to pressurize their friends or relatives to contribute; at the same time the free gift gives due honour to the contributors. It is clear that by introducing money into the transaction, any free contribution is devalued; the contribution, instead of being an anonymous and disinterested gift of life and health, becomes essentially a gift only of that amount of money that could purchase the relevant quantity of blood. Intrinsic value is replaced by pure use value.

Anderson's discussion is seriously deficient in that it does not treat the government as an economic agent in the same way as firms or consumers are treated under the market. The self-interest of government may lead to at least two forms of 'government failure'. By this we mean the failure of government to deliver the socially desirable forms of activity, either because of their interaction with other interest groups or because of their own desire for self-aggrandizement. The first form is considered by Stigler (1971), who points out that government activity is also subject to economic behaviour and interests. He considers it in the context of regulation in the sense of restrictions on the entry of rivals or on their abilities to trade. The general principles can be extended to other forms of interest such as gaining or avoiding laws, taxes or contracts. To get their wishes the firms have to 'bid' for various government activities, either very directly in the form of traditional 'pork-barrel politics', whereby contracts are awarded to firms that have been useful to the ruling group in government, or in more subtle forms of 'buying' regulation which favours them. Stigler puts this process firmly into the context of the theory of the firm, and sees it as the outcome of the 'costs of producing regulation', in the form of campaign contributions which the firms have to provide, more direct support in the form of design of campaigns, or undermining opponents of the government party, and other costs of overcoming the objections of other interest groups. These are set against the 'profits from regulation', which are related quite directly to the benefits of higher profits for the firm through restricted entry or privileged trading position.

An example of the benefits of gaining regulation is a private waste management firm assisting the campaigns of councillors who would contribute to the refusal of a rival's application for planning permission on a waste disposal site. This process is also present within government in the form of sponsoring of Members of Parliament by trades unions. The example of the trucking industry in the USA given by Stigler (1971, pp. 8–9) shows the interplay of the interests of the railway industry and the severity of restrictions on trucking during the 1930s. The restriction on entry to the trucking industry by the granting of licenses to firms provides Stigler with a particularly clear example: new trucking firms were prevented from entering and competing, and furthermore, since the license was for the firm as opposed to the individual vehicle, the system allowed those firms holding licenses to expand by adding more trucks. The tight restrictions on entry to the airline industry, by the policy of not granting licenses to duplicate carriers on the majority of routes to keep down the number of flights and hence the noise nuisance, are also mentioned as a good example of apparently good environmental legislation in fact being heavily in favour of protecting the existing competitors, not protecting the process of competition. The protection of professionals such as lawyers, doctors and dentists by the restriction of entry provides a further example of this aspect.

The costs of obtaining regulation fall into those direct costs of lobbying and paying sums into campaign coffers, but also the costs of overcoming the relevant opposition. Thus in the case of the restrictions on the weight of trucks in the USA, the restrictions tended to be tighter where there was a considerable rail network against which trucks were competing, but looser where there was substantial agricultural production since the agricultural lobby required large trucks to shift its output.

In assessing costs, one of the most important aspects is the concentration of the interest group; a concentrated small group with a strong interest, such as a major firm, will have low costs of communication between the members of that group and low costs of information gathering, since presumably the interested parties will have the information already as part of the requirements for their work. The potential benefit is also large for each contributor. Conversely, the consumers, whose rubbish disposal (for example) is going to cost more by 1 cent per person per week as the result of regulation, would have high communication costs, there being many of them, and a small individual benefit.

The second form of government failure, the potential for self-aggrandizement and self-serving within the civil service, is considered in the classic text by Niskanen (1971), which is interestingly summarized and extended in Stiglitz (1986, pp. 169–176), or in Vickers and Yarrow (1988, pp. 29–35 in the context of the whole question of who monitors government activity). The key idea is that civil servants maximize some combination of low stress and power. The low stress ensures that they do as little as possible, but more important perhaps is their desire for promotion and power in the form of a large department. Thus there is an incentive to maximize the size and scope of their department, and not to keep it at the minimum size at which it could operate efficiently. Because they take the operational decisions, and Members of Parliament do not have the time or the access to their operations to discover how efficient they are, this desire for aggrandizement can lead to expansion beyond the optimal. Clearly, this suggests that a tightening of civil service budgets will in general lead to activity at a more nearly optimal level – a doctrine that has clearly been much in evidence since 1979.

We return to the fact that there is no market signal that can give a clear view of the efficiency of the operation since the output is not traded, and in some cases is not tradeable in any sense. Thus each side can accuse the other of various forms of inefficiency and mismanagement, as shown in the recent debate about the National Curriculum in the UK. If the government holds an anti-civil service view, there is no reason why it might not reduce necessary levels of service below the tolerable, for the same reasons as it might allow the civil service to overexpand if it held pro-government views.

3.4.4 Summary

The discussion of this section provides a different basis for considering the attributes of different transactions. Anderson's approach is rather different, and considers that there are three domains of transactions, each of which operates under different rules. The private market operates on impersonal lines, and its virtue is at least partly its lack of intrusion into the lives of participants. Dissatisfaction is signalled by 'exit', i.e. not purchasing. In personal relationships, intimacy and sharing are key factors, in contrast to the purely individualistic approach in the market. This raises interesting questions about the morality of those selling techniques that involve the use of personal intimacy to achieve market transactions. The questions of the ethics of personal services, in their widest sense, including advice to businesses, is raised, and may clarify the resistance to pure market norms of some practitioners; the discussions surrounding the recent opening up of advertising for lawyers and the commercialization of medicine provide topical examples.

In consideration of social-democratic (political) relationships, Anderson pursues a different approach to that implicit in welfare economics. It is not just those services where the market fails because they are 'public goods', or where externalities produce public goods aspects, as in both education and transport, that should be provided publicly, but also those where direct consideration of the morality, as defined by social norms, suggests that price signals will cause socially unacceptable deprivation. Thus while the failure of insurance-based schemes on grounds of adverse selection may predispose one to a national health service, the argument from Anderson would probably be that we have decided as a society that health care should be available to all irrespective of their abilities to pay, and that as such health is a 'social-democratic good'. The neglect of the potential corruption of government, by self-interested lobbying or by self-interested civil servants, provides an antidote to the potentially over-idealistic view of government as a corrector of social wrongs.

The section concluded with a brief summary of the views of Stigler in relation to the economic nature of government and government regulation. These provide a less benign view of government activity, as does the work of Niskanen in relation to the ability of the people in controlling the civil service, via Parliament.

3.5 CHAPTER SUMMARY

Since the perfect market has been dismissed as a myth, one may ask why it is included at all. Firstly, it is included because it appears to hold sway among the politicians. Their faith in markets seems to extend to anything that can vaguely be called one, and to regard market forces as invincible and some sort of god-substitutes, omniscient and all-benevolent. At least under unalloyed market forces, they seem to believe that 'all is for the best in the best of all possible worlds', in the words of Voltaire's ridiculous philosopher Pangloss. It is the thesis of this book that even for strictly functional managerial purposes a wider and more aware approach is needed, particularly for the service industries. This is because so many of these industries are very far from the sort of definition of quantity, cost and output that is implicit in any perfect market. Indeed, many of the service industries are responses to problems of supply of public goods; others provide private goods, but a failure to understand either their personal or social-democratic characteristics leads to strange misunderstandings of the environment in which production is taking place. Equally, dewy-eyed optimism about the behaviour of public agencies, or the ability of interest groups to manipulate political processes, is misplaced.

The second major reason for including the perfect market paradigm is that it does highlight certain characteristics of profits, costs and revenues, the entry dynamics of firms, and the hiring of factors of production, which can be used in less idealized analyses. In particular, it provides a paradigm for the interrelated decisions about price, costs and the hiring of factors depending on both the price of the good and the cost of the factor.

FURTHER READING

The material that we criticize here on the 'perfect market' can be found in any of the major economics textbooks.

For further information on the notions of different modes of human exchange see:

Anderson, E. (1990) The ethical limitations of the market. *Economics and Philosophy*, **6**, 179–205.

Sahlins, M. (1974) *Stone Age Economics*, London, Tavistock Publications.

For information on the problems of information asymmetry see:

Strong, N. and Waterson, M. (1987) Principals, agents and information, in Clarke, R. and McGuinness, T. (eds) *The Economics of the Firm*, Oxford, Basil Blackwell, chapter 2, pp. 18–41.

For a more complete and advanced treatment of these issues and those of Chapter 5, see:

Ricketts, M. (1987) *The Economics of Business Enterprise*, Hemel Hempstead, Harvester Wheatsheaf.

Key texts on the ideas of regulation are:

Posner, R.A. (1971) Taxation by regulation. *Bell Journal of Economics*, **2**, 22–50.

Stigler, G.J. (1971) The theory of economic regulation. *Bell Journal of Economics and Management*, **2**, 3–21.

Demand

4

4.1 INTRODUCTION: MARKET DEMAND AND FIRM'S DEMAND

In a book devoted to managerial economics, the inclusion of a substantial chapter on market demand needs justification since few firms have such control of the market that the market demand is their prime interest. They should normally concentrate on the demand for their firm's services, which may be much more volatile since it depends on their competitive position and may change rapidly depending on the actions of rival firms. However, the nature of market demand gives pointers to the evolution of the firm's demand, and in the more dynamic context, it is much easier to develop a market position in an expanding market than in a static one. The evolution of market demand is therefore of material interest.

This chapter first considers the traditional approach to demand. This considers demand for a 'product', assuming tastes are given and unchanging, and focuses on the relationships between price and income and the quantity demanded. This is complicated for the services by the great difficulty of specifying output in terms of quantity, and defining the 'market'. But even for physical products in the modern context of highly differentiated and technologically developed goods, this theory seems bald and difficult to apply. In section 4.3.1, Lancaster's theory, in which goods are considered as bundles of attributes, is examined as a response to analysing the complexity of goods. This is a more promising approach for the service industries, since services are bound to be differentiated products by virtue of location and accessibility, and usually the qualitative aspects that the service interaction introduces.

Since so many services are related to time saving, and in others the use of time is part of the service, in section 4.3.2 we consider the approach of Becker, who treated goods and time as an input into a domestic production process which then leads to consumption. This approach allows for the valuation of time. This is a necessary input into modern approaches to the analysis of location and demand for travel as incorporated into the gravity model, which is explained in section 4.3.3.

All of these approaches rely to a greater or lesser extent on the assumption that tastes are given and fixed. Section 4.4 considers various relaxations of this assumption. These include Tibor Scitovski's view that we need to consider the quite different pattern of consumption based on the search for stimulation, Peter Earl's view of the consumer as a 'scientist' learning new forms of lifestyle, and Hilary Silver's view that structural changes in society and the pattern of work are the principal influences on demand.

The discussion at the end of the chapter aims to set these various approaches into the context of managerial decisions – particularly the relationship between the approaches in terms of their assessment of how price will affect demand, and secondly their implications for market segmentation, and product and price differentiation.

4.2 ECONOMIC ANALYSIS OF MARKET DEMAND

The traditional textbook analysis of demand stresses the relationship between price and quantity, *ceteris paribus*. The things that remain constant are incomes, tastes for and prices of other goods. There is good justification for this from a managerial point of view, in that price and quantity are the only two items which are in any way under the control of the firm. However, failure by the firm to be prepared for the exogenous changes in demand which might come through changes in the other factors, such as tastes, prices of other goods and incomes, is quite likely to be fatal, for example, a mistimed investment programme incurring heavy costs when demand is about to decline. Furthermore, when estimating the demand, we have to be able to take such changes into account, otherwise the estimates of the relationship between quantity and price are corrupted by these other influences.

At the level of market demand price is always likely to be inversely related to quantity, i.e. an increase in price will cause a fall in quantity, *ceteris paribus*, as shown in Figure 4.1. The reason for thinking that price will always vary inversely with quantity, *ceteris paribus*, is that consumers are assumed to want to maximize satisfaction from their income; they will therefore not choose to pay more for a product than they need, and will substitute other products, if these give better value for money at the margin. This can be formally stated in terms of either marginal utility theory or in terms of marginal rates of substitution. (These formal demonstrations can be checked in any of the major economics textbooks.) The key psychological insight is that as you consume more of anything, the additional units give progressively less satisfaction. Thus, if the final units of consumption give less satisfaction than previous units, if the price increases, the satisfaction-to-price ratio of the last units declines, and it may be worth switching to the consumption of other goods where the satisfaction-to-price is higher. If the decision is finely balanced anyway, at the limit if the goods are perfect substitutes and have exactly equal satisfaction-to-price ratios at the initial price, there will be a rapid switching of consumption to the now cheaper good. If there are no substitutes, then the effect of a rise in price is similar to a fall in income of a comparable amount. The imposition of VAT on fuel is held to be such a situation by its opponents, and, particularly for

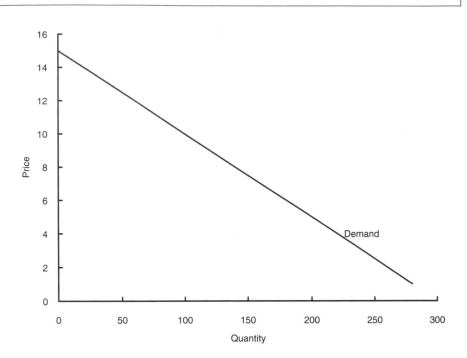

Figure 4.1 A demand curve.

pensioners, whose incomes are often very low anyway, this is a potentially serious problem.

This inverse relationship of quantity with price has two possible exceptions. Firstly, if consumers are judging quality by price (and we should include 'snob goods' where the quality is defined by price, since it is the price that makes the good desirable, as in diamonds and fur coats, or gold Rolex watches) then the desire for quality may be such as to negate this inverse relationship. This is clearly an important exception, since many services involve both lack of information about the quality of the service, and severe consequences from poor quality of service. Bad financial or medical advice or poor maintenance of a vehicle can have dire consequences for the health of the consumer. Our ignorance of the goods and services we consume may in fact be such that we do not trust anything that is 'too cheap', and so this aspect may be vital to selling the item in the first place. Once reputation is established, the normal inverse relationship is likely to return.

The second case seems unlikely in the modern context: where the item is the cheapest available product or service that satisfies a particular requirement, it is just possible that a rise in the price will so reduce consumers' incomes, that they will actually consume more of the good than before the price rise; this is the so-called 'Giffen effect'. Potatoes in the Irish potato famine and rice in Bangladesh are the usual examples cited. It is difficult to think of similar necessities in the context of services in modern Europe. Fuel for pensioners, or public transport for some groups, might be relevant in terms of being necessities and forming a significant part of consumers' incomes (fuel accounts for 47% of pensioner household expenditure in the poorest groups). However, it seems unlikely that consumption would actually increase, because the key aspect of the Giffen good is that other more expensive products have to be given up and replaced by the Giffen good, which is still the cheapest option for satisfying the particular need. In the Irish or Bangladeshi context, this would imply that the demand for meat would actually decline, and more of the basic staple would be consumed because of the dire effect the price rise had on incomes combined with the fact that the staple is still the cheapest foodstuff.

Before discussing the possible shape of the demand curve, we need to define the price elasticity of demand:

$$\text{Price elasticity} = \frac{\text{Proportional change in quantity}}{\text{Proportional change in price}} \qquad (4.1)$$

The calculation of price elasticity is set out in Appendix 4.A. It is essential to understand this concept before proceeding; readers who are not fully conversant with it are urged to work through the appendix carefully before resuming reading the chapter.

A measure for price elasticity is useful for several reasons:

1. It provides the only way of describing the change in quantity demanded as the result of a change in price that is not entirely dependent on the particular units of measurement used.
2. The elasticity of demand tells one which way total revenue is moving with a fall in price.
3. The elasticity of demand can be linked to the marginal revenue, a concept we shall use later. This approach gives a plausible basis for estimating whether the firm is profit maximizing, without all the problems of having to estimate a demand function. (A demand function is the set of relationships which links quantity demanded to price, income and prices of other goods. In theory, it should include tastes, though these defy precise description and therefore quantification.)

The elasticity of demand is determined by the relative desirability of other services and products, given present levels of income, prices of other goods and tastes. This means that it is related to the ease of substitution, and the need for the service or product. Thus, telephone services are substitutable by letter or by personal visits, and can be much reduced by taking the effort to plan what is to be discussed. Thus in the short run, when consumers have little time to change their technology, the demand may be relatively inelastic (the proportional change in quantity being small compared with the proportional change in the price of phone calls), since writing a letter involves considerable time and the greater expense of a stamp as compared to a phone call. Visits are likely to involve considerably greater expenditure of time by both parties to the call, and if that is costed, the call is still likely to be worth while. (It should be noted that both of these alternatives are only partial substitutes; letters frequently confirm phoned decisions, and phone calls are the best way to organize meetings, and hence visits.)

A good illustration of the use of these ideas is in the estimation of the price elasticity of a derived demand. **Derived demand** is where the demand for something is due to its use as an input into something else. For example, the demand for petrol is almost exclusively derived from the demand for car travel, as is the demand for garage services. Since either of these is only a small part of the total cost of travel, the derived demand is likely to be very inelastic. Indeed, if in the short run there are no substitutes, we can say that the elasticity of demand with respect to a proportional change in the price of the input is the elasticity of demand for the final service multiplied by the ratio of the cost of the input as a proportion of the selling price of the final service. So in the case of car travel, with an elasticity of demand of perhaps -0.33, and the cost of petrol being about one-third of the total cost (for which we need a value of time as we shall see below), the elasticity of demand would be $\frac{1}{3} \times -0.33$ $= -0.11$, which is indeed the value of the elasticity found during 1974 when the price of fuel doubled.

In the longer run, changes in the technology available to the firms or consumers influence the demand very considerably. In the context of telephone services, for example, the combination of improved lines, giving sufficiently error-free transmission, and the wide availability of computers with modems and faxes, has blurred the distinction between phone and letter. The fax is now cheaper per unit than a letter and very much quicker, and computer networks operating over telephone lines have altered everything from banking and stock-broking to pornography. These may be seen as the result of the huge changes in unit cost that have taken place.

Given this approach we should *not* expect straight lines (or smooth curves) in real-life market demand curves. Where the price of a particular good rises and puts it at a competitive disadvantage compared with an alternative way of satisfying the particular need, we might expect an increasingly rapid decline of demand as price rises. Conversely, if the price falls, it may cause little change in demand, until the price is low enough to encourage a switch from other goods. There is no reason for this to occur at only one point. It might occur over several price ranges, giving a graph like the one in Figure 4.2.

4.2.1 *Ceteris paribus* 1: Tastes

The foundation of consumer behaviour in modern micro-economics remains the proposition that tastes are 'given' for each individual and that they can be analysed separately for each individual; technically, this is expressed as being 'additively separable over individuals'. This may be justifiable in the short run, since each individual may operate as if individually in his/her choice of goods and services, while the pattern of development of tastes may be determined socially. This does not allow us,

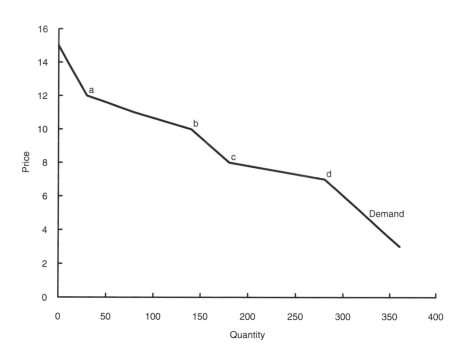

Figure 4.2 A demand curve with competing goods.

however, to develop any understanding of fashion; indeed fashion is seen as an aberration in this context in economics, a serious defect in the economics of the service industries, which include fashionable shops, restaurants, holiday facilities, sports, etc., and even the advertising agencies that go to fashion the fashions.

4.2.2 *Ceteris paribus* 2: Incomes

The normal way of thinking about the influence of income on the demand for services is to consider their income elasticity. This, like the price elasticity, is a purely descriptive device, which, if we are to use it for prediction, implies that the set of relationships established in relation to prices and incomes is relatively stable. It describes the relationship between a proportional increase in income and the proportional increase in quantity demanded such that:

$$\text{Income elasticity} = \frac{\text{Proportional change in quantity}}{\text{Proportional change in income}} \quad (4.2)$$

It is usual to categorize goods or services according to their elasticities, as shown in Table 4.1. Thus we would expect, and would find, that the demand for hotel services is income-elastic, i.e. they are a luxury good, as are holidays abroad, air travel and train travel, but not bus travel.

However, these broad statements conceal severe methodological prob-

Table 4.1 Categories of goods and services

Income elasticity	Category
Negative	Inferior good
Zero	Necessity
Unitary	Normal good
Positive and greater than 1	Luxury good

lems in the measurement of the units of output for almost any service. Taking the case of air travel for example, what are the units of quantity? They could be passenger miles, but this would eliminate the distinction between budget travel by APEX or charter flights and the much more expensive full-price tickets, let alone between the various grades of full-price tickets. It does, however, capture a measure of distance; within this, it is further distorting the value of transatlantic trips compared with trips within Europe, for example (trips to the USA being very much cheaper per mile due either to the fares war in progress, or perhaps to competition forcing prices down to an appropriate markup above costs). These difficulties are acute in most services; consider a category such as restaurant meals. Thus the quoted figures for income elasticity may not relate to the theoretical ideal of changes in quantity but to changes in **expenditure**. This can make very large differences to the observed magnitudes of the elasticities.

4.2.3 *Ceteris paribus* 3: Prices of other goods

In many cases the changes in demand will be related neither to changes in the price of the service in question nor to the income of the consumers, but will be the result of changes in the prices of other goods or services. It will be shown in the analysis of time values that only very large taxes on the car will significantly increase use of public transport, and the use of parking charges and restrictions is perhaps the simplest way of achieving this. This may be measured by the **cross-elasticity of demand**, the proportional increase in quantity demanded divided by the proportional increase in price of the other good. The relative levels of car ownership in urban and rural areas may be taken as an indicator of the cost of public transport. In more rigorous studies, it is notable that cross-elasticity for private and public transport is extremely sensitive to the relative cost of each. Unless the trips by each take approximately the same time, very little change can be expected if one increases in price. This of course is exactly as one would expect, but I remember vividly the senior transport executive official who was bemoaning the failure of the public to respond to the improvements in the speed of public transport that had been achieved with no increase in fares. When asked how fast car trips were in comparison, he replied that they took half the time! He was therefore expecting people to shift out of their cars because the bus trip was now only twice as long, rather than three times as long! It is, however, very easy to follow his example; all his ingenuity and effort had gone into improving the service, and if you put in that sort of effort, you should expect to get results, even if taking a more rational perspective, you should not.

The cross-elasticity of demand provides the only method of defining markets in this approach to consumer demand. Goods or services with significant positive cross-elasticities (i.e. as the price of prescriptions goes up, hypothetically, purchases of alternative medicine, both in the form of consultations and medicaments, might also increase) are substitutes; those with significant negative cross-elasticities are complements (if prescription charges go up, visits to the doctor might go down). In either case, the goods are within the same market sector under this definition. This is, however, a rigorous test for defining markets, and the more intuitive test, that the products fulfil related functions, was one of the stimuli to Lancaster to develop his theory of demand, as set out in section 4.3.1.

4.2.4 Rationality assumptions

In addition to the assumptions mentioned above, that consumers have declining marginal utility and that they are individualistic, conventional economics assumes that they are fully rational and fully informed. This implies that consumers will respond sensitively to relative price changes among competing goods or services, and will be aware of any changes in relative price. Price inflation, where all prices rise by the same proportion, will leave quantities unaffected if incomes also rise by the same proportion. All price rises are thus considered to be real price rises; inflation is implicitly, if not explicitly, assumed away. This certainly runs counter to the daily experience of many of us, who continue to buy the things we have always bought until some major dissatisfaction creeps in. This implies that many people are less sensitive than the theory suggests. We might also expect the job of the firm in monitoring the effects of price changes to be much more complicated by the delays caused by this learning process of consumers. This time dimension is ignored in most economics literature except that relating to the adoption of new technologies.

Many of the extensions and critiques of the economistic tradition set out below try to make the consumer more human by altering the assumptions of perfect rationality, or independence from others. It is perhaps worth emphasizing that this attack on the assumption of consumers' independence to take account of social pressures is perfectly fair; what is not fair from the theoretical point of view is to say that economics ignores the context. The emphasis of all consumer theory in economics is on marginal decisions; these are decisions given all the surrounding parameters, including the availability and prices of different products and hence consumption technology. What economic analysis can no more provide than any other empirical work is detailed and accurate prediction of major changes: what would happen if petroleum suddenly became really scarce? How would people react if we banned cars from city centres, or increased the number of Health and Safety Inspectors so that building sites, factories and restaurants were regularly inspected and prosecuted? This would greatly increase the numbers employed by the Health and Safety Inspectorate, but would it also increase consultancy in the field, and employment of lawyers, etc. and by how much? Would it merely improve management or really increase building costs?

In simple treatments of welfare economics, there is also an assumption that only private goods exist. This is, however, a result of the simplification, not the underlying theory. However, as shown in the previous chapter, it does indicate a real limitation on economic calculations, since the mechanisms of allocation by price cannot work for public goods, nor indeed where there is pollution or beneficial externalities. This problem will be returned to briefly in the discussion of the liberalization of transport in Chapter 12. This problem re-emerges in the estimation of the productivity of the public sector. In gross national product calculations, the output of all forms of public sector employment, except those in the trading companies, can only be included by inserting their cost to the public purse. Thus, with no tangible output, it is by definition impossible to calculate whether their productivity is increasing or not. The burden on teachers, for example, can be increased by forcing them to prepare their own materials, as appears to have been done under the National Curriculum, and imposing a further load of testing, but this will not show up as increased productivity, because the only measure of output would be number of pupils taught, or some such, which is not positively affected by such changes in workload.

A further area on which traditional economic texts are silent is the framework of law and social custom which permits economic activity to take place. It is obvious that with the present poor level of crime detection, it would be rational to thieve or swindle to make money quickly and easily, and hence maximize one's satisfaction. The wide range of social behaviour observable across the world, in terms of the acceptability of bribery, the degree and context in which telling the exact truth is expected and acceptable, attitudes to other races or groups, etc. seems to indicate that our norms are socially determined, and that the real problem with crime is perhaps not that one will be caught, but that it only needs to be suspected for the suspect to become a social outcast. All these norms are socially learned, but equally they are very powerful forces in both economic and social life. An example of this directly impinging on service industries is the need for truthful packaging and advertising. Recent legislation and practice has greatly increased the rigour of this in some areas, and with it the need for servicing these requirements.

4.2.5 Summary of the traditional approach to demand

Demand is influenced by the price of the good or service, and the price of other goods and services, particularly those for which it is a substitute or complement, and by consumers' incomes and tastes. A demand function relates the quantity of the good or service demanded to all of the above variables. A demand curve relates quantity demanded to price, other variables remaining constant. Under these conditions, only defective information, which is not included in the theoretical framework, or Giffen goods would show other than an inverse relationship between quantity demanded and price. The constancy of other variables is referred to as the *ceteris paribus* condition, literally 'other things being equal'. The extent of changes in quantity as the result of a change in price are indeterminate from a theoretical point of view, and could vary from very little to very large. Such changes in the quantity demanded as a result of a change in price, or price of another good or consumer income are measured by the elasticity of demand: the proportional change in quantity divided by the proportional change in price, price of the other good or income. The classical approach to demand provides no method of defining whether a class of products, even those as obviously close as swimming pools within easy reach or similar sized cars, can be viewed as one product or not.

Tastes are considered as 'given'. Interdependence with others, i.e. social pressures, or a systematic process of learning to enjoy different activities, and hence goods and services, are not considered. The process of choice between goods in the conventional theory is one of continual adaptation to any changes in relative prices and to changes in incomes by marginal adjustments to quantities purchased. This implies very high degrees of both awareness of price changes and ability to compute the 'utility maximizing response'. It should be remembered that none of these limitations may be a serious limitation; in the short run the changes from these sources might be small, and price and quantity relationships might hold. The long run may be very difficult to forecast, since we do not know the vagaries of fashion, or the goods and services that may be on offer. Nevertheless, these limitations seem potentially so restrictive that we now look at some of the attempts to get round them.

4.3   ELABORATIONS OF THE TRADITIONAL THEORY

This section is entitled 'elaborations of the traditional theory' because all of the contributions aim to make the conventional analysis more effective. They thus retain the underlying view of the consumer as a fully rational, well-informed individualist with given tastes.

The first extension of the theory we shall consider is the approach of Lancaster, which was designed to overcome the problem that all goods and services were considered separately even though they were clearly closely related, such as the swimming baths or cars mentioned above. The same logic of course would imply that all solicitors or doctors were perfect substitutes, except for locational differences, whereas again one knows that they differ in both interpersonal and technical skill. Lancaster shifted the basis for demand from products and services to the characteristics that such things might embody.

Lancaster's work could be seen as deriving from the work of Becker, whose approach was to see the household as a productive unit, using various purchased inputs along with their own time to achieve the satisfactions they sought. This is interesting in itself, but we require it for the framework it gives us for the valuation of time. It is, in its full formulation, considerably more difficult to understand than Lancaster's work, and our discussion of Lancaster will lay the groundwork for a review of Becker's contribution.

Even before Becker, the inter-industry linkages in demand had attracted the attention of Leontieff. He assumed that demand is very largely the result of the structure of industry in an area. This provides the basic forecasting method for many sorts of tourist impact study, and even for some modern pollution studies.

Since services are very frequently locationally specific – shops in the next town or even the other side of town are not substitutes, whereas those close to each other or at similar distances from the customer may be – an understanding of the main locational models is essential for managers in service industries. The principal model is still the 'gravity model'. It uses ideas similar to the inter-industry demand model in its basic assumptions about demand for access, but in adding the transport dimension, and thus the value of time, it provides an approach to considering the mechanisms of substitution which are used more widely in models of monopolistic competition. These will be considered in Chapter 9.

4.3.1 Lancaster's approach to characteristics

Given the wide range of characteristics bundled together in a modern consumer durable, or service such as a package holiday, explanations that consumers trade-off between 'package holidays' with no way of explaining or analysing the differences between such holidays seems a major weakness in economic theory. Thus Lancaster's approach to the explanation of choice by looking not at the finished goods but at the constituent characteristics seems very attractive. This approach claims to provide a way of considering demand from the point of view of these apparently more fundamental constituents, so that we could model the choice of package holiday, or indeed other types of holiday as compared to the package, by considering the desires of the consumer, the consumer's budget allocation, and the **characteristics** of the holidays on offer and their prices. Firstly, we will show how this is done, and then take a critical look at its implications.

For reasons which will become clear later we will use as a fictitious example a simple canned food, let's say bolognese sauce. Let us say we have three varieties: Carners, a conservative British product, with that strange red substance that passes for tomatoes, a lot of meat and virtually no garlic; Pommodorio, on the other hand, indeed Italian, with a substantial amount of tomato and some garlic, but rather little meat; Aiolio, another Italian product, with approximately equal amounts of tomato and meat and substantially more garlic than even Pommodorio.

The approach is to construct a set of axes, one for each characteristic; we will consider just two, and chart the characteristics onto this space.

Thus, taking our example, Table 4.2 lists the proportions of meat and tomatoes in a 500 gram tin.

The proportions of the two ingredients are shown for each variety as a ray from the origin, and the point to which a single tin corresponds is shown as a white square in Figure 4.3. If one can mix and match so as to get the optimum between each ray, a budget line is drawn, in this case the amount one could buy for £1.00. This is clearly a fictitious item but could be made up from a proportion of each of the two relevant products, either side of the tangency point between the budget line and the indifference curve. If that is not possible, and it would usually not be, there is no budget line; the items that are within the budget allocation are indicated by points on the 'product rays'.

How is the consumer regarded as choosing between these options? We

Table 4.2 The proportions of meat and tomatoes in three varieties of bolognese sauce

Weight in grams	Meat	Tomatoes	Price
Carners	300	50	£1.10
Aiolio	200	300	£1.00
Pommodorio	450	50	£0.80

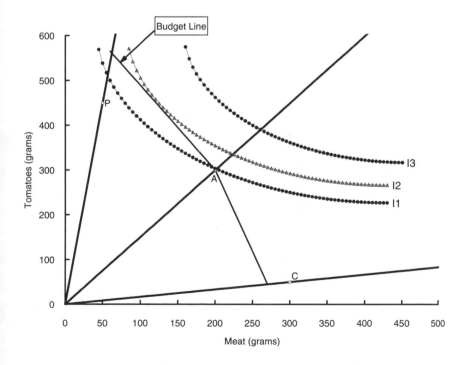

Figure 4.3 Lancaster's characteristics approach to demand.

can examine this using conventional indifference curves. These are contours along which the consumer is indifferent between the various combinations of characteristics. The consumer is regarded as having a preference for a particular combination of meat and tomatoes, and would be willing to move away from this preferred situation but would require ever increasing amounts of the other characteristics to compensate for moving away from that optimum. Thus the indifference curves are indeed convex to (i.e. curved away from) the origin. We assume that more of both meat and tomatoes is better, in other words that the consumer is not satiated at any point, and thus that higher levels of satisfaction are gained as the curves are further away from the origin. Curves I1, I2 and I3 in Figure 4.3 therefore show increasing levels of satisfaction.

As we can see, the highest possible indifference curve, I2, is reached if the consumer buys a combination of Aiolio and Pommodorio, as indicated by the point of tangency between I2 and the budget line. If it is not possible to combine the products, the budget line between the 'product rays' is irrelevant, and the item is chosen where the highest possible indifference curve intersects with the budget points on the product rays. In this example, there would be an indifference curve between I1 and I2 which would intersect the point at which the budget line meets the Pommodorio ray, and so at these relative prices, this would be chosen.

Let us examine the consequence of a change in prices. For example, assume the price of Aioli were to come down to 80 pence per tin. The budget line would pivot to pass through a point very close to the point at which I3 passes through the middle ray representing the combination of characteristics of Aiolio, and it would then become the preferred purchase. It would still be possible to get a mix-and-match combination of Aiolio and Pommodorio that would give higher satisfaction, since it is evident that we could construct a further member of this family of indifference curves which would be higher than I2, and which would be tangential to the new budget line. This would nevertheless involve the purchase of more Aioli than with the previous higher price. Thus the normal price/quantity relationship is preserved when we consider characteristics rather than goods. Pretty and complicated: does it in fact give us much more understanding of demand?

Unfortunately, very little; it is possible to construct such an indifference map in theory, but in practice it often seems to look quite different; Bowbrick (1992, pp. 244–265) shows various cases in which this does not hold empirically. In particular, his mapping of experiments with the sweetness of iced tea show that a fixed amount of sugar is preferred, with apparent indifference over a wide range of strengths of tea! It would seem very plausible that in the context of holidays, 'sun', in terms of both hours and temperature, might show a similar pattern for many people; one would hazard a guess that a temperature between 27 and 30 °C would be optimal for many for a seaside holiday, with temperatures above or below being less satisfactory. A decline in satisfaction when more of a good or service is consumed is the result of 'satiation' – being sated with a product – and the assumption of Lancaster's analysis is that this will not take place over the relevant range of variables. For real-world suppliers it is not a problem, unless they are being blinded by ill-formulated market research based on this approach, or its bowdlerized equivalent, that a good or service is good because of the sum of its attribute scores. They will be supplying a particular variant of a service, and sensitivity to the needs of their customers will alert them to the problem of overstepping the point of satiation. (We should add a word of caution, as will be shown below when considering the work of Scitovski and Earl: this point of satiation may not be a fixed point. As people gain experience of many services, their requirements change. Repeating previous studies is usually most unsatisfying, for example.)

In other situations, notably services, certain qualitative aspects may be the dominant influence, but may be unscalable; thus, we could not put them on a chart of this sort because the axes would be impossible to define. The beauty of views and the quality of walking in hills, for example, would be very difficult to scale. Indeed, they would only be possible to scale as 'attributes' rather than as 'characteristics', attributes being our subjective reaction to characteristics. Once this is done, we no longer have an independent measure on the axis and the scientific rigour inevitably disappears.

The approach becomes complex to the point of uselessness if the characteristics have different importance according to the presence or absence of other characteristics – in other words, if they are interdependent. This is clearly the case in holidays: the positive attributes for a 'Four Ss' holiday (sun, sea, sand and sex) are completely different from those for mountaineering, sailing or sightseeing. This problem is also serious in the context of other services since all are likely to be both sensitive to aspects of 'quality' which one could not scale, and may be further heavily contextually determined: for example, for a knee injury, I would like a certain famous knee specialist, even if his services carry with them a long wait; for an infection the family doctor will do fine, provided he or she can recognize something serious that would escape me, and provides the right care for the rest, and can be seen quickly.

The closely related approach due to Rosen (1974) has been widely used in estimating the value of such things as extra space in the house, proximity to the city centre or bus routes etc. and has been used to estimate the value of different characteristics in cars (Leech and Cubbin, 1978). Rosen assumes that all desired levels of all characteristics are catered for by the products and services available, and that the firms are charging marginal cost. Following traditional cost analyses of the competitive firm, marginal cost will rise with increasing output. Thus consumer demand and the costs of production uniquely determine the market valuation of the characteristic. Because there is a complete range available, you can estimate the value of a bit more of characteristic 'x' by the price difference as compared to the rival product, which has all other characteristics the same but a bit more of 'x'. This would mean that one could collect statistics on characteristics of goods and services, the price people were willing to pay, and, using multiple regression, get values of the characteristics.

The interpretation of such statistics is, however, immediately clouded if the situation is complicated by interdependence since, like Lancaster's approach, the assumption is that characteristics are valuable in themselves; thus more of a valued characteristic is better. If the characteristic is valuable only in the presence of another, it might be possible to capture this in the analysis, but the complications of several characteristics varying according to the amounts of other characteristics, and indeed possibly moving from being valued to being disliked according to the strength of other characteristics, become extremely difficult to model. The danger is that such problems are simply averaged out, and a characteristic which is strongly sought in some circumstances and shunned in others leads by a process of averaging to a characteristic that has little value.

Unfortunately, therefore, Lancaster's contribution, while aiming to fill a need, cannot do so because of the complexity of characteristics. This is partly due to the fact that one cannot scale the relevant characteristics, and partly due to the unstable nature of their costs and values due to the impact of interdependencies in supply and in demand. If one takes the problem of satiability seriously this has the same effect.

4.3.2 The value of time: Becker's contribution

Gary S. Becker was awarded the Nobel Prize for Economics for his contributions to the application of economics to the field of personal and social relationships, including population and education as well as the area with which we shall deal here, the value of time. His original paper (Becker, 1965) introduced the idea of the household as a productive unit, using purchased goods in combination with time and skill to produce what he calls 'basic commodities' – the term he uses to define the activities that actually produce satisfaction. Thus, purchased inputs of foodstuffs, pre-prepared to a greater or lesser extent, are further prepared to make meals. The activity of preparation is seen by Becker as a production process exactly analogous to that of the firm, with both direct inputs, like the raw materials for the meal, and capital in the form of the tools used to prepare the food, from knives to stoves and other mechanical aids, and the human capital represented by the cook's experience and ability. If we follow this view, one of the factors that is required is the time to make the meal; indeed, in the original article all purchased goods require time to enjoy. This means that income (with which to purchase goods) and leisure (the time to enjoy them) are complements.

We explore this approach to the value of time. Layard and Walters (1978) provide the clearest review of the theories relating to 'values of time'. They do this in the context of the value of leisure and hence the supply of hours of work. They tackle the problem in a very formal manner, which requires real familiarity with the formal structures they use to enable the reader to make full use of them. This is an attempt to follow their argument with a minimum of formalism, while not losing too many of the major points. They start from the point of view of explaining the decline in the hours worked by males in the USA in recent history. Is this the result of the positive income effect of higher wages and a high income elasticity of demand for leisure, resulting in a backward sloping supply curve? At the simplest level their theory considers the potential working day as 24 hours, and any leisure time to be time out of work. This is done using traditional utility theory. From this formulation we get two interesting results:

1. The wage rate defines the rate at which goods can be transformed into leisure, i.e. 1 hour of work = w of income = a quantity of goods depending on the price level. Since the hour at work entails the loss of 1 hour of leisure, 1 hour of leisure is equivalent to the loss of goods to the value of w.

   but

2. Since the enjoyment of goods involves the use of leisure time, leisure and income are complements.

   Thus

3. As the wage rate rises, with the normal assumptions about diminishing marginal utility, the income effect can be expected to overcome the substitution effect towards more work, and the labour supply curve will slope backwards, at least after some value of the wage rate.

The difference in the pattern of work for men (declining hours worked with rising wages) and women (rising hours worked for increasing wages) is explained by the ease of substitution of machines for the time required for work in the home, but which require income to purchase. The substitution effect of the price of machines compared with the wage dominates the income effect. This framework gives no way of incorporating the pleasure or displeasure given by work. This can, however, easily be incorporated into the equation. The substitution becomes not simply a matter of the amount of goods that are sacrificed for the relevant amount of leisure, but of this weighed against the pleasure of work and leisure.

Even this framework does not include the major contribution made by Becker (1965) in his article on the value of time. This contribution was to incorporate both the price of the goods used in consumption and the time required to consume or use them. The combination of the value of time and the value of goods he called the 'full cost' of the activity, and the activity which results from the application of time and goods he called a 'basic commodity'. The household is seen as producing basic commodities by the use of time and purchased inputs. It is the consumption of these basic commodities which gives satisfaction, not the purchase of goods which are only inputs into their production. Formally, the idea of the combination of basic commodities which exhausts the household budget is expressed as:

$$\sum_i (P_i a_i + wt_i) Z_i = 24w + T_0 \qquad (4.3)$$

where $(P_i a_i + wt_i)$ is the inputs to basic commodity Z_i, P_i is the price of good i, a_i is the quantity of those goods, w is the wage rate, t_i is the time required and Y_0 is unearned income. That is, the price of goods multiplied by the input of goods, plus the wage rate multiplied by the time required for the production of basic commodity Z, summed over all basic commodities, must be equal to the 'full income' (i.e the income that could be earned if one worked for 24 hours per day plus the unearned income Y_0).

Thus:

1. If a fall in P_i is compensated by a fall in unearned income (so that utility remained constant) there would be substitution to Z_i from other basic commodities. If Z_i happened to be relatively time consuming compared to other goods this implies a substitution of time for income. 'In this connection the fall in the relative prices of goods inputs to recreation appears to offer some explanation of the secular decline of working hours in the United States'.

2. If substitution is allowed between time and goods inputs, the above effect might be reduced, by the substitution of the now cheaper goods for the time element in Z_i.

3. This general approach can be modified to account for varying wage rates per hour (e.g. overtime) and complementarities between certain sorts of leisure time and earning power (rest and efficiency at work), while still retaining a determinate result.

This whole analysis underlies the valuation of time for the estimation of travel demand. But before proceeding we should notice that this analysis correctly interprets the 'value of time' not as of 'time *per se*' but of 'time spent in alternative activities open to the consumer'. Thus 'negative values of time' are not inconceivable: (i) in prison, no alternative valuable use is available; (ii) lack of resources may permit only very poor uses of time. This analysis assumes independent utility functions, contrary to Earl. It also fails to analyse the situation where a good is consumed but consumption does not prevent other uses of time, e.g. expenditure on pleasanter offices improves the quality of work time; eating chocolates can be done while doing almost anything else.

Beesley (1965) used exactly these ideas of the trade-off of goods, in the form of expense, for time to obtain a value of time spent travelling. Becker's theory suggested that the value of time was the value of the opportunity cost of time in use 'a' rather than in use 'b'. This would be influenced by the other costs of uses 'a' and 'b' such as the prices of goods used in each, and by the level of income (by virtue of wage rates and unearned income) which determines the level of access to the goods inputs into the process of consumption. Thus for the value of time spent travelling we would expect:

1. A rise in fares (or car running costs) will encourage the substitution of other activities for travel, and hence will shift the demand for travel.

2. It is, however, the opportunity cost of the other activities open to the travellers that will influence the value of time spent travelling as

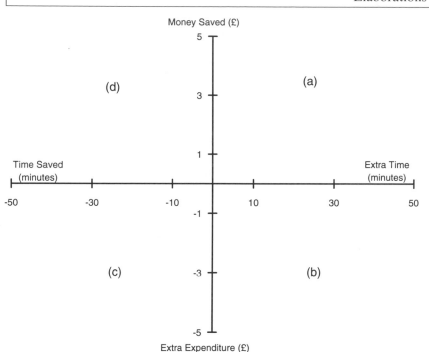

Figure 4.4 Measurement of the value of time by observed trade-offs.

opposed to time spent in other uses. This will vary with real incomes, and might be expected to vary with social conditions (urban or rural, for example) which give rise to different opportunities for using time. It will therefore not be surprising if homogeneity of income and location were to give the best results in measuring the value of time.

Beesley was looking for just such a group to assess the value of time. Clerical grade civil servants in the Ministry of Transport in London, where Beesley was working, suited admirably; most of them had no option but to travel by public transport, thus eliminating the final element in Becker's model, that of the quality of the experience in itself (car travel being frequently regarded as more relaxing than public transport). He found a group of people who had options of going by bus, by train or by tube, taking different lengths of time and with different costs. Their choices could be graphed as shown in Figure 4.4 and interpreted as follows:

- Quadrant **a** implies accepting spending longer on travelling in order to save money; for each individual the value of his or her time must be less than that indicated by the trade-off shown.
- Quadrant **b** is apparently illogical since it implies spending both extra time and extra money; if many observations fall into this quadrant it would probably indicate that some other variable was playing an important part in the choice, for example comfort. In fact only 69 out of 1109 subjects fell into this area.
- Quadrant **c** implies spending less time but paying for it by greater

expense, thus to each individual making such a choice, his/her value of time must be less than that indicated.

• Quadrant **d** is an uninteresting, because obvious, choice since it costs less to go by the faster route.

Beesley was able to find a value of time which resulted in only 27% misclassifications. The value was 31% of hourly income for the lower paid clerical officers, and 37% of hourly income for the higher paid executive officers.

All subsequent efforts at getting a value of time have suggested that the particularly simple situation studied gave very specially good results. Once the car is brought into the picture the values of time change in unpredictable ways. This could be for reasons of comfort and status, both of which were largely avoided by the particular choices facing the clerical officers. It could also be because of the potential for joint trips, and the flexibility that the car gives to change plans. The figure of one-third of hourly income is, however, still the official value of leisure time for transport studies.

Studies of higher income groups such as air travellers suggest much higher values (figures of 1.5 times hourly income have been found). The difficulty is in avoiding the effect of nervous travellers; the opportunity cost of travel time is very high if the result of too much time spent travelling is that you miss your flight.

Further studies showed that time spent walking to the bus or train stop, or waiting for the bus, was perceived as twice as long (or twice as unpleasant) as time actually spent travelling. These two values have been used to calculate the 'full cost' of travel; this is more usually known as **generalized cost**. The equation for this would be:

$$GC = aT + bW + F + P + M \qquad (4.4)$$

where a is the value of time, one-third of the average hourly wage rate; T is the total time taken for the trip from door to door; b is the excess value of walking and waiting time – if walking and waiting is twice as expensive as travelling time, $b = a$, if it is three times as expensive $b = 2a$; W is the walking and waiting time; F is the fare if travelling by public transport or the direct cost of the trip if travelling by car (this is usually only fuel costs since oil and tyre wear are not usually perceived as directly related to distance travelled. It does *not* include the overhead costs of car owner- ship: depreciation, road tax, or insurance; these do not vary with the number of trips made); P is parking charges if appropriate; M is the modal penalty – it has been found that public transport has to be about 10 minutes faster to be equally attractive, and hence to gain 50% of the market of those with access to a car.

4.3.3 The gravity model

Where the choice between service outlets is based on their accessibility to the consumer, the gravity model provides a method of analysis. It also provides the basic method for forecasting traffic flows in urban areas when new facilities, be they road or public transport, are to be built. It is based on the common-sense premise that consumers will prefer destinations that are equally attractive in themselves if they are closer, but that they will take account of the attractiveness of the destination. The structure of the model is closely akin to many of the models of monopolistic competition that we shall consider in Chapter 9.

The basic assumptions of the gravity model are that the numbers of people who will choose to travel to a service will be in direct proportion to:

1. its attractiveness; and
2. the potential of the zone of origin to generate trips;

but in inverse proportion to:

3. some function of its distance from them.

However, these simple assumptions are to be put into practice for urban areas with many different possible destinations and so we shall need a set of notations. The urban area is divided up into zones. Typically, it is convenient to use Census Enumeration zones so that the data from the Census can be used directly. We will use the following notation:

- T_{ij} represents trips from zone i to zone j.
- O_i represents trips originating in zone i.
- D_j represents the attraction of zone j as a destination.
- $f(d_{ij})$ represents the function of distance from zone i to zone j. This is known as the deterrence function.

Our simple assumptions would then transform into an equation as follows:

$$T_{ij} = \frac{k O_i D_j}{f(d_{ij})} \tag{4.5}$$

To use this we need some estimate of the number of trips likely to originate in zone i, as well as the approach to estimating the attraction of zone j. We will discuss the distance deterrence function later. The number of trips expected to originate in a zone has been the subject of much research by the major transportation consultants and the Ministry of Transport. It is based on the Census data for the zone and the large data collection exercise undertaken as part of any transportation study. It may be of interest to note that however complex such studies may seem, it is very much cheaper to collect only enough data to calibrate these models than to collect the data required to estimate zone to zone trips directly. The method of prediction is essentially to divide the population into categories, using household size, number of workers and car ownership to get estimates of trip rates for each category, and to apply these to the numbers of households in each category in each zone according to the Census. For shopping models, a similar process is carried out, often using regression based models from the family expenditure survey to match to the Census data.

The attractiveness of the destination, D_j, is in many ways more difficult to estimate. It is often done tautologically, by using the number of trips finishing in the zone, as estimated from traffic data, or simple factors are applied to office space and other such destinations. It is perhaps worth pointing out that for London at least, the Ministry of Transport did not know the amount of office space in Central London, and believed that no one else did either; the collection of this data will be a major problem for any future London study. It is always a problem in such studies. For shopping centres it is less difficult to estimate the shopping floor space, and this is the most frequently used variable for forecasts of the attractiveness of a shopping centre. Studies of consumers suggest that the actual (or reputed) value for money of the centre is also important. With modern leisure shopping centres with particularly attractive environments, one would expect these to have some influence also. This sort of refinement is extremely difficult to incorporate, as it amounts to *ad hoc* adjustments, since there are usually only relatively few centres on which any statistics could be based. This exactly mirrors the problems associated with Lancaster's approach to consumer choice, since many of the attributes are also difficult to measure.

The distance deterrence function has two aspects which need discussion: the measure for 'distance', and the form of the function and the value of its parameters. The best measure of distance is generally thought to be 'generalized cost'. In the context of transport studies this is the only one that allows policy variables such as parking charges, public transport subsidies, or rises in fares, road pricing and the like to be analysed. In the shopping or leisure context, it is perhaps less crucial, unless such transport policy aspects are important. Second best to generalized cost is probably total trip time, since this correlates with the cash cost of the trip, which is usually distance related but with an extra weighting on congested areas. It at least allows for some of the aggravation of walking and waiting time, even if this is heavily under-represented, and of course it allows for travel time. Distance *per se* is probably the worst of the measures, its only justification being that it is cheap to collect the data – requiring only a map. It is clearly useless if the model is to estimate transport demand case, as it does not allow for the quality of road or the levels of congestion; it may be acceptable in the shopping or leisure facility context, since the gravity model is unlikely to give very accurate results anyway because of the problems of scaling attractiveness, particularly for facilities that have not yet been built.

The distance deterrence function has to be calibrated to the data. There are many functional forms that it can take, the most usual being the exponential function, but it can also be a simple power function, e.g. $(d_{ij})^{-\gamma}$. The process of calibration is an interactive one, and depends somewhat on another aspect of the model, namely how far the model is to be constrained. The difference between constrained and unconstrained is a major conceptual difference, and this will now be explained.

An **unconstrained gravity model** is a **combined trip generation and destination choice model** – one where the interaction between the origin and destination zone is truly multiplicative. Thus, the bigger the attract-iveness the more trips will be generated; if the attractiveness is decreased then the model will actually predict that fewer trips will take place. Such a model is liable to be very difficult to calibrate accurately, since the item we have identified as the weak link, the attraction measure, now becomes crucial in generating trips. However, if that is the sort of model you wish to put forward – one where the attractiveness of the destinations affects the number of trips – this is really the only sort of model to use.

A **constrained gravity model** is a model that implicitly assumes that a certain number of trips will take place – a residential zone will generate a certain level of shopping expenditure or private/public transport trips – and the model is about the **choice of destinations or modes**. The model may be constrained only in relation to the origins; this implies that we have accurately forecast the trips originating from a zone and that we wish to share these out between the destination zones, but we do not know the numbers of trips we expect in each destination zone to any degree of accuracy. A destination-constrained model makes the reverse assump-tion; for example we might know how much expenditure we expect in each shopping area, but not know accurately which zones are generating it. A doubly-constrained model shares out the trips so that both the predicted origins and the predicted destinations are accurate.

Let us take as an example an origin-constrained model; as stated above, this is constructed so that trips are shared out between destinations. Thus, we know O_i and we wish to model the distribution of this fixed total between the possible destinations. One way to do this would be to say that what we are looking for is a relative measure of the attractiveness of the destination allowing for its distance. We could thus rewrite the attractive-ness element of Equation (4.5) as:

$$D_j (d_{ij})^{-\gamma} \tag{4.6}$$

and if we express this as a proportion of the attractiveness of all destinations, we would get a relative attractiveness as follows:

$$\frac{D_j (d_{ij})^{-\gamma}}{\Sigma D_j (d_{ij})^{-\gamma}} \tag{4.7}$$

To calculate the number of trips, going from i to j we need to multiply this term for the relative attractiveness of zone j by the number of trips we expect to start from zone i. This gives:

$$T_{ij} = O_i \frac{D_j (d_{ij})^{-\gamma}}{\Sigma D_j (d_{ij})^{-\gamma}} \tag{4.8}$$

The difficulties of calibration of such a model come from the fact that the item for which we need a figure, the deterrence function, will not just affect D_j, but its relative attractiveness to all the other zones. The model has therefore to be calibrated by a trial and error procedure, gradually moving to an acceptable result. The process is illustrated in Figure 4.5.

The doubly-constrained gravity model ensures that both the estimates of trips originating from each zone and the trips expected to finish there are consistent with the forecast numbers. It is correspondingly more complicated both in its formula and in calibration, but the principles are identical to the singly-constrained model.

Discussion

The gravity model is widely used, particularly for public choices in relation to transport or planning policy. Its importance to the manager is therefore largely one of understanding the tools and constraints of public policy. The constraints may be binding – if you want to set up a supermarket, you need planning permission. It is thus often necessary to know the way in which the authorities are analysing the problem. The authorities'

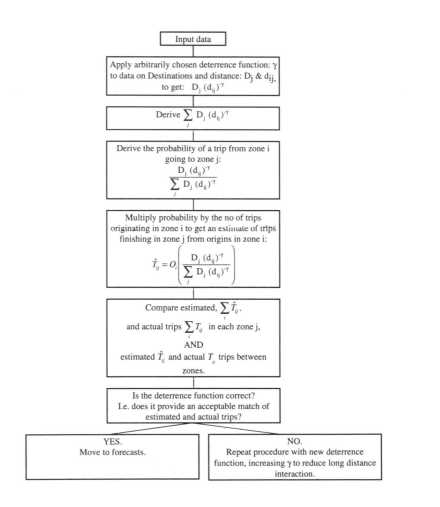

Figure 4.5 Calibration of the singly constrained gravity model.

models may also provide material of interest to the estimation of the demand for your services; for example, changes in transport policy may affect your competitive position, either adversely or favourably.

Consideration of the specification of the gravity model in the light of the problems identified with Lancaster's approach to demand is fruitful, and shows up many of the potential problems with the estimates derived from gravity models. For example, although the transport models have a fair record for the accuracy of their predictions, they are not necessarily well adapted to evaluating all sorts of policy; they use generalized cost models with single values of time, so that the probable increase in value of time relative to expenditure that would be predicted by Becker's model is ignored; this might give odd results in evaluating road pricing schemes. They would certainly not reveal the consequences for different income groups, and the notion that it would be the socially highest value uses of the car that would survive the imposition of sufficiently high prices to change the level of congestion indicates a touching faith in the relationship between social value and the level of pay received.

It is finally worth noting the very strong assumptions that these models incorporate in relation to the elasticities of demand. The unconstrained model has implicitly a very high elasticity of demand with respect to facility creation or enhancement. The constrained model has a zero elasticity of market demand in total, but a varying elasticity with respect to particular destinations; the elasticity will be greater as the deterrent effect of 'distance' declines, since small changes will bring a greater range of alternative destinations into contention. The elasticity of use of a particular shopping centre (the ratio of the proportional increase in the number of users to the proportional change in travel costs) will also depend for any particular zone on the particular configuration of alternative origins and destinations with which it is comparable. The more zones that are directly competitive (i.e. which offer a similar level of attractiveness allowing for the cost of transport), the more likely it is that a small favourable change will attract considerably more trips. It is the provision of a realistic structure for modelling this sort of interdependence that makes the gravity model of interest in spite of inevitable crudity in its formulation.

Finally, a note on bibliography for the gravity model: there is a vast range of literature discussing it at various levels of detail, much of it turgidly mathematical. For an excellent simple introduction, which shows how it works and gives lots of worked examples, and which provides a good discussion of many of the basic points, David Foot's (1981) *Operational Urban Models* is excellent; for a much more advanced treatment: Alan Wilson's (1974) *Urban and Regional Models in Geography and Planning* is still well worth considering.

4.3.4 Sectoral interdependence of demand

One of the reasons given in Chapter 2 for the growth in service industry employment was the hiving off of the service element into separate units, rather than its retention within the manufacturing firm or plant. This clearly indicates the importance of the linkage between that unit and the service industry for demand. Input–output analysis provides a method for analysing such interdependence. It is also the basis for local area impact studies, particularly important in relation to tourism and other regional economic studies. The demand for freight transport is also modelled on this basis.

The idea is very simple: trace the purchases in the economy through their various industrial groups to assess their final impact. For example, how would the layoffs following the closure of Swann Hunter's shipyard on the Tyne affect the local shops, cinemas, clubs, lawyers' practices, etc.? To do this one would need to trace the amount of income from Swann Hunter's that went into the local firms. Thus, one would need two surveys: firstly, a survey of the purchases by the industry from various local suppliers and an estimate of their purchases outside the region, and, secondly, an estimate of consumer spending and its distribution between various sectors. At a larger scale, to assess the impacts of national changes on national demand, input–output models are used as part of national income forecasting methods.

For the inter-industry purchases, the easiest source of information is usually VAT returns, since these must itemize all the payments for purchased inputs, and, providing one can allocate the destination firm into an industry, this then provides a detailed breakdown of purchases. VAT sales receipts provide a cross-check, assuming that both firms are surveyed. The results are aggregated into a table called a **transactions matrix**, which looks approximately like Table 4.3, which is adapted from Iain McNicoll's (1992) study of the Shetland economy. Since we are interested in service industries let us look first at 'Business Services and Communications'. Following down the column with that title, we find that they purchased £71 000 of inputs from Agriculture. Presumably, this would largely be food, but it could be premises on agricultural holdings etc. The purchase from 'Marine and Other Manufacturing' is £15 000, and could be almost anything; from 'construction' £333 000, presumably for repairs; new buildings should come under 'Investment' in the final columns; the expenditure on 'Government Services', which includes three rows from the original table – Local Government, Education and Health – is confined to expenditure on 'Local Government'; this is the contribution to the business rate. Central Government taxes come into the row 'Other Value Added'. This forms part of the expenditure for inputs outside the region.

The expenditure on 'Transport' and on 'Distribution' is, however, subject to special accounting procedures. Since almost everything requires transporting and selling through the distribution system, except large flows between industrial buyers and sellers, to allocate items to 'Transport' on the basis of 'Transport' buying everything and then selling it on to whatever industry is appropriate, would completely mask the set of relationships the analysis is trying to reveal. The only purchaser would be Transport, unless the firms had their own fleets of trucks (or boats in this

Table 4.3 The Shetland input–output table, 1987/88 (£000s, current producers' prices)

PURCHASES FROM \ SALES TO	Agric & Fish Farm	Fish'g	Fish Proc	Knit	Marine & Other Mfg	Constr & Quarry	Hot & Cat	Electr & Water	Trnspt & Distrib	Oil Rel Act	Bus Serv & Comms	Govt Serv	Other Serv	House-holds	Total Inter-mediate sales	Final Demand — Invest-ment	Exports	Tourist Expend	Central Gov't current expend	Total Gross Outputs
Agriculture & Fish Farm.	712	3465		301	291	293					71	59		583	5775	1072	22894			29741
Fishing			7655		9		2					21		247	7934		9840			17774
Fish Processing					136		8							229	373	158	16931			17462
Knitwear				6	21									584	611	213	5638	272		6734
Marine & Other Mfg	918	3159	287	35	610	1096	76	2	354	3550	150	391	21	1468	12117	47	243	302	43	12752
Construction & Quarries	404	31		29	229	1703	291	180	1319	446	333	2801	132	1341	9239	31001	1980	18		42238
Hotels & Catering	12	29	20		116	291		107	674	1442	126			1640	4457			2195		6652
Electr. & Water	804	502	72	20	72	104	107	63	536	301	151	2320	191	2040	7283			9		7292
Transport & Distribution	1279	167	261	161	223	2707	140	124	5244	15162	542	2181	897	22181	51269	204	4763	452	210	56898
Oil Related Activities	89														89		204767			204856
Business Serv. & Comms	1156	228	198	113	207	669	220	137	2819	3321	954	1036	399	7511	18968	132		18		19118
Government Services	84	105		85	60	172	360	449	761	29977	161	18194	175	1902	52485				18974	71459
Other Services	432	157	10	25	156	66	102	93	480	355	221	1495	642	12414	16648			179	996	17823
Households	12146	3153	7709	2598	4323	13381	2016	1643	17847	22362	10762	18164	6231	372	122707			415	15961	139083
Local Purchases	18036	11252	15750	3550	6453	19898	3615	2691	30461	76916	13471	46662	8688	52512	309955	32695	267056	3833	36343	649882
Imports	8280	2413	700	2769	3489	13256	2111	2761	7108	33584	1865	19993	4423	54376	157128					71459
Other Value Added	3425	4109	1012	415	2810	9085	926	1929	19329	89117	3482	12208	4712	32216	184775					184775
Unrequited payments										5150		-2793		-21	2336					2336
TOTAL INPUTS	29741	17774	17462	6734	12752	42239	6652	7381	56898	204767	18818	78761	17823	139083	656885					

Source: McNicoll, Small area input–output analysis: A case study of Shetland for 1987/88; published by the Scottish Office, 1992.

context), and the only seller Transport. Thus what is done for both of these is to regard the purchase from 'Transport' or 'Distribution' as being just the value they add, i.e. the costs of that transport, or the markup charged by the distributor (whether retail or wholesale). The rest of the transaction is considered as a transaction between the industry selling and the industry purchasing.

Purchases from 'Local Government' are the payment of rates. Purchases from 'Households' are the payment for work done, i.e. the wages, salaries and profits payed to Shetlanders by the various firms making up the industries. It will be noticed that 'Households' come within the internal matrix, both in terms of purchases and sales. This is perfectly valid, and means that the income and expenditure by households is being treated as a fixed pattern like the purchases and sales of the industries. This is not the only way to regard this item. It may be regarded as primary input, along with 'Imports' and 'Other Value Added', and, on the purchases side, as part of 'Final Demand'. This latter approach would be appropriate if one wished to be able to treat it as a separate item which can be modelled by reference to other information, such as independent forecasts of consumer expenditure patterns, which might change with changing economic situations. For example, the collapse of the car market during the recession would not be correctly forecast by the method employed in this study. Following this method, expenditure on cars would be assumed to follow the fixed pattern of expenditure on cars at the survey date, and so would be expected to decline in proportion to the decline in consumer incomes, whereas it has declined by very much more than that.

'Primary Input' consists of those items bought from outside the Shetlands, and which therefore will not contribute to the circulation of money in exchange for goods and services in the Shetland economy. Indeed, they will take money out of the economy. 'Final Demand', on the other hand, consists of the purchases not under Shetlanders' control, which put money into the Shetland economy. These all therefore need to be forecast separately.

How is this useful for forecasting? The idea is to record the changes that might happen to one industry, and hence forecast the effect of these changes on the economy as a whole, and more specifically on its component parts – for example, the purchases of £3 465 000 worth of fish from 'Agriculture and Fish Farming' and a further £7 655 000 worth from 'Fishing' by 'Fish Processing' and the purchase of £3 550 000 from 'Marine Engineering and Other Manufacturing' and over £15 million worth of transport and distribution services by 'Oil Related Activities'. In general, however, in a small economy like that of the Shetlands, most of the linkages come through the payments to and expenditure by 'Households'; in other words local knock-on effects may be small but are principally due to falls in incomes. Even this will, however, be much attenuated by the level of expenditure by households outside the region. Following down the 'Households' column one can see that out of a 'Gross Input' in excess of £139 million, £86.5 million goes straight out of the economy, £54,3 million in imports and £32.2 million in taxes.

Even with the relatively small linkages in a local economy, if one industry's final demand changes, there will be effects felt through the system. To simplify the analysis and gain an understanding of the process, we will construct an entirely arbitrary input–output table (Table 4.4).

Table 4.4 Input–output table

Sales to:	1	2	3	Final demand	Total gross output
Purchases from					
1	**5**	**11**	**12**	22	50
2	**15**	**22**	**15**	3	55
3	**20**	**5.5**	**11**	11.5	48
External	15	16.5	18		
Total gross input	50	55	48		

To complete the next stage we need to have a set of coefficients to indicate the proportion of any change in the output of a particular industry that will be purchased from any other industry. In other words, we want to find out how much the inputs bought from other industries will change. This we can do by expressing the figures of 'purchases from' as a proportion of the total gross input (these figures are in bold type in Table 4.4). Thus, Industry 1 purchases 5 units out of its gross input of 50 from other firms within Industry 1, i.e. 5/50 = 0.1; its 15 units from Industry 2 make a coefficient of 0.3 (15/50), and its purchases from Industry 3 give a coefficient of 0.4. These coefficients are set out in Table 4.5.

Table 4.5 Technical coefficients, input–output example

	1	2	3
1	0.1	0.2	0.25
2	0.3	0.4	0.3125
3	0.4	0.05	0.23

Now it is obvious that if the demand for Industry 1 were to increase by 10 units, and the pattern of input purchases were to stay the same, then purchases from other firms in the industry would initially increase by 1 unit; purchases from Industry 2 would increase by 3 units, and from Industry 3 by 4 units. But of course those increases have impacts on all the industries, as well. So the second round purchases will be as follows: the further 1 unit increase in demand for Industry 1 would increase demands for Industry 1 by 0.1, Industry 2 by 0.3, and Industry 3 by 0.4. The three units' increase in Industry 2's output would increase Industry 1's by 0.2 × 3 = 0.6, Industry 2's by 1.2 and Industry 3's by 0.15. Finally, in this second round of purchases, the four units of increase in demand for Industry 3's output will lead to purchases of 1 unit from Industry 1, 1.25 units from Industry 2 and 0.92 units from Industry 3. Totalling these second round purchases for Industry 1: $0.1 + 0.6 + 1 = 1.7$ units. And so we start on the third round, and so on. Fortunately, computers programmed by mathematicians can solve this process in one by multiplying the change in final demands by the Leontieff matrix (Table 4.6).

Table 4.6 Leontieff inverse matrix

1.673 148 1	0.624 092 2	0.796 514 1
1.334 395 4	2.222 742 8	1.335 332 4
0.955 816 9	0.468 537 7	1.799 184 7

What does this matrix mean? For each 1 unit increase in output required from Industry 1, you would get a final increase in gross output from Industry 1 of 1.67 units, from Industry 2 of 1.33 units and from Industry 3 of 0.96 units. Why should there be such increases? It almost sounds like a money making machine. In fact, it is the result of double counting: every unit of output requires purchased inputs and these come into the firm's turnover; here we are adding up changes in turnover, and, like the amazing figures produced to scare the public about the disastrous effect of strikes, these are gross exaggerations. They include all the purchases counted as if they were final output. To give an example: if a civil engineering consultancy is hired to do the final design and site work for a motorway, it will usually purchase the services of lawyers, landscape architects and quantity surveyors, and may even subcontract some of the civil engineering work such as specialist bridge or piling design. If it is the main contractor in the actual construction it will hire all sorts of firms to provide plant, soil stabilizing netting, concrete, aggregates, steelwork, etc. Let us say the prime contractor, the civil engineering firm, is paid £50 million for the contract, and pays £100 000 to landscape architects, who further subcontract £50 000 to nurserymen and contractors. (We will not consider all the other links suggested.) What input–output analysis is doing is to count the £50 million, plus the £100 000, plus the £50 000 since these are the payments made to each of the firms. The real income element of this can be found by applying the technical coefficient from the previous matrix, which represents the income payments per unit of gross output; in Table 4.3 for Agriculture and Fish Farming this would be: £12 146/£29 741 (thousands) = 0.40.

The actual effect on local incomes, the equivalent of the Keynesian multiplier, is usually less than 1.2, of which the 1 is the initial injection of cash, for example a farm subsidy, or the expenditure by tourists in an area. As much of that immediately goes out of the area in the form of taxes and imports, it is not surprising that the overall effect is small. The employment effect could be calculated if the ratio of employment to gross output (or income) were available.

Given the small scale of the effects at local level, one might question why input–output analysis is given a place in this book. There are basically two reasons: firstly, it is important to realize how small these effects are, and input–output analysis gives almost the only basis for doing so; secondly, it is the methodological basis for many types of *ad hoc* multiplier studies, where the multiplier is traced through the specific paths of purchase and hence impact. Two recent studies of this type may be cited to show its ongoing application. Johnson and Thomas (1990) used such a study to show the local employment impact of the Beamish Museum in Northumberland. They show that the maximum probable level of employment generation is 55% above the basic employment in the museum itself. Their alternative estimate, which results from employment diverted from elsewhere by the opportunities at Beamish, is that it contributes only 99% of the direct employment. A methodologically excellent study is provided by MacDonald and Swales (1991); unfortunately their data failed them and so its results are hypothetical.

Some points on terminology are worth noting. Most studies will use the terms: 'direct', 'indirect' and 'induced' in relation to employment, output or income effects. The first is more or less self-explanatory; the direct impact is the initial impact created by the expenditure. The direct employment from the Beamish Museum was 115 people at the site, and 15 people in associated activities (things like printing, providing food for the restaurants, souvenirs etc.). The indirect employment is those jobs created by the inter-industry linkages, where these are defined by the purchases of goods and services, but it excludes the employment created by the spending of income. In Beamish this amounted to 35 extra jobs. The induced effect is those extra jobs created by the spending of income generated by the 'direct' and 'indirect' jobs. In Beamish this amounted to 13 extra jobs. The ratio of 'direct and indirect' to 'direct' output, income or employment is called a type 1 multiplier. If the 'induced' effect is also included it is called a type 2 multiplier, i.e. the ratio of 'direct, indirect and induced' to 'direct'.

Common to all these methodologies are certain limitations which should be borne in mind when assessing their appropriateness:

1. They are demand driven. They assume that output can be produced and that it will be produced by the same industries as before. Thus, for example, the supply side change, like the 'tie-up' policy for fishing, which one might hope to model using the Shetland input–output table, would require special estimates to be made of the changes in final demand resulting from the policy, so that its impact could then be traced through the system. (Under the 'tie-up' policy boats are kept tied up in harbour for a certain proportion of the time to reduce overfishing.)
2. They use fixed coefficients. This implies two things: firstly, if prices remain constant the structure of inter-industry demand remains constant in terms of the proportions of items purchased from different places; this implies no technical change. Secondly, if there are relative

price changes, there is unit elasticity of demand for such items, so that the value of inputs purchased remains the same! That is a pretty strong assumption, and where there are substantial price rises in only some sectors, the model should probably be examined carefully. If the technical coefficients (in the sense of the relative quantities of inputs required to produce a given amount of output) are fixed, as was originally assumed by Leontieff, then the transactions matrix should be adjusted by the full measure of the price rise. This would be offset by any price elasticity in the demand for inputs.

3. An input–output study, like any other sectorally based study, can be distorted by the wrong classification of firms, or by the presence of large but atypical firms in the area. As long as the pattern of links persists, it will not cause distortion, but as the sort of impact study analysed here will be dealing with special facilities and their impact, these distortions are quite likely, and it is wise to be on one's guard against their effects. For example, in the Shetlands study, one of the industries is 'Tourism'. It is a matter of common sense that if a huge new Trust House Forte or other chain hotel is planned, this will have radically different linkages as compared with an industry based on bed and breakfast and family guest houses. The hotel may have almost no linkages with local suppliers, in contrast to the B&B; even the staff may not be locally recruited. In places like the Highlands of Scotland the demand may be so seasonal that even chambermaids are brought in from outside the area.

This section on the sectoral interdependence of demand has been included in order to show how demand may be forecast using input–output analysis. The examples largely refer to the social impact of either the opening or closing of a facility. It could be argued that this has little to do with managerial economics, the economics of decisions within the firm; however, the firm operates within a local authority area and may be crucially dependent upon the local authority for planning permission and very possibly for access to various grants, and even specially favourable loans through enterprise trusts. The social arguments cannot be ignored, and as such this aspect of demand is important.

4.3.5 Demand and time

The problem of peaks and troughs in demand stems directly from the inability to store the output, and is in many cases exacerbated by the need for the customer and supplier to be present at the same place and time. Activities are part of a lifestyle; for example it may be difficult to get away from work to play squash in the afternoon, and so for many a squash court in the afternoon is a completely different service from a squash court in the evening. The extent to which these differences can be managed and money can be made by price discrimination is a recurrent concern in service industries. Fuller consideration will be given to this in Chapter 9, under the heading of 'Price discrimination' (section 9.3).

4.4 ALTERNATIVE THEORETICAL APPROACHES TO DEMAND

In contrast to the previous section where the consumer was considered to be omniscient, individualistically rational, and subject to diminishing marginal utility, the ideas introduced in this section consider different approaches to the consumer. Scitovski in 1947 had pioneered the modern theory of 'externalities' which we discussed in Chapter 3, based on a strictly conventional view of the rational individualistic consumer. His late work, *The Joyless Economy*, provides an interesting view of the consumer torn between boredom and overstimulation, who changes as he or she masters new activities. Since many services provide such stimulation, it seems worth including this view. A kindred view, based on the work of a different psychologist but containing the idea of the learning consumer, is that of Peter Earl, whose book *Lifestyle Economics* provides a much less mechanistic view of the consumer and interesting insights into alternative ways of looking at behaviour. Both of these are important in their emphasis on the learned nature of tastes and their social determination. Moving on from that in what might be seen as a logical progression, we look at the suggestion of Hilary Silver that much of service industry provision is in response to changing demographic and social patterns. This brings us to a view of demand based on need; the political Right might wish to see this eliminated, but it seems likely to persist in spite of them. The contradictions between this and the rational individualistic consumer, and the difficulties of catering for demand based on need within the economic framework complete this chapter.

4.4.1 Distinction between stimulation goods and commodities

Tibor Scitovski distinguishes between 'comfort' and 'stimulation' goods. Comfort in this context comes partly from the satisfaction of physiological needs – you are warm, well-clothed and well-fed, sitting in a comfortable chair – but this is only a limited proportion of the satisfaction of comfort, as illustrated by the widely different definition of the poverty level in different countries, and the fact that it is undoubtedly possible to survive on our poverty level Social Security payments. It may not be possible to live in 'comfort' on them for two reasons: firstly, the payments may be too low to gain acceptance in society so that the basic need for 'social belonging' may not be met. The comforts described above almost certainly imply a certain social context which involves acceptance. Secondly, the payments may be the result of loss of income from unemployment, and this involves giving up aspects of consumption that have become habitual. The widespread nature of 'addiction' is stressed by Scitovski, and it is clear that everything from attachment to a daily bath or shower to grief for a lost partner may be explained by mechanisms close to that involved in addiction. The loss of status involved in losing a job is thus likely to be threefold: you lose the status of belonging to a social group, you lose income which may involve direct losses of habitual consumption patterns, and very probably, you lose the stimulation that a job may entail.

Stimulation, on the other hand, involves the appropriate amount of novelty. Too much novelty involves stress, and lack of enjoyment; too little involves boredom. The transition from stimulation to stress, from maximum enjoyment because of just the right amount of new material to being overwhelmed by it, is quite sudden, and is probably a familiar experience to students of economics. As stimulation is the result of learning new things, the stimuli that give rise to it are therefore continually shifting, since once the situation has been mastered, stimulation is only obtained from a new and more testing one. To give a personal example, when I started hill-walking, I felt exposed and anxious on steep slopes, particularly if they had cliffs below them; now the height of delight is a path a couple of feet wide with '800 metres of beetling cliff above and 800 metres of vertical drop below', as a local guide book put it. In terms of excitement the initial experience on the hills and more recent experiences were probably similar, though objectively very different. This is a cruel compression of Scitovski's account of the psychology of consumption and his resulting critique of much of the approach to growth in the G7 economies and the policies that go with it; *The Joyless Economy* is a readable book, full of ideas but without technicalities, and the reader is urged to seek it out.

The importance of these ideas for the service industries is extensive. They give some strong implications that we should not be looking for a 'representative consumer', the homogeneous version of economic man which forms the basis for much of the theory of monopolistic competition. We shall naturally return to this topic. These ideas emphasize that which is known to every advertising agency and marketing expert, that social status and belonging are vital elements in a service or product, and thus that we had better consider this in our pricing and marketing policies. Finally, since the process of learning is very often a service function, whether it be by business consultancies 'stimulating' management to look at new ways of doing things or providers of leisure activities giving new challenges to their clients, and since stimulation is a need which is continually self-renewing, it provides a strong suggestion that the service industries will not suffer from market saturation in the way that goods industries may. Equally, firms that try to stand still will suffer from a loss of custom unless they continually adapt their offerings to the new level of expertise of their customers; 'menu fatigue' – boredom with an unchanged menu – is not just a problem in restaurants.

4.4.2 Lifestyle choices

Peter Earl's (1986) book *Lifestyle Economics*, subtitled *Consumer Behaviour in a Turbulent World*, approaches the problem of consumer behaviour from the perspective of a different school of psychology, the Kellian school of 'personal construct theory'. The main focus of this view of the world is that people develop a set of constructs – that is, ideas about the functioning of the world – which they use to guide them in their decisions. Like the 'arousal theory' on which Scitovski based his approach, personal construct theory encompasses situations where we feel comfortable, i.e. where our constructs prove adequate for our life situation, in which case we shall be looking to 'extend the range of our competence', looking either for new areas in which to apply our constructs, or new constructs to extend the way we cope with the existing environment; this appears to be parallel to the search for stimulation. Where 'arousal theory' would look at behaviour in situations of stress as 'comfort seeking', personal construct theory also encompasses those situations where the old rules do not seem to be working at all well, because the environment has changed, or possibly because our old rules were inadequate, and we have made perverse choices; we are in need of establishing comfort around us by finding a new set of constructs that will enable us to cope with our new circumstances.

Much of the question of controlling the environment is dependent upon the way we are interacting with our social group, and Earl (1983, pp. 182–183) sums up five ways in which we interact with other members of society:

1. Other people can help us to form theories about the nature of things by offering advice and information.
2. Other people can help us to test theories, either directly (e.g. 'What do you think of . . . ?'), or indirectly where we can observe their experiences in particular circumstances.
3. We find some people particularly interesting and wish to clarify our image of them.
4. In industrial societies social interaction in the workplace is necessary if we are to obtain income with which to explore other activities, or test out skills.
5. If we are prepared to accept on trust what others have told us to be 'common-sense things which everyone knows' we can confidently proceed to more adventurous activities. Social codes and customs, as well as the legal framework and reputations of people and products, enable us to save time and take a lot for granted.

This emphasis on social interaction, and the strong base in the obviously realistic premise of 'bounded rationality', puts Earl's approach into immediate conflict with the traditional approach to demand based on individually separable utility functions and perfect information. The term 'bounded rationality' encompasses the limitation on our ability to process information. We aim to be rational, but can only be so within the limits of our ability to understand the world about us; by 'understand' we mean in this context that we can (i) perceive what is happening accurately, (ii) have a theoretical structure which will allow us to handle this information and (iii) have the computational ability to apply this theoretical structure.

The process of choice suggested by Earl is also quite different from the full information marginal decision making techniques implicit in the traditional analysis. Earl stresses the impact of bounded rationality, such that a decision on a complex matter will be taken by a selection process based on target levels of certain key variables. He suggests on the basis of psychological literature that between five and nine variables are the most that people can handle (Earl, 1986, p. 177). Thus, in choosing a consumer durable, such as a car, or more still in relation to true lifestyle choices such as whether to live in the country or the town, some method has to be found for selecting across many different characteristics. This in Earl's view may be done in two stages; firstly, a strategic decision reflecting the basic criteria and the outline of the direction we wish to follow, and, secondly, the tactical decision, as to which particular appropriate house or car should be selected.

The strategic decision is seen as one which involves serious implications for many other aspects of the consumer's world view. Thus, choosing a house involves implications for the expense and hence the disposable income after purchase, the amount of commuting time and hence the time available for other activities and the access to those activities, and there may be real choices as to which activities will be favoured by a particular choice. (Long-distance commuting may facilitate one's passion for horse riding or bird watching, but severely restrict the feasibility of regular opera and theatre going.) The style of house also has implications for the sort of people who are going to be impressed by one's choice, and hence who will be attracted into one's social circle, and those who will find it offputting. For example, if you want to marry money, you had better think up some excellent reasons why a council flat in a slum area famous for its drugs and violence is the right residence. Even if your partner can be convinced, the parents from whom the money may eventually come are unlikely to be, and may even withdraw the funds. These multiple connections make the decision almost impossibly difficult, and may push the consumer towards taking the choice that would be favoured by his or her reference group rather than the individualistic choice implied by traditional theory. Earl points out the contradictions in the neat division between strategic and tactical decisions, such that one can take decisions in this hierarchical fashion: choosing a house, at price 'X' in a particular area leaving enough money to pursue such and such activities; the combination of house and activities requires such and such a type of car which can be purchased for so much money, leaving enough for. . . . However, it is immediately obvious that any slippage in any one of the above has implications for the others; unforeseen expenses, failures of one of the elements to provide the characteristics sought, or changes in life circumstances, particularly unemployment or such things as family breakups, may all cause such severe spillovers into the other areas of activity that what seemed a neat tactical decision becomes a decision about saving as much of the lifestyle as possible, or choosing a new one.

Within the tactical sphere, Earl can be more specific about the decision structures likely to be adopted and favours the view that choice is made on the basis of a non-compensatory elimination process, based on critical levels of various characteristics. This he calls a 'characteristic filtering rule'

(Earl, 1986, pp. 183–188). This differs from all the approaches which imply that 'everything has its price', in that here there is no compensation for failure to meet one of the levels of aspiration for a characteristic. A neat example is provided by the reader of a motor car magazine who wrote in to say 'I am over six foot and cannot get comfortable in the driving seat of either the Golf or the Escort. No matter how superior the Golf or the Escort may be "mechanically" that is of no consequence if I find myself permanently uncomfortable in them' (Earl, 1986, p. 247). This is in contrast to the theory of consumer behaviour incorporated in Lancaster and in the theory of demand set out above, where preferences can always be reversed by a sufficient fall in price of the rejected article or characteristic.

Thus in Earl's view, the range of choices is narrowed down by elimination. In the choice of housing, a person may only consider houses with two or more bedrooms, views of open country, near a limited range of schools, and below a certain price. This may eliminate many houses where bedrooms could be added, or where the local school is only marginally worse but all other attributes are significantly better, etc. Earl supports this imperfectly rational approach both with discussion of the psychological processes and with reference to some market studies. In the psychological context there is strong emphasis on fitting things into the limited frame of reference that is at the person's command, and certainly not extending that frame of reference in too many ways at once. Many marketing studies use an approach which is explicitly one of compensation; the 'hedonic price' of a good is the sum of its scores on various characteristics. This implies that a very high score on one characteristic will outweigh slightly low scores on many others. This Earl regards as implausible, and points out the poor predictive ability of such studies. He quotes a study by Reilly *et al.* (Earl, 1986, p. 240), and more particularly a series of reviews of different brands of car within certain categories. The very choice of a particular set of cars for comparison implies this sort of clear categorization of multi-characteristic artefacts into groups which will be instantly recognized by consumers, and within which they themselves will be choosing. Earl regards this form of discussion as demonstrating the use of criterion levels of achievement in particular characteristics in a **non-compensatory fashion**. For example, no matter how fast a car may be, even in the context of sports cars, this does not make up for poor handling, or comfort, except for a very small minority of buyers.

If several potential purchases satisfy the requirements, compensating methodologies – where implicitly the sum of desirability of different attributes is the decision criterion – may be used, or the 'mould' may be tightened; that is to say the levels of characteristics to be achieved may be raised.

It is interesting to apply the notion of non-compensating filters to travel choice. Beesley's study of the value of time provides a successful study based on full information trade-off theory. However, the situation was chosen so that there were no complex choices. There is no problem of bounded rationality in choice of Mode A, ten minutes faster, against

Mode B, fifty pence cheaper. The choice might be more complex if it involved car trips, because issues of comfort, prestige and personal safety would enter into the decision; it would certainly become more complex if it involved joint trips with other members of the household. The complexity and poor fit of the trade-off model in more complex situations, as shown by subsequent value-of-time studies, suggests that either the theory is deficient and other choice methods are being employed, or that the structure of the trade-offs is much more complex and cannot be captured by the data or its method of analysis. Subsequent studies of the multiplicity of trip functions within any trip by car drivers suggest this, but of course still do not suggest which method of choice is being used. Thus we know that in many cases the main earner's trip to work may involve dropping the children at school, his or her partner off to a job, and then proceeding to the place of work. This does not tell us whether marginal trade-offs are being used or whether a decision process more akin to that suggested by Earl is appropriate. It does suggest that changes will have to be fairly large before any response in behaviour will be evident, since it is unlikely that a complicated chain will be altered by a small change in, say, the price of petrol. A change in regulations such as the loss of parking places might well force an alteration, and with it a significant change in the daily organization of the household. The only way that this can be analysed is to set out a research design that enables the process of decision as well as the outcome to be followed.

What are the implications of Earl's approach as compared to the traditional approach to demand?

1. There may be large areas of consumption where habit is more important than marginal price changes, since habitual consumption forms part of our range of competence and frees our limited energies for the extension or consolidation of that competence.
2. Social interaction, in the form not only of 'keeping up with the Joneses' but also of using the Joneses as role models and sources of information in consumption, becomes an important aspect. Thus we have a conceptual model for 'reputation goods' which is integrated with our overall model of consumption rather than the explanation of an awkward exception.
3. If target ranges of particular characteristics are being used in the selection of individual goods or services, there is likely to be saturation on some items, and there will certainly be saturation if other items do not match up to the required levels. Thus an excessive price tag combined with very fast spin speeds may exclude many washing machines from consideration if the target range is a lower price with an adequate spin speed. This could be simulated in the traditional analysis by choosing extreme forms of the indifference curves, but the extra complexity implicit in the traditional analysis would then lose any justification.
4. There has not been space to discuss the extra dimensions of understanding of individual consumer behaviour which integration into a

wider psychological framework permits. People's persistence with failed strategies, alias the failure to regard sunk costs as sunk, their hostility when faced with confusing situations, and the potential for explaining life-cycle and product-cycle developments, are all areas that Earl explores.

As an example we might cite his explanation of the failure of income tax cuts to improve educational standards. In traditional economic models the decision by an individual to invest in more education is based on the higher income achievable in the future. (By 'invest' we mean spending time in school or university, which prevents earning during that period, as well as any cash expenditures on education.) Thus income tax cuts allow a person to retain more of his or her higher earnings, and so should encourage more investment in education. Earl's argument is that the decision to invest in education is not a simple trade-off between cash invested and potential future earnings. It is also a personal commitment to a life-strategy based on education as a key to success. The cut in income tax makes all 'successful' people better off, but this does not change their success or failure rating. If, however, unemployment is high, and the person who has made a commitment to education fails to get a job, this represents a failure of strategy and a major blow to his or her conceptual structure. If the individual does not invest in that conceptual structure, there is no failure; indeed the failure of others is a sign of his or her wisdom. Thus high unemployment provides a strong disincentive to educational achievement, and the high rewards for those with jobs may be a relatively weak stimulus.

4.4.3 Sociological explanations of demand

The basic argument of Hilary Silver (1987, p. 28) is set out in her introduction. This argument seems so plausible that it is included here:

> Although some economists of time recognize that consumption and non-economic behaviour have durations, they have not considered the social relations of consumption – the ability or inability to pool or redistribute consumption-related labour – which may influence both an individual's and the social stock of time. . . . People can free time committed to social and cultural activities, consumption, and unpaid work with access to the labour and time of others. This can be obtained from either paid or unpaid sources. The unpaid sources are in the household or socialised labour pool; the paid source is in purchased consumer services. For those with higher incomes, where only a time constraint is effective, demand for final consumer services will rise; for those with lower incomes, who are subject to budget constraints as well, access to others' labour may be obtained by non-market means. . . . Socialisation or collective consumption is often, although not always, more productive than having the consumer expend his/her own labour.

This is particularly the case for those services which are clearly time saving, as opposed to services such as education and medicine where the customer has to be present in order to benefit from the service; the service is thus, like the enjoyment of goods in Becker's model, time consuming at least at the point of consumption. The service may involve the use of the expertise of others, as in both education and medicine, to save the consumer from the very large expenditure of time in acquiring the expertise. Directly time-saving services are particularly those of domestic service, child care and restaurant meals.

Silver then goes on to show how female labour force participation has increased in the USA and how this has increased the pressure to obtain the extra labour indicated by the expansion of child care facilities, restaurant meals and perhaps domestic service. Furthermore, the decline in family size has also reduced the available domestic labour supply via the reduction in the availability of grandparents who after having the relatively small families will be back at paid work and thus not free to mind the children.

A neutral application of the theory of household division of labour would suggest that this shift of women to full-time work would increase the amount of work done by the men in the household. This appears to be the exception rather than the rule, and to be present to a significant level only where there are children or where the women are on shift-work (Silver, 1987, p. 34). Thus women's intensity of work increases and in particular the time spent on housework declines by some 30 hours per week with relatively little apparent effect on cleanliness, etc. In spite of supposed falling marginal utility of money, and thus the traditional declining willingness to work longer hours as income increases (the traditional explanation of the fall in hours worked over the last century) most workers in surveys wanted longer not shorter hours, including married women with children (Silver, 1987, p. 32).

These developments in the reduction of the available pool of household labour have caused huge increases in the number of child care places in the USA from less than 200 000 places in 1960 to 1 021 202 places in 1972, evenly split between commercial and not-for-profit places. Even where child care is with relatives there is now generally payment: 79% of working mothers pay for their child care. The same logic is applied to the enormous growth in eating places, with rises in expenditure between 1952 and 1982 of 220% compared with a 160% rise in total consumer expenditures; restaurants have become more varied and specialized and fast food outlets have increased restaurant productivity enormously. The take-away business has also grown, even more rapidly than fast food outlets (Silver, 1987, pp. 34–35). Employment has approximately doubled between 1970 and 1985 in the time saving services of hotels, eating/drinking and repairs (Silver, 1987, p. 39).

The developments in the UK in child care parallel those reported in Silver, with local authority nurseries and playgroups increasing from 21 000 in 1966 to 36 000 in 1990, and registered day nurseries and playgroups increasing from 75 000 to 555 000 over the same period. Registered childminders increased from 32 000 to 238 000 (*Social Trends*, 1992, table 3.12). The expenditure on domestic help as a proportion of total expenditure has however roughly doubled between 1980 and 1990 for all types of consumer, single adults or nuclear families with children (Brooks, 1992, p. 58). Expenditures on restaurant meals over the same period seem to have accounted for a roughly constant proportion, with only single adult males having a noticeably larger proportion of income devoted to this than any of the other groups (Brooks, p. 55). The dominant factor in most of the demand for these services seems to be the increase in income, with income elasticities of expenditure of around 2 for hotels, restaurants, registered day nurseries and registered childminders. Household services had an income elasticity of about 1.3. The most surprising result was the weak relationship with registered playgroups, which had an income elasticity of only 0.42 (Brooks, p. 12). This is, however, not in real conflict with Silver's hypotheses since playgroups are very often part-time and cooperatively organized and are therefore more related to education than to child minding and work reduction. The fact that income seems to be a dominant factor in no way negates Silver's hypothesis, which is that the gaining of extra income by female work will lead to this extra consumption. To distinguish between pure income elasticity and a situation where time constraints are the driving force would require much more detailed statistics.

4.4.4 Social-democratic demand

Demand for services from the public sector cannot be ignored even within the context of marketed services since the interdependencies of demand between the public and private sectors are important. Indeed the trend is for private sector organizations to provide much of government services on a contract basis. This section will therefore pull together some of the aspects of Chapter 3 and the view expressed in Silver's (1987) article, that much of the needed resources for such 'needs' as child care will have to come from government. The present era seems to be caught between the acceptance of the view of Anderson (1990) in relation to solidarity and the views of Stigler about the corruptness of the government process, and the perceptions that government handouts lead to perverse incentives. Thus we have the conflicts between the desire to provide universal health care, and the failure to provide a satisfactory system of signals to ration that health care on the assumption that demand for it is otherwise limitless. This section gives extremely brief consideration to the methods of forecasting public sector demands, and to the interaction with the ideas of Stigler on regulation, Niskanen on government overexpansion, and those of moral hazard and adverse selection that result from such 'free handouts'.

Forecasting

Once it is decided to provide some service, a forecast is made of the requirements in terms of cash and human resources. These are usually based on a level of need according to age group or some such independent variable which is considered a good basis on which to extrapolate. This is therefore very closely akin to the methods of input–output analysis, in that some aspect of the structure of the population is used, usually in conjunction with certain socio-economic variables drawn from the Census, to estimate, say, the requirements for education or for services to the elderly by applying a fixed 'rate of use'. Thus if 75% of the children of parents in Class A or B go to higher education, this rate is applied to the predicted numbers of children of such parents to obtain their contribution to the required number of university places. Since education is not a public good in the strict sense of being non-rival and non-exclusive, we will retain the term 'social-democratic good'. These forecasts are then translated, after a process of argument among the local or national politicians, into programmes for the provisions in question. These are quite likely to meet strong local opposition, particularly if there is re-allocation to be made by closing schools or hospitals, because of changing demographic structures. The political process as outlined in Stigler (1971) then takes place to take the final decision. This clearly is not the pure exercise of 'voice' within the democratic process, and is one source of dissatisfaction.

Moral hazard and the forecasting process

It is evident that the forecasts made by government agencies rarely prove accurate. They are either, as in the case of school closures, vitiated by the political process, or suffer from the effects of moral hazard. This occurs because the very act of providing a programme makes it worthwhile for people to notify their eligibility; for example, in the case of the mobility grants for the disabled, the programme has been heavily underfunded because the extent of disability that would qualify for a grant was greatly underestimated. This is indeed because of moral hazard, since the establishment of the programme causes a change in the behaviour of the participants. It should be pointed out, however, that while there may be abuses of the programme by false claims of disability, this will not be the major cause of such overspend: there is simply no incentive to collect statistics on levels of disability unless there is a programme for which they are needed. Furthermore, without the criteria that such a programme sets up, it is very often difficult to define whether a person will qualify or not.

Moral hazard and more widely definable perverse incentives are of course likely products of a system where individuals can gain much at no cost to themselves except for the trouble of claiming. Thus, whether they are significant or not, the problems of young women 'getting pregnant to get housed', or much more widely the problems of people on social security who become poorer when taking anything but a well-paid job, discredit a scheme. These perverse incentives are not confined to the recipients of a scheme; as we saw in Chapter 3, Niskanen (1971) was able to make a good case that the incentive for government servants was to overexpand. More generally, once there is no incentive such as that provided by the private market to sell if it is profitable and to stop selling once it ceases to be profitable, there is no incentive structure to guide public provision on the levels of output. Indeed, within any public service there is much demoralization when budgets are cut, since there is very often no mechanism by which the employees can improve their situation by (for example) improving the service, whereas in the private sector they would at least have that option and the corresponding rewards for success and efficiency.

To summarize, the notion of demand in this context has really very little to do with the notion of demand in private sector traded goods or services. It is entirely fixed by the often arbitrary process of government; this process should be recognized by all private sector institutions that depend on government demand, and they should therefore try to ensure that it will be very costly politically to reduce their budgets. This implies considerable effort in 'marketing', both to the public as voters and to the relevant officials and councillors or MPs who can influence the future course of the programme. Stigler's (1971) account of the process is essential reading for those who wish to have a conceptual framework for this activity.

4.5 CHAPTER SUMMARY

This chapter has considered the traditional approach to demand, which looks at the consumer as a perfectly informed and fully rational satisfaction maximizer. This approach stresses continual changes in quantities as adaptations to price changes, and provides a useful descriptive tool for the responsiveness of changes in quantities to a change in price in the form of price elasticity. The emphasis given to demand curves – the relationship between quantity and price, given the level of incomes, prices of other goods and tastes – sometimes obscures the fact that conventional economic theories of demand give equal importance to the changes in incomes or in the prices of other goods. The problem with this approach is that few of us can recognize ourselves in the fully informed rationalist of economic theory. Economists often stress that this is not important in aggregate, if this approach gives good explanations of how people behave.

Before discussing approaches which attack one of the fundamental assumptions behind traditional demand theory, such as the approaches of Scitovski and Earl, we considered various extensions to the traditional approach which make it more realistic, or have particular use in connection with the service industries. The first such approach was Lancaster's use of characteristics as the basic elements which were demanded, and the closely related approach of Rosen; this seems promising but, as we discovered, it is impossible to operationalize, because the characteristics in which we are most interested are only possible to scale by considering people's evaluation of them; in other words we cannot measure their objective properties, only their subjective ones, and this destroys the accuracy of the measure. Just as its parent, classical demand theory, assumes that both goods and persons are independent, and that adding a bit more of good 'x' will increase satisfaction by a certain amount, Lancaster has to assume that adding a bit more of characteristic 'y' will add satisfaction, and will do so whatever the levels of other characteristics. We may, however, doubt this; the empirical example of the value of the park depending on the type of area, and the users of that park, is one cogent example.

Becker's integration of the time taken to use goods or services and their prices was used to show how the values of time are derived to obtain a value for 'generalized cost' for transport studies, or use with gravity models for shopping centre forecasts or potentially for use of facilities. Gravity models were discussed, both because of their use in forecasting shopping and transport flows, and also because they provide a basis for thinking about choice under monopolistic competition or oligopoly, particularly the distinction in the mechanisms of choice implied by the unconstrained gravity model, where the inherent desirability of the facility and the distance interact to generate demand, as opposed to the constrained gravity model, where the level of demand is fixed but the destination is chosen in relation to its relative attraction.

Forecasting techniques such as gravity models often use fixed coefficients; for example, a trip rate per household of a particular income group and size would be used in a transport model. The most complex of these fixed coefficient models is probably the input–output model. This is explored in order to understand the sort of limitations of such models, and to gain insight into the methods used in forecasting regional impact of public policy changes, or the introduction of new facilities. Since many of these facilities are in the service sector and the effect of changes is also principally felt by the service sector, the regional multiplier study is important to understand.

All of these models are based upon the idea of the fully rational well-informed consumer whose tastes are exogenously given. Providing the decisions are truly marginal, and the changes implied by the decision are small, this approach will yield similar results to one based on the idea of the consumer evolving as the result of learning from experience and interacting with others in society. Scitovski emphasizes the search for stimulation, and the interaction implied by this, and the continual change of tastes that such a search implies. Earl also emphasizes the continual change in tastes as the consumer learns or is subject to changes beyond his or her control. In his context, the inability to know everything and the importance of social contacts to provide information lead to different types of decision taking than the classical economic man. Many of the decisions are taken on the basis of filtering techniques rather than trade-offs in the normal sense. While this may provide a sensible basis for market research, we need to consider whether it invalidates the demand curve as an exploratory device and as a framework for thinking about pricing.

Earl's work suggests, firstly, that income changes may be much more important than price changes. Secondly, as price is one of the attributes on which the consumer will take a decision, if that decision is going to be taken by looking only at alternatives within certain ranges of values for each attribute, it is possible to price too low; a consumer might then ignore the service or good because of an assumption that anything that is cheap cannot be of suitable quality. Equally, although not stressed above, a consumer who discovers that the price was too high may feel 'ripped off' and the firm may lose a lot of goodwill by this. Thus while the firm may get away with small deviations from the 'proper price', it would be liable to rapid loss of custom if the word gets round that it is a 'rip-off' or simply bad value for money. This also suggests the importance of the firm's image building exercises through advertising, and this also seems to provide a more plausible approach than the traditional one for thinking about price policy.

His approach also provides an integrated framework for considering the notion of 'reputation goods' – goods (or services) that one cannot test out by experience. For example, it is very difficult to evaluate the quality of a doctor, physiotherapist, business adviser or lawyer. Most cases will sort themselves out in the absence of active incompetence, but one would like to feel better treated than that so that good rather than merely passable solutions are found, and so that one is not the victim of one of the cases that is difficult. We normally decide on such goods by a process of inquiry among social contacts, hence the term 'reputation goods'. Earl would stress that things of vital importance like lifestyle are also socially influenced, and that as such a system of thinking about demand without the social dimension is unlikely to be a good framework.

We still have not answered the question: does it invalidate the traditional view about price? The answer is probably not, with the exception of a firm that clearly underprices. It will suffer a very different fate from that suggested by traditional economics; it ought according to the traditional view to clean up the entire market, if it can produce enough. Earl's view suggests that unless it can persuade a lot of customers that all the other goods or services are overpriced, it may simply get ignored. A firm that overprices dramatically is likely to lose out when the bubble bursts; there might be a delay, but the traditional view would hold in the longer run. When the firm is charging a little bit more or a little bit less than it perhaps should if the ideal fully informed public existed, Earl's view would suggest that it may suffer much less than under the traditional approach; it may still fall into the same decision group, and if it has some clear advantages, it may come out with a larger market, even though it charges more. This suggests a lower than expected elasticity of demand. Equally, if the overpricing puts it into another group altogether, it may not be able to compete on the required qualities, and hence it will suffer from a higher than 'expected' elasticity of demand. This supports the idea of target prices, as suggested within the marketing literature. Apart from dramatic underpricing, the results are to introduce variation to the traditional view rather than to give qualitatively different results.

Market demand introduced by the sort of social developments suggested by Hilary Silver, seems plausible, but may operate over a longer time-scale than that of the firm's decisions on price and quantity. Traditional modes of analysis would therefore pick up both price and income effects on the services in question, and this would be sufficient for firms to decide their policies. It may however, help in assessing a market in an area that is relatively deprived. The final section of the chapter simply points out that 'social-democratic demand', as suggested by Silver under the rubric of social struggle, is a very different problem to that of market demand. The forecasting of it is fraught with problems because of moral hazard, and the rationing of it is equally problematic since price signals are absent.

FURTHER READING

The basic material can, again, be found in any of the major economics textbooks, whether on general economics or managerial economics.

For a critique of Lancaster and associated market research models, and for a challenge to simplistic views of human market behaviour, see:

Earl, P. (1986) *Lifestyle Economics*, Brighton, Wheatsheaf Books.

and on the challenge to simpler views of demand, see:

Scitovski, T. (1976) *The Joyless Economy*, New York, Oxford University Press.

For the value of time, a basic introduction is provided by:

Layard, P.R.G. and Walters, A.A. (1978) *Micro-Economic Theory*, Maidenhead, McGraw-Hill, pp. 304–313.

and the best simple introduction to the notions of how a value is derived empirically is provided by:

Beesley, M.E. (1965) The value of time spent travelling. *Economica*, **32**, 174–185.

For further work on the gravity model, see:

Foot, D. (1981) *Operational Urban Models*, London, Methuen.

APPENDIX 4.A

4.A.1 Elasticity calculations

$$\text{Elasticity of demand} = \frac{\text{Proportional change of quantity}}{\text{Proportional change of price}}$$

$$= \frac{\Delta Q}{\Delta P}\frac{P}{Q} = \frac{(Q_1 - Q_2)}{(P_1 - P_2)} \times \frac{P}{Q} \tag{4.A.1}$$

It would be useful to introduce some notation at this point:

ΔQ = a change in Q. Thus, in this case we could take any particular value of the quantity in Table 4.A.1, and the change in Q would be the difference between that quantity and another over some specified range. In this case it would be convenient to take each line of the table as a step and use the difference between one line and the next. Thus $\Delta Q = 20$. On the same basis, $\Delta P = -1$.

For Table 4.A.1, both ΔP and ΔQ are constant, as the demand curve is a straight line. We can therefore work out $\Delta Q/\Delta P$ first; giving $20/-1 = -20$. This can then be used with the different levels of price and quantity in the table. For example, at $P = 14$ and $Q = 20$:

$$\frac{\Delta Q}{\Delta P} \times \frac{P}{Q} = -20 \times \frac{14}{20} = -14 \tag{4.A.2}$$

It can be seen in Table 4.A.1 that the elasticity varies continuously; this is because although the slope of the line $\Delta Q/\Delta P$ is constant, the values of P and Q are not. The proportional changes are therefore altering rapidly.

Table 4.A.1 Calculation of elasticities

	Calculation of elasticities of demand			
Price	*Quantity*	*Elasticity*	*Total revenue*	*Marginal revenue*
15	0	$-\infty$	0	15
14	20	-14.00	280	13
13	40	-6.50	520	11
12	50	-4.80	600	9.5
11	60	-3.67	660	8
10	80	-2.50	800	6
9	100	-1.80	900	4
8	120	-1.33	960	2
7	140	-1.00	980	0
6	160	-0.75	960	-2
5	180	-0.56	900	-4
4	200	-0.40	800	-6
3	220	-0.27	660	-8
2	240	-0.17	480	-10
1	260	-0.08	260	-12
0	280	0.00	0	-14

The markets and hierarchies paradigm

5

5.1 TRANSACTIONS COSTS AND INFORMATION ASYMMETRY

It is ironic that in perfect markets where there are no problems of availability of information, there is no need for firms! Each stage of production could be carried out by subcontracting, and, given the flexibility and the perfect information provided by the market to increase or decrease production and/or prices, this would be the optimal form of organization since only a minimum of overheads would be carried by the firm. It was Coase in 1937 who first pointed out that one reason why such a situation would not work was that the collection of information and the setting up of contracts was a major cost to industry, and that this would increase with the number of transactions implied by the form of subcontracting suggested above. This transaction cost theory of the firm was developed subsequently, largely by Oliver Williamson (1975). He links the problems of setting up contracts on the one hand to the limited abilities of the human species in processing information and in communication, and to the well-developed capacity to deceive, and on the other to the need to make capital expenditures which are specific to a particular contract; these could be investments in physical or human capital. Since at least some service industries show a substantial individual subcontracting sector, for example the individual jobbing builder, gardeners, self-employed consultants and accountants etc., it would seem important to explore this approach, particularly as it has implications for the relationship between employer and employee as well as between firms.

Let us start with a concrete example of this problem. Some of the difficulties of setting up contracts are vividly illustrated by the unfortunate experience of a hospital in Edinburgh. As required by government legislation, they arranged for competitive tenders for contract cleaning. Part of this was naturally the cleaning of the windows. The firm that won the contract did so with a quotation based on the belief that they were required to clean the windows and external glass doors inside and out. The contracting hospital had wanted all internal glass surfaces cleaned as well, including many partitions both within and between wards. This went to court, since both parties stood by their interpretations of the contract. The alternative was to renegotiate, but of course this could have been greatly to the advantage of the contractors since they would already have a foot in the door, and could potentially renegotiate on terms favourable to themselves.

This example illustrates two facets of the difficulty of contracting: firstly, the problems of communicating what is to be done, and, secondly, the potential, once one party is committed, for 'opportunistic renegotiation'. These ideas need to be explored further. The particular contract was perhaps unusual in that what was to be done could have been explicit from the outset. The problem was in communication only, one of **language** in Williamson's terms (Williamson, 1975, p. 22).

Pure communications problems of that sort are one source of information asymmetry, but it may be impossible to predict the exact outcome at the start of the contract, either because of **complexity** or **uncertainty**, or both (Williamson, 1975, pp. 23–24). For example, the computerization of accounting procedures often involves using subcontractors to help to customize the software. This, however, implies that the accounting procedures already in place in the firm can simply be applied to the new accounting system. This is rarely the case, and even if they can be used in this way, it is often very wasteful to do so. But the firm does not know the required extent of redesign of procedures; this may lead to job redesign, and hence renegotiation of contracts of employment and retraining of staff. None of these can be specified in advance, since they can only be specified when detailed knowledge of the workings of the firm and expert knowledge of the new accounting package come together, and this is only achieved by the expert working with the company on the project. The information asymmetry is bilateral; the firm knows its existing accounting needs; the expert knows the new accounting package; only the process of information exchange coupled with organizational skills allows the development of a good set of procedures which, it is hoped, will save money and/or give the basis for development of new levels of managerial control, and hence flexibility and efficiency of the firm. There are thus three levels of information asymmetry: the firm knows its accounting procedures; the consultant knows the computer system; and neither party knows how good the expert will be in developing new and elegant solutions to the firm's problems.

These limitations on the ability to know are the basis of the concept of **bounded rationality**. As the result of the obvious implausibility of perfect information models and under the influence of the ideas of Freud and others on the role of the subconscious, the idea of rationality as a whole was often attacked. This brought difficulties with ideas of democracy as well as the more limited ideas of consumer and producer rationality. It is also in fundamental conflict with the way most people view the world. It is not the normal experience that nothing works to any set of rules, and yet in the absence of rational behaviour, this would presumably be the outcome. The concept of bounded rationality suggests that people in general act rationally, but within the limitations of their perceptual, communication and information processing abilities.

Opportunism (Williamson, 1975, pp. 26–28) can be defined as 'self-seeking with guile' or 'involves making 'false or empty, that is, self-disbelieved, threats and promises' in the expectation that individual advantage will thereby be realized'. Williamson contrasts it with 'stewardship behaviour', which 'involves a trust relation in which the word of a party can be taken as his bond', and 'instrumental behaviour'; this is 'a more neutral mode in which there is no necessary self awareness that the interests of a party can be furthered by stratagems of any sort'. To continue our previous example, the potential for opportunistic behaviour on the part of the consultant is probably greater than for the firm, since it is the firm that is paying. The consultant can claim that the job is time consuming and challenging, whereas his past experience makes it easy; he may persuade the firm to take on overelaborate systems, unnecessarily costly to buy and install, and which the firm's management is not in a position to use. He may even be able to get a quasi-permanent consultancy, by withholding information so that he has to be called back to do a particularly 'difficult' bit every month when the accounts are reconciled. The firm could be opportunistic, however, by insisting on a fixed price contract and deliberately understating the difficulty of the job.

Opportunism is a particular problem in market transactions where one individual or firm has to commit resources to investments that are only of use if the contract to supply the other party continues. This problem is described as **asset specificity**. It would encompass anything from the specialized machinery to make parts unique to a particular machine, to learning software unique to a particular firm. Once that commitment is made it gives the supplier the opportunity to renegotiate the terms of sale to its advantage, providing it has either patents or significant skill advantages in production, and the buyer a similar opportunity to renegotiate if there is an alternative potential supplier. If neither can avoid the contract, the potential for strife is endless since there is no just price in such a situation.

In the 'perfect market', opportunism is assumed away because information is perfect. In a very fragmented market, precisely the type of market implicit in the perfect market paradigm, it may run riot; the individual seller may be one among so many that he need fear no repercussions from his opportunistic behaviour since he may never have to deal with the same clients again. Eventually such behaviour may destroy the market, because it simply becomes too risky to purchase anything, unless the price is so low that no seller wishes to supply the goods. The survival of such a market depends on the ability of buyers to recognize value for money; thus, unlike modern electronic equipment, for example, it must be possible to see whether a product is of good quality and will last, or not. In a slightly less fragmented market, where repeat purchases are important, the market solution may dominate since suppliers of poor quality goods will not get repeat purchases. Thus, Cheung (1983) quotes the example of the market in Hong Kong for laying hardwood floors. This is a market where there are many individual workers who act as private contractors, and where there are very clear quality standards and rates for the job. Thus, although the craft is highly specific, the assets are not specific to the contract, because there are so many of these contracts, and a market can develop. Note that this is advantageous for contractors and their clients, since it avoids having the costs of the independent floor layers on the contractor's books even when they do not have work to do. It is also advantageous for the workers because by shopping around for jobs they can keep busier, and hence better paid, than they would otherwise be. In so far as practice makes for speed and efficiency they can also do more work in any given time, and as it is piecework, also reap higher rewards in that way. The key factor is that the **frequency of the transaction** makes it worth setting up the market standards.

5.1.1 Hierarchies

It was stressed above that the hiring of labour for each aspect of a job in the absence of such markets was an impossibly onerous task. A **hierarchy** is essentially a form of labour contract where the worker surrenders to the hirer the right to use his labour as the hirer dictates, within the limits of the contract of employment. Thus, while the contract may stipulate certain limits on the types of task that will be required, it leaves the details of the work to be decided later, as the situation requires. This clearly saves a lot of effort for both sides in the setting up of contracts, but it also has implications for the quality of work. The long-term relationship implied by this sort of contract means that reciprocal obligations are built up; the worker's quality and speed of work can be monitored and rewarded, but if the conditions of employment are too onerous, the hirer will lose his or her best workers. Apart from the benefits in terms of cost reduction in the labour contract, there are also benefits both in terms of reputation and in internal information of being organized as a firm rather than a set of individual contractors.

In an environment where information about quality and price is expensive to acquire, the hirer, whom we may call the firm in this context, also has a clear interest in maintaining its reputation for decent quality work and fair price levels. Such a reputation will keep it at the top of clients' search lists for appropriate contractors; it therefore saves enormously on advertising and publicity and the costs of searching for work, which may take up a very large proportion of a consultant's time. With the greater number of workers – if communication within the firm is good – development of a better technique by one worker can be taught to the others and so improve the efficiency and hence competitiveness of the firm.

The potential for opportunistic behaviour on short-term contracts comes from the specificity of investments by both firm and worker. In the service industries, investments by the firm may be in computer systems, special tools to simplify the servicing of electrical appliances, etc., and specialized staff training is almost ubiquitous – or should be. From the workers' side, many of the same investments may be required; certainly the effort of starting a new job where one knows nothing of the structure of the firm or the relationships that have been built up with clients is considerable, and however much training is offered, skills are acquired only with practice. Both sides therefore have an interest in the stability of the relationship, and this stability is itself a major guarantee against opportunism, since recognition of opportunistic behaviour will at least spoil chances of promotion, and might lead to dismissal. The prospect of promotion is supposed to guarantee the 'willing compliance' of the worker with the aims of the firm. It may pay the firm to restrict entry to lower levels of the hierarchy so that it can guard against the problems of communication across firms as to the quality of the worker. If it only promotes from within the firm, it can use 'experience rating', that is to say judgements of quality based on experience, rather than the vagaries of references and interviews, both of which are subject to opportunism. (Glowing references may be supplied if a firm wishes to be rid of a bad worker, while the potential for opportunistic self-promotion in interviews is very obvious.) The internal promotion mechanism thus provides both an incentive to ensure the willing compliance of its workers and some protection against opportunism (Williamson, 1975, chapter 4, pp. 57–81).

What Williamson does not stress is that it also provides an incentive to be economical with the truth if that truth conflicts with the views of one's superiors, and may cause a firm to become introverted by the lack of new blood at the higher reaches of management. Both lead to a 'house style' which makes for easy communication, but potentially perverse directions for the firm. Furthermore, firms which do not manage the interdepartmental rivalry appropriately may not only lose new ideas from outside but may also experience all the problems of information asymmetries as departments try to get rid of poor workers onto other departments and otherwise exploit their departmental rivals, for example by overcharging for their services if an internal transfer pricing system is in operation. These are all part of the problems of 'control loss', which is the traditional explanation for limits on the size of the firm, and can be contrasted with the control exerted by competition in the market.

5.1.2 Hierarchical structures and control loss

The traditional argument against the expansion of firms to very large size, in spite of the absence of production factors which would cause rising marginal costs, revolves around the loss of control and the excessive complexity of a very large firm. Williamson (1967) provides a neat paradigm for this: information is passed between levels of the hierarchy, in the form of discussion, or orders being handed down, or as reports handed up about the progress of the operation. If at each level of the hierarchy a proportion of the information is lost, then even with only a few levels there is a substantial loss of information. If a proportion a is lost at each level of the hierarchy, the total loss of information is $a^{(n-1)}$, where a is the proportion of information lost at each level and n is the number of levels in the hierarchy. For example if a were 5% and n were 5, the control loss would be just less than 19%; if a were 10%, this rises to 34%. This is, however, a very simplistic model of the way a hierarchy might work, although it certainly fits with experience of such organizations as the Civil

Service. The control loss in a well-run corporation is probably relatively small, since each level of the hierarchy has separate functions, and it is therefore only a very small proportion of the information at each level that needs to be passed on, yet it is not only actual communications that cause information loss, but the failure to communicate. When the shop manager fails to tell the staff that there is a special offer on certain goods, a carefully laid marketing plan may be vitiated.

Williamson's model also shows how costs rise as the levels of the hierarchy increase because of the numbers of supervisory workers, and their increasing pay levels as they rise in the hierarchy. This means either that the lower levels must receive below average pay, or that the costs of output must increase to cover the costs of the management. This is no problem if the value of the output goes up at least proportionately. For example, in the information based services such as education, and in the various consultancy activities such as medicine, law, accountancy, management consultancy and design, the quality of service depends on a combination of the quality of the individual giving the advice, and the backup that such an individual receives from the organization; that backup is dependent upon the availability of specialist materials and equipment and/or specialist information from members of the organization. It seems highly plausible that the range of size of, say, accountancy firms reflects the different needs of the client for such specialist features. Small firms simply requiring accountancy services and auditing, with basic advice on taxation and debt collection, could almost certainly be as well served by a small accountancy firm with correspondingly low overheads, as by a large firm. The large corporation, where accountancy requirements will include management accounting advice, auditing of complex computer systems, control of overseas branches and international transactions, are likely to demand much more specialist advice.

But even if the specialist advice is deficient, the scale of the task will require more than the staff of the small accountancy firm could manage, and will thus require a firm that has developed experience of managing large tasks. This special experience is largely the development of techniques to avoid the control loss implicit in such a hierarchy. Particularly for auditing a complex business where accounting may be designed to obscure the real situation, the development of the skills in the team to know what must be communicated upward to team leaders and sideways to other colleagues is a 'skill' that will distinguish the good team from less effective ones. This aspect is probably a sufficient reason for large firms; the availability of in-house specialists is more dubious as a reason, since these could be bought in from small specialist firms.

It is interesting to consider whether it is the balance between control loss and increased expense, as against the provision of in-house specialists, that explains the relatively small size of law firms in the UK as compared with accountancy firms. Major accountancy firms can tackle the very large jobs of auditing the largest domestic and multinational firms. Within the accounting firm there is considerable specialist expertise on computerization, VAT, corporation and income tax, international transactions etc., as well as management accounting and management consultancy. There is thus a relatively flexible pattern of consultation within the firm to gain specialist knowledge, and one of the benefits of hiring one of the 'majors' is their potential to bring that knowledge to bear, even on small jobs. As the need for accounting services is frequent, accountancy firms can use their internal specialists frequently, and because of this and the variety of cases that they will meet, their knowledge should be finely honed by practice. The ability to consult internally raises the quality of the work of non-specialists, and these in turn will act to gain more work for the specialists because the non-specialist staff will refer more complex cases to the specialist divisions as separate consultancy exercises. Thus every employee is acting as a salesperson for the specialist facilities of the company.

Law firms have an alternative structure; even the major city practices are relatively small, and usually have a high degree of specialization. Other firms will contact them for specialist advice on a subcontracting basis. (The same is also true of the property development and civil engineering industries, where teams of consultancies are common and the very large integrated consultancy such as Ove Arup is the exception rather than the norm.) Since the need for specialist legal advice is relatively rare, and the continuous employment of a specialist cannot be justified within a normal law firm, any member of staff thus employed within the firm would tend to be less expert than external specialists, and the information advantages point towards a market solution – i.e. subcontracting – rather than a hierarchy solution in the large firm. This is a self-reinforcing cycle. Because the specialist firms have a better reputation, they will be consulted for the difficult cases, which further enhance their reputation, and consequently make it more difficult for the non-specialist firms to justify the retention of specialist staff, who would tend to be underemployed, and hence less experienced.

The same considerations probably determine the range of sizes of firms in the building industry, where small firms of general builders can undertake relatively small jobs and not incur the heavy overheads of the large firms; there are also relatively small and very specialist firms – experts in stonework repairs or underpinning of foundations – and the major national builders who tackle both large civil engineering works and major housing schemes.

The advantages of using the market rather than hierarchy appear to have dominated in the case of engineering draughtsmen. Major civil engineering firms in the London area used contract draughtsmen almost exclusively; this may have been enforced by the desire of the draughtsmen to gain higher wages, since the trend developed at the time of extreme shortage of draughtsmen during the 1980s. But it is also to the firms' advantage in that they are freed of the need to retain draughtsmen on their payrolls when work is slack. It is not known whether the engineering firms saw how convenient this would be during the recession that followed.

Reading Williamson (1975) one might think that hierarchy dominates markets as a form of organization in almost all situations; however, both his own cost arguments (Williamson, 1967) and information arguments point to the superiority of markets where transaction costs are low.

5.2 ORGANIZATIONAL STRUCTURE OF THE FIRM

Information costs are also used to explain the internal structure of the firm, and in particular the progress of the multidivisional firm as a form of organization. In this section we look at the implications of having a unitary structure in terms of the control loss as compared to the multi-divisional structure. We will also consider the situations where the multidivisional structure is not appropriate.

The **U-form firm** is a structure in which the divisions are set up along functional lines, such as production, marketing, finance, personnel and purchasing. All report to the Chief Executive's office. The necessary coordination between these different functions takes place at that level. It can be imagined how difficult it is to run a firm as large as General Motors in this way, when the financial decisions for an engine plant have to be referred to the Chief Executive's office before decisions are handed back down to the production teams within the plant. This was the situation in the early 1920s; not surprisingly, it created a crisis and forced a major reorganization by General Motors. The form that this took was to separate out the various product divisions of the firm into units, each with its own U-form structure. This was the start of the **M-form**, i.e. multi-divisional form, of organization.

The particular problems created by large U-form firms relate to the overloading of the Chief Executive's office, which has to look after both the day-to-day tactical decisions and any strategic issues. Naturally, strategic issues tend to get crowded out and the firm drifts on, taking only tactical decisions. Because of the functional specialization rather than product and hence market specialization, the performance of the firm in each market is often poorly monitored. This follows from the aggregation of the data for each product by functional specialism; thus, financial details would be reported firm-wide rather than for each product. If this is repeated for production information, it can be seen how difficult it would be to trace down situations where the costs were running out of control for a particular product. A further major problem may be the loyalties to each functional division, so that bitter warfare ensues between Marketing and Finance, Personnel and Operations, etc. These naturally make it much more difficult to analyse the problems of the firm, let alone to develop sensible strategies to overcome them.

The M-form firm operates quite differently. Each product division is likely to be a separate profit centre, and each profit centre operates almost as if it were a separate firm. It has its own Production, Marketing, Finance, Personnel and Purchasing divisions, and these report to its managing director. The managing director of the profit centre will rep-resent it at board meetings with the Chief Executive's specialist staff, along with the managing directors of all the other profit centres. The essential responsibility of each profit centre is for the profitability of that division. Decisions about modifications to product lines, purchasing or production techniques are left to the management team of the division, subject of course to reporting to the Chief Executive's office, where these would have an impact on other divisions in the company.

Under the M-form system, the Chief Executive's office is responsible for the strategy of the firm, and in particular for allocating investment funds to the profit centres. These should be allocated on the basis of the profitability of each investment programme. In some cases, the allocation of investment funds is based not on the programme but on the profitability of that division. This is strictly no longer an M-form firm; it is rather a holding company where the Chief Executive's office is simply a fund-holding agency – an internal capital market.

The M-form results in what are effectively individual single-product firms linked by a capital market, the Chief Executive's office. This capital market has the advantage of better information than the normal capital market, since it can investigate the profit centres in as much detail as it wishes, and as these are all part of the hierarchy, the benefits of the individuals in the profit centre cooperating fully with the Chief Executive's office are obvious — no cooperation: no promotion.

The M-form firm is likely not to be superior to the U-form firm when certain conditions prevail (Cable, 1988, pp. 18–21):

1. If there are few customers and products, it is likely that the linkages in operations and marketing will be too great to allow each division the autonomy implied by the M-form.
2. When the divisions are producing output for another division of the firm, i.e. they are different stages of a vertically integrated production process, it is extremely dangerous to allow them to behave as independent profit centres. If the earlier stage maximizes its profits, it will be selling its output to the second stage at too high a price. Conversely, the second stage division will wish to beat down the price of the first stage as far as possible. There is no 'fair price' in this situation unless there are alternative suppliers outside the firm, in which case their prices would provide a market price that should be used for transactions between divisions.
3. This problem of vertical integration may take the form of a variety of outputs coming from an integrated production facility, for example where these are the result of process industries, such as the wide variety of petrochemicals coming out of an oil refinery. Both problems of pricing of the output of the first stage, and problems of organizing production coherently are likely to occur. It could be said that the splitting of track management from operations in the privatization of British Rail will suffer from these problems.
4. It is almost a subset of item 3 that where industries are subject to very rapid technical, and hence product, changes, the details of coordination would be greater than that implied by an M-form structure.

In some modern contexts a new form of organization is developing where the support functions are being treated as profit centres and are 'purchased' by the various product divisions. This is the basis for the reorganization of the Société Nationale des Chemins de Fer (SNCF).

5.3 AGENCY RELATIONSHIPS

The presence of information asymmetry and opportunism implies that there is a monitoring problem in any organizational structure. This may be resolved in many ways, ranging from setting up an organizational structure where conflicts of interest are minimized, to the setting up of contracts and monitoring systems which constrain the agent to follow the principal's wishes. This section is devoted to a basic introduction to this area of economics.

The terms 'principal' and 'agent' will be used repeatedly, and so a definition will be useful:

> The **principal** is the owner of resources or the person responsible for their use. The **agent** is the person hired by the principal. Thus the principal might be the owner of the resources which the agent is to use or the senior manager to whom the agent will be responsible.

We shall start the discussion on the assumption that the principals are the shareholders and the agent is the managing director of the firm. There is evidently a potential clash of interests between these two groups, since the managing director could appropriate all of the profits if the principals were extremely unobservant, and this might be in his interests. It would clearly not be in the principals' interest! The subject of this section is an assessment of the various ways in which this conflict may be resolved.

The principals' interest is taken to be the maximization of their real income, which is the combination of the dividend payments on the shares and the increase in value of those shares over the year. In general, share prices appreciate if the City is convinced that the firm will be paying increased future dividends because it is investing wisely and is selling its products in a growing market. Marsh's (1990) pamphlet puts forward a strong case that the City does as good a job as is possible in valuing shares, given the uncertainty about the future, and that it does so taking a long-term view as opposed to the short-term approach of which it is often accused. He points out that, 'The figures for ICI's share price in August 1990 imply that the market was anticipating a long-term dividend growth of about 13 percent in nominal terms . . . these figures would imply that of ICI's current market capitalization, only 8 percent is attributable to the current year's dividend; only 29 percent can be explained by the present value of the dividends expected over the next 5 years; and only 50 percent by the value of the dividend expected over the next 10 years. Similar figures for the Wellcome Group would be 1.4 percent of the current year, 6 percent over the next 5 years, and 11 percent over the next 10 years' (p. 11). Furthermore, stock prices appreciate when industrial firms announce investment plans, again implying that a long-term view is being taken.

From the shareholders' point of view, therefore, the manager should maximize long-run profits. What alternative goals might managers have? They might maximize their perks or their personal incomes; they might maximize the size of the firm by maximizing sales, particularly if they thought that would increase their own incomes; or they might maximize profits, but would probably not be willing to take too many risks, since their income would depend on the existence of the firm, and therefore its demise would threaten them more than it would the shareholders. This holds true if their income is profit-related: they would probably be unwilling to take a high risk of a fall in profits and hence income, even if the potential profits were excellent. The shareholders can be expected to have a portfolio of shares precisely in order to guard against such risks.

There are two basic approaches to the analysis of principal and agent problems, which come under the general term **agency theory**. The first looks at the relative incentives of the owner–manager as compared to the manager who owns only a small part of the business or who shares in only a small part of its profits; the second looks at the problem of providing the relevant incentives to management, given that their interests are likely to be different from those of the principals.

The first approach derives from Jensen and Meckling (1976), and shows that the incentive to take perks is much greater for a manager than for an owner–manager. The logic is quite simply that the owner–manager faces a direct trade-off between income and perks, which in the absence of tax differentials is on a one-for-one basis; each pound's worth of perks taken means a pound of profit sacrificed. If on the other hand the manager has 10% of the shares of the firm, each pound's worth of perks taken only loses him 10 pence in profits. There is thus apparently always a conflict of interests between the manager who would want to take perks and the shareholders who would want to maximize profits.

The approach taken by Strong and Waterson (1987), following Shavell (1979), revolves around the question of moral hazard, which we discussed in Chapter 3. The problem for the principal – in this case the shareholders – is that they can only observe outcomes. They cannot observe effort, and the world is an uncertain place, so they cannot know whether the outcome is the result of maximum effort by the agent or simply a matter of luck. They would therefore like to engineer a contract which would maximize their likelihood of a good result. This contract must reflect the fact that the agent usually has more at stake than the principal, since the agent's income is predominantly dependent on the firm. The principals will therefore be relatively risk-neutral – in other words, they will want to maximize the expected profits even though these may be the result of a risky venture; the agent, on the other hand, is likely to be relatively risk-averse, as outlined above, in that he would not wish to accept a large fall in income as the result of failure of the risky venture. The apparently obvious solution of making the agent's pay entirely dependent on profit will therefore work perversely. The agent would avoid what were to him excessively risky ventures, even though they would be optimal for the principals. The contract will therefore have to provide for a substantial fixed salary, as well as a certain amount of bonus payment based on profit. The design of such schemes is sensitive to the goals of each party and to the probability of different payoffs.

5.4 EXTERNAL CONSTRAINTS ON MANAGERS

As even the best-designed contract will not ensure a perfect solution, since the motives of the agent remain hidden from the principal, we need to consider what other mechánisms control managers. There are at least four major mechanisms:

1. Bank loans will require tests of credit-worthiness, and will signal managerial confidence.
2. Takeovers: the threat of takeover results from failure of management to maximize the value of their firms.
3. Managerial labour markets may act as incentives to profit maximize.
4. Product markets may act as a constraint on behaviour.

We will consider each of these in turn.

When the firm applies to banks for substantial loans, it must submit to searching investigations of its credit-worthiness, and it signals to the world that it is confident of its ability to repay the loans. The loans, indeed, inevitably push the firm into a situation where if it does badly it risks bankruptcy, since the bank would call in the loan if it defaults on repayment. Thus, the manager is constraining his freedom of action to take out profits from the firm, since these will be needed to repay the banks. This is well known to the City and to the shareholders, and it therefore acts as a signal of confidence and a promise of growth. Thus taking out a loan and increasing the firm's debt will normally cause the share price to increase.

Takeovers occur when the buyer believes that it can use the target firm's assets to greater effect than the target firm is managing to do. This may be because the target firm is managing less efficiently; in other words, the predator believes it has a better management system which will enable costs to be cut or the products to be better marketed. The great exponents of this process in our times are the Hanson Group and the BTR Group. Alternatively, it may be that the target firm is well managed, but that there are 'synergies' of which the predator can take advantage; for example, the target firm may have an excellent product but a weak marketing system, or it may even have a perfectly adequate marketing system but its product may fit into the predator's product lines so that the marketing costs could be greatly reduced. Thus, takeover disciplines management that is either being slack in its duty to the shareholders or simply lacks the context in which to maximize the value of the firm.

Managerial labour markets are said to provide a strong incentive to maximize the value of the firm. Fama (1980) produces a model which suggests that the manager's pay will be set according to that manager's ability to increase the value of the firm (that is, his marginal product). However, because of the information problems within the market, the principals can never be sure whether they are observing an increase in the value of the firm as the result of the manager's effort or as the result of generally favourable trading conditions. There is therefore a substantial random element in this process. Nevertheless the process is repeated year by year, and so any luck at one stage tends to be corrected at the next and so the manager's reputation will be a good guide to his potential.

This does not in fact mean that his salary will necessarily go down to the level at which it would be had he not had the luck, since it could be expected to follow a 'random walk'. This is a process where the chance elements at each stage are randomly distributed. It therefore does not necessarily – indeed, it does not usually – correct itself completely. Thus if a manager is lucky in year one, this gives him a start and in year two he may or may not be lucky again. If he is lucky, it pushes him up to a yet more favourable position and in the third year it would only be exceptionally bad luck that would bring him back to an average salary. It can be seen that this process could lead to either long-run good fortune or long-run bad fortune, simply by chance. This random walk process is present in all share markets and accounts for the twin propositions that some funds will do better than average over quite long periods but very few beat the average in the very long run (see Brealy and Myers, 1991 pp. 290–292).

Finally, product markets act as a constraint on managerial behaviour in two ways. Firstly, if the product is in decline, whether temporarily or in the long run, this puts pressure on the firms within the market and as profits decline so managerial discretion declines with them. Secondly, if a cosy situation develops between firms, all of whom are managed in an unenterprising way, this would allow any firm, whether a breakaway or a new entrant, with a particularly enterprising management to make substantial competitive gains and therefore to put the other managements under pressure.

5.5 SUMMARY

The concept of information asymmetry is now fundamental to modern economics. By its application to the problem of developing contracts it suggests the conditions under which the firm should develop. The presence of specialist information within the firm may allow that firm to gain significant market advantages. In some cases, these advantages go towards the creation of very large firms – as in accounting. In others, the degree of specialization required for excellence can only be achieved by a few relatively small specialist firms who operate on a subcontracting basis.

Information asymmetry also lies at the heart of the principal and agent problem. The divergence of interests in each case is clear, and demonstrated by the work of Jensen and Meckling (1976); the impossibility of developing an ideal contact was shown, but this may not be disastrous since there are other market constraints that help the principals to avoid being 'cheated' by management, and thus force the management to follow behaviour that approximates to long-run profit maximization.

FURTHER READING

Strong, N. and Waterson, M. (1987) Principals, agents and information, in Clarke, R. and McGuinness, T. (eds) *The Economics of the Firm*, Oxford, Basil Blackwell, chapter 2, pp. 18–41.

For a more complete and advanced treatment of these issues, see:

Ricketts, M. (1987) *The Economics of Business Enterprise*, Hemel Hempstead, Harvester Wheatsheaf.

Costs in the service industries

6

6.1 INTRODUCTION

This chapter will consider the application of the economic theory of short-run costs to the service industries. This theory forms the basis for pricing decisions under conditions where demand has changed but the level of capital investment has not adapted to meet the new level of demand. The full implications of much of this material can therefore only be seen in the context of market structures and issues such as regulation, which will form the subject of later chapters. For profit maximization, the basic premise of economics that if revenue can be increased by more than costs, profits will necessarily increase, even though it will not guarantee solvency, is seen as a useful guide to managerial behaviour. The problems lie in the application of this rule.

Section 6.2 gives a very brief review of the 'traditional' view of short-run costs such as is found in any textbook on managerial economics. Section 6.3 gives two examples of probable marginal costs in the service industries, and section 6.4 goes on to show why the attempt to calculate marginal costs seems so sterile and so difficult to apply in that context. Methods of deriving cost elements are discussed briefly. The problems of application are shown to derive from difficulties with the definition of units of output. Firstly, the intangible nature of many service outputs makes it impossible to define a unit of quantity except the value of the services consumed, an output measure of input which is thus unsatisfactory. Secondly, the differences in units of supply from those of demand, such as the provision of a bus service compared to the taking of a bus trip, make it impossible to define a short-run marginal cost applicable to both producer and consumer. Section 6.5 discusses the particular problems of statistical cost analysis in the service industries. Section 6.6 outlines the reduction of costs by overtrading and thus allowing a fall in the quality of service. Section 6.7 considers one case in which short-run marginal cost calculations may be of direct use in decision making; this case relates to situations of the purchase of perishable inputs with the risk of not being able to sell them increasing with quantity purchased.

6.2 TRADITIONAL APPROACHES

The discussion of short-run costs is normally in the context of the firm producing an output that can be measured in quantity units per time period (defined as appropriate for the analysis), where this output is dependent upon inputs of capital equipment, labour and other purchased inputs.

The period for which the capital is fixed defines the 'short run'. Thus, although capital is fixed in supply, both the other inputs are continuously variable in quantity and very possibly in proportion. There are thus fixed costs, the average value of which declines as output increases, and variable costs which result from hiring increasing amounts of inputs (staff or materials) in order to produce more.

However, since the capital available is fixed, it is traditionally said to be likely that output will initially increase more than proportionately to the quantity of inputs; thus, increasing inputs by 10% will increase output by more than 10%, because the original level of inputs is too low to work effectively. For example, if agricultural demand is very low, a farmer might only take on one worker, although five would be the normal number. That worker will have to cover so many jobs that the addition of a second worker would more than double the output. After a while as capacity is approached, output will increase less than proportionately, because diminishing returns will already have set in.

Marginal costs are defined as the increase in total costs resulting from the production of the marginal unit of output. The pattern of change of variable costs leads to the familiar initial fall and subsequent rise in marginal costs, and the corresponding fall in average costs, pulled down by both declining marginal and average fixed costs (see the definitions in Chapter 3). The average costs then rise when marginal costs have risen above them. While this view may be appropriate for agriculture, it is rarely found in studies of industrial costs, where constant marginal costs are the norm (Johnston, 1960; Andrews, 1949). This is normally explained by the relative fixity of input requirements in relation to capital available in the modern industrial context, so that increased output per unit time in relation to labour and materials is nearly impossible. The notion, often canvassed in years gone by (see Dean, 1976, p. 20 ff) was that costs would rise through loss of quality as capacity was reached through a combination of the use of older and less efficient 'standby' plant and increases in defective items through the attempt to rush production. Dean points out that such standby plant is not common and is in general reserved for special jobs for which it may be essential, that the skills required to operate it decay with lack of practice, and that most firms would not wish to prejudice their reputation by rushing output to the point of increasing defective items.

The continuously variable proportions of the various inputs also allows decisions to be taken about the quantity of inputs in a very neat way. The marginal cost of a unit of output is made up of the cost of the relevant marginal input, divided by the marginal product, i.e. the amount of output for which that final unit of input is responsible. This one can imagine in relation to agriculture, where, for example, one might increase the output of wheat by a certain amount by the addition of an extra bag of fertilizer per hectare; the marginal cost of that extra output would simply be the cost of the bag of fertilizer divided by the number of units of extra wheat produced. If some units have to be used in fixed (rather than variable) proportions, the marginal input is the combination of inputs required in fixed proportions with their corresponding costs. Thus in manufacturing you might need so many minutes of labour per aluminium blank to turn out a piston; the cost of input would have to be the combined cost of labour and the aluminium blanks. If marginal cost is not the result of such continuously variable processes, such that it fluctuates between the cost of the next unit of input and zero until the level of output is reached where a further unit of input is required, a rather different approach is needed, which is discussed under the term 'marginal revenue of service' in Chapter 9. In this case, then, it is impossible to calculate the purchasing of factors of production in this way, and marginal productivity theory falls as an explanation of the purchase of inputs in the short run.

Although the precise use of marginal productivity theory as an aid to purchasing decisions may be impossible, the principle of marginal equivalence derived from it may be useful in checking the allocation of resources in production. The **principle of marginal equivalence** states that the firm should get equal output per pound spent on the marginal unit of each input. For example: would extra training offset the need to buy a more sophisticated and easier computer package? Would cleaning bills be cut by providing each cleaner with better equipment such as vacuum cleaners, polishers etc.? Theoretically, both of these decisions can be taken by the application of the principle of marginal equivalence, but the difficulties are immediately apparent. In the first case, the principle might give a result that it would be better to give more training; however, the more sophisticated computer package may allow the same work to be done more easily, and may allow other things to be done with a resulting rise in the quality of work. The principle also assumes that you can fully appreciate what the consequences will be: the more sophisticated computer package may have flaws. The graphics handling of the package on which this book was written is appalling, although it is supposed to be a full 'Windows' package; furthermore, it cannot communicate with the latest version of the spreadsheet package bought at the same time, an apparently detailed point but one which enormously reduces the benefits of the overall environment. Some of the benefits of the switch were thus vitiated by choosing the wrong word processing package.

The principle of marginal equivalence can be extended to include qualitative aspects such as the type of advertising or publicity, or changes in the quality of service designed to increase revenue rather than just maintaining the level of production. The question then becomes: is the marginal unit of expenditure (on advertising, for example) yielding the same increase in revenue per pound as an equivalent expenditure on some other input (say publicity or representatives' commissions)? The principle here has to be very carefully applied, since it is not only the expenditures which are being varied but also the revenue, and so one has to consider what price changes will be necessary to accompany the policy, and whether the production side can cope with the extra demand. Indeed the latter problem, of 'systems effects', is very common: solution of the problem at one point merely reveals that it was potentially present at either a previous or a subsequent stage. In transport terms, the improvement of one junction may merely reveal that the blockage there was preventing a blockage from occurring at the next junction. It is no accident that the principle of marginal equivalence was developed from the context of agriculture, where small additions and substitutions of inputs are possible. In other contexts, where small changes may alter or fail to alter the capacity of the system as a whole, or change the quality of the output, and where there may be uncertainty as to the effects, it can be a dangerous principle to apply since it may encourage the decision maker to focus too closely on the local decision, and not sufficiently on the wider context. It may, however, provide a useful check that in taking a wider view, the allocation has not become distorted; the principle should still hold if the optimum approach is being followed.

6.3 SHORT-RUN COSTS IN THE SERVICE INDUSTRIES

Let us now try to establish how these costs might look for a couple of service industries, taking the examples of a shop and a bus company running fare stage operations. The basic structure of costs normally recognized in economic analysis are:

- Fixed costs: those factors of production which cannot be altered in the short run, notably the buildings and such heating and lighting as are required, capital goods in the form of machinery and tools, and employees working in management. These would involve the shop itself, its fittings and the manager, and here is the difficulty: normally the shop staff would be counted as variable costs, but in both these cases, and indeed in all service industries, the staff must be hired in **anticipation of providing the service**, along with any necessary equipment such as tills for the checkouts. Because the service cannot be stored, if no one comes to the shop to buy, or passengers do not board the bus, that staff time will be wasted, and cannot be recovered. Thus in most service industries, staff time is a fixed cost. The exceptions to this are where output can be expanded either by overtime payments or the hire of freelance or other contract staff to cover particular services. This is frequently employed in the hotel and catering industries for banquets and the like.
- Variable costs: inputs which vary directly with output because they can be bought or hired as required to make the output. Typically these would consist of the energy, raw materials and semi-finished goods

needed as input, and the operatives required to turn these into output. In the context of a shop, this makes sense: the variable costs are the purchased and storable goods for sale. In the case of the bus operation, they are zero; even the fuel must be provided in anticipation of sales, and if sales do not occur, the fuel is wasted by operating an empty bus. (For contract hire, some of the hire may be possible to service on a marginal basis by employing temporary staff, but this does not apply to the fare stage operation.)

- Joint costs may be present in either fixed or variable costs, where one set of machinery (or other capital) or a group of workers (or other variable costs) contributes to the production of more than one output. A hotel kitchen may provide food for room service, restaurant, bistro or bar meals, etc. Allocation of these overheads to any particular output will *always* be arbitrary. This is one very good reason why marginal costs – even if these are zero – should be used in pricing and output decisions. Allocating more of the joint costs to a service than it will bear will price that service out of the market and the joint costs will then have to be allocated to other services. There is then a risk that these, too, will become overpriced. The extent of joint costs in health care is one of the major problems of trying to provide a system of health care where prices for each item reflect the full costs; since the allocation of joint costs is arbitrary, any such pricing system is arbitrary!

Since marginal costs are the variable costs attributable to the marginal unit of sale, marginal costs for the bus operation will by definition be zero, and for the shop will equal the wholesale cost of the stock.

6.4 THE ANALYSIS OF SHORT-RUN COSTS

That there is a zero marginal cost in many service industries, and only the direct cost of inputs in others, suggests that all costs (other than directly purchased inputs) can be regarded as long-run. In practice, it is necessary to monitor costs month by month, or even more frequently, in most service industries in order to understand what is affecting the profitability of the business. This cost analysis is, however, directed more towards technical control and subsequent use of this knowledge in planning and long-run pricing decisions than towards the day to day pricing decisions implied by traditional analysis. It is, therefore, directed towards verifying that anticipated costs and actual costs coincide, to ensure that management slack is not increasing in different departments. Management slack can come from excessive overtime payments, wastage of materials or pilfering, as well as from the failure to seek out more efficient modes of operation in the long run. It is frequently difficult to model whether the realized totals reflect changes in patterns of trading or managerial slack. For instance, in any bar or restaurant, the patterns of consumption will influence the profits; large quantities of champagne are likely both to put up order costs and profits, whereas large quantities of beer will do the opposite. Not all shifts are so simple: increases in waiter-service meals as opposed to cafeteria style meals can cause shifts in both stock orders and staff requirements. These therefore need careful analysis.

The problems of joint costs will be considered in the next chapter, on planning and investment, since decisions relating to these will usually be taken in that framework. The methods of analysis of costs will be examined briefly since their use shows up some of the problems discussed above.

There are three basic approaches to the calculation of cost functions:

1. The accounting approach. This involves using data from the accounts to cost those elements that vary with output, in order to calculate the changes in cost to be expected for the relevant changes in demand.
2. The engineering approach. Where the design of the (manufacturing) plant is used with known costs of inputs to calculate costs for different levels of output, by changing design parameters – for example, the size of vessels or the type of machinery – a very wide range of options can be tested. In practice, it is usually found that the real costs are very different from those predicted. This approach, being essentially a design approach and thus affecting long-run decisions, will not be discussed further in this chapter.
3. Statistical cost analysis. This involves using the recorded costs and output and calculating the relationship between the two.

For managers, there is often no alternative to the use of the accounting approach. The aim remains to gain an analytical understanding of costs, if possible, to calculate the change in costs resulting from a change in output of one unit. For example:

• Bus operations: carrying an extra passenger from A to B
• Shops: selling an extra item, or the serving of an extra customer
• Electricity: selling an extra kilowatt hour
• Business consultancy: taking on a particular extra job
• Lawyers, doctors, accountants: a further consultation

From a managerial point of view, this approach has the advantage of concentrating the mind of the decision maker on the variables that can be controlled, providing they can solve the problems of deciding on the relevant units. However, it has two major disadvantages. Firstly, it may be argued that the use of the accounting approach may lock the decision maker into an existing suboptimal organizational structure, for example by assuming that only full-time workers can be used, or that no flexibility is possible in using workers nominally employed for one purpose to carry out extra tasks. This is, however, a risk of any analysis based on existing situations, and is part of the human condition. The intuitive leaps gained from using an inappropriate basis for analysis are likely to be a poor basis for decision making. Secondly, the accounting approach is also prone to the omission of relevant costs as the result of wrong analysis. A parallel monitoring of the changes in total costs, with or without using statistical cost analysis, would provide a check on this, and the disaggregated nature of the approach allows such monitoring.

The definition of the level of output from past records for cost analysis is difficult in the context of manufacturing, due to potential changes in quality. It is much more acute in the service industries. Most services are a bundle of intangible attributes which vary markedly through time (a bus trip in one hour's time is not the same as a bus trip now, whereas the television made now will probably be indistinguishable from that made in one hour's time, and may form part of the same order), and in quality, as the result of the elements of personal interaction involved in most trans-actions. (Purchases can be spoiled by the incivility of staff, or interactions with unpleasant fellow customers.)

In addition to problems of defining quality, in service industries the definition of quantity is often very problematic, firstly because of the intangible nature of many services and secondly because the unit of output as seen by the customer may differ from the unit of supply as seen by the provider.

An example of the problem of intangible output is provided by the use of 'consultations in diagnostic related groups' at present being foisted upon the health service. This seems likely to be an extremely poor measure since (i) differences in cost resulting from the severity of the condition within diagnostic related groups is likely to vary by more than the variation between many of the different diagnostic groups, and (ii) the difficulty of establishing what is wrong and an appropriate treatment is likely to vary considerably with the individual's self-awareness and ability to communicate with the doctor. There may be no substitute for the time taken by various grades of staff as a measure of the output in this context, but this assumes that the input is a satisfactory measure of output. If the units of input are of very different qualities, such as senior partners and juniors working on a consultancy case, these units will not give a good measure of units of output, and one is reduced to the circular notion of the total value of the input as the unit of quantity; as value is quantity times price per unit, this is far from satisfactory.

The second problem is that it may be difficult to establish units of output because in many cases the unit of purchase may be radically different from the unit of supply. A bus passenger wants a seat from A to B at a particular time of day, and the intangible aspects of smoothness, quiet, civility, punctuality, etc. The bus company has to think about the putting on of a 'service', of which the section A to B may be only a small part, and which may require much larger outlays in terms of buses and driver hours than is apparent to the passenger; it may require two buses and four drivers to run a route. Similarly swimming pools are either open or closed; the swimmer only wants a session in a pool for a portion of a day. Thus from the operator's point of view, picking up an extra passenger has no cost other than the delay to the bus by stopping, which may not be relevant since an allowance will have been made in the route timings. If the bus later fills up, the cost of that passenger may be seen as the forgone revenue from passengers not able to board because the bus was full, a concept of only limited value to the operator.

The simple view of a different unit of supply from that of demand, essentially the result of indivisibility of inputs and unstorability of output, is insufficient. The units of consumption may be infinitely variable due to the very large number of combinations of services that may be used in any one activity. Whereas the first type is a problem of the jointness of supply, this second is one of jointness in consumption. Thus, for example, we have to ask whether the marginal unit of consumption is a trip to a shopping centre (or several centres on a particular day), a trip to a shop, or a trip to purchase a particular item. Work at the Transport Studies Unit at Oxford University on multipurpose trips and time budgets suggests that this may be a much underestimated area in the determination of demand for transport, particularly in explaining the relative inelasticity of demand for car trips. It is clearly a problem in any tourism and recreation research (as illustrated by the potential benefit of cutting entry costs for facilities such as swimming pools and retaining a reasonable profit on both cafeteria and such ancillary services as shops. Once the overt purpose is purchased – e.g. going for a swim – demand for drinks etc. may be relatively price-inelastic and related to the numbers of customers). This problem could be expressed theoretically as clear units of demand at the most disaggregated level, with externalities in consumption to explain the bundles purchased.

For many purposes, the analysis of this situation is carried out by using the unit of output as seen by the provider and the degree of utilization of that output is expressed by the **load factor**. This is simply the proportion of capacity actually utilized. Thus, contrary to the experience of the London commuter, the load factor of most suburban trains in the rush hour is only just over 50% because the journey in the peak direction is overfull, and the trains are usually almost empty for the return trips. Load factors are thus extremely important in estimating the break-even levels, and/or profitability of the facility, but do not alter the calculations of marginal cost. The appropriate profit maximizing decisions relate to the marginal revenue of service (MRS) and the marginal cost of service. The load factor is useful in exactly the way that average total costs are useful: to indicate whether the firm will be in profit or loss. The marginal cost of putting on a service is essentially a long-run decision involving decisions about investment of capital, in machinery, facilities and staff. The MRS will be discussed under Monopoly in Chapter 9 and Oligopoly in Chapter 10.

The use of the accounting method for costing hotel bed spaces is exactly analogous. It is, however, critically important to determine which cost elements can be made to vary precisely with the number of guests as opposed to the number of bed spaces. Hughes (1980) suggests that labour hours are essentially related to the number of bed spaces, not the number of occupants, in other words that all costs except 'consumables' such as coffee and milk for the coffee maker, fresh soap, etc. are fixed, as was suggested above for the bus and swimming pool cases. This he supports from discussion with hoteliers, who stated that their labour was hired for the season at the start of the season (Hughes, 1980, p. 4) and he provides further evidence from the analysis of the change of staffing with turnover (p. 26, table 4.1). This may reflect the isolation of the Pitlochry labour market, and might be less appropriate for hotels and guest houses in large cities; furthermore, while staff costs will be essentially fixed, up to the point of full utilization of staff time, there is likely to be a level of occupancy which will demand overtime payments. These would be properly included in any calculation of marginal cost, but it is worth pointing out that it is unlikely that marginal cost will approach average costs, and that such expanded output will be other than extremely profitable. The total staff input per sleeper night was on average 0.68 hours, with a range of 0.40 to 0.82 hours, the lower and higher figures reflecting above and below average occupancy rates (p. 20, table 2.3). The level of consumables is extremely low and we can thus be sure that the higher occupancy would be very profitable even if the extra hours needed were paid at double or triple the usual rates.

As any revenue above marginal cost will contribute to profits, the wily customer can try to bargain to reduce the charges towards this level if there is known to be spare capacity in the hotel. Since these costs are so low compared to the very large costs of running a hotel, there is a lot of leeway for tour operators to try to force low prices from the hotels in a recession. In so far as they are successful in forcing 'distress prices', they will equally certainly bankrupt the hotel quite rapidly.

6.5 STATISTICAL COST ANALYSIS

The problems associated with using statistical cost analysis for assessing marginal cost can be seen in the work of Joel Dean based on data from 1931 to 1935 inclusive (first published in 1942, and subsequently in Dean, 1976). This approach was to take literally the relationship that $MC = dTC/dQ$, and after careful elimination of such variations in costs as were due to pure price changes, to regress quantity on total cost, and thereby derive a relationship for marginal cost as its first derivative. In one department, Ladies Medium Priced Coats, a falling marginal cost was noted. In all the others it was shown to be constant. As Dean notes (1976, p. 292), this decline in marginal costs may indicate a fall in the standard of service, although this seems unlikely since his data was monthly cost and sales, rather than daily sales as discussed above. It seems plausible that Ladies Coats, being a fairly seasonal purchase, will have short periods when extra staff need to be drafted in; if these extra staff add less to the costs than average staff costs per sale, the total costs will increase with additional sales but less than proportionately. This seems very likely since the staffing associated with the organization and design aspects of the department would be fixed. A similar pattern is observable in catering establishments where 'casual' staff are recruited to be on standby for such peak sales as banquets (their poor training is often very obvious compared to the restaurant staff, for example). On this basis it is unclear why the same fact should not be observed in the other two departments examined; a plausible explanation would be in the relative stability of sales through the periods, such that planned staff expansion could match the expansion of sales.

From a managerial point of view this approach seems excessively coarse grained, since it includes only broad categories of costs, or in some cases only total cost and total output. The need for long runs of data also makes it very difficult to use, given the changing nature of many retail conditions. It is difficult to work out whether this is a long-run or short-run marginal cost. Following the argument of Hughes, staff will be substantially fixed in numbers and hours in the medium term, with careful scheduling to meet known peaks and troughs in demand. The use of long periods of data thus reflects a mixture of the costs of such scheduled changes in staff in relation to expected changing levels of demand, and the unplanned over or under provision. This problem was partially overcome by Dean since he used total costs against the number of transactions and the value of the trans-actions. He found that factors such as bad weather and higher or lower sales than predictable from the total sales in the same month of the previous year (the basis for the store's forecast sales figures) affected the number and hence value of sales but not the total costs. These factors were therefore left out of the equation, thus including only (i) input costs, and (ii) planned staff cost changes (see Dean, 1976, pp. 281–283). The first aspect would seem to be a short-term element, the second a medium- or long-term element. The marginal cost thus produced does not therefore analyse either situation clearly.

6.6 DEFICIENCY GAINS

The potential for reducing costs by cutting the levels of service (as noted by Dean) is present in most service industries. Memorably called 'deficiency gains' in the context of university education, to distinguish them from the gains achieved by finding more efficient means of service delivery, these are almost always present as a means of cutting costs in the short run. A supermarket can fire a few cashiers, and even fail to stock shelves adequately by saving on the accuracy of deliveries, but if there is competition in the market, these gains will tend to be followed by falls in revenue as the customers find better outlets. In services such as education, such results may take a long time to show through, and may indeed only register as a reduction in student recruitment, if other destinations not affected by the same pressures are available to them.

6.7 A RISK-BASED MARGINAL COST

The notion of short-run marginal cost may have some use in relation to the purchase of perishable inputs. This would apply to the catering and retailing industries, but seems unlikely to apply to others. To the consumer in (let's say) a grocery shop, the extra purchase will clearly be a particular item – more margarine, coffee, etc. If we accept this as the definition of output, then clearly the only cost that is going to vary precisely with output in a shop is the purchase of that item from the wholesaler. Thus we might say that the marginal cost is the cost of purchase to the shopkeeper of the extra item purchased by the consumer. However, this is only true in the context of durable goods. For perishable goods, there is a considerable problem of wastage. Thus while $MC =$ wholesale price may be an adequate description for non-perishable goods, for perishable items this is by no means so clear. The greengrocer may go to the wholesale market daily; in so far as he buys material that must be sold the same day, his problem is no longer so simple; he must now choose whether to buy an extra crate of (let's say) peaches, and estimate whether they are over- or under-stocking. More precisely, he needs to work out the probabilities of selling various proportions of the crate. Suppose each crate has two dozen peaches, and costs £2.00 wholesale; he thinks he can sell between 10 and 12 crates, each crate potentially realizing £4.80. Considering then the last two crates, he believes he has a 50% chance of selling the first, and no chance of selling more than the second. For points in between he thinks the probabilities work out roughly in proportion. Thus the average probability for the first crate will be 0.75, and its probable value to him will therefore be £4.80 × 0.75 = £3.60, a comfortable profit over the £2.00 it will cost. The average probability of selling the second crate will be 0.25, giving a value to him of £1.20, below the cost. He should thus buy the first and not the second crate. This may be seen as an example of rising marginal costs; the first 10 crates, assuming his estimates are correct, have a constant marginal cost per peach of 8.333 pence; the final peach of the second box has an equivalent marginal cost of 16.66 pence, with points in between being given by dividing the cost per peach by the probability of selling it.

One should notice that this process would not aim to eliminate wastage, but to find a level of probable wastage that will maximize profits. It may be noticed that pushing sales towards saturation point at the prevailing prices will increase the probable level of wastage, and hence will actually increase the marginal cost of sales.

6.8 SUMMARY

Because of the inability to store the input or output, such apparently variable costs as labour are normally fixed costs in the service industries. Short-run marginal cost is thus likely to comprise only those purchased inputs that serve for a particular unit of output. The definition of units of output is likely to be difficult and in the context of personal services is likely to be measurable only in terms of either the units of input – hours of labour used – or the total value of output. Definition of units of output is also complicated by the difference in units seen from the managerial perspective and the consumer's point of view. Both viewpoints incorporate jointness: of supply for the manager, and in demand for the consumers. The joint supply can be seen in the operation of a bus service from A to B from the hours of 07.30 to 19.30, and from the consumer's point of view in taking a bus at a particular time for only part of the route. The jointness in demand may be seen in the decision to rent a hotel room as part of a holiday. The marginal unit may therefore only be expressible from the managerial viewpoint as the marginal cost of service, and the profit maximizing output is given by the equality between this and the expected marginal revenue of service. This is essentially at least a 'medium term' decision, where substantial inputs are fixed but during which the decision will fix other inputs. It therefore does nothing to detract from the view that short-run marginal costs are likely to be very low or zero. This does not invalidate the use of marginal analysis, but means that the emphasis for short-run analysis shifts from the cost side to the demand side, the side which determines the marginal revenue. Decisions on the level of service and the methods of production, and hence costs, are long-run decisions, and these are the subject of the next chapter.

FURTHER READING

Follow up the references, if appropriate.

The investment decision | 7

7.1 INTRODUCTION

This chapter considers costs in the long run from the point of view of the firm's decisions to allocate funds for investment. Since the previous chapter established the strong probability of low or fixed marginal costs in the service industries, and the inability of the firm to avoid many of the costs that are normally considered variable costs even in the short run, investment decisions may be divided into two categories: in section 7.2, the 'routine' medium-term decision whether to pursue the present pattern of service provision, expand or contract is very briefly outlined. Section 7.3 discusses the major new project decision, whether to open up new lines of service, invest in major new equipment or R&D programmes. Like the short run and long run in economics, these are defined by characteristics rather than time period. The two processes will run concurrently, but the firm's management procedures usually involve a different approach to the consideration of the two situations.

Section 7.3 first considers the process of discounting to allow for the distribution of cash flows through time. The important question of how a project can be defined is then tackled. The circumstances in which it is appropriate to use internal rates of return rather than net present values are outlined. This particularly involves the examination of the treatment of joint costs and revenues. The section will then examine the key concepts used in capital investment appraisal: capital investment, running costs and revenues. The relationship between cash flows and depreciation and the concept of 'economic depreciation' are introduced. The potentially dire results of failing to use this technique, where start-ups or projects involve substantial advertising and/or research and development expenditures, are illustrated.

Section 7.4 considers the incorporation of uncertainty into the analysis of capital projects. The distorting effect of including uncertainty as a higher rate of discount is noted and contrasted to the alternative use of sensitivity analysis. This is linked to the suggestion by Peter Earl of 'surprise' as compared to the Expected Utility hypotheses of von Neumann and Morgenstern. This section may be considered to be too sophisticated and too detailed given the level of detail in the rest of the work. It is included because the material is more difficult to obtain elsewhere, and is often explained with such a high level of mathematical sophistication that it is a closed book to managers.

Section 7.5 considers the integration of investment appraisal and strategic management of enterprises. The difficulties of strategic management and the lack of formal links between strategy and investment appraisal are noted. However, it is suggested that a consistent approach to the accounting, design and management of service delivery is required, which integrates the monitoring and learning functions into the planning and investment appraisal routines.

7.2 ROUTINE REPLACEMENT DECISIONS

If labour costs are not simply short-run decisions, as implicit in the traditional analysis of economists, but are actually part of planning the delivery of a service, at least into the medium term, such decisions should be part of the investment appraisal approach, and should theoretically be subsumed under the discussion of project appraisal. It is, however, clear that no firm could operate on this basis, since it would be impossibly cumbersome. The normal procedures for replacement of staff or minor pieces of equipment are therefore to do so on a routine basis, buying in an exact replacement from the market. This is tantamount to saying that the decision has been taken in the past, and that if it was valid then, a repeat will be valid now.

If the decision is about minor adjustments in terms of expansion or contraction, it is sometimes very obvious; for example, a restaurant may be profitable, but working below capacity; there may be no work for the number of waiters originally hired, and so one or more may be laid off. This has no apparent wider implications, unless the amount of training required is very high so that considerable care has to be taken to avoid losing staff and then replacing them. In such cases a small analysis of the relevant cost implications will enable a decision to be taken. In many cases, however, the decision may raise questions about the capacity of the whole organization to function, as might be the case on the borderline of firing a chef, since there are usually only a small number of chefs, and thus the capacity change may have implications as to the type of meals that can be served, etc. Here the only technique will be to use project analysis, since it affects both costs and revenues, and probably the reputation of the establishment. It is thus truly an investment decision.

7.3 PROJECT APPRAISAL

Whenever the future development of the firm, or branch, is at stake, project appraisal forms the basis for analysing the flow of costs and revenues that will result from any decision. It is seen as a means of examining the consequences in a dispassionate manner, so as to take 'good' decisions. This clearly sweeps the agency problems within the firm under the carpet. Typical 'agency' behaviour such as the overestimation of costs and underestimation of revenues in the formal analysis because it will give the local management leeway against targets, or its contrary – the underestimate of costs and overestimate of revenues in order to get the project passed in spite of the rules imposed from above – affects the overall management of the firm and its strategy. Control of this behaviour forms part of the decisions of higher management in relation to the firm's strategy, which is dealt with in section 7.5. It is assumed that students of managerial economics will also be studying courses on business finance, where more detailed work will be done on project appraisal and discounting, and the relationship between performance and share prices, etc. This section can do no more than sketch the outline of the topic for those who will not be taking such courses.

7.3.1 Discounting

The principle of discounting future cash flows can be seen as a reflection of the fact that 'riskless' investments can be made in the money markets, which will ensure that money invested will grow at the prevailing rate of interest into the future. Thus, if £1 can be invested in a bank at a rate of 10%, in one year's time it will be worth £1.10, in two years £1.21, and so on.

Similarly, if there were no risks involved to either the borrower or the lender, and no costs involved in setting up the transaction in the form of records, contracts, etc., we could borrow money now against a repayment in the future of that money plus the accumulated interest on it. Thus if the same 10% rate of interest prevailed, if we could guarantee to pay £1.10 in one year's time, we could expect to borrow £1.00 now. Thus we can say that £1.10 in one year is worth £1.00 now. This leads us to the convenient formula for the present value of any future cash flow (whether negative or positive):

$$PV = A \; \frac{1}{(1 + r)^n} \tag{7.1}$$

where PV is the present value, A is the amount expected in year n, r is the rate of interest, expressed as a decimal (e.g. 10% = 0.1) and n is the number of years, where the present is regarded as year 0. This formula is applied to all net cash flows for each year in project analysis.

Choice of investment criterion

Investments are acceptable where the **net present value**, which is defined as the sum of the present value of revenues less the present value of costs, is greater than zero. Since this criterion is both theoretically sound and easy to use, particularly with modern microcomputers, other criteria such as the payback period and the internal rate of return are entirely redundant.

The **payback period** requires that the capital investment be recoverable over a given period or less; it is therefore an invitation to short-termism. The **internal rate of return** is that discount rate that reduces the net present value to zero; judgement of the desirability of a project on the basis of internal rates of return again encourages short-term thinking, since the very high rate of return will reduce costs or revenues in the longer term future to very small values. Indeed, the results may be spurious, particularly in the presence of any costs occurring late in the project. In these cases, there are usually at least two internal rates of return, a high one which values the near future revenues highly and discounts the future costs, and a low one which gives the long term its due, including both costs and revenues. In at least some cases, there will, however, be no second internal rate of return, and the very high value will actually be accompanied by a negative net present value using a sensible discount rate, because only by discounting the future costs at a very high rate of interest can one make them sufficiently insignificant for them not to determine the outcome of the project evaluation. The quick and dirty **first year rate of return** provides a quick check, but since it ignores the whole problem of the future development of the business, it can scarcely be taken as a serious criterion for project evaluation.

The mechanics and the practical and theoretical aspects of choice of interest rates, the adjustment of the process to account for different periods of projects, its use where there are only cost savings, the treatment of tax, and so on are well rehearsed in all of the textbooks on managerial economics, or much more fully and appropriately in those on corporate finance (for example, Brealy and Myers, 1991), and it seems redundant to repeat them here. However, as each industry is subject to different uncertainties, and the treatment of risk is often less than full, it seems important to deal with this here at greater length.

7.3.2 The definition of a 'project'

Projects have to be defined in relation to the areas of the business that will be considered and in relation to the length for which the project will be deemed to run. Defining project life is often difficult, but is perhaps less important operationally because of the effect of discounting, which tends to reduce the value of far distant costs and benefits very considerably. Methods for correcting for different lengths of project are given in Brealy and Myers (1991, pp. 109–110).

The problems of defining a project are perhaps most vividly illustrated from the definitions that were permitted by the World Bank and other funding authorities on the combination of projects relating to the Itaipu Dam in Brazil, its electricity generating capacity, the steelworks and the railway that was needed to ship the steel. Each project was defined separately and separate funding accordingly sought. This ingenious device allowed the profits from the steel mill to be allocated to the steel mill in the first instance, thus justifying its construction. The electricity generating stations and the vast dam itself were defined as a separate project, and one of the major benefits was the profits from the steel mills, which were to use the very large local iron ore deposits. Since, however, the Itaipu Dam is some 1400 kilometres from the nearest major city, this electricity generation was not ideally located other than for the steelworks. Thirdly, in order to transport the produce of the steel mills, a railway was required; once again its major benefit was the profits from the said mills. In a world with excess capacity in steel production, the profits from the steel mills were dubious anyway, but if the project had been properly defined, to include all the necessary infrastructure costs, i.e. both the dam and its generating stations, and the railway, it would clearly not have been viable. In this way are private contractors' fortunes made and Third World countries plunged into serious debt. The international banks thought they would also do well out of it, since no country had refused to repay its debts or the interest – at that time.

An intrinsic part of project definition is the decision about the baseline from which the project will be evaluated. This is particularly easy in the context of the decision to set up new service outlets or new networks, since there are clear running costs and investments, staffing needs and well-predicted revenues. The definition of the baseline for a major refurbishment is however more difficult, since it is usually possible to continue to generate revenues with smaller scale investments. Two complementary approaches are often followed: firstly, a 'zero-base' budget is assumed and each project is evaluated against the option of closing down the outlet; and secondly, the incremental expenditures and revenues of the more expensive project(s) are treated as if they were separate investments and evaluated to see whether the 'phantom projects' thus generated have positive net present values. This is done to guard against a situation in which almost all the profit comes from the initial lower level investment, such that the higher investment evaluated in total has a positive net present value, although the increased investment is in fact not worthwhile.

The key factor in defining projects is that they must include all the costs and all the benefits (alias revenues in a purely private project). Decisions on these boundaries are particularly difficult where there are joint costs or revenues, such as the firm's central management functions, which will only be marginally affected by the project, or jointly generated profits from the use of other services offered by the firm, such as ongoing flights offered by the same airline. These should not be ignored. In more humble contexts, companies should not be surprised if they get into difficulties if they justify a new service purely on its own costs and revenues, and then find that they need to increase the overheads of the whole company because the management and central ordering and engineering facilities can no longer cope.

A good example of the problem of the identification of project boundaries is furnished by Pappas and Hirschey (1987, pp. 417–419). Continental Airlines had to decide whether or not to continue a particular flight that was producing low profits. The airline correctly considered only the 'incremental costs'. They therefore ignored whether the flight was making the expected contribution to overheads. They also ignored such apparently direct costs as ground crew for the flight where such ground crew were paid in order to service other flights and would otherwise be idle. They correctly included the profits generated on other flights by passengers using the flight in question as the first leg in a longer trip with Continental Airlines, that is the net profit (over incremental costs) from passengers from the feeder flight using other flights. Since these other flights would presumably run anyway, the net profit is the complete fare, less only those direct costs from having an extra passenger (the cost of the airline meal?).

If each flight is dependent on the others' feeding in sufficient of its passengers to affect its viability, the only boundary that can appropriately be drawn is that around the whole group of flights so affected. The procedure of partial evaluation may be dangerous, but is correct *if* it is only the one flight at risk. In view of the consequences of taking too wide a boundary, it is desirable to take some risks in defining the boundary narrowly. If the lack of that flight, and the passengers it brings to ongoing flights, would make these unprofitable, then their impact on other connecting flights in the whole sector needs to be reassessed. At each stage the choice of the project boundary becomes an even more complex decision, since presumably the wider the sector the more such interconnections there will be. Potentially, the project boundary would widen to include the airline's complete operations and the costs of the decision could outweigh the costs saved by it.

While it is dangerous to widen the project boundary, ignoring the interconnectivity of a network is equally dangerous. There is an obvious potential domino effect. You cut the least apparently profitable route; this makes other routes unprofitable, so you cut further. This logic also applies to shops or other retail outlets considering reducing the range of goods or services carried: a shopper coming for one item is quite likely to buy others. All these are examples of either joint costs or benefits. Network-based services are obviously very prone to such problems, but by no means uniquely: consider the restaurant kitchen that also provides bar food or room-service meals; the tax expertise in accountancy firms, which is available to clients whose main interest is in hiring a tax consultant and those whose main problem is auditing, etc. To summarize: the ideal definition of a project is to include all costs and revenues that are directly affected by the project, and to exclude all others, but to stop the analysis if its costs are becoming higher than its benefits.

7.3.3 Definition of capital costs, running costs and revenues

For all costs, certain rules of valuation apply, whether they are capital costs or running costs. The value of any item or person should be estimated at the **opportunity cost**. This is their value in the next best possible use; in other words, it represents the opportunity forgone by spending the money or using the staff time on the project rather than on its next best use. In most cases the market cost will provide the best estimate of this value. In some cases, however, the firm will have unique resources, usually staff whose experience is unique and who can therefore design or develop things uniquely quickly. Where this is the case, two possible valuation methods can be suggested: firstly, if others could learn those skills, how much would they cost to hire and train, and how long would the new recruit require to do the work (and consequently what other costs would be incurred in the project)? This provides a market value for the person in the particular context. The other means of valuation requires that the direct costs of the unique resource be included, a person's salary and overhead costs, *and* that the profits from the project be ascribed to them, and these profits be compared to the opportunity cost of that person, in terms of the profits generated by the best alternative use. For example, your firm has a uniquely experienced software designer, whose gross salary costs amount to £30 000; two possible projects are being evaluated. Assuming that both would require this unique resource, it is clear that the opportunity cost of using the person on Project A is the profit forgone on Project B. Thus one can ignore the special value of the key resource and choose the project with the higher net present value, because the projects are the only two to use the key resource.

Spare resources that cannot be disposed of, for example ground crews needed to service flights before and after a possible new flight, have zero opportunity cost, unless there are competing projects. These are referred to as **sunk costs**: that part of any expenditure which cannot be recovered by resale once it is made, and which cannot be avoided if it is a direct input. In this case the opportunity cost of one project is the profit forgone on the other, exactly as in the case above; we can therefore ignore such sunk costs since an evaluation of the profitability of the alternatives without any special estimates will tell us which project appears preferable. An alternative way of expressing this situation is to say that we wish to calculate the **long-run marginal cost** (LMC). This is defined as 'the increase in total costs due to the increase in output', achieved in this case by the project. The difficulty with the concept of LMC is that it is usually assumed to be continuously variable, whereas in reality it can often only be estimated as an incremental cost.

The definition of each of these items seems self-evident. **Capital costs** are those 'once and for all time' items associated with the project: any necessary machinery, land or premises to be purchased or refurbished. **Running costs** are those expenditures that will be incurred throughout the life of the project, such as the staff costs and the cost of purchased inputs. The **revenues** are the results of sales from the output of the project. On closer analysis these headings are not necessarily so self-evident; we will accordingly look at each in turn.

Capital costs

The purchases of capital inputs are often the trigger for a project evaluation. However, there are items that often come into running costs which are very clearly of a 'once and for all time' nature, at least in the levels of expenditure required.

Firstly, for many projects, where the aim is to launch a new service, there is a choice between allowing such a service to build up in its own time or to use advertising and publicity to ensure that it is known and achieves market penetration as quickly as possible. Such advertising is a capital rather than a running cost.

Secondly, particularly with a service, there are often major start-up costs relating to staff training, and the absorption of the service delivery into management structures. These are again capital costs, not running costs, even though routine staff training may be such a cost. The self-deception involved in putting such items through as running costs can have severe consequences. These are particularly likely in relation to computer programs; two examples illustrate this:

A catering operation bought a new suite of programs for meal planning, costing and materials ordering, and checking and updating of the purchase ledger. To run these programs, more sophisticated hardware was necessary. Not only did the guarantee period of a year on the software and hardware run out before the programs were put to use, but the new and the old systems of accounting had to be run simultaneously for a time since the management could not trust the new system to operate effectively. While the latter might have been a wise precaution in any case, the lapse of time before the programs could be used was a clear example of the failure to incorporate all the necessary costs into the analysis. It was due at least in part to two favourite corporate failures: the Board, being largely ignorant of the details of management and particularly of the new technology, were unwilling to let it go ahead despite the professional manager's recommendations; he thus felt it necessary to try to disguise the true costs. The second corporate failure came from the manager, who was himself ignorant of the requirements of the new technology; he did not appreciate either the requirements of the technology in terms of staff training – 'They can just pick it up on the job . . .' – or of the changes in monitoring and job description that such a system would involve. Ideally, a trusted middle manageress (in the particular case) should have been given the task of mastering the system, working out the staff training and reallocation of duties, gaining staff acceptance for these, then introducing the system appropriately; such expenditures as staff training should have been included in the costs of the new approach. However, at no time did the manageress have the spare capacity to do this and so the system was introduced painfully and wastefully – though with the great advantage that no one could calculate the costs since they were spread through various items of staff time, and emerged as staff sick leave due to stress.

A similar failure to plan the purchase and introduction of new technology occurred in the production of an encyclopedia by one of the major scientific publishers. An administrator was hired. A request for a computer was put in along with software that would allow all the monitoring of articles and letter writing to be carried out. The administrator had no experience of this software, and since the Managing Director of the conglomerate suddenly had the idea that too much was being spent on computers lying idle in offices, he put an embargo on further purchases. Thus, the computer was only delivered as the project gained momentum, and the administrator was wholly unnecessarily stressed in having to learn the software and undertake the heavy duties of administration that were coming on stream. Such failures always have long-run echoes; parts of the software that could have allowed much more effective monitoring were never really learnt; and the monitoring of such huge projects is crucial. Once under full pressure of work, it is very difficult to make use of information that should have been sought from elsewhere in the conglomerate about the organization of such ventures. This type of training, and the use of expertise in the system, was never applied; the wheel was duly reinvented, probably without the benefit of such known technology as ball-bearings.

Working capital

Many ventures fail because of the lack of working capital. For example, in retailing it is sometimes possible to organize payments to wholesalers (or manufacturers) so that goods are sold before they are paid for. The retailer therefore makes money off the stock by putting the revenues into an interest earning account, and delaying payment. Rumour has it that the shops at London Heathrow are not viable at the high rents charged by the British Airports Authority if this source of income is not included in the calculations. The shops are of sufficient importance to the manufacturers to allow the shops to negotiate a 3-month delay in payment for produce; the turnover is approximately weekly, so the shops have an equivalent income from interest of just less than one-quarter of a year's turnover. Even if the legend is without foundation, it illustrates the importance of forecasting working capital requirements.

More commonly, of course, the delay between payment to suppliers for goods or work done and the receipt of income from customers for the services derived from those inputs, implies a need for working capital, with implications both for interest charges or receipts, and capital limits if these are important. Furthermore, the higher the turnover, the more working capital is needed – a real problem if the bank will not allow the overdraft to expand to match.

Resale value of capital assets

In many contexts it is possible to estimate the residual values of the capital assets used in a project; these should be estimated and must be inserted at the end of the project life. Values should be market values where possible. This will be discussed further below in the context of depreciation.

Depreciation

Depreciation is defined as the loss of value of a capital asset over a particular period, almost always a year. This is very often defined by accounting convention, with a view to assessing tax liability and reducing it where possible. This is, however, *not* a good indication of the decline in economic value except by pure chance. The value of a capital asset may be defined in two ways, which should be equivalent only if the firm has no special advantages: firstly, it may be defined by its value on the open market; and, secondly, by the value of the future profits that will flow from it.

The use of the latter criterion gives us a measure of the economic depreciation of the asset to the firm. This is particularly important where the profile of profits leads to an increase in the value of the asset in the first years. The classic example is the development of a significant brand for a product. This normally takes years to develop, and during that period the advertising and promotion expenditures are appreciating in value. Almost any service, except those consultancies set up to sweeten redundancy, will tend to have a period during which it is becoming known and thus during which the value of profits is increasing; this profile will lead to negative economic depreciation over that time period. Biggadike (1979, p. 55) shows, in his important study of corporate diversification and new entry in the manufacturing sector, just how long such losses on entry may persist; in his study the median value for the time between entry and coming into profitability was recorded as 8 years. Brealy and Myers (1991, pp. 270–276) show how economic depreciation can be calculated (p. 271) and discuss it in relation to the investment in supermarkets by a supermarket chain. They show how perverse incentives may be set up for managers if accounting rather than economic depreciation used in combination with a return on book values of investments is set up as the criterion for management performance. The straight line accounting depreciation causes low returns to be recorded on the asset in the first years, because the rate of return is measured by the ratio of the **economic income**, which is the sum of profits and capital appreciation, to the book value of the assets. Thus, putting in a large loss of value of the asset when it is either static in value or even increasing reduces the income considerably compared with its true value. At the same time the book value of the assets is the amount paid less the total depreciation allowed to that date. The total depreciation is low as the asset is new, and so at one and the same time the income is being underestimated and the book value overestimated, thus giving a lower rate of return. For older assets, where the economic depreciation should be high, the rate of return is grossly overstated by the accounting measure; here the capital value of the asset has been much reduced by previous excessive accounting depreciation, and economic depreciation is higher than accounting depreciation – and the economic income is correspondingly overestimated. This procedure would lead to underinvestment if accounting rates of return are being used either (inappropriately) as an investment criterion or as a means of monitoring managerial efficiency.

Calculation of economic depreciation is extremely simple (Table 7.1). To illustrate it we will use the case of a shop. Profits are revenues less operating costs. To simplify the table, we include costs of refurbishment and the manager's salary in operating costs. Profits are expected to be zero in the first year, and to rise in years 2 and 3, reaching a steady state 'for all time' in year 4; this is equivalent to saying that the shop will be sold as a going concern with profits expected at £23 000 in each year indefinitely. This means that the shop has a constant value of £230 000 after year 4, if the interest rate is expected to remain at 10%. It therefore has no economic depreciation. More interestingly, in years 1, 2 and 3, it appreciates, since during these years clientele is being built up and with the build-up come increasing net profits, and hence increasing capital value.

Table 7.1 Economic depreciation in a shop

Year	0	1	2	3	4 and subsequent
Cash flow (£000s)	−200	0	15	20	23
Present value (£000s)	−200	0.00	12.40	15.03	15.71
Present value of profits at start of year (£000s)		200.23	220.25	227.27	230.00
Loss of value over the year = economic depreciation (£000s)		−20.02	−7.02	−2.73	0.00

Note: 'Negative depreciation' means 'appreciation'.

Taking each line of the table in turn:

- The cash flow in year 0, the start of year 1, is an expenditure of £200 000 for the purchase of the shop. By the end of year 1 no profit or loss has been made on operations. At the end of year 2, a profit of £15 000 has been made, rising to £20 000 in year 3, and to the final steady state figure of £23 000 in year 4.
- The present values of each of these cash flows is given in the next line; for example in year 2, £15 000/1.1^2 = £12 400; in year 3, £20 000/1.1^3 = £15 030 etc.
- The present values of profits at the start of the year is the value of the profits discounted back to the start of that year; thus in year 1 it is the present value of the profits in years 1 to infinity. In year 2, it is from year 2 to infinity, etc. These figures thus represent the amount a buyer would be willing to pay for this stream of profits, assuming the discount rate of 10%.
- The final row, the loss in value in that year, is the result of subtracting the present value in year 2 from that in year 1. This loss in value would be the exact equivalent of the economic measure for depreciation. Here it is negative, meaning that the shop is appreciating in value.

As Brealy and Myers point out, this value would be the correct value for calculating depreciation. It is difficult to use for tax purposes, however, as it is based on estimates, and hence could be arbitrarily calculated each year. (It should be pointed out that this arbitrary calculation is precisely the technique used to revalue property portfolios; this may be the reason why the shares never fetch the price equivalent to the stated value of the assets; the discount to the asset value seems likely to be a measure of the stock market's lack of trust in this process.) There is no reason, according to Brealy and Myers, why the structure of expected economic depreciation should not be used for accounting and tax purposes, i.e. the firm could agree with the Tax Office at the start the pattern of depreciation for an investment. This would potentially reduce the worst of the disincentives that the alternative systems of depreciation provide, particularly if they are used in conjunction with the need to achieve a good return on capital in each year.

It will be noted that depreciation emerges from the calculations of net present value. It is not necessary to insert depreciation into the calculations, except insofar as there are real expenditures to maintain the usefulness of the asset, such as refurbishment costs. A fully costed set of cash flow and expenditure patterns will include allowance for the costs of the capital, and the interest charges at the rate of discount. Thus, the capital is implicitly being paid off in the process of calculating the net present value. Here the present value of the profits amounts to £200 230 as against a present value of purchase of the shop of £200 000, and hence we have a truly marginally profitable net present value of £230. Equally, this does *not* mean that a capital sum of £200 000 would be sufficient to start up the business; the actual amount required would depend on the means of financing and the running costs that were being incurred in advance, by however small an amount, of the receipt of revenues in the first year. Such items as interest on the capital and advertising expenditures, as well as staff and stock, could increase the sum enormously; to avoid early failure, it is essential to calculate the capital requirements properly. It is generally believed that many of the new businesses that fail during the first two years do so because they are undercapitalized, particularly in view of the losses likely for that period.

Running costs

For investments that replicate existing systems, reasonably precise estimates of running costs may be available. For new systems based on designers' criteria, there are always likely to be underestimates of cost. Breakdowns, for example, involve net increased costs since the time is irrecoverable, and the cash costs of repair are additional. Some unpleasant surprises are avoidable with foresight; the matching of all aspects of capacity for delivery of the service, from the personnel required for processing orders to the accounting and billing systems, is one major area that may cause problems. Small mail order firms whose goods achieve cult status can fail precisely for this reason. The fatal spiral comes about through excess orders, which then cannot be filled because the suppliers cannot supply the quantity required in time. The staff that should have been filling the orders, sending them out and putting the cheques etc. through the system, are then needed to return the cheques, with the appropriate apology, often asking whether the customer wishes to have the product after some delay. Whether the customer does or not, the staff time has to be paid for and is increasing costs because of mailing the apologies, with no revenue to compensate. It is obvious that this can exhaust working capital rapidly. If the suppliers are able to fill the orders in time, sufficient unplanned expansion can cause problems. If no one can be found to replicate the founder's control functions, the organization of despatch and billing can rapidly break down, particularly as there are liable to be acute bottlenecks with computer facilities. The cost of replicating the system to cope may be much greater than expected, particularly if the scale of expansion is too great for the slack in the existing system, and too small to justify full replication. The stress and difficulty of the operation may also lead to unpleasant errors such as failing to allow for taxation, or coming into a level of turnover that requires VAT registration. Here, however, we are essentially anticipating two subsequent sections – section 7.4 (The treatment of risk in project analysis) and section 7.5 (Investment and the strategy of the firm), which, as we will see, often means considering the impact of the particular project on the firm as a whole, and on its future profile of cash flows.

It is important to include the appropriate allowances for taxation and any regulatory considerations in the analysis of running costs.

Revenues

It may appear easy to estimate the revenues from a project, but there are two key problems. One has been mentioned under the heading of 'jointness', where the revenues from one project may affect the revenues elsewhere in the firm, and the investment may be crucial to the firm's survival in a particular market. Thus, the opportunity costs of not investing may be not zero revenue, as is usually implicitly assumed, but the loss of revenue on existing operations: again, the problem is one of defining the project boundary appropriately. The second major problem concerns the issue of forecasting the quantities demanded at any price. This is the core of the chapters on different market structures. In each market structure the problems of demand forecasts are different, since the issue of response of rivals, or its absence, is crucial.

No aspect of demand would appear to be separable from these considerations. Though they will not be explored here, two points are so important that they deserve mention. Firstly, the timing of the build up of demand is likely to be crucial at the project level. Even in simple situations, without issues of connectivity (see the section on depreciation for further treatment of this), it seems to be quite likely that it will take 18 months before demand builds up. Secondly, simple rules of thumb assuming constant demand per unit of service delivery are almost bound to be wrong. For example, each bus on a route may carry the same number of passengers on average, but if an extra one is put on, this number is likely to decline (although this depends on the elasticity of demand with respect to service levels and the proportional increase in service levels). This problem is discussed in section 9.2.4, 'The marginal revenue of service'. The same should be expected from increasing the density of shops in an area or increasing the density of alternative insurance packages available in the range.

7.4 THE TREATMENT OF RISK IN PROJECT ANALYSIS

7.4.1 Introduction

Before discussing the treatment of uncertainty in project analysis, it is essential to note that even 'impartial' approaches will include some implicit attitude to risk. A large firm, for example an oil company engaging in exploration, may be **risk neutral**. This stems from its particular situation. The special factors are as follows: (i) the risks of gains or losses are small compared to its financial power, (ii) it has sufficient confidence in its basic data that it will be successful in a certain proportion of cases. Its expertise allows it to assess both this probability and the size of any find it might make, and hence to estimate the **expected present value** of the exploration, that is the net present value of the operation multiplied by the probability of success. (iii) The number of projects is sufficient to cause the expected and actual present values to converge. The same might hold for a large service company developing a mass market for (let's say) some new telecommunications facility. It may 'know' that 1 in 1000 people will want to take up the facility, and that this will make its cold calling expenses worthwhile. The same might well not be true of the staff who have to make the calls; if their income depended on the number of successes they had in selling the facility, the risks of failing to find a new subscriber for long periods might make them require either very high rewards per subscriber, or to be paid mainly through salary with little or no commission. In other words they would be **risk averse**; normally this is ascribed to the disastrous effect on one's lifestyle of having no income, which does not offset a small chance of a very high one. For some, especially those with a moderate silver spoon in the form of private income, the opposite might be true; the increase in the quality of life resulting from a normal salary might be so small compared with becoming 'seriously rich' that they might prefer the small chance of a very high income, even with a substantial risk of no income. They would therefore be **risk seekers**. These issues are relevant to situations where projects are 'one offs', and may predetermine the profitability or indeed demise of the firm.

In section 7.4.2, we consider approaches to risk based on situations where the firm is risk neutral. Section 7.4.3 considers situations where risk neutrality cannot be assumed, and so some means of adjusting the outcomes is required. The dominant paradigm is based on the assumption that the probabilities attaching to different outcomes can be estimated, and that the firm's attitude to risk can then be independently estimated. This enables us to calculate an 'expected utility' for each outcome. Section 7.4.4 applies the criticisms of Earl and Schoemaker to this approach, leaving it in some disarray for many, if not most, projects. In section 7.4.5, we look at the alternative approach, by 'lexicographic choice', which is easy to use but conceptually less powerful before moving in section 7.5 to the question of relating the project to the strategy of the firm.

A distinction is made in almost all the writings on this topic between **risk**, which relates to a situation in which there is enough information to attach probabilities to each outcome, and **uncertainty**, where there is no information about the size of the outcome or therefore the probability of achieving any particular outcome. Tautologically, uncertainty is not amenable to analysis. It is of risk that we shall be speaking.

7.4.2 Approaches to risk under risk neutrality

In Brealy and Myers' (1991) great textbook on corporate finance, risk neutrality is assumed throughout. This is perfectly logical in the context of large diversified corporations, or in the stock market, where risk can be reduced to the desired level by the choice of portfolio. The suggested means of treating uncertainty in the context of the investment decision of the firm are summarized in the following subsections.

Risk premiums on interest rates

Banks may impose higher interest rates on projects that they perceive to be risky. This may provide one measure of the risk; it must however be remembered that if the loan is secured by some collateral, the bank may not be concerned about the risk attaching to the project, and so the bank's interest rate may or may not include a risk premium that is appropriate to the firm. It may be possible to calculate a risk-adjusted interest rate for large firms with substantial share capital. Firms in high risk industries whose shares have a high variability as registered by the beta (β) coefficient, which in turn usually reflects high variability in their profits, can be shown to have higher company costs of capital because of the lower valuation of their shares. Thus, a risk premium attaches to their borrowing (Brealy and Myers, 1991, pp. 193–207). Brealy and Myers specifically advise against further adjustment of interest rates by 'fudge factors' to account for risk (pp. 197–199), and they show how to derive 'certainty equivalent' measures (pp. 201–204); they add a further caveat against using the same implicit adjustments for risk when the risk varies through time (pp. 204–205).

Sensitivity analysis

This involves the examination of each of the major categories of expenditure to check the effect of optimistic and pessimistic assumptions about each category on the net present value of the project. It seems almost certainly worth carrying out simple tests of how the revenues respond to changes in market size or penetration, or how the costs vary if there are problems with certain components. This may reveal where the projects are vulnerable, and where extra information would bring high payoffs. It suffers from two major problems: firstly, it is difficult to know whether the risks identified are independent (for example, would a lower than predicted growth of market size lead to a lower penetration than anticipated?); and, secondly, it is very difficult to attach realistic probabilities to the different outcomes, so that even if they are independent it is difficult to derive a single final expected value to the project on which to base a decision. We shall see that this reservation about the realism of attaching probabilities to outcomes is serious, and possibly fatal, to the economists' favourite approach using expected utility theory. If sensitivity analysis is based on such valid probabilities, it would still need some method of assessing the relative value of high-value small probability outcomes, as against extreme low-value (hence possibly fatal) outcomes, with low probabilities; the subjective expected utility approach provides such a method. Sensitivity analysis with no adjustment for the relative severity of impact of different outcomes implies complete risk neutrality.

Decision trees

These allow exploration of the alternative tactics and sets of **sequential** decisions that can be employed on a project. At first sight it might appear that all potential outcomes should be listed, and the sets of decisions that could lead to them mapped out. However, a little experimentation shows that the size of the resulting tree can rapidly grow into a chaos of intertwining branches and that the aim of gaining insight into the decision will be lost. As Brealy and Myers put it, 'Decision trees are like grapevines: They are productive only if they are vigorously pruned' (p. 236). They also show very clearly how decisions based on project evaluations can be reversed, if the ability to get out of situations by selling up the capital equipment, and/or increasing the expenditure at a later date when more is known about the success of the project, is included (pp. 229–237); to express this in the terms used in this book, we might say that it is vital to distinguish between fixed costs and sunk costs.

7.4.3 Expected utility

At the start of the previous section we used the concept of 'expected value', the sum of the values of the outcomes of a particular action, multiplied by the probability of each outcome occurring. This is only acceptable if the firm is risk neutral; it implicitly gives equal value to the two schemes shown in Table 7.2. Both schemes have a 'planned' and most probable outcome of providing a net present value of £1000. Scheme 2, however, very clearly has a much higher downside risk. This might well be thought to be an unacceptable level, which is not offset by the higher probability of achieving the relatively high payoff of £10 000. How should such decisions be tackled?

Table 7.2

Scheme 1

i	NPV	Probability	$p_i(NPV_i)$
1	0	.3	0
2	1000	.5	500
3	10 000	.2	2000
	Expected value $= \Sigma\, p_i(NPV_i)$		2500

Scheme 2

i	NPV	Probability	$p_i(NPV_i)$
1	−3000	.3	−900
2	1000	.4	400
3	10 000	.3	3000
	Expected value $= \Sigma\, p_i(NPV_i)$		2500

1. Decisions are a sequential process, and are in reality explorations into possibilities and ways of coping with surprises. Thus we might, as a first effort, explore the ways in which the firm could cope with the loss, and indeed the higher gain. Could extra advertising, for example, or a higher payment to agents and sales staff, actually reduce the risk of a £3000 loss? The question immediately comes back, 'If so, why not do it and increase the overall profitability of the scheme?' One of the major benefits of the sorts of analyses discussed here is to reveal problems and their solutions. There is a possibility that although this strategy would be feasible under the pressure of losses, and the obvious threats involved, it would not be possible to motivate people to take on the extra work if all were going according to plan, i.e. the planned £1000 net present value were being achieved. Let us assume away such issues.

2. We could alternatively use 'expected **utilities**', i.e. some direct measure of the acceptability of each of the outcomes. We shall see below that these involve the use of some fairly strong assumptions about the way we can calculate such things.

3. We could re-examine the schemes on a variety of criteria, among which would be some aspects of risk such as the potential losses. We would reject schemes that fail on any criterion, until we are left with only one scheme, or are sufficiently confident of all the schemes remaining to choose by their net present values. Such filtering approaches are called **lexicographic** choices. These are discussed in section 7.4.5.

4. If the decision is to be taken by the Board of Directors or by a group of managers, they could simply take a **vote** on the acceptability of the schemes based on the evidence made available. Unless the vote is unanimous, if there are three or more schemes, there is a risk that

only a minority will be satisfied and that the decisions will not reflect the overall preferences of the group.

This section examines the approach using **expected utilities**. By 'expected utility' we mean a measure of the decision maker's expected satisfaction. These are calculated in such a way as to be consistent over a wide range of risky alternatives.

This approach is quite clearly normative. Its proponents would claim that it enables decision makers to gain consistency in their decisions: 'It should be remembered that the output of a decision analysis is not an instruction on which choice to make. The output is understanding. The analysis is meant to bring me an understanding of where the balance of my beliefs and preferences lies' (French, 1986, p. 346; see also p. 14). The approach is usually seen as stemming from work by John von Neumann and Oskar Morgenstern (1944), who showed that a measure could be derived providing a cardinal scale for the 'utilities' of values of outcomes that were uncertain (known as the VNM Utilities). The scale of values for the utility of different payoffs aims to provide an assessment of preferences, which can then be inserted into analyses where there are various possible outcomes, and each outcome can be associated with a probability of occurrence. The context, the method, the assumptions, then the interpretation are discussed in the following subsections.

The context

This method is appropriate when there are several alternatives, each of which has an expected payoff, and it is possible to assess the probability of each payoff with some confidence. For example, under the two schemes set out in Table 7.2, the risk neutral decision maker would be indifferent as to which scheme should be chosen. Sensible decision makers might take a very different view, and so the problem is to discover their valuations. To do this we need to know the decision maker's valuation of gains and losses of different sizes.

It is intuitively obvious that for a small firm a loss of £1 million is an irredeemable catastrophe; paradoxically, a loss of £10 million may be little or no worse. Similarly huge profits will be welcome – even more profit may again only represent a small gain in perceived welfare. To put it in the sort of image suggested by Kellian psychology, as advocated by Earl (1984, 1986), taking one step into a world of riches for which one has no competencies, by virtue of making an unexpected £1 million, is little different from taking two steps into such a world by making £10 million. A smaller gain that allows one to extend the range of one's competence in desired ways might be relatively much more valuable. It is a measure of these relative valuations that we are seeking.

The method

To do this we cannot simply ask, 'What's a million pounds worth to you?', particularly as we are looking for values not for a million pounds for certain, but a million pounds with some risk attached. To do this we make two important assumptions about human capabilities (which are expressed formally below). These are that decision makers can firstly envisage the value to them of different gains or losses, and secondly truly understand the implications of the probability with which such gains or losses might occur.

If that is within their capabilities, we could ask them how much they would accept instead of a particular gamble. That gamble would take the form of a 'lottery' in which they would receive £x with probability p, or £y with probability $1 - p$. For example:

> 'How much would you accept instead of participating in a lottery where you would have a 0.5 probability of losing £5000 and a 0.5 probability of gaining £15 000?'

Let's assume they said £1676.

> 'How much would you accept instead of participating in a lottery where you have a 0.6 probability of losing £5000 and a 0.4 probability of gaining £15 000?'

Answer: £108.

The analyst would then choose arbitrary values for the −£5000 and the £15 000. Let us choose 10 and 2000, respectively. The **utility index** is then calculated as $p(10) + (1 - p)(2000)$. Thus in the two examples above the 'certainty equivalent' value for the first lottery (£1676) had a utility index value of $(0.5 \times 10) + (0.5 \times 2000) = 1005$. The utility index for £108 would be 806 $(0.6 \times 10) + (0.4 \times 2000)$. We can then create a graph, or a detailed table, showing the equivalent values for subjective utility and cardinal utility. The latter can always be calculated if we know the outcomes and their probabilities, and so we can derive the graph or table, the equivalent subjective values. Table 7.3 and Figure 7.1 illustrate this for a wider range.

Formally expressed, the decision maker decides the value of the certain sum x at which he would be indifferent between accepting it or a lottery of −£5000 occurring with probability p and £15 000 occurring with probability $(1 - p)$, for various probabilities. The outcome −£5000 is allocated the arbitrary utility value of 10 and £15000 is allocated the value 2000.

We can now use these figures to evaluate the preferences of the decision maker for the different outcomes of the schemes suggested above. The net present values can be regarded as the certain equivalents of a possible lottery, and we can thus look up the corresponding utility index. For example, a net present value of £10 000 would give us a utility index of just less than 2000 – in fact of 1940 or thereabouts. The utility index is then multiplied by the probability of achieving that net present value. We are in effect recreating a new lottery using the preferences revealed by the decision maker (Table 7.4).

Table 7.3 Table of subjective utilities

Probability[a] p	Expected value of lottery[b] $E(V)$	Certainty equivalent value[c] x	Utility index[d] $E(U)$
0.01	14 800	10 300	1980
0.05	14 000	9600	1900
0.1	13 000	8800	1801
0.2	11000	6800	1602
0.3	9000	4997	1403
0.4	7000	3308	1204
0.5	5000	1676	1005
0.6	3000	108	806
0.7	1000	−1384	607
0.8	−1000	−2777	408
0.9	−3000	−4032	209
0.95	−4000	−4579	110
0.99	−4800	−4939	30
1	−5000	−5000	10

[a] p is the probability of receiving −£5000 (i.e. having to pay £5000) and $(1 - p)$ is the probability of receiving £15 000

[b] $E(V)$ is the expected value of the lottery, i.e. £$\{-5000 \cdot p + 15\,000(1 - p)\}$

[c] x is the certainty equivalent value of the lottery; i.e. the valuation the respondent puts on that particular lottery

[d] $E(U)$ is the utility index, i.e. the arbitrary value of the lottery in this case $\{10 \cdot p + 2000(1 - p)\}$

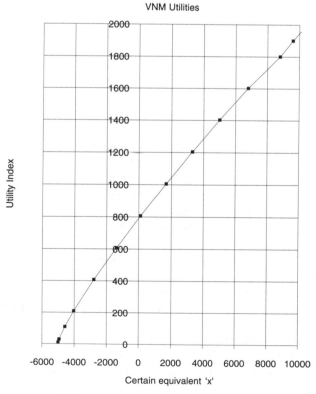

VNM Utilities

Figure 7.1 Expected utilities.

Table 7.4 Evaluation of schemes using expected utilities

Scheme 1

i	NPV NPV_i	Probability p_i	Expected value of the NPV $p_i(NPV_i)$	Utility index for that NPV U_i	Expected utility $U_i p_i$
1	0	.3	0	800	240
2	1000	.5	500	919	460
3	10 000	.2	2000	1910	382
		Expected Value $= \Sigma p_i(NPV_i) = 2500$		$\Sigma p_i(U_i) = 1082$	

Scheme 2

i	NPV NPV_i	Probability p_i	Expected value of the NPV $p_i(NPV_i)$	Utility index for that NPV U_i	Expected utility $U_i p_i$
1	−3000	.3	− 900	410	123
2	1000	.4	400	919	368
3	10 000	.3	3000	1910	573
		Expected Value $= \Sigma p_i(NPV_i) = 2500$		$\Sigma p_i(U_i) = 1064$	

This would indicate that the less risky scheme is preferred. The numerical difference may seem small but we shall see that only rankings have any meaning. The units of difference are impossible to interpret.

What we have done is to provide the decision maker with a mirror of his/her preferences which specifically takes into account the relative values of big gains or losses, and the probabilities associated with them. By using the uncertainty inherent in this sort of lottery, we are able to chart preferences. The particular set of figures presented shows a person who is very risk averse; at no point does the 'certainty equivalent value' approach the expected value. Thus in our question and answer example, the combination of a 60% chance of making a loss of £5000 or a 40% chance of a gain of £15 000 is only valued at £108, although a risk neutral decision maker, with a unitary marginal utility of money (i.e. £1 is worth the same at any level of wealth), would value that lottery at £3000 $[(0.6 \times -3000) + (0.4 \times 15\,000)]$.

Much of the debate around this approach centres on the question of how these two elements – the marginal utility of money at different levels of gains and losses, and the uncertainty, as represented by the probabilities and the range of payoffs in the lottery – interact. (The measure to be used for the element of risk, uncertainty, in the sense of random variation within limits, does not appear in the texts that I have examined. The equivalent measure for the riskiness of a share, the standard deviation of its daily movements in value, is not available to us.) How do risk and the payoff interact? Since we use the probabilities as multiplicands to produce the index, we are assuming these to be truly perceived. Thus, presumably, what we are recording is the utility of the outcomes. For example from Table 7.4 we can see that the 0.01 probability of winning £15 000 leads to a certainty equivalent only £61 different from the full monetary value of the loss of £5000. At the other end of the scale, with a 0.99 probability of winning £15 000, either the threat of a £5000 loss is overwhelmingly powerful, or it is the low valuation of the £15 000 gain that leads to a certainty equivalent £5000 below the face value of the £15 000 gain.

The assumptions

The assumptions on which this approach is built amount to five, which themselves might be summarized as meaning that people can be perfectly consistent in their choices of lotteries, whatever the level of prize or probability. The five assumptions are (following Schoemaker, 1982, p. 531):

1. Preferences for lotteries are complete and transitive. Thus the decision maker will always be able to say that lottery 1 is either preferable to lottery 2, or that she is indifferent. Furthermore if lottery 1 is preferred to lottery 2, and lottery 2 to lottery 3, lottery 1 will always be preferred to lottery 3.
2. If there are three prizes $x1$, $x2$ and $x3$ of increasing attractiveness, there will always be some probability p of receiving $x3$, and probability $(p - 1)$ of receiving $x1$, which will make $x2$ equally attractive to receiving the lottery.
3. If $x1$ and $x2$ are equally attractive then the choice of lotteries $\{p.x1$ and $(1 - p).x3\}$ or $\{p.x2$ and $(1 - p).x3\}$ are also equally attractive.
4. If two lotteries have identical objects as payoffs, but differ only in the probability of those payoffs, the lottery with the higher probability for the more desirable payoff will be preferred.
5. In compound lotteries, where each lottery has a lottery as the payoff, this structure will not influence the order of preference as compared to the implied lottery obtained by multiplying through the probabilities in each branch.

There seem to be two schools of thought in the interpretation of these assumptions. Schoemaker (1982, p. 533) states:

> The cardinal nature of VNM theory must thus be interpreted carefully. ... One reason is that preferences among lotteries are determined by at least two separate factors; namely (1) strength of preference for the consequences under certainty, and (2) attitude

toward risk. The VNM utility function is a compound mixture of these two.

On the other hand, French (1986) treats the decision maker as one who can always understand the implication of probabilities and for whom they represent relative likelihoods, and can thus be used without modification to weight the value of outcomes to him/her. This implies that the utility values are the relative values of outcomes under certainty, which can then be weighted by their probabilities to get an expected utility value of each action. Mathematical notation makes the distinction clear; Schoemaker is suggesting that:

$$EU_i = \Sigma f(p_i \, u_i) \tag{7.2}$$

whereas French is suggesting:

$$EU_i = \Sigma \, p_i \cdot f(u_i) \tag{7.3}$$

This view is tantamount to saying that it is not the uncertainty that causes the change in utility, but the variation in the value of the outcomes, and the probabilities enable us to weight these values to get a consistent, and hence rational, decision. The way the utility value is derived, without modification of the probabilities, suggests that the interpretation by French is more appropriate. As decision makers we want to avoid 'fatal outcomes', and so we value them strongly negatively, but uncertainty is a fact of life, and so we decide as best we can how strong our expectation of the fatal outcome is, and weight it accordingly. The Schoemaker view corresponds to the assumptions of much of capital theory, and seems to be closer to the meaning of the words 'risk aversion', but it makes the utility indices much less useful, since each index is specific to a combination of payoff and probability. Thus, given the considerable problem of fatigue and consequentially irrational choices by decision makers who are asked to provide more or less complete utility maps, it means that the choices have to be set up around the decisions so that both payoff and probabilities coincide with those in the decisions; this would be tantamount to saying 'Do you like this result or that one better?', an altogether simpler approach, but yielding little in the way of extra insight.

Within the context of the firm's investment decision, it may be that the usefulness of the approach depends on the way in which the investment programme has been elaborated. If it is the result of complex forecasting techniques, based on good data, such that the chains of logic would be difficult to disentangle, and hence intuitive grasp of the outcomes is almost impossible, then the expected utility approach has much to commend it. It can certainly help to disentangle such complex networks, and by gaining a consistent picture of the ranking of outcomes, and demanding that decision makers should not be 'risk averse' in the sense of disliking certain probability structures, it can introduce coherence into otherwise very difficult decisions. See French (1989) for several excellent case studies.

Whichever interpretation is preferred, all that is being assumed is that the decision maker can indicate preference by indicating the sum they would be willing to accept 'for sure' in place of the lottery. (Negative values of the sum indicate a willingness to pay rather than face the negative payoff. This is of course equivalent to insuring against undesirable events. Negative 'expected values' represent the actuarially fair insurance premiums.)

7.4.4 The criticisms

One of the major criticisms of this approach is implicit in the discussion above. If the utility index is in fact a 'compound mixture' of the value of the outcome and the attitude to risk *per se*, to ignore the risk element in it is fallacious and misleading. This is a statement about the nature of decision makers' abilities in two directions. Firstly, can they disentangle the risk from the decision to be made? Secondly, Schoemaker (1982) points out that probability is a relatively recent concept, and there is considerable doubt about people's ability to interpret probabilities. If this is so, the method of deriving the index is bound to give inaccurate results. French (1986, pp. 222–253) has a most interesting discussion of this, and takes the view that it represents a person's best view of the likelihood of an event, and as such is the best data available to that individual. Furthermore, it allows revision of the probability following further information, and because of the considerable work on probability, this revision can be made logically consistent. This does not invalidate Schoemaker's point, however, and leaves the index suspect, particularly if it is derived from very different scales of data.

These criticisms would not be serious if we could rely on a utility function which showed increasing risk aversion throughout its range (because of increasingly low marginal utilities of money). This is the context explored by Markowitz (1952). Unfortunately, he suggests a doubly inflected curve, such that at low levels of payoff people would prefer a risk to get a higher payoff (offered £1 for sure, or a 10% chance of £10, many will choose the latter); at high levels (say at £1000 for sure, against the 10% chance of £10 000) people become increasingly risk averse, and choose the generous sure payment over the chance of a fortune. Conversely, going downwards, if it comes to owing £1000 for sure against a 10% chance of owing £10 000, or more still £1 million against £10 million, people may prefer to take the risk, whereas for small sums they will take the small debt for sure. As shown by Hay and Morris (1991, pp. 461–462) this has very unfortunate results for the stability of some decisions, leading to widely differing results for very small changes in estimates of either payoff and/or probabilities.

In summary, it is clear that this approach would require considerable awareness by the decision maker of its limitations.

7.4.5 Lexicographic decision procedures

This term refers to the simple choice by elimination required in any decision to reduce the number of options to a manageable total. Earl

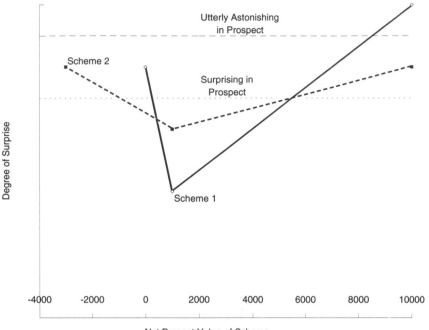

Figure 7.2 Analysis of risk by potential surprise curves.

(1986) proposes such techniques strongly in relation to the consumer's decision, particularly in relation to consumer durables. Earl (1984) suggests that they are the way the firm will choose between investment strategies. They are in many ways the verbal equivalent of linear programmes, in that the decision maker chooses limiting values on various criteria within which acceptable strategies must fall. These might involve a limit on the rate of build up of labour, so that training and absorption into the firm's structure can function smoothly, or the maximum amount of capital that can be spent, or the amount of profit that must be generated. It might also include the acceptable level of risk. It is, however, likely that the measures of risk would be much more intuitive than the rigorous expected probability measures suggested above. These might be related to the 'potential surprise curves' developed by Earl (1986, pp. 213–217), on the basis of work by Shackle; these are explained below.

The essential characteristic of **potential surprise curves** is that the consumer/decision maker must be able to decide whether results other than the planned outcome are likely or not; Earl calls this 'surprising in prospect' or 'astonishing in prospect', i.e. perceived as highly unlikely. There may be sufficient different outcomes envisaged to give a curve, or simply three outcomes, such as were suggested in the schemes above. For purposes of exposition, let us follow Earl and suggest that a curve can be envisaged. This scores each outcome, in our example profits and losses, to the level of surprise associated with it. This is illustrated in Figure 7.2 (following Earl, 1986, p. 224).

As set out, the diagram is only different from the diagram one could draw of the gains and losses and their associated probabilities needed in order to carry out an analysis using expected utility in that 'surprise' is substituted for 'probability'. This is, however, misleading; the text makes it clear that Earl would expect a much more intuitive approach, using the word intuition in its proper sense, meaning 'immediate apprehension by the mind without reasoning; immediate apprehension by sense; immediate insight' (*Concise Oxford Dictionary*). This would involve a mixture of interest in the result because of the importance of its consequences, in this context the size of gains or losses, and because of the likelihood of occurrence of these results, the surprise. In other words, it is the representation of a filtering process, that involves two separate decisions for each scheme. Firstly, is the loss about which one would not be excessively surprised too great to be acceptable? If so, eliminate the scheme. Secondly, is the gain about which one would not be excessively surprised sufficient to make the scheme an attractive gamble? If not, again reject the scheme. This leaves open to intuition the combination of level of gain or loss and probability that is acceptable, and this is a deliberate feature of the analysis, since Earl would subscribe to the criticisms of subjective utility theory that were outlined above: that decision makers firstly cannot ascribe accurate probabilities and secondly that the utilities associated with losses or gains will not be independent of the 'probabilities' with which those are likely to occur.

Let us try applying it to our two hypothetical schemes. The probabilities of 0.2 and 0.3 associated with the extreme outcomes of the schemes hardly seem likely to be considered 'utterly astonishing'. The decision maker would therefore ask whether the loss of £5000, in Scheme 2, was tolerable or not. If not, then Scheme 2 would be rejected. The same question would be applied to Scheme 1: would zero profits from the scheme be intolerable? If so, it too might be rejected, or the standard might be lowered to accept it. On the other side, would the gains of £10 000 be sufficient to make this an attractive gamble? If not, then Scheme 1 would fail on the positive test. This would leave no scheme available! Three options exist: (i) find a better scheme, (ii) revise expectations downward, either towards greater acceptance of risk, and take the gamble on Scheme 2, or towards the acceptance of lower maximum gains, and accept Scheme 1, or (iii) do neither and continue with the status quo, if that is an option. (If so it should of course have been evaluated, since it might have a higher net present value than either scheme.)

The objections to this approach are easy to identify; its intuitive nature does not permit logical examination. Firstly, how do we know what is meant by 'unsurprising'? Presumably there is a set of interconnected reasons behind the likelihood of any scenario occurring; if we apply probabilities, we may be able to apply conditional probabilities as we follow the logic of 'surprise', and hence refine our understanding. Here we cannot.

Secondly, why is an outcome 'unacceptable'? This objection is, however, not very much different from asking 'why is a particular lottery worth £x?' in the expected utility framework, except that in the latter we can check whether preferences are transitive, i.e. whether the decision maker is valuing inferior lotteries more highly than superior lotteries. There is thus some check on the consistency of preferences, which would in general be absent here.

Thirdly, given the arbitrary nature of cut-off points, it may eliminate schemes prematurely, particularly when it is applied at earlier stages of the evaluation, and particularly at that early stage, there may appear to be many other schemes in contention, and thus the elimination may not be re-evaluated. This is, however, an unfair critique. The point was made above that decision trees only yield results when pruned. This is almost certain to be the sort of pruning that is carried out. Crude pruning on a lexicographic basis will therefore in fact be common to both approaches.

These objections seem quite powerful; is there anything to be said in favour? Only that the subjective expected utility approach may be 'non-sense on stilts', if the decision maker is not able to handle the approach implied in it, particularly if the results are in fact very case contingent, either because of unreliable valuations of the outcomes or because of the truly joint valuation of risk and return. If decision makers cannot use probability estimates 'correctly', subjective utility is a misleading 'technocratic' approach which, because of its elegance and intellectual difficulty, prevents decision makers from examining their intuition – their gut feelings. These gut feelings are very often set up by experience, and hence recognition of patterns of which they are only vaguely aware, and which they are therefore unable to explain. Thus, the scientific approach may actually be eliminating a different sort of information.

The second major objection to subjective expected utility approaches is that they are very difficult to adapt to situations where effects are interconnected, and thus probabilities are not independent. It must, however, be remembered that lexicographic approaches may simply be ignoring this interdependence in the estimation of surprise, or they may have included it in the 'gut feel' of the manager.

7.5 INVESTMENT AND THE STRATEGY OF THE FIRM

Strategy has been defined as 'a complete set of responses to all the possible states of the world', and we might add, 'and/or a set of rules to govern such responses'. This, however, illustrates neatly the impossibility of fully rational strategic thinking. We neither know enough about the world system, nor usually about the firm's own operations, to model such a complete set of responses. Thus, strategy in fact has to be interpreted as being the major directions in which the firm is to move in the medium or long term. The sort of issues that might be considered would be the expansion or contraction of product lines, the movement into new markets, the development of new services, or major changes in the technology of service delivery, including the closure and amalgamation of branches.

Such changes always require some element of investment, and therefore one would expect there to be a close link between investment appraisal and strategy development. This is not usually the case. Investment appraisal usually requires detailed information, but this is very often precisely the thing that is lacking in strategic decisions. For example, the decision to develop an electronic point of sale (EPOS) system for a retail chain must initially be fraught with major uncertainties as to its costs or benefits. It is therefore difficult, and potentially very misleading, to apply discounted cash flow (DCF) techniques to such a decision.

The normal way in which strategy is implemented is to take a decision on goals, such as the development of an EPOS system, and then to elaborate this decision into a set of investments. Initially these may not be evaluated by DCF techniques, since the uncertainty is too great to provide either costs or benefits. Nor are these costs and benefits so great in the initial stages that this is important. Thus the first stage is to conduct the research and development on the project, and for obvious reasons of budgetary control, this is usually done within a budget, but this is likely to be the only financial constraint imposed. Part of the outcome of this stage is the approximate measurement of costs and benefits. The next stages, where large-scale investment is required, are then subjected to DCF techniques, since over-ambitious or clearly ill-judged programmes would be potentially disastrous. It is likely that these initial phases of implementation will still involve further development of both management and design of hardware and systems, and will therefore show low profitability. Indeed, we would expect at this stage to have to include some of these 'running' costs under investment costs for the firm as a whole, as suggested in the section on economic depreciation. It is important at early stages of a new venture not to undervalue the learning aspects of the project; it is often only as such projects are developed that one realizes the full potential within them (see Kester, 1984 on the valuation of the options that initial developments reveal).

One of the chief issues surrounding such strategic decisions is the degree of learning incorporated into the process. The most commonly advocated form of monitoring is a 'post-audit', a detailed financial review, usually after one year of operation. The difficulty, even after such a short time, is to allow for the changes in the economic environment, as well as the modifications usually incorporated into the design. The problems of the post-audit are essentially no different from those of enforcing the penalty clauses in a construction contract. They are only practicably enforceable in cases of gross failure; with more normal levels of failure, there is usually ambiguity as to whether the failure was one of design or specification, which caused modifications to be requested by the client, or whether the failures were due to the contractors. A further problem is that the design of the audit should not be purely financial; and indeed the organization that is interested in continual improvement should be as interested in the errors of design, whether these emerge in the one-year period, or in the longer term. Thus the incorporation of overcapacity in one area, and even more importantly the undercapacity in another, have somehow to be learned, along with the correct balance of products and services for the particular area.

Because of the synchronous aspect of supply and consumption in services, the capacity considerations are particularly important. If insufficient capacity is provided, some of the demand may shift to other times where utilization is lower, and appropriate pricing policies should assist this, but often the demand that cannot be satisfied at the time will be lost. Furthermore it must be remembered that the capacity of any facility is determined by its lowest capacity item. Thus a consultancy, where report production is the final stage of each project, may be late on its presentations by virtue of insufficient printing capacity despite lavish computer facilities and adequate staffing. The extremes of peaking that are liable to occur in such operations may, however, best be satisfied by subcontracting; a good example of this is provided by the extensive use by hotels and restaurants of temporary staff for special functions. There is often an unofficial network which involves reciprocal loans of staff to cover such eventualities. It is, however, much more difficult to circumvent the lack of parking space for a store, or bottlenecks in delivery or supply systems, and they need corresponding care in their design.

In section 7.3.2, it was emphasized that the proper definition of a project boundary was a key aspect of any investment decision. One of the major strategic dimensions is the framing of the appropriate subdivisions of the firm. Many investment projects will emerge from the perceptions of the branch management as to what 'their business' requires; if that business is defined so narrowly that it ignores significant interactions with other parts of the firm – it might actually be in direct competition – the investment decisions are likely to be distorted. For example, a major refurbishment of the 'bistro' area of a restaurant may divert custom from the restaurant. The decisions as to whether this reduction in the value of the investment is sufficient to cause it to be refused and whether it would affect the whole strategic direction of the facility by emphasizing one area at the expense of others are both characteristic of high level strategic decisions.

There may be substantial issues of 'agency' in any such decisions; ambitious managers will play the system to improve their image, and this may not be in the firm's interests. The adjudication of such cases, and the settling of them without causing loss of motivation among the staff, requires real understanding of the situation, the ability to empathize with the staff, and the powers of communication to explain the situation as a whole. As discussed in Chapter 5, there is no magic solution to agency problems. A rigorously punitive technique to meet targets puts all the risks onto local management, and thus encourages excessive caution; a 'go-for-growth' approach will tend to reward managers for excessive optimism, and lead to irresponsible expenditures. The solution lies, if anywhere, in the sophistication, knowledge and skill in communication of the senior management.

7.6 SUMMARY

It is the contention of this book that most costs in the service industries have to be treated as 'long run'. That is to say, they involve investment decisions rather than the sort of decision implied by the short run, to buy in extra staff or other inputs to increase output. This follows from the need to have the facilities in anticipation of the arrival of customers, since 'production' only takes place when both supply and their demand are present, because a service cannot be stored. The appropriate pricing structures can alleviate the problem of peaks but this merely sets different parameters on the investment decision, and does not alter the fact that it is one.

It was emphasized in the context of investment decisions that the choice of project boundary is not trivial; indeed inappropriate choice can lead to overall disaster as the result of locally correct decisions. The estimation of costs is largely a technical matter, but involves the overriding economic principle of the use of opportunity costs; this implies proper definition of costs into a marginal cost (the incremental cost of the management accounting literature), and the examination of market costs, both for purchasing and for resale at the end of the project. The definition of revenues is subject to the same considerations: it should be incremental revenue, i.e. marginal revenue, and it must be judged against a realistic alternative, which is not likely to be zero revenue. The process of discounting and its use was only briefly sketched. However, its application in defining 'economic depreciation' was emphasized. The destructive consequences of using rates of return based on inappropriate values of both capital and income were mentioned.

More emphasis was given to the nature of decisions under uncertainty, since these are often ignored. As a start, it was recommended that simple sensitivity analysis be applied; this is a useful planning tool, since it may help to isolate the areas in which a strategy is vulnerable, and suggest possible responses. With uncertain outcomes, there are two basic situations: firstly, the company may be large enough and confident enough of its field to be 'risk neutral'. Here the number of projects is sufficient and the experience of the company great enough to work on the 'expected net present value' of the project, using a discount rate that is appropriate for the industry. In many service sector applications this is not a valid set of assumptions. Thus uncertainty has to be tackled by more fundamental analysis. The rational form is that of 'subjective expected utility', which is horribly complicated but allows for a detailed analysis of the issues. It is, however, not likely to be applicable to situations where there are a lot of interdependencies between the policy variables. The 'lexicographic approach' is much less demanding, but does not allow for any real analysis of the outcomes.

In section 7.5, the question of strategy and strategic decisions was discussed briefly. There seems to be no satisfactory way of formally incorporating these issues into the framework of investment analysis. The normal procedure is to choose only those projects for analysis that cohere with the strategy of the firm, but it was argued here that this is only a part of the issue. It was suggested that the key factor was the incorporation of strategic issues of coordination and learning into the process of facility design and monitoring. The investment appraisal process should merely be an articulation of this approach.

FURTHER READING

For the investment decision in general, see:

Brealy, R.A. and Myers, S.C. (1991) *Principles of Corporate Finance*, 4th Edn, New York, McGraw-Hill.

For the management science approach and the use of subjective utility, some very interesting case studies are provided in:

French, S. (1989) *Readings in Decision Analysis*, London, Chapman & Hall.

A rigorous and very tough 'introduction', requiring considerable mathematical logic, is provided by:

French, S. (1986) *Decision Theory*, Chichester, Ellis Horwood.

Costs and industrial structure

8

8.1 INTRODUCTION

This chapter considers long-run costs as a foundation for considerations of market structure. The sources of economies of scale are set out and examples in the service industries are given. These are likely to be related either to the nature of facilities to be provided, for example by the utilities and other network-based services, or to economies of specialization gained from easy access to skilled manpower whose skill relies upon learning by doing, and hence the number of related cases seen (heart operations for a surgeon, tax problems for accountants etc.). Economies of scale in selling costs, such as advertising, are also likely to be relevant for the service industries, and may be the key to understanding the extent of large firms even in situations where the skills of operatives in the local branch are actually the key factor in creating this quality.

Section 8.3 looks at the importance of entry barriers and sunk costs, briefly reporting the work of Geroski and others, before considering the approach adopted by Sutton. This views the patterns of response by existing firms to entrants as a result of the market situation, and in turn this response forms the future market structure.

8.2 LONG-RUN COSTS

The long run is that period in which all the factors of production have had time to adjust to their optimal level given the level of output. This is more commonly expressed as being the period in which capital can be invested or disposed of. Like the short run, it is an economic abstraction and assumes that technology is known. Most of the discussions of long-run costs also assume that firms are operating as if they had to assemble all the capital etc. at the same date and thus faced the same set of costs for the same range of capital. The long run is thus a 'counterfactual' construct in two ways: firstly, it assumes that technology is given and known to all the participants; and, secondly, it assumes that the costs of a given array of capital and labour are the same for all firms. In reality, since technology is the full range of ways and means in which the different factors of production can be combined to make the output, it is the gradual change in technology that is responsible for much of the growth of output in the economy, and this technology is embodied both in the individuals that make up the firm and in the procedures used by the firm to manage its capital and labour through all the stages of the production and distribution process, as well as embodied in the capital equipment. In computer terms, you cannot run the hardware without software, and you cannot run 1990s software on 1960s hardware. Technology cannot therefore be commonly available to all since it is a historical development, both in generally available knowledge – the knowledge embodied in machinery – and in the particular knowledge embodied in the management and workers of a particular firm.

As shown in Chapter 2, the service industries have not been immune to technological change as a source of growth. As the change in technology is a continuous process, the 'very long run', where technology is considered to change, is actually contemporaneous with the 'long run'.

Long-run costs in the limited economic sense are, however, of interest since they represent the limits of the possible in terms of cost reduction with the existing technology. If there are substantial economies of scale, it is to be expected that concentration will be high or will increase in the industry and that this may bring monopoly power and higher prices.

The predatory ability of an incumbent firm is also likely to be related to any cost advantages it may enjoy; the nature and presence of cost advantages is thus of interest to competitors. To the presence of economies of scale – advantages available to any firm able to reach the required size – one must add the advantages of **sunk costs**. These are costs which, once incurred, cannot be recovered by the sale of the assets purchased. Thus if a machine may be bought and installed for £10 000 and can only be sold for £6000, there are £4000 of sunk costs and the opportunity cost of the machine if it becomes surplus to the requirements of the firm is only £6000. R&D which does not result in saleable patents or goodwill, and advertising expenditures for failed brands or in excess of the goodwill associated with a brand are both good examples of sunk costs. If such costs are of value to the firm, but have no market value outside it, their value to the firm is a cost advantage that any competitor will have to overcome. The problem this could raise for new entrants to a market is self-evident. The problems of entry-deterrence have long been of interest, since it is seen as reducing competition; there has been a recent upsurge of interest in these questions (Geroski, 1991; Geroski and Schwalbach, 1991a; Rosenbaum and Lamort, 1992).

8.2.1 Economies of scale

Economies of scale are usually discussed in relation to manufacturing industries, but the emergence of very large service sector firms, previously thought to be impossible except in the case of public utilities, raises the question of how such firms continue to develop. The examination of the ideas surrounding economies of scale thus forms the basis of this section. This is followed by a discussion of the importance of sunk costs.

Economies of scale are said to exist at the plant level when average costs of output from plants operating at optimum capacity with optimal capital investments are lower for larger than for smaller plants. Economies of scale may also exist at the level of the firm, even when absent at the level of the plant, when the above holds true for firms.

A subset of economies of scale are economies of scope, where two or more outputs can be produced more cheaply by one plant or firm than the same level of the two (or more) outputs can be produced by separate plants or firms. The multiple products of oil refineries or the savings on travel costs from 'one stop shopping' both provide examples.

The sources of economies of scale are usually listed as follows:

- Indivisibilities in the size of capital goods: capital goods may only be made in certain sizes, thus attempts to produce output by underutilizing capital goods will cause increased costs.

- Economies of containers and pipes: the volume of a container and the potential flow through a pipe increases in proportion to the volume contained; thus, according to the cube of the dimensions, the cost tends to increase as the surface area of the vessel or pipe increases, i.e. as its area, which is proportional to the square of the dimensions. This leads to a cost-to-volume relationship summarized by the 'rule of 2/3': for a unit increase in volume/flow, the costs of construction increase by two-thirds of a unit. Since the friction produced by flow through a pipe or by a container moving through air or water is also proportional to its surface area, this rule also applies to energy costs of moving materials in pipes or ships.

- Plant wide economies: these will occur where there are combinations of machines of different capacities; a balanced minimum cost production process will only occur if all the machines are working to capacity.

- Specialization of labour: larger scales may permit labour to be allocated to specialized tasks, thereby gaining proficiency.

- The principle of massed reserves: if breakdowns occur randomly, the level of spares needed can be reduced for large numbers of machines. The same principle applies to the holding of stocks of output to meet surges in demand; a firm producing for several markets is unlikely to face such surges of demand from each market at the same time, and can therefore reduce the stock of output.

- Transaction cost economies: bulk buying and regular routine orders can reduce the costs of purchasing. This would be particularly true if the firm holds monopsony (sole purchaser) power over its suppliers, enabling it to force down prices.

- The length of production runs: as each run involves an investment in tooling up, longer production runs will reduce the average cost of this investment.

- Economies of scope: these occur as the result of the use of by-products of the 'main' process, and/or as the result of being able to use equipment more efficiently because demand for the two outputs is complementary, allowing the equipment to be used for the second output when there is low demand and hence slack production time for the first.

- Economies of multi-plant operation: it may be much more economic to operate each plant at its optimum capacity, closing plants down when demand falls off, than to operate each plant at part of its capacity. This naturally requires that the cost of transport between local markets is not excessive. It may also be cheaper to use the technical expertise developed in one area to open up plants in other areas, to apply the same production technology but with better access to local markets, reducing transport costs. Providing the transport costs are not excessive, it may also be cheaper to use neighbouring plants to provide spare capacity than to provide significant spare capacity at each plant – an application of the principle of massed reserves across several plants.

There are also effects which seem to favour the growing firm, and which are therefore somewhat different to the above items which affect the scale of the firm, whether growing or not:

- Economies of sunk costs: R&D expenditures and the goodwill coming from advertising are examples of sunk costs; clearly, the more units over which they can be spread, the lower the average cost of these outlays. The firm may be benefiting from costs sunk in previous periods and no longer appearing as a cost.
- Learning by doing: both management and labour learn how to produce output more cheaply as they go along. There is debate as to whether it is possible to make this a continuous process such that there is a given proportional decrease in cost for each doubling of output, or whether such learning economies come to a halt after a certain level of production is reached.
- Economies of growth: the process of growth may itself create beneficial effects; it may be easier to attract high quality management, and lower cost capital. Equally, firms may overreach themselves and fail to integrate new management and new parts of the firm, particularly if acquired by takeover.

How far are these applicable to the service industries, and how far do they explain the growth of large firms in this sector?

Indivisibilities in capital goods take a particular form in many public utilities and make them natural monopolies. At the point of delivery the capacity of the local systems – the telephone lines, sewers, water pipes etc. – is sufficient to provide for the delivery of the service to the consumer, and as such duplication of those lines is an unnecessary expense. This has, indeed, in general been the case. The duplication of exchanges and trunk lines by BT and Mercury is not as clear a waste of resources since with interconnection ensured by government regulation, the capacity of both lines and exchanges needed to be upgraded. In view of the costs of billing from one system to the other, and the probable unnecessary duplication of some lines, it may well be that an optimally run BT would have remained cheaper. However, that would leave it a statutory monopoly, and as such with little incentive to run optimally; it was felt that competition, however contrived, would provide this spur and would more than offset the extra costs. The potential for this to be extended in the future by cable television operators and others remains to be seen. It is highly probable that no rival company would have tried to enter the market without the protection provided by the regulator, Oftel. This protection was based both on prices – BT's rates were set so that Mercury could both charge less and make a profit on operations – and on interconnection. BT could have made entry impossible if Mercury had only been able to connect to its own subscribers. As outlined below, it would have lacked the crucial 'economies of connectivity'.

One suspects that in the absence of competition, BT would not have opened up its lines to 'value added networks', data transmission, or, as we are promised by the cable companies in the future, the provision of entertainment along with phone facilities. In other words, complacent management would not have taken advantage of the potential economies of scope.

The superior performance of electricity utilities that were subject to competition over those protected by regulation was recorded by Primeaux (1979). These were almost certainly natural monopolies. Millward (1986) documents further cases of private versus public firms' costs, but it is only Primeaux's study that considers the competitive environment as well as the question of private as against public ownership. (The only exception is the implication in Savas' report on Minneapolis waste collection (Millward, 1986, p. 140) in which Savas showed that the costs of the previously inefficient public City Sanitation Division converged rapidly with those of the private operators. This gives anecdotal support for the importance of competition in these discussions.) The importance of the style of regulation, as indicated by the much tougher stance towards loss making by the Tory governments of the 1980s, is argued by Bishop and Thomson (1992).

To the above list of sources of economics of scale, we should perhaps add one that seems to be unique to the service industries:

- Economies of connectivity: where a network gains in desirability to the consumer by the range of persons or places it connects to, and perhaps the frequency and convenience of these connections.

These economies are clearly the basis for the growth of telephone and airline networks; the decline in places connected has probably reduced the attractiveness and hence the growth of British Rail, although the improved frequency and speed of connections on some routes will have made some amends. The lack of information resulting from the dispersal of fare stage bus services among many companies in many British towns has also been a source of loss of connectivity of the bus services, and may have been partly to blame for the decline in numbers of passengers carried. These economies are called 'network externalities' by Katz and

Shapiro (1985); they develop a model of adaptation by firms in the context of computer manufacture.

In the computer industry, the change in the cost of processing power has led to the loss of economies of scale in the form of indivisibilities in the size of capital goods. The switch to microcomputers has left many of the large computer bureaux in a state of serious decline.

The development of the very large computer software houses may reflect economies of specialization – their experts being able to concentrate on individual aspects of the task of software development – but it seems more probable that it reflects the ability to reap the benefits of a successful software product because of the indivisibilities inherent in R&D. The research and development of a software package is clearly the major cost. The higher the output, the less the cost per unit, and the higher the profits; these can then be re-invested to keep the golden goose in lay, by providing better manuals, improved facilities and the elimination of bugs. This virtuous circle is further enhanced by personal and professional recommendations, the increased availability of service outlets as the density of users increases, and with this increased density also the advantages of contact in the passing on of 'wrinkles', so that less expert users gain the advantages of the 'learning by doing' of others.

As such economies of scale to the producer are so important in their effects on the service industries, both by encouraging the development of large firms and by fostering the development of many small firms servicing the developments, it would perhaps be worth giving them a name. They should perhaps be called:

- Economies of density of use: their essential characteristics appear to be the three that are summarized above: increased word-of-mouth recommendation by experienced users, increased density of service outlets reducing costs to consumers, and enhancement of the usefulness of the product by the passing on of useful techniques among the community of users. All of these make the product more desirable to the consumers and thus reduce the producer's costs of publicity and servicing.

   They are not the same as Leibenstein's 'bandwagon effects', which are essentially spurious fashion elements, though these may be important in addition. Nor are they the same as the fall in average cost per passenger kilometre which occurs in railway operations in areas of relatively dense population (Caves and Christensen, 1980).

Although the economies of containers and pipes appear to relate to construction costs, their use is very largely in the service industries, particularly the transport industries including the pipeline transport that is usually listed under the production industry owning the pipeline. The combination of these economies and economies of connectivity have revolutionized the shipping and trucking industries.

Plant-wide economies occur particularly in conjunction with the specialization of labour in many of the service industries, notably in garages, but also in the specialization that occurs in the larger medical and accountancy practices. Law practices still appear to cling to the alternative means of achieving this specialization by themselves, consulting experts outside the practice. If this is a logical structure, as opposed to a slow take-up of modern practices, it could be due to the greater level of specialization to be expected in the law, such that it would take an impossibly large practice to satisfy the needs of a significant proportion of the specialist questions internally.

The impact on the potential monopoly power of hospital trusts due to the ownership and use of specialist equipment and the presence of specialist staff is a source of concern to many following the introduction of internal markets into the NHS. It seems to be well-established that it requires very considerable experience (as well as the necessary personal qualities) to develop the skills needed for the most specialized forms of surgery. There is thus a potential problem: if they develop this skill, and the market is allowed to work, the trusts will use it to strengthen their position by monopolistic practices, and thus raise the costs of hospital treatment unnecessarily; however, the patients lose the benefits of progress if hospital trusts are prevented from developing this degree of specialization, and the present structure whereby the decision making is largely in the hands of the District Health Authorities, whose main interest is to stay within budget and so minimize costs, might well prevent the development and even maintenance of the most specialized centres. These have higher costs for routine operations even within their specialist fields since the most specialized equipment is not needed for such operations. They are also 'overstaffed' for such operations, since, as in the case of the machinery, fewer staff are needed for routine operations, but staff must be available for the more specialized ones. They might be more expensive also because of the higher pay of top consultants, although this difference in pay may be a small proportion of the total costs.

This situation is an example of **unsustainable natural monopoly** – to be viable, the facility requires to monopolize the local market for both specialist and routine operations, but it is vulnerable to the 'abstraction' of the routine operations by cheaper, smaller scale facilities. If this is the case, however, it indicates that the routine operations were subsidizing the more specialized ones. Thus the solution would appear to be to raise the price of the specialist operations, and keep the prices of the routine ones at the normal level. If this then prices the specialist centres out of the market, it is an indication that 'society' is unwilling to pay. This discussion will be extended in Chapter 13; as it stands, it is simplistic because it includes neither the question of pricing in the presence of joint costs, nor the question of whether 'society' can be said to choose in this context.

The ownership of very specialized equipment in the form of computer systems and staff is also, in conjunction with the presence of buyer power, arguably the basis for the development of chain stores of very significant size. Their computing and distribution networks have elements of economies due to 'specialist machinery'. The corresponding specialization of labour to run it, and the concomitant sunk costs of training the workforce to use the systems, raise the costs still further. The systems enable such stores to reduce the costs of their ordering and to coordinate them effectively, thereby enhancing their buyer power. That this is considerable is shown in the Monopolies and Mergers Commission report (1981) and the subsequent Office of Fair Trading report (1985).

8.3 ENTRY BARRIERS, SUNK COSTS, ENTRY AND EXIT

Barriers to entry of new firms into an industry would provide protection for the incumbent firms against the unpleasantness of competition. While there might be outbreaks of 'destructive competition' (which will be discussed in relation to oligopolistic behaviour in Chapter 12), the predominant mode of behaviour could be expected to be comfortable collusion. The nature of barriers to entry have thus been of interest to economists both in relation to management, for whom the height of such barriers gives an indication of the protection they might enjoy, and in relation to the work of the competition authorities. Thus both barriers to entry and the level of entry as an indication of such barriers is of interest. The interest in exit stems from the same concerns: if exit is difficult, entry becomes much riskier, since the losses resulting from failure are greater, hence the interest in the relationship between entry, exit and sunk costs.

Bain's original work on the subject suggested that there would be industries where entry was 'blockaded' as the result of ownership of unique natural resources, or for the duration of the life of patents. The former are relatively rare, and would include, in the service industries, the ownership of uniquely accessible sites, although this is not the absolute barrier implied by the term 'blockaded'. Unique sites of historic or other interest might provide further examples. The blockade by patents is of course subject to the inability of other firms to invent round them, and only lasts for a period of 22 years.

The presence of very high capital costs, implying economies of scale and hence limited numbers of firms in the market, was a further source of such barriers. This was, however, disputed by Stigler, on the basis that the level of capital costs was not the issue; a rival might well be able to raise such capital and enter. The problem for Stigler should be seen in terms of 'first mover advantages' (see Clarke, 1985, p. 72). Sunk costs are a key factor, and high capital costs might well turn out to be sunk costs since they might have little resale value outside the industry. Other first mover advantages might be the development of a market by advertising a new product for which brand loyalty was built up, and which would thus mean that future entrants would need to invest much larger amounts in advertising in order to break into the market. This might be exacerbated by the heavy use of advertising by the existing firms, causing the expenditure on advertising to increase for any entrant if they are to have a significant 'share of the voice'. Since advertising is very clearly a sunk cost – there can be few things less saleable than a failed advertising campaign – raising the amount of advertising required raises sunk costs. This argument is however contestable: while such heavy advertising increases the risk, it may also be a symptom of the effectiveness of advertising in causing customers to switch brands. In so far as this is so, it will allow an entrant to gain market share and hence reduce the costs of entry.

Recent work on this topic has concentrated entirely on the manufacturing sector because of the lack of information available from government statistics on the service sector. Nevertheless, its conclusions are of considerable interest. Firstly, it is no surprise that entry is much less frequent in industries where economies of scale are known to be very important, such as steel, cement and others (Geroski, 1991b, p. 84; Schwalbach, 1991, p. 129). Secondly, entry is deterred in those industries with high levels of sunk costs, as measured by both the investment in machinery, which cannot be resold without loss, as opposed to investment in buildings, which can be resold under the conditions prevailing at that time (Kessides, 1991, p. 41), and the availability of a rental market, which allows current costs to be substituted for capital costs (Kessides, 1991, p. 42; Mata, 1991, p. 57; Rosenbaum and Lamort, 1992, p. 301). The effects of the sunk cost of advertising are also shown to be negative but the advertising intensity of the industry tends to be positively related to entry, thus giving support to the idea that while advertising costs form a barrier, the ability to inform by advertising in a particular industry (shown by its advertising intensity) allows entry more easily than in industries where this option is less available (Kessides, 1991, p. 43; Yamawaki, 1991, p. 181). The hypothesis that advertising rates are a barrier to entry because of their nature as a sunk cost finds support also in Rosenbaum and Lamort (1992, p. 301). This effect was not found significant in relation to exit rates, however.

Entry occurred at average rates of 6.5% new firms per year in manufacturing industry over the eight countries reviewed in Cable and Schwalbach (1991, p. 258), and with an entry rate for services double that of manufacturing in Belgium (the only country with data available for the service industries) (Cable and Schwalbach, p. 258). However:

> In terms of market share, entry is much smaller – on average only 2.8 percent in manufacturing industries across the eight countries, and within the very narrow range 1.1–3.2 percent except for Portugal (5.8 percent) and the Belgian service sector (4.4 percent). This of course reflects the fact that the entrants' relative size is on average less than one-fifth (18.1 percent or 19.7 percent in Belgian services) that of the incumbent firms', though with a notable exception in the case of the United Kingdom where entrants are shown to be 45 percent of the size of the incumbents. (Cable and Schwalbach, 1991, pp. 258–259)

With the small market share, it is unlikely that entrants will seriously affect the competitive structure of the industry, particularly in view of the short life of most entrants. The five-year survival rate was around 70% for entrants to the UK manufacturing industries in 1975–1978 (Geroski, 1991a, p. 29). Ganguly (1985, in Geroski, 1991a, p. 28) shows failure rates for all entrants including service industries, based on VAT registrations and deregistrations, peaking at between 15 and 16% in the 6 months around $1\frac{1}{2}$ years from entry. The failure rate still lies at 8% in the 6 months around 3 years. After 6 years it is only 2% of the original cohort, but that cohort will be considerably diminished by then.

This pattern is somewhat different for the large entrant. Much of the sales achieved by entrants are accounted for by a few very large entrants. Geroski (1991a, p. 29, table 2.11) shows that the less than 1% of entrants employing more than 500 employees accounted for 34% of all sales by entrants in the first year. Interestingly, their survival rate for the first year was not very different from the small firms with less than 99 employees, and in aggregate they had a faster loss of employment than the rest.

As stated above, only Belgium had data for the service industries. We may however hazard some observations on the nature of entry:

1. The failure to attract further entrants to the telecommunications industry, the very few new generating companies in the electricity industry, and the recent withdrawal of the only entrant into railways (Stagecoach's passenger wagons on Scottish lines) contrasts with the vigorous entry into the mail delivery service and the bus industry, both in coach and urban fare stage operations. These contrasting patterns seem to reflect the differences in capital requirements to enter, and indeed in sunk costs. The second-hand market in buses and coaches has provided a means to both entry and exit in those industries. The apparently huge numbers entering and exiting from retailing at the small-scale end of the market contrast with the very few firms entering at a large scale; significantly those large-scale entrants are all major foreign firms expanding into the UK market.

2. Entry into management consultancy and retailing, as well as other forms of small self-employed low-capital forms of enterprise, may well reflect the alternative of unemployment. As noted by Geroski (1991, pp. 14–15) it is not clear *a priori* whether entry will be pro- or anti-cyclical; the evidence from his figure 2.1 indicates that it is marginally pro-cyclical, in other words that the attraction of growing markets and apparently profitable opportunities, even with the relative difficulties of recruiting staff and the rising costs associated with upswings in the business cycle, outweigh the flight from unemployment as a motive.

3. In the financial and business consultancy fields particularly, as well as the franchising field in retailing and hospitality, some of the entry may reflect new forms of industrial organization where the 'firm' is replaced by a set of main and subcontractors. This issue was discussed in relation to transaction cost theories in Chapter 5.

8.4 SUNK COSTS AND MARKET DOMINANCE

The approaches discussed above are all developments of Bain's original concept of 'barriers to entry'. A radically new approach is presented by Sutton (1991). This incorporates the idea that the type of market influences the sort of competition to be expected and hence the level of entry, which in turn conditions the development of the industry's structure. The two major influences are the level of sunk costs which potential entrants must be able to recover if entry is to prove attractive, and the sharpness of price competition to be expected after entry. If these can be expected to reduce profit margins to a level at which it will be impossible to recover sunk costs, the combination of sunk costs and the post-entry competition can be expected to deter entry. Throughout, Sutton discusses situations in which sunk costs are significant and marginal costs below average costs.

Sutton distinguishes three main situations. The first is where **commodities** are produced – standardized undifferentiated products such as wheat, cement, sugar, salt, etc. – in which price competition can be expected to be fierce, since purchases are based purely on price. Since marginal costs are below average costs, any excess capacity will cause losses by some firms, who are likely to cut prices to try to increase sales. The ensuing price war is likely to lead to a combination of firms exiting the market and being taken over. The process is likely to continue until a virtual monopoly results.

The second type of market is characterized by genuinely differentiated products – i.e. those with real differences in characteristics or quality, such as the products of specialist engineering firms or prepared foods – and by the presence of purchasers who are expert enough to know what they are buying and what is on offer. With this sort of product differentiation, purchase is not solely on price, and price competition is less severe than in the first case, and so sunk costs can more readily be recovered. Thus, more firms will co-exist in the market and entry of new firms may persist, until the fall in market shares eliminates profit for each firm – or at least until the entrant could not expect to cover his or her sunk costs. In general the larger the overall market, the more firms there will be.

The third major case is where products are differentiated largely by image created by advertising (and publicity). While price competition may not be so fierce as in the first case, increases in market size, because of economic growth for example, may increase the market of the dominant brand, particularly if the firm keeps up the pressure of advertising, rather than allowing room for new entrants. Two mechanisms are at work in this case: firstly, advertising is a sunk cost, and so if larger markets require more advertising, sunk costs grow with market size, thus entrants have to be able to invest larger and larger amounts as the market grows; and, secondly, the entrant has to be able to break through the brand loyalty created by the past advertising expenditures of the dominant firm. Whether a single firm now remains dominant or whether a few others join the 'first mover' in the big league depends on the ability of the first mover to satisfy the whole market and prevent the increased size from allowing a second (or subsequent) contender to put a product onto the market which attracts a different segment or appeals to the desire for variety. However, provided that advertising continues to be effective in attracting the new consumers in the market, there is every reason to think that the sales in the industry will remain predominantly in the hands of only a few firms.

Sutton also shows that a market might be split between the brands which sell direct to the consumer by advertising, where a very small number of firms are likely to dominate, and a much more competitive market in which the buyers are the professionals from chain stores for their own labels.

8.5 SUMMARY

The presence or absence of economies of scale is clearly an important determinant of the market structure in all industries, including the services. The presence of the very large airlines, telephone companies and accountants, and the increasing concentration of firms in the bus industry, all indicate the importance of this concept.

The traditional account of economies of scale and their impact on the numbers of firms fails to take account of the response of the industry in terms of competition. As shown by Primeaux, this can be a more potent force than scale economies. Sutton demonstrates for manufacturing that we should consider a combination of the effects of sunk costs and competition when analysing the likely industrial structure or decisions about entry into a particular industry. There seems every reason to adopt this paradigm for the services also.

FURTHER READING

A very good introduction to economies of scale and their importance in industrial structure is provided by:

Clarke, R. (1985) *Industrial Economics*, Oxford, Basil Blackwell.

A much more detailed and newer treatment of the subject is provided by:

Geroski, P.A. (1991) *Market Dynamics and Entry*, Oxford, Basil Blackwell.

A major challenge to one's understanding of the dynamics of market structure is provided by:

Sutton, J. (1991) *Sunk Costs and Market Structure: Price Competition, Advertising and the Evolution of Concentration*, Cambridge, MA, MIT Press.

This is regarded as one of the great works of recent times, but is written with considerable use of mathematics in the theoretical section. The case studies are enlightening and easy to read.

Monopoly and monopolistic competition

9

9.1 INTRODUCTION

Monopoly, strictly defined, is the situation where there is only one seller in a market and where that seller is safe from new entrants because of major barriers to entry. This is a rare situation, unless government has intervened to put up the barriers, as in such government services as the police, prison services, the army, etc. However, as these do not operate on commercial lines, they are of limited interest in the context of this book. What is of more interest is the situation where there is a firm that has considerable control over its markets because of patents, market power or product differentiation. This would clearly be the case for major privatized utilities, such as gas, electricity and (we are told) in the near future, British Rail. Less obvious but nevertheless a monopoly are the village store or the village pub, where there are no alternatives, and possibly local stores, restaurants or other services where these are strongly differentiated so that they actually have very separate markets; this is more normally characterized as monopolistic competition, a key difference being the barriers to entry.

The key factor in monopoly, as opposed to the subject of the next chapter, oligopoly, is that under monopoly the firm does not have to consider the responses of other firms in the market. Under oligopoly there are just a few firms and so the actions of each firm have a direct impact on the others. The firm has to consider their probable responses when it embarks on any policy.

The second key factor, which is implicit in the opening paragraph, is that the firm has to decide on its price. It will face a trade-off between the quantity it can sell and the level of its price, and it is the basis for this choice that forms the subject of this chapter.

We will consider first the simple case of a monopolist producing a single product, and how such a firm should maximize its profits. Because in service industries the unit of supply is different from the unit of demand, we discuss how to maximize profits under these conditions using the notion of the marginal revenue of service. In most cases, a firm does not produce just one sort of output; even such apparently simple producers as British Rail sell train trips both at different times, different speeds and with different class facilities. For such producers, the question of how to price the various output is clearly crucial, and we therefore discuss the issues surrounding price discrimination.

The chapter then continues with a discussion of monopolistic competition. This appears to apply to almost all service industries, in that it deals with services that are differentiated, possibly only by space – they are accessible to different people because of their different locations – and yet there are many competing firms. This clearly relates to the situation analysed under the gravity model, although we shall see that it is by no means certain that we should be looking upon it as monopoly, rather than as oligopoly. We conclude the chapter with a discussion of the implications of consumer ignorance for such competition, and on how to decide on the level of advertising expenditure.

9.2 MONOPOLY

As stated in section 9.1, a monopoly is strictly the situation where you have just one single seller. This in fact disguises the potential for competition from other 'industries', because they produce products or services that are substitutes as far as the consumer is concerned. For example, we may consider gas and electricity, oil and coal as substitutes for heating, though scarcely for lighting. Thus we might expect the demand for gas to be relatively elastic if at that price the cost of using gas to produce heat is comparable to the cost of that heat produced by other fuels; if it is either clearly cheaper or clearly more expensive the demand is again likely to be much less elastic since it will be working in a range where there are no substitutes. If the price is comparable only to oil and coal, the demand is likely to be less elastic since switching fuels requires considerable investment in new plant; furthermore, both have some disadvantages in terms of convenience and cleanliness. These considerations help to define the type of demand curve we should expect, and warn us not to expect a straight line or smooth curve over large ranges of price.

9.2.1 Marginal revenue

As the firm faces demand that is price-sensitive, if it raises its price it has to expect a fall in the quantity demanded. Thus the firm will lose a certain quantity of sales and hence revenue, but it will earn more on what it sells. Conversely, if it wishes to increase the amount it sells by reducing its price, the firm has to remember that the gain in revenue is *not* just the increase in demand times the new price; it must also take account of the reduction in revenue that it is going to incur as a result of the price change affecting all of the demand that it would have enjoyed at the previously higher price. Let us define this more precisely.

The change in total revenue resulting from a change in demand is known as the **marginal revenue**. This is most appropriately defined for each possible unit of output; we are therefore considering the change in total revenue that will occur if we reduce the price by just enough to increase demand by one unit. The precise derivation of the formula given below is set out in the Appendix 9.A. The formula for marginal revenue is:

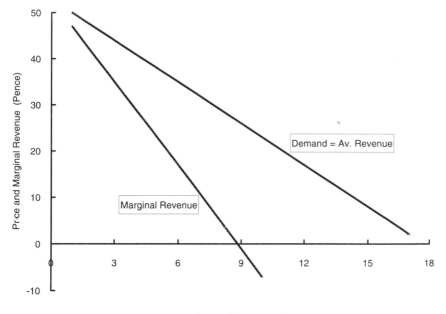

Figure 9.1 Demand and marginal revenue.

$$MR = P + Q \cdot \frac{dP}{dQ} \qquad (9.1)$$

In words, marginal revenue (MR) equals the price (P) of the marginal unit plus the quantity (Q) sold (before the price change) times the amount of change in price that is required to sell that extra unit (i.e. the differential of price with respect to quantity). Since we are talking about a single unit change, it does not normally matter whether the quantity is measured before or after the change; indeed if we are deriving it by calculus from a demand curve, this does not come into question. The relationship between the demand curve and the marginal revenue is shown for a straight line demand curve in Figure 9.1. (It will always – for a straight line demand curve – start at the same intercept on the price axis, and have twice the slope; in other words it will cut the quantity axis at a point half-way between 0 quantity and the point at which the demand curve cuts the quantity axis.)

9.2.2 Profit maximization: MR = MC

To maximize profits, output should be set to the point at which marginal revenue equals marginal costs. This is a tautology, since marginal revenue is the increase in total revenue and marginal costs is the increase in total costs – both with respect to quantity; it is clear that if one increases revenue by more than one increases costs, profits are increased. This will continue to happen as long as marginal revenue remains above marginal cost, and stops happening, therefore, at the point at which they are equal.

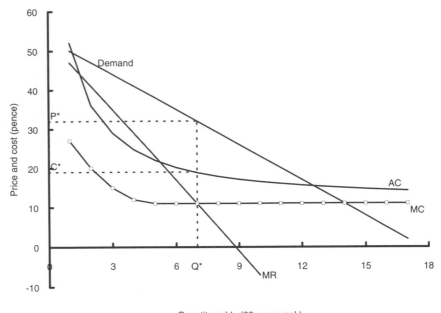

Figure 9.2 Profit maximising output and price under monopoly.

This general rule holds equally when marginal costs are zero or when they are positive. Price is then set at whatever the market will bear for that output. This is shown by the point on the demand curve for that quantity (see Figure 9.2).

9.2.3 Profit maximization: The optimal markup

Clearly this implies that in order to maximize profits the monopolist needs to know the demand curve and his cost function so that the relevant mathematical calculations for deriving marginal revenues and marginal costs can be undertaken. As demand curves are notoriously difficult to derive, this bit of economic theory seems condemned to the bin marked 'Useless Theory'. Fortunately, however, one can transform this set of conditions into a rule for calculating the markup on the basis of the elasticity of demand. It will be recalled from Chapter 4 that the elasticity of demand is:

$$\frac{P \cdot dQ}{Q \cdot dP} \tag{9.2}$$

and one might therefore reasonably expect that marketing managers would be able to provide a good estimate of the percentage increase in output that would result from a percentage cut in price. This formula, which is derived in Appendix 9.A, is as follows:

$$\frac{P - MC}{P} = -\frac{1}{e} \tag{9.3}$$

In words, the markup over marginal cost, expressed as a proportion of the price, should be the reciprocal of the elasticity of demand (expressed as an absolute number, i.e. ignoring the minus sign).

Remember that in the absence of very marked changes in the slope of the demand curve the elasticity declines as quantity increases. In other words, in the absence of sudden changes in the competitive position of the service in question, we can say that if the markup is causing too large a decline in demand compared with the change in price, we have set the markup too high; conversely if very few buyers are deterred we have probably set the markup too low. For example, if we consider the running of some facility such as access to the celebrated Wookey Hole cave, where marginal costs are zero, we should be deterring 1% of our customers for each 1% price rise. This follows from the fact that with a zero marginal cost, price minus marginal cost is equal to price; price divided by itself is equal to one; therefore, the elasticity of demand should also be unity, implying that for a 1% increase in price we get a fall of 1% in customers.

The application of this formula needs to be considered carefully. It makes assumptions implicit in the construction of a demand curve which may be dangerous in practice. Firstly, it assumes that the demand curve will be stable; for example, in the context of fuel prices, we would expect a rise in the price of one fuel to lead to a relatively small fall in demand for it in the short run, since most customers will be locked into it by virtue of the investment they have made in suitable boilers and heaters: paying £5000 for a new domestic heating system to save £100 per year because the cost of the fuel has changed is irrational. When it comes to choosing a new boiler, choosing one that uses a cheaper fuel is not irrational, however. Thus, while the short-run effects may be rather small, the same stimulus can cause a complete revolution in consumption patterns in the long run. For example, the increase in fuel prices in the USA caused a major shift from 'gas guzzlers' to smaller Japanese cars. This would be even more significant if the change in price causes a major shift in the opportunities for suppliers. Secondly, there is an implicit assumption that the elasticity of demand will change in an orderly fashion as prices alter. This would by no means necessarily be true for large changes in price, particularly if these cause the service to shift from being the preferred option to being a poor substitute for one that is now cheaper. This is particularly likely in such things as intermodal transport choice.

The application of the formula for the profit maximizing markup is vital also to an understanding of price discrimination and to the pricing of retailers who sell many different items. Every attempt should therefore be made to understand it before proceeding to the next section.

9.2.4 The marginal revenue of service

The **marginal revenue of service** was mentioned briefly in Chapter 6. It refers to the fairly frequent problem in service industries that the unit of output for the supplier is not the same as that for the customer. The examples of buses, trains and hotels were given. Now that the marginal revenue of the normal variety has been defined, referring to the effect of a price and quality change on total revenue, we can define the marginal revenue of service more closely:

> The marginal revenue of service (MRoS) is the increase in total revenue resulting from increasing the output of a service by one unit, with price and quality remaining constant.

An example from bus operation will help to make this clear:

> Assume that a monopolistic bus company has a potential demand at the existing fare level of 180 passengers per hour, and that this is fixed and will remain unaltered by the frequency of the service. Its bus fleet consists of double deckers with a useable capacity of 80 passengers. The first bus it puts on will be full and will thus have an MRoS of 80 passengers times the fare. Similarly, the second bus will also take 80 passengers, and have an MRoS of 80 × fare. The third bus will, however, take only the remaining 20 passengers, and thus $MRoS_3 = 20 \times$ fare. The buses may run at 20-minute intervals and each may take on average 60 passengers but this does not alter the fact that the **increase in revenue** from the third bus is only 20 × fare.

This example is clearly not realistic; if as suggested in Chapter 4 the value of time is important in assessing transport demand, it seems unlikely that the time savings available from a more frequent service will not attract at least some extra passengers. Thus a more frequent service will increase the total number expected, in much the same way as a cut in fares. We can define an elasticity to account for this notion:

$$\text{Service elasticity of demand} = \frac{\text{The proportional increase in the number of customers}}{\text{The proportional increase in the level of service}} \quad (9.4)$$

A typical value for bus operations might be +0.4 (Goodwin *et al.*, 1984, p. 9). Thus we might modify our previous example to take account of generated traffic:

> Let us assume that the bus company predicts 180 passengers per hour with a half hourly service; adding the third bus enables a 50% increase in service to be provided, increasing the frequency from one every half hour to one every 20 minutes. Thus with a 50% increase in service, we might with our elasticity of 0.4 expect an increase of 50% × 0.4 = 20% in the number of passengers, i.e. from 180 to 180 × 1.2 = 216. The $MRoS_3$ now becomes 216 − 160 = 56 passengers × fare.
>
> A further bus would increase the number of passengers by 0.4 × 0.33 × 216 = 29 passengers. Thus $MRoS_4 = 29 \times$ fare.

The decision to supply each of these buses would therefore depend on the marginal cost of putting on the service. If it were less than 20 × fare the third bus in the first example, and the fourth in this, would be put on, since if MRoS is greater than the marginal cost of service (MCS) it will increase profits.

This logic may be applied to the decision to open and staff further areas of a restaurant on a particular evening, extend the length of opening of a hotel, run a transport link, etc. In many cases, for example in the provision of a different type of insurance, care has to be taken to ensure that one is not including the revenue from customers who would be purchasing alternative policies offered by the firm; this would be exactly equivalent to the bus company using the average number of passengers times the fare as the marginal revenue of service, and is clearly misleading; indeed to use the criterion of average revenue = marginal cost is a recipe for suicide, alias bankruptcy, in an industry where marginal costs are approximately constant and there are fixed costs to be covered.

9.2.5 Profit maximization: Integration of MR = MC and MRoS = MCS

This represents a twofold maximization problem of the type beloved of mathematicians, but often very difficult to solve in the absence of neat equations. An approximate solution would be given by maximizing revenue, such that MR = MC. If MC is zero, the fare would be set such that the elasticity of demand is unity, following the rule for the optimal markup with zero marginal cost.

Thus $e = -1$, and so each 1% rise in fare should deter 1% of passengers. If MC is not zero, the fare should be set on the basis of the rule for the optimal markup, and then with the expected numbers of customers, estimating the MRoS and MCS. For example, on an airline, it might have been decided that the way to attract customers was to provide a lavish meal, drinks, etc.; thus each passenger might cost a substantial sum. This cost would be used to set the fare level, by MR = MC, and setting the fare (or using the optimal markup and the estimate of the price elasticity of demand). Then the appropriate level of service would be decided by taking the net marginal revenue for each passenger to be (fare − marginal cost), and then working out the MRoS and the MCS; the latter would of course *not* include the costs previously included under MC. (This procedure would probably be simpler than the estimation of the cost of service by including these marginal passenger costs, since these would vary with the number of passengers and the rest of the service cost would not.)

9.3 PRICE DISCRIMINATION

A monopolist will always be able to make more profit if he can divide up different markets and charge different prices in them. By different markets we mean markets where the demand curves, and hence the elasticities of demand, are different. Typical examples are the ones we meet every day, where British Rail discriminates between business travellers willing to pay high prices for peace and calm, normal passengers from whom they can extract a second class fare, and schoolchildren, students and pensioners who could not afford this and whom they therefore charge

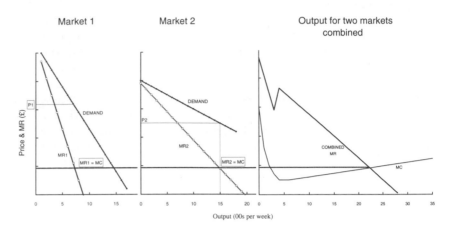

Figure 9.3 Price discrimination in two markets.

an even lower fare. These markets may be separate in demand, but the supply is largely joint, i.e. the same inputs – engines, station staff and rolling stock – go towards providing the service. The monopolist must therefore work out the appropriate markups over marginal cost. Whether it can be done simply as in the last section depends on whether marginal cost varies with quantity, and if so, whether it varies with joint quantities or not. In the simplest case where marginal costs are constant the firm simply works out the markups for each market separately, as in the previous section. Thus it does not matter if the marginal costs are the same in each market.

The problem comes when the marginal costs vary with joint quantities. If so, the marginal cost with the combined quantities needs to be calculated, and adjusted for each market if that is required. For example, it might be that the marginal cost of passengers might vary because of quantity discounts on inputs, for example food or cleaning, but that they were different in the first and tourist classes. Thus the marginal costs for the combined numbers would have to be calculated, and the relevant corrections made for the different costs in each class. These figures for marginal cost could be applied in each market using the optimal markup rule.

Formally, the process is to add the marginal revenue curves – that is to say, to add the quantities at each level of marginal revenue; this marginal revenue is set to equal marginal cost. This process gives one an overall marginal revenue; the individual marginal revenues for each sub-market are then set equal to this overall figure, and the quantities and prices at that level of marginal revenue are calculated. This process is illustrated in Figure 9.3.

If marginal costs are constant over the whole range, then of course this process is similar to the one mentioned above. If however the marginal cost varies, the procedure using Equation 9.3 can be used provided that one can insert the appropriate marginal cost; that is the marginal cost for the combined outputs.

Price discrimination depends critically on being able to ensure that the purchasers of the cheap tickets cannot re-sell them to those who would have to pay a higher price, thereby collecting the extra profit for themselves. In general this is much facilitated by the fact that you cannot store services.

As formulated, the process does not take account of the people who would switch between high and low prices. If this is a significant problem, the higher price needs to be reduced as compared with the full profit maximizing level, and the lower price raised. The exact formulation is quite complex, and would depend on being able to estimate the rate at which people would switch at different relative prices. It is therefore likely to remain a matter of judgement as to how much prices are adjusted. This is not a trivial problem; for example, a restaurant that has full restaurant meals, a cafe service and bar meals faces exactly this problem in assessing its prices.

Similarly if there is a question of developing a market for the future, the short-run profit maximizing price is likely to be too high, since it will discourage the expansion of sales. This would be particularly true in cases where the number of users is a positive advantage to the new consumers – as in computer systems or telecommunications.

9.4 PRICE DISCRIMINATION UNDER REGULATION

If prices are regulated, such as those of British Telecom, the process of pricing follows the same lines as normal price discrimination except that the monopolist has to remain within the constraint set by the regulator. This process is outlined in Vickers and Yarrow (1988, pp. 101–107).

We shall be returning to this concept when discussing the pricing by a retailer for whom there will be different markups for different products, but who must retain an overall value-for-money level across all products in order to compete against other retailers.

9.5 MONOPOLISTIC COMPETITION

Monopoly power is said to occur whenever a firm can differentiate its products from those of other firms so that it retains some control over price and quantity. For example, local shops can increase their market by reducing their prices or choose to charge higher prices and make more profit per item sold. However, it is clear that in the case of local shops, hairdressers, small building concerns, lawyers' and accountants' offices, and indeed almost any other privately provided service that one cares to think of, there are not the barriers to entry that would go to create a real monopoly. We therefore have what is called monopolistic competition.

Strictly speaking, monopolistic competition involves a situation where each firm has a downward-sloping demand curve, because its product is noticeably different from the products of other firms, and yet where it is competing generally against all those other firms. We will see that this assumption may be extremely restrictive, and we may wish to consider it more in the light of a rather open oligopoly where competition is much keener with a small number of close rivals than the competition implied here with all other firms in the industry. It is nevertheless worth considering monopolistic competition, since it forms a substantial body of literature and it looks as though it should be significant for the service industries and, more importantly, the process of entry of new firms is relatively easily understood by considering it in this context first.

E. H. Chamberlin first elaborated the theory of monopolistic competition in 1933. He distinguished small-group monopolistic competition, which we would now call 'product-differentiated oligopoly', and large-group monopolistic competition, which is what we would now recognize under this term. It may be easiest to explain this as a transition from monopoly to a more competitive market by the entry of firms, and so that is how it is explained here.

Figure 9.4 reproduces Figure 9.2, for pure monopoly. Let us now consider what would happen if, as the result of the attraction of the high profits shown there, a second firm identical to the first except that its products fit a different market niche, should enter the market. Clearly if it enters successfully, it will share the market with the existing firm; let us say for simplicity that it takes half the market. Because of the properties of marginal revenue curves, the marginal revenue curve enjoyed by the original firm before entry now becomes the demand curve for each firm, and we need to construct a new marginal revenue curve for this demand curve. This will start at the same point on the price axis, and will cut the quantity axis half way between the origin and the point at which the demand curve cuts this axis. As can be seen, this will lead to both higher prices and costs.

This, however, is not the only change that is taking place. The original firm now faces some relatively close substitutes for its services. Thus, either firm would be able to gain a very considerable share of the market by cutting its price, always providing that the other did not follow suit. The demand curve that we have drawn represents a share of the market demand, which is what happens if all firms change their prices together. Going through the relevant market price, there is also another demand curve which represents what would happen if the individual firm cut its price and others did not follow suit. This is of course why it is so important to have a generalized competition with all firms in a relatively large group rather than just two firms as we have sketched here, because if we have competition among many firms it is not implausible that the individual firm should be able to cut its prices without causing severe losses to the others. If we therefore reproduce the diagram for the new firm (simply for clarity) and insert the new, more elastic demand curve and its appropriate marginal revenue curve, we can then see that the firm might choose a new price and quantity combination based on the more elastic demand curve in the hope of a much larger market share (Figure 9.5). However, what is sauce for the goose is sauce for the gander and so the other firm is likely to think along the same lines. We could therefore expect the price to fall to this new lower level, but the market demand will only expand along the

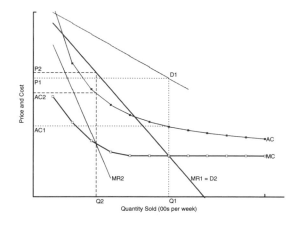

D1 = The demand curve of the firm initially dominating the market.

MR1= D2 = The marginal revenue of the firm dominating the market initially, and thus the demand curve of both firms after the new entrant takes half of the market. (The marginal revenue of a straight line demand curve always declines at twice the rate of the demand curve, and thus is equivalent to halving the market. This implies that a monopolist with a constant marginal cost and a straight line demand curve, will produce half the level of output of the firm forced to produce at price equal to marginal cost.)

MR2= The new marginal revenue curve for half the original market.

MC = The marginal cost curve.

AC = The average cost curve, both of which are assumed not to change with the increased competition.

Hence, P1, Q1 & C1: the price, quantity and cost in the initial monopolistic market.

P2, Q2 & C2: the price, quantity and cost in the market, once it is shared.

The rise in price in spite of the fall in quantity, is exactly what we would expect when we have chosen to indicate a natural monopoly, since the average cost falls over the whole range of output. In the longer term, the capital stock of the firms should adjust to give the same price as in the initial position, providing adaptation is possible, in other words there are no economies of scale, and assuming that the other facet of monopolistic competition, the desire to price cut does not come into play. It would be likely to do so and is illustrated in Figure 9.5.

Figure 9.4 Monopolistic competition and the effect of entry of a new firm.

steeper 'share of market' demand curve, because all firms are cutting prices together.

This process of price cuts is accompanied by the process of new entry discussed previously. The result is therefore to have more firms producing at a lower price, and with lower profits. This process can continue until no profits are being made, and therefore there is no incentive for further firms to enter.

9.5.1 Spatial monopoly and monopolistic competition

One of the major aspects of differentiation in the service industries is that of location, and this has formed one of the core elements of monopolistic competition theory throughout. A service is identical only if it is the same service, delivered from the same place. To anticipate the conclusions of this section, we may say that the more closely identical services are, the more likely it is that price competition will be important. Thus identical services provided from approximately the same location are likely to be

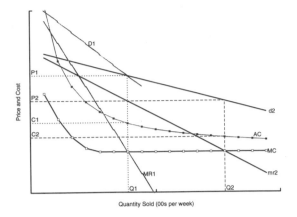

D1   =   The share of market demand curve; the demand curve that would exist if all firms changed their prices together.
MR1 =   The marginal revenue curve for the share of market demand curve.
d2   =   The demand curve that would exist for the firm, if all other firms kept their prices constant, and it alone cut or raised its price. The 'Ceteris Paribus Demand' is a convenient term.
mr2 =   The marginal revenue curve for the Ceteris Paribus Demand.

P1, Q1 & C1: The price, quantity and cost under the share of market demand.
P2, Q2 & C2: The price, quantity and cost if the firm cut its price alone, and other firms did not follow suit.

In this case the improved profits are very obvious. Price cutting thus looks to be the obvious option unless retaliation is to be expected; in view of the very large numbers assumed in monopolistic competition, retaliation is not to be expected, but other firms are likely to think in the same way. If they do the firm will find its demand falling along the share of market demand curve, D1, and all firms will be worse off, but the consumers will be better off.

The final equilibrium would be where the market demand, D1, and the Ceteris Paribus Demand, d2, intersected at the point where the Ceteris Paribus Demand was tangential to the Average Cost curve, AC, and where the Ceteris Paribus Marginal Revenue curve, mr2, and the marginal cost, MC, curves intersected at that quantity. There would therefore be no incentive for new firms to enter since average costs are only just being covered, or for existing firms to cut their prices, since marginal revenue equals marginal costs.

Figure 9.5 Monopolistic competition: the incentive to cut prices.

priced identically, whereas identical services separated geographically may charge quite different prices. The major issues in this area of work relate to the way customers will trade off better facilities for lower transport costs, or either of these for lower prices – in other words how to choose the best combination of location, store type and pricing structure, if one considers retailing. Similar considerations will apply to almost all services going direct to the consumer. For producer services, the service may be sufficiently 'one-off' for such considerations not to apply. Secondly, it may be important to know whether we should expect service providers to be able to retain monopoly power, because they crowd out the market sufficiently cleverly. Could one, for example, set up a chain of local stores located cleverly enough so that no other local store could come between, and so that one could continue to make some 'excess profits'?

Let us start, as most economists do, with the work of Hotelling (1929). He suggests that one can look at this problem by considering the location of ice cream sellers on a beach. The customers are equally spread out along the whole length of the beach and buy just one ice cream each per day from the closest ice cream seller. The number of ices they buy does not vary with the closeness of the seller. The ice cream is sold at a fixed price, so price competition does not come into it. From a social point of view, if there is one ice cream seller, it would be best that he should locate at the centre of the beach where overall distance walked will be least. If there were two ice cream sellers, socially speaking, they should locate at points a quarter of the way along the beach from either end. Would they actually do this?

Let us take two situations as starting points: Firstly, suppose one seller is already installed in the centre of the beach. Where could the second seller locate in order to gain as large a share of the market as possible? The answer is right next to the first seller. If he moves away, and the first seller stays still, he will get all of the market between himself and the end of the beach he is nearer, and only half of the market between him and the first seller at the centre of the beach. So the maximum he can get is half of the market, if he is right next to the first seller in the centre of the beach. To check that this is a stable equilibrium, let us consider our second case: what would happen if they arrived at the social optimum, one quarter of the way along from each end to start with? It would then give each of them half the market, and give the maximum social welfare because overall distances walked to get ice cream would then be at a minimum. But it would pay each of them to move towards the centre, since if the other did not, the mover would gain all of the market towards his end of the beach, and half of the market between him and the other seller. Take the situation of one staying still and the other moving to the centre: the latter, the mover, would have the half of the market from the centre to the end of the beach, and half of the market between him and the quarter point where the other sap was still standing, making 5/8 of the market. If Sap stays still, he can do even better, moving beside him, but towards the centre, in which case he would get 3/4 of the market. However, even the good sap would not stand for this and would step to the inside of the mover, and so take just less than 3/4. This little dance would go on until they reached the equilibrium position back to back in the centre.

If a third seller joined them, there would be no equilibrium, with a rotary dance taking place for the spaces just outside the centre. With four sellers, they would move to two groups of two, back to back at the quarter points. Indeed, it is not possible to say generally whether there will be an equilibrium, and unfortunately it seems that introducing price flexibility does not make the existence of equilibrium any more probable. Equilibria will exist where transport costs are high enough to ensure that no firm can undercut another's price by a sufficient amount to take over its whole market. Thus for example for 'corner shops': once sufficient have disappeared, so that there are relatively few, and often only one of each type of local shop in each vicinity, the access problems that allow local shops to survive in spite of the major price advantages of the large supermarket chains are such that no local shop can charge a sufficiently low price to undercut its rivals to the point of driving them out of business.

Does the lack of equilibrium matter in business as opposed to economic theory? The answer must be that it is likely to do so, since equilibrium in this sense is a situation in which one can expect the other firms not to change prices, which might force one to change one's own. It implies, in fact, a situation where there is no resting place but monopoly or annihilation. At a purely intuitive and casually empirical level, this seems to approximate moderately closely to the rapid demise of the small shop. It suggests that the small shops drive each other out of business if they are too densely set on the ground, and that they cannot raise their prices, since to do so would be to push their customers towards ever more frequent use of the supermarkets, or would allow other local shops to enter. The latter situation would lead to an unstable position where there would probably be no equilibrium until one of the shops went out of business. We will see, however, that there might be reason to think that such situations lead to 'accommodation', rather than the all-out pursuit of profit maximization, so that the basic assumptions of the model would be violated – but this implies oligopoly, not monopolistic competition.

The other message that comes from this sort of model is that we should perhaps be abandoning the notion of monopolistic competition in favour of product (or spatially) differentiated oligopoly. This is the implication of the so-called 'address branch' of spatial competition theory (Archibald *et al.*, 1986). This is based on the idea that each consumer and firm has an 'address' as in the Hotelling model sketched above. This does have two disadvantages; firstly, it suggests strongly that competition will not be general, but will be at least 'chain' in the sense that price changes by one firm will affect its nearest neighbours; if they react, that may – or may not – cause similar reactions from their neighbours, hence the name 'chain competition'. If it does not go beyond the neighbouring firm, we have local oligopolies, *not* monopolistic competition. Secondly, at a much more advanced level, the address branch is mathematically intractable – in other words the maths gets horribly complicated – and often leaves one with results of a tautological nature like, 'It depends on this, this and this, and their relative magnitudes'. A practical version of the address model is the gravity model discussed in Chapter 4. As mentioned there, however, it is extremely difficult to operationalize a gravity model which includes measures of price differences and other qualitative aspects within it. Unfortunately, the alternative, the **representative consumer** model (e.g. Dixit and Stiglitz, 1977), which assumes a consumer (or set of identical consumers) with preference for variety centred on a particular product variant and with preferences declining as the characteristics vary increasingly from that variant, appears highly unrealistic for most of the questions one might wish to model. It is of course the version implicit in Chamberlin's monopolistic competition model.

9.6 RETAIL PRICING

The article by Bliss (1988) provides the only appropriate treatment in the economics literature of the pricing decision by a retail firm. This section follows his lead. The article also provides an interesting example of the use of the representative consumer model to simplify the analysis, and to set up the framework for the more complex analysis using the address model (neither term is used by Bliss); the address model turns out to give different results, as one would expect.

Bliss considers the basic elements of the model of retailing to revolve around the following assumptions:

1. Shops face two sorts of cost: a marginal cost, which is the sum of wholesale costs and the holding costs (see section 6.7); these are, as we said in Chapter 6, sufficiently constant so that pricing according to perfect competition rules of price = marginal cost would cause losses, given that the firm's overheads would not be covered.
2. The overheads are joint costs between all the different goods being sold.
3. The consumer also faces joint overhead costs in the form of the transport costs required to get to the shop (and we might add in the form of any waiting for service in the shop or at the checkouts).
4. The pattern of demand in the choice of quantities of goods to purchase in the shop is normal; the higher the price of any particular good, the lower the quantity demanded in aggregate, and the more is demanded of rival goods.
5. The consumer thus faces a two-stage decision process: (i) he or she must decide which shop to patronize, and this is based on the perceived 'value for money' of the shop, a trade-off between the set of prices in the shop and the quality of service; and (ii) once in the shop, he or she must decide which goods to buy. This is based in the normal way, on the relative prices actually found.
6. The shop correspondingly has three decisions after the location decision: (i) what level of service to provide by expenditure on decor and staff (the decision about fixed costs, as in Chapter 7); (ii) what level of prices to charge overall, in other words what 'value for money' to aim at; and (iii) what price to charge for each particular item, given choice (ii) about the value for money of the shop as a whole.

The store's final decision is one of constrained optimization; given the value for money, how do the individual items get priced? This is therefore akin to the problem facing BT: given a set of prices which must on average not exceed the prices of last year plus or minus a given percentage (i.e. +RPI −X, where X is determined by Oftel), how are the individual prices for services to be changed to maximize profits subject to this constraint? (This process will also give the socially preferred set of prices, subject to the constraint, providing that they are satisfactory on income distribution grounds; see Vickers and Yarrow, 1988, pp. 101–107 for a moderately advanced treatment of this – Equation 9.5 is a simple transformation of theirs – and Chapter 3 for a brief discussion of the income distribution question following Posner, 1971.) The solution in the BT case is to charge prices for each item which are above the marginal cost by a margin that is some factor of the reciprocal of the elasticity of demand for that item, i.e.:

$$\frac{P - MC}{P} = -\frac{k}{e} \tag{9.5}$$

where k is the factor by which profit maximizing is constrained in order to bring prices down to the level required by the constraint of having to provide value for money. (Note that this ignores the interactions between the price of one good and the quantity of other goods demanded. This would be a serious omission if the impact on demand of the other good were large. It is not ignored by Bliss, but this makes the formula he uses very difficult to interpret in an operational fashion.)

The version of 'value for money' used by Bliss is one based on fully informed and rational consumers, and so it relates to the average cost of the complete 'basket of goods' that they purchase. Most consumers are not that rational, or well-informed about prices, and so it is an interesting question whether one should use this measure, and compare it to rival stores; in other words should one take the average amounts of items sold as the basis for making comparisons with other stores, or should one restrict it to a few goods which are thought to be 'comparators' for the public. As a personal opinion, the author would suggest doing both; if the two came out with very different answers one would want to know why, and then long discussion and consideration would be in order, preferably followed by well-controlled experiments in different stores.

Bliss points out that it is possible that rational profit maximization might involve selling some goods at below cost price, if one is taking into account cross-elasticities (which the above formula does not). This would follow the normal rationale for this activity, that it attracts people into the store by contributing to their view that the store is very good value for money. At first sight it would appear extremely dangerous to follow this line, since one would expect that such goods would have to have a very high elasticity of demand, so that the markup from the above formula would be close to zero; to this one would then add the effect of these goods in contributing to sales of others, and thus the markup would actually be negative! The danger of this 'give away policy' would seem to come from the elasticity of demand, which might prompt very large purchases of the item, and hence cause very large amounts to be given away, and the store to make losses. But these would be more than offset by the correspondingly large expansion in demand for the high markup goods which would be bought as the result of the positive cross-elasticities. This might be the situation with cut price sugar: high demand elasticity because of universal availability at similar prices, and complementarity with cake and jam making materials which might have a good markup. The problem is that one cannot stop people coming to 'take advantage' of the low prices, and then going elsewhere for the other items. This is however not the only possible outcome; the loss leader strategy would be a success provided that the cross-elasticity was strongly positive, and that the marginal revenue from the complementary items purchased outweighed the effect of the subsidy on the cut price good.

The internal pricing model is developed by Bliss on the basis of the representative consumer. This should not do violence to the facts since the store cannot distinguish consumers once they are through the doors. Decisions about 'value for money' and the level of service, however, would be taken on the wrong basis if one uses a representative consumer model. The critical factor in these decisions is the extra customers that will come to the store as the result of optimal decisions on these two items. Thus one needs to consider the different transport costs, and income levels, in order to see which consumers might switch from other stores to one's own, and this needs the sort of considerations that the 'address model' uses. The question might be formulated as follows:

> In each zone, what percentage increase in people coming to the store could we expect from a cut of $x\%$ on overall prices? Summing this over all zones, how much extra gross profit does that bring in? Does that more than offset the $x\%$ fall in revenue that one might expect from all existing customers?

It is important to remember that the fall in prices will cause a fall in revenue, probably uncompensated by any fall in costs, since the amount each existing customer buys will not fall and thus neither wholesale nor holding costs will fall. A zero elasticity of demand for existing shoppers has been assumed (an $x\%$ fall in revenue from an $x\%$ fall in prices); that is a very pessimistic assumption, but we would probably not expect the elasticity to be greater than unity for existing shoppers. (It might be, particularly if it encouraged them to shift demand from other suppliers.) The demand generated by the new customers, and by the diversion of the demand by existing customers from other shops, will involve extra input costs, and so it must be estimated not in terms of revenue but in terms of gross profit: the net increase in revenue minus the increase in costs. This is called the net marginal revenue (NMR) in many economics texts.

How should one estimate the likely diversion of customers from elsewhere to one's own shop? One way to do this would be to assume that customers were fully rational, and that they therefore went to the shop which provided the cheapest combination of travel and purchase costs. The total costs and the value of time taken in the alternative shops could be estimated using the method set out for 'generalized costs' in Chapter 4, and this could be added to the purchase costs of the 'shopping basket'. The effect of this change of prices on the catchment area, given by the zones in which it was now cheaper to shop at one's own shop rather than others, could then be estimated. Alternatively, if a gravity model is available, this process is equivalent to reducing the zonal travel times by the amount of the savings from price cuts. The costs of all trips to the zone could therefore be reduced by that amount.

Considering the impact of price changes by inserting them into the framework of a gravity model would provide an interesting test of the degree to which competition would be concentrated on a few centres rather than dispersed as predicted by the Chamberlin model, or the representative consumer models. The very direct impact on closer shopping centres resulting from the opening of hypermarkets (Seale, 1977) suggests that we should take the implications of the address model seriously. This implies that although monopolistic competition may be a useful way of considering certain aspects of competition, we should really consider oligopolistic behaviour to be more probable. To this we turn in the next chapter, after considering the impact of imperfect information.

9.7 IMPERFECT INFORMATION

The role of information in determining demand and hence the appropriate behaviour of the monopolistic firm has not been discussed. Some account of this has been taken by the insistence on the use of elasticities rather than the demand curve as a measure of demand, but the literature goes further. The starting point is the observation that if there is ignorance of prices and availability, some monopoly power (a negative slope to the demand curve) will be present. Unfortunately, from this observation one can develop many different models according to the particular assumptions made about the behaviour of consumers and their methods of search for information. Economists seem particularly interested in the question of whether one can expect a distribution of prices at different outlets, or whether there will be a single price, and if so whether this will approximate to the competitive price or the monopolistic one, and whether there will be monopoly profits or none under free entry. As students of management, we might be interested in this from the point of view of the optimal strategy of the firm, and we will attempt to discuss this – initially in relation to retail outlets (any service selling a range of items or services to the consumer, thus including jobbing builders and repair services); it will be followed up with a brief discussion of professional services such as doctors, lawyers and accountants, where these are operating on a market basis.

Full information theory would suggest that neighbouring firms may be in 'chain competition' and therefore oligopolists rather than monopolistic competitors. However it should be borne in mind that the costs of keeping an eye on the prices of neighbouring firms, and the difficulty of estimating how consumers view 'value for money' in a store as a whole, are considerable. Smaller stores particularly may ignore oligopolistic interdependence and thus behave as monopolistic competitors, even if they are actually in head-to-head rivalry with closely neighbouring stores.

Assuming for the moment that we have lots of identical monopolistic competitors, it will clearly pay each of them to raise their prices if they can do so by a amount small enough to avoid prompting any consumer into searching for cheaper outlets. If the stores are identical, it would pay all of them to raise prices by this small amount. If they all do, the consumer would not find cheaper prices elsewhere, and so the cycle could start again. The eventual result would be to raise the price to the full monopoly price level, at which the resistance of the consumer to further prices rises would be operating. Thus the outcome would be that all stores charged the same monopoly price. Should this occur, it would also be very socially wasteful, since it would presumably cause monopoly profits, and hence would cause the entry of further firms into the market, and would continue to do so as long as monopoly profits could be made (Stiglitz, 1979). The outcome is thus the same as that experienced under Retail Price Maintenance (RPM) – too many stores selling at excessive prices.

This model however makes the amazing assumption that the firms know the small price rise they can get away with, and that this will be the same for all firms (a consequence of the assumption of identical firms). Neither assumption is plausible, and we certainly observe a distribution of prices. Thus, what we have to model is a situation of a variety of consumers, with some search routine that is plausible, and this implies sources of information that are plausible. The response of stores is also to be modelled, and clearly this is also subject to information difficulties, firstly in understanding the consumer behaviour that is actually taking place, secondly in responding to it in the optimal manner, or at least a satisfactory one, and thirdly in that the firm's response be within the compass of boundedly rational firms. The difficulty then arises that there are innumerable possible search routines, and that mathematically the models will become complex since we will be dealing with the interaction of probability distributions relating to the types of firm, the search procedures of consumers, and with address models, the different costs of search for consumers varying by location, tastes and incomes and the variety of store locations.

Models using a variety of consumers, some of whom search and some of whom do not, tend to come to the conclusion that there will be a diversity of prices, and that high price firms will survive, although lower price ones will have much larger sales (Wilde and Schwartz, 1979). There is likely to be a gap in the distribution of prices above the competitive price. This emerges because the firms operating a 'low price strategy' will have a higher probability of being chosen by those consumers who 'shop around', in other words who search for the best prices. The gap emerges because the consumers take the cheapest supplier; this is to be expected since the goods are assumed homogeneous and so there is no question of differences in quality of shop or in delivery conditions influencing consumers to buy even where they know it is more expensive. Thus it does not pay to be marginally more expensive than the cheapest since it will only be by chance that such a shop will be chosen rather than the lowest price shop, and such a chance selection does not make the small extra price that is being paid profitable over the relatively small number of shoppers buying. For the clearly higher priced shops, however, assuming a relatively large number of casual shoppers (i.e. those who simply go out and buy without seeking more information), and/or a sufficient range of shops so that they may get chosen even by price conscious shoppers, the higher markup per item makes up for the smaller number of items sold.

Such a model is of course dangerous in that it assumes a homogeneous good, which implies no differences in after-sales service, delivery times etc. Such product differentiation would become extremely important at the 'competitive equilibrium' in that a substantial number of stores would presumably be selling the same product at the same price, to consumers who were in general well informed (as well as others who came in by chance). Their choice of store would thus be conditioned by the relatively small differences created by the product differentiation. Depending on price sensitivity (and advertising advantages), this might lead to some price dispersion due to product differentiation at a 'competitive price' which reflected the desire of different consumers for the characteristics over which the product was differentiated.

A model of price dispersion for 'reputation' goods is provided by Satterthwaite (1979). Reputation goods are those whose quality is not discernible by looking (search goods), or by a single experience such as in the case of canned foods or restaurant meals, but which – like doctors, dentists, accountants or lawyers – can only be evaluated after a long period and then only with a high level of uncertainty since the advice given is rarely demonstrably wrong, and even if it is, the blame for misdiagnosis is often in doubt. Thus, one relies largely on reputation. In this context, we may get the perverse result suggested by Satterthwaite, that the higher the number of firms, the smaller the probability that any one consumer will have acquaintances with significant experience of any individual firm, and therefore the less the likelihood of being able to make a confident choice of firm. In so far as this means that the consumer will not have the confidence to switch firms in the event of some dissatisfaction because of inadequate information about the other firms, switching as the result of price rises, for example, will be reduced, and prices may rise as a response from the firms.

In the service industries, the questions relating to information acquire particular importance, since many of the service industries provide their services to the general public, whose main function in life is not to be informed about prices and qualities, unlike a professional buyer in the industrial context. Despite widespread awareness of this problem, it is extremely difficult to model it in sufficiently general ways to give useful and robust results. Lack of information is not however a sufficient reason for government involvement; government involvement involves costs, and built-in perverse incentives. Given the diversity of interest groups and the diversity of tastes, it may be that the acquisition of information should be left to consumer groups. Equally, however, the provision of disinformation should presumably be controlled; bodies like the Advertising Standards Authority are likely to be a useful part of government, assuring the basic legal framework without which the market cannot function.

9.8 ADVERTISING

The purposes of advertising are much discussed in the economics literature, since much of that literature is trying to retain the notions of full consumer rationality. Under such a world view, the only function of advertising is to inform the customers about new products or about new locations where products or services are available. In more realistic world views, where consumers have bounded rationality, and hence do not have full information about all the products and services available, advertising clearly has both the functions which casual observation suggests: to inform, and to alter consumer tastes for products or services. Advertising for cinemas, restaurants and holidays provides interesting examples of the different extent of each. The principal aim of cinema advertising is to tell people of the programme and the time of showings at the particular cinema. The major advertising of the film is done by the production and distribution company. Restaurant advertisements usually contain the minimum of information such as locality, the type of cuisine, and often cues as to the type of restaurant in terms of quality – the aim being to draw attention to itself and to provide 'notification of the existence of a seller'. Even the nationally advertised chains provide a fair degree of information in their ads. Holidays on the other hand are advertised sufficiently to try to attract the customer to find out more.

Given these different mixes of persuasion and information, and the very clear importance of the quality of any advertising campaign, does economics have any useful guidelines on the decision to advertise? Well, it certainly has a view. It turns out that for a fairly general model of monopolistic behaviour, of the sort discussed at the start of the chapter:

$$\frac{\text{Advertising expenditure}}{\text{Sales}} =$$

$$\frac{\text{Elasticity of demand with respect to advertising}}{\text{Elasticity of demand}} \quad (9.6)$$

This is known as the Dorfmann–Steiner theorem. It is derived in Appendix 9.B. Let us explain it a little; the only term that appears strange is the 'elasticity of demand with respect to advertising', henceforward shortened to **advertising elasticity**. This is defined as:

$$\text{Advertising elasticity} =$$

$$\frac{\text{Proportional change in quantity}}{\text{Proportional change in advertising expenditure}} \quad (9.7)$$

where the 'proportional change in quantity' is the proportional change at a given price. As one would expect, and as shown in Appendix 9.B, this is equivalent to saying that one should expand the advertising budget up to the point where the net marginal revenue from advertising (the **net** increase in total revenue due to a unit increase in the advertising budget) equals the marginal cost of advertising. If advertising can actually be increased to give single units of output, then it amounts to saying that markup over marginal cost should equal the cost incurred in advertising to achieve that extra unit of output. More commonly, advertising can only be increased in discrete units – for example an extra newspaper advertisement; an approximate value of the marginal cost of advertising can then be calculated by dividing the cost of the advertisement by the number of extra sales it produces. Thus, a bus company should continue to advertise up to the point where the cost of the advertisement divided by the number of extra passengers equals the fare; a training course should continue to advertise up to the point where the cost of the advertisement divided by the number of extra students equals the fee for the course less any extra expenses caused by the extra student (such as accommodation and hospitality costs if these are borne by the provider).

Careful thought needs to be given as to whether the 'marginal costs of production' are short-term marginal costs (assuming the service will be provided at that level anyway) or long-term marginal costs (assuming that all the costs of expansion of the service will need to be met, including capital investment, staffing and management).

Thus the two factors which enter into this equation are the sensitivity of the service to advertising, and the profit per unit of service as given by the reciprocal of the elasticity of demand. In very intuitive terms, if you get substantial expansion of sales, providing they make a profit it will pay to advertise; if you are making a very large profit per unit, it may pay to advertise even if there is only a small expansion in sales. It is interesting to conjecture which of these is the dominant aspect of the large advertising budgets of building societies, pension and life insurance funds, and to a lesser extent health insurance.

What will cause the sensitivity of sales to advertising to be high? Firstly, if no one is informed of the product, it will not sell, and so we might expect that informing a large proportion of the potential market hitherto unaware of the existence of the service will give a large potential gain from advertising. If it is a service entering a market in which existing offerings are relatively homogeneous, a small differentiation of the service may suffice to cause a relatively large change in customer loyalty. This formulation assumes that advertising expenditures will shift demand in the case of monopolists or monopolistic competitors, so that they will be able to increase both price and quantity at equilibrium. However, there is a general belief that very small levels of advertising may have very little effect, since they may not be noticed, and very large advertising expenditures may face diminishing returns since all the customers who might purchase will have seen the advertisements many times over. Thus this formula holds for the position where the effectiveness of advertising is declining, in the same way as the formula for the optimal markup holds for the situation where marginal revenue is falling from above the marginal cost curve to below it.

It seems clear that there are industries where advertising pays and others where it does not. Clarke (1985, p. 120, table 6.1) shows the wide variety of advertising to sales ratios. In 1968 the industries with the highest advertising to sales ratios seemed to be those to do with repeat purchases of goods, with differentiation being essentially on the basis of image, including toilet preparations, soap and detergents, pharmaceuticals, cocoa, chocolate and sugar confectionery etc. One is tempted to remark that it is a matter of such indifference as to which one buys that the small differentiation by advertising creates a large difference in sales. It is clear that at the other end of the scale come the producer goods industries where very well-informed buyers are not likely to be influenced by advertising, and so it can fulfil its role neither as information diffuser, since they are already well informed, nor as creator of differentiation by altering a person's views on a product because opinions depend on more solid information than advertising jingles. The much more complex approach adopted by Hay and Morris (1991, pp. 128–151) is also thought provoking in relation to the estimation of the advertising elasticity.

As it stands, the formula implies that advertising is a current expense, and the returns it brings occur in the same time period. This is contrary to much of the empirical work on advertising, which suggests that advertising expenditures have impacts lasting several years, and should therefore be analysed as a capital expenditure. Fortunately it is not difficult to do this (as shown in section 7.3.3, failure to do this will cause underinvestment by the firm, and is one of the plausible reasons for short-termism in UK industry):

$$\frac{\text{Advertising expenditure}}{\text{Sales}} = \frac{\text{Advertising elasticity}}{(\text{Discount rate} + \text{Rate of decay})} \cdot \frac{1}{\text{Elasticity of demand}} \quad (9.8)$$

where the discount rate is the rate of interest used for investment analysis by the firm, expressed as a decimal, thus a 10% rate of interest would give a discount rate of 0.1; and the rate of decay is the rate at which an advertising campaign loses its effectiveness, thus if a campaign loses 15% of its impact by the second year, assuming no renewal of it, the rate of decay would be 0.15. This would give a total on the denominator of $0.1 + 0.15 = 0.25$, and would thus represent the equivalent of multiplying the short-run advertising elasticity by 4 to get the long-run advertising elasticity.

It should be noted, however, that this improvement is not all one-way; if one is working with the long-run elasticity for advertising, one should also be working with the long-run elasticity of demand, which is usually considerably higher than the short-run elasticity.

Treating advertising as a capital good also allows us to consider whether the literature on advertising as a quality signal in itself is important to the service industries. Certainly many of the service industries which deal in domestic servicing, building and decorating, repairs, etc. have a problem of assuring quality, and some are relatively infrequently used, so that information on the quality of the firm may be thought to go out of date. Thus the ability to reassure customers, as well as remind them of the firm's services, would be an advantage. The logic is as follows: if advertising is an investment, there is no point investing in this aspect of the firm's activities if personal experience, supplemented by enquiries among friends, is going to negate that positive message. The repeat purchases on which the firm may depend, and which increase the effectiveness of the advertising, coupled with the spread of positive information, which further increases the effectiveness of advertising, thus rely on quality, and thus it will pay the advertiser to go for high quality if they are going to advertise. The consumer can therefore rest assured that high quality firms will advertise, and that firms advertising will be of high quality. This is of course like the discussion of the 'market for lemons' in Chapter 3, where in a single period market the firms that take advantage of others' quality can ruin the reputation of the high quality firms and the market. Once repeat purchases become important, then this is no longer so likely, since experience will become important. Thus the combination of persistent advertising and the persistence of the firm should give a reliable signal of quality. If, however, the service is one used so infrequently that no body of knowledge is built up in the population, the situation is akin to the single period market, without repeat sales, and advertising is no more a guarantee of quality than the cries of the hawker of 'genuine Rolex watches' on the street corners of the Far East.

Before leaving this topic, it is important to note two things: firstly, that any of the formulae rely on the ability of the firm advertising to be able to deliver the service to those wanting it. It has been pointed out before that investment in advertising and failure to deliver can be a source of rapid failure. The advertising is an extra expense, and there is potential expense in servicing the demand one cannot satisfy (as in mail order firms), or if one gets overcrowded, as in restaurants, the quality declines and the customers are disappointed, and so take away and spread negative messages about the service provided.

Secondly, we have not discussed the balance between advertising and other selling expenditures. The formal treatment of this can be found in Reekie and Crook (1987, p. 307); it does not, however, seem to this author to be a very useful approach since the estimation of the sort of curves implied seems wholly impossible. What one can say from general theory, however, is that one should expand all activities to the point where a pound spent yields the same marginal benefit; thus if switching the cost of an ad in a national paper could yield a really good article giving publicity, and this was judged to be more effective, then clearly profits would be better served by so doing. It is easy to fail to observe this tautology in practice, however, since it is always easier to continue as before than to alter course.

To summarize, there are reasons for thinking that advertising would be profitable in services (i) where the potential for attracting customers is considerable because a large number of them will not otherwise be aware of the service, and (ii) where that service is otherwise weakly differentiated from other similar services. There is, furthermore, a formula for the optimal expenditure on advertising which is applicable to monopolistic contexts, i.e. those where one can ignore the retaliation by other firms. This formula relates the sensitivity of sales of the service to advertising and the profit level on each unit sold to the amount of advertising expenditure as a proportion of sales. This can further be modified to account for the investment nature of advertising. This approach, considering advertising as an investment, also gives some credibility to the notion that high quality firms advertise, since the effectiveness of such investment will depend on their ability to provide a satisfactory service.

APPENDIX 9.A

9.A.1   Monopoly pricing: Derivation of the optimal markup for profit maximization

$$MR = \frac{dTR}{dQ} = \frac{d(P \cdot Q)}{dQ} = P + Q \cdot \frac{dP}{dQ} \tag{9.A.1}$$

Marginal revenue (i.e. the increase in total revenue from the sale of one extra unit of output) equals the rate of change of total revenue with respect to output, which equals the rate of change of price times quantity with respect to output, which equals price plus quantity times the change in price from one extra unit of quantity sold.

We can express both MR and the optimal rate of markup in terms of the elasticity of demand; we can manipulate the expression:

$$MR = P + Q\frac{dP}{dQ} \tag{9.A.2}$$

By multiplying the last term by P/P we would get:

$$MR = P + Q\left(\frac{dP}{dQ} \cdot \frac{P}{P}\right) = P\left(1 + \frac{Q}{P}\frac{dP}{dQ}\right) = P\left(1 + \frac{1}{e}\right) \tag{9.A.3}$$

where e is the elasticity of demand.

We can think of the markup as a percentage of the selling price, i.e.

$$P = \frac{P - MC}{P} \tag{9.A.4}$$

Since for profit maximization MR = MC, we can substitute MC for MR to get:

$$\frac{P - MC}{P} = \frac{P - MR}{P} = \frac{P - P\left(1 + (1/e)\right)}{P} = -\frac{1}{e} \tag{9.A.5}$$

Thus if the price elasticity of demand were -2, the markup as a proportion of price should be 1/2.

APPENDIX 9.B

9.B.1   Derivation of the Dorfmann–Steiner theorem

Most sources use calculus to derive the theorem, as was done in the original. Martin (1988, pp. 202–203), however, shows it without using calculus, and we will follow that path here.

The decision to advertise can be viewed as one in which the firm increases advertising to the point where the increased revenue from advertising equals the increased cost. The increased revenue is the price of the units sold, P (assuming no change in price) times the increase in the number of units, i.e. ΔQ. The increase in cost comes from two sources: the marginal cost of producing the increased units $c\Delta Q$, plus the increase in the number of advertisements, ΔA, times the cost per advertisement, PA, in equation form:

$$P\Delta Q = c\Delta Q + \Delta APA \qquad (9.B.1)$$

We can take $c\Delta Q$ across to the left-hand side, and take out ΔQ to give:

$$\Delta Q(P - c) = \Delta APA \qquad (9.B.2)$$

Dividing both sides by ΔAP gives:

$$\frac{\Delta Q}{\Delta A} = \frac{(P - C)}{P} = \frac{PA}{P} \qquad (9.B.3)$$

and multiplying both sides by A, the total number of advertisements, and dividing by Q, gives:

$$\frac{\Delta Q \cdot A}{\Delta A \cdot Q} = \frac{(P - C)}{P} = \frac{A \cdot PA}{P \cdot Q} \qquad (9.B.4)$$

The first term of Equation 9.B.4 is the advertising elasticity of demand; the second is the optimal markup, which is equal to the reciprocal of the price elasticity of demand; on the right-hand side, the numerator is the total expenditure on advertising, and the denominator is the total revenue, alias the total sales.

For those with calculus, this result can be found in most texts on managerial economics, e.g. Reekie and Crook (1987, pp. 315–320).

FURTHER READING

The ideas of profit maximization under monopoly can be found in any economics textbook, although the 'optimal markup' is less commonly shown.

The idea of a marginal revenue of service and the dual optimization problem is treated mathematically in:

Straszheim, M.R. (1974) The determination of airline fares and load factors: Some oligopoly models. *Journal of Transport Economics and Policy*, September, 261–273.

The author would be grateful to find other simpler and more accessible texts!

Price discrimination is handled by almost all managerial economics texts, but only

Bliss, C. (1988) A theory of retail pricing. *Journal of Industrial Economics*, **xxxvi** (4) (June), 375–391

handles the question of retail pricing in a theoretically satisfactory way, although it requires good mathematics to understand it.

Oligopoly

10.1 INTRODUCTION

The key factor in oligopoly is the rivalry between firms because of their small number. Rivalry is the term used for competition where the actions of one firm have a direct impact on the other firms. Thus, for example, if one firm drops its price in order to increase its output the rival firms will suffer a direct and noticeable fall in their demand.

This implies that, as in monopolistic competition, we have to consider two aspects of demand, the market demand which gives the amount purchased if all prices move together, and the firm's own demand if it manages to alter its price and other firms keep theirs constant. The difference between monopolistic competition and oligopoly is that under oligopoly it will be extremely unlikely that the rival firms will not respond, whereas in monopolistic competition they would only change their prices or output because it was a sensible thing for them to do individually; they would be so numerous that no firm would feel the direct impact of any other individual firm's policy changes.

This chapter will look at oligopoly in three main ways:

1. We will look at what are called naive approaches, where the firms are assumed to believe that their rivals will not react to their policy changes – and here we will look at Cournot oligopoly where the policy variable is the quantity produced, and Bertrand oligopoly where the policy variable is price; we will examine these particularly in relation to the marginal revenue of service as identified under monopoly.
2. We will consider briefly two simple deterministic views of the way rivals will respond; this will lead us to examine the so-called kinked demand curve view of oligopoly, where the motivation is the jealous protection of the firm's market share, and the problems of collusion in the form of cartels.
3. We will consider what happens when rivals are expected to respond but according to strategic decisions made by all the firms concerned. To do this we will introduce the notions of game theory and its application to collusion, and entry deterrence by various strategic ploys, including the establishment of a reputation for aggressive response to entry. The chapter ends with a discussion of advertising decisions under oligopoly.

10.2 NAIVE APPROACHES: COURNOT AND BERTRAND

The first of the two 'naive' approaches we shall discuss is that of Cournot, who put forward the first model of oligopolistic competition; this makes the assumption that competitors decide on the quantity to put onto the market, and the price is determined by some process of bidding according to that quantity. The second approach comes from Bertrand, who countered some years later with a model in which the rivals set the price, and the market demand decided the quantity. We shall see that this has very different results from Cournot's model. Under Cournot, a price somewhat lower than the monopoly price is achieved; under Bertrand, price is driven down to the level of marginal cost, a level that makes it the most aggressively competitive of markets. Both are called 'naive' models because the rivals do not seem to learn of their impact on the other's policies, and operate as if there was going to be no impact. This does not invalidate them altogether, however, firstly because there are situations where one has to make such assumptions, and secondly because the mechanisms identified within these models form the basis for thinking about the possible reactions of rivals in a less naive way.

10.2.1 Cournot: Rivalry on quantity

The oldest model of oligopolistic rivalry was developed by Cournot in 1838. He assumed that there were two identical firms and they decided how much to produce and put onto the market; the market would decide the price by the normal process of supply and demand. We will add the assumption that they have zero marginal costs; this just makes the analysis simpler. It is easy to incorporate a positive marginal cost or indeed different marginal costs for each firm. Each firm assumes that its rival's output will be kept constant for the next period.

Let us therefore consider the situation of a firm – firm A – which was acting as a monopolist and was producing an output Q_1. Let us put it in its original context of firms selling bottled spring water in France, so that we shall talk of output in terms of cases and the value in terms of Francs. A second firm now enters – firm B – and assumes that firm A will keep producing Q_1. It therefore faces a demand curve equivalent to the market demand curve minus Q_1 and calculates its profit maximizing output given that demand curve. The market will then determine the price, given that combination of outputs. This is illustrated in Figure 10.1.

This of course has altered the situation for firm A, whose price has now gone down from 50 to 25 francs. If firm A now assumes that firm B's output will remain constant at 25 cases, it will face the demand curve minus 25. So it can work out its optimal output given that new demand curve; this would be 37.5 cases. This process can obviously be repeated until an equilibrium is established; although we should never assume that there will be an equilibrium as the result of such interactions, there is one in this case.

Rather than repeat that process indefinitely, we can work it out by the

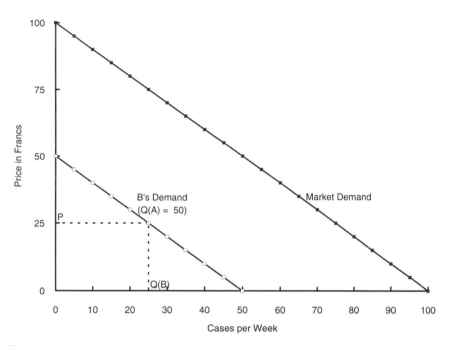

Figure 10.1 Demand and price under Cournot oligopoly, immediately after entry of firm B.

use of **reaction functions**. A reaction function is the set of optimal responses to any rival's policy. In this case, it is the reaction of firm B to each possible level of output by A.

Since firm B has a demand curve which is the market demand curve less the committed output produced by A, we can calculate the marginal revenue and hence the appropriate output for firm B for all possible levels of A's output. Let us assume a demand curve for the market, as illustrated in Figure 10.1, of:

$$P = 100 - Q \tag{10.1}$$

If we call the output of firm A Q_A, and the output of firm B Q_B, we can then simply substitute $(Q_A + Q_B)$ for the quantity Q in Equation 10.1 to get:

$$P = 100 - (Q_A + Q_B) \tag{10.2}$$

By substituting the above equation into Equation 9.1 for the marginal revenue, bearing in mind that Q in the context of firm B's marginal revenue is Q_B, since it is only on their own output that reductions in price affect the firm, and that dP/dQ is -1 (from Equation 10.1, we can see that for each unit change in Q there is a unit change in P):

$$MR_B = P + Q_B \cdot \frac{dP}{dQ} = 100 - (Q_A + Q_B) + (Q_B) \cdot (-1) \tag{10.3}$$

Thus:

$$MR_B = 100 - Q_A - 2Q_B \qquad (10.4)$$

and since $MR_B = MC = 0$, this gives us our reaction function for B, since it represents B's optimal output response to any level of output for firm A:

$$0 = 100 - Q_A - 2Q_B$$

$$Q_B = (100 - Q_A)/2 \qquad (10.5)$$

A few of the values for this reaction function are set out in Table 10.1. The whole function is illustrated in Figure 10.2.

Table 10.1 Illustration of B's reaction function

Q_A	Q_B	Price
0	50	50
10	45	45
20	40	40
50	25	25
80	10	10
98	1	1

Since firm A faces exactly the same conditions as firm B, firm A's reaction function will have exactly the same form as B's, but with the subscripts interchanged:

$$Q_A = 50 - Q_B/2 \qquad (10.6)$$

This is shown plotted on the graph in Figure 10.3 with firm B's reaction curve from Figure 10.2. It is now a simple matter to trace the path of adjustment of output as each firm responds to the other. The path chosen starts with the position of firm A as the profit maximizing monopolist, with an output of 50 cases. It can be seen that the result converges to an equilibrium position where both produce 33.3.

This is a **Nash equilibrium**: an equilibrium in which neither party can improve its situation given the other party's strategy.

To summarize, the Nash–Cournot equilibrium for a duopoly at constant and equal marginal costs is at 1.3 × the level of output of a monopoly. It can therefore be seen that profits will not be as high as in a collusive monopoly. In the above case, a collusive monopoly will share profits of 2500 francs (50 francs × 50 cases of output), whereas the duopoly shares 2222 francs profits (price of 33.3 × 66.6 cases of output).

This may seem a sterile exercise, since it is usually prices that are fixed and customers decide how much to buy at those given prices. While this is true for manufacturing and most services, firstly it may be that firms will target an output level and know enough about the demand conditions to estimate the price required to achieve that target level, and secondly (and for us more importantly, perhaps) in almost all services we have to work with the marginal revenue of service given a price, and this is equivalent to

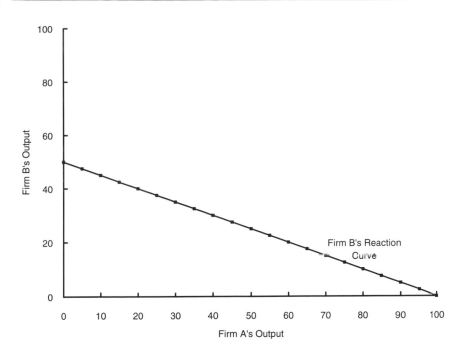

Figure 10.2 Cournot oligopoly, firm B's reaction function.

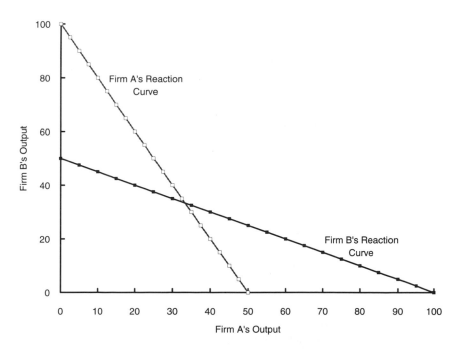

Figure 10.3 Reaction functions under Cournot oligopoly.

fixing the output in Cournot oligopoly. We will now examine a model for this derived by Straszheim (1974) for airline operations, in a simpler version by the author for bus operations.

10.2.2 Cournot oligopoly in service industries

Let us assume that bus passengers would arrive at equal intervals throughout the hour and that buses depart at equal intervals, and that potential passengers are indifferent as to the company or the type of bus. The passengers would be likely to take the first bus that arrived, and so the share of the route passengers for operator X is likely to be equal to the share of that operator's buses on the route:

$$\frac{n_x}{T} \tag{10.7}$$

where n_x is the number of buses put on by operator x and T is the total number of buses on the route. Assuming a single fare, and costs that are independent of the numbers of passengers per bus, the formula for profits per bus is:

$$\pi = \frac{K \cdot f - C}{T} \tag{10.8}$$

where π is the profits per bus, K is the total number of passenger trips per time period on the route, f is the fare per passenger trip and C is the cost of running the bus.

The specification of a full demand model for bus travel on a particular route would require more detail than is likely to be available to the operator, since it must have substantial cross elasticities with the generalized cost of motor and pedestrian travel, and be very dependent on the changing opportunities in the urban area, including the alternatives in terms of bus travel itself. The assumption of a fixed demand for travel, with the firm's demand dependent on the proportion of the route supplied, in the fashion set out above, may therefore be a useful heuristic device.

The total revenue of the company with $(n - 1)$ buses is:

$$TR_{(n-1)} = \frac{(n - 1) \cdot K \cdot f}{T - 1} \tag{10.9}$$

whereas with n buses the total revenue of the company is:

$$TR_n = \frac{n \cdot K \cdot f}{T} \tag{10.10}$$

Thus the marginal revenue of service for the extra bus from $(n - 1)$ buses to n buses will be the difference in total revenues, i.e.:

$$MRoS_n = TR_n - TR_{(n-1)}$$

$$MRoS_n = \frac{n \cdot K \cdot f}{T} - \frac{(n - 1) \cdot K \cdot f}{T - 1} = \frac{K \cdot f (T - n)}{T(T - 1)} \qquad (10.11)$$

This can be illustrated by choosing a value for the marginal cost of service, and graphing the two reaction functions. Let us again assume a duopoly, with equal MCS = 20 fares. We therefore set MRS = MCS = 20f; and let us also assume as in the previous example that there are 180 passengers per hour, thus $K = 180$. It will also be convenient to express T in its two components, n the number of buses put on by firm B, and a the number of buses put on by firm A. Thus $T = n + a$. Thus making those substitutions, Equation 10.11 becomes:

$$20f = \frac{180 f a}{(n + a)(n + a - 1)} \qquad (10.12)$$

Dividing both sides by 20f, and cross-multiplying we get:

$$(n + a)(n + a - 1) - 9a = 0 \qquad (10.13)$$

The normal method for quadratic equations gives the solution:

$$n = \frac{-(2a - 1) + [(2a - 1)^2 - 4a(a - 10)]^{1/2}}{2} \qquad (10.14)$$

This reaction function is symmetrical and so can be plotted onto both axes to give the two reaction functions in Figure 10.4.

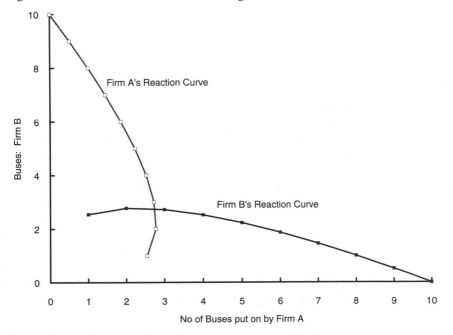

Figure 10.4 Reaction functions of Cournot oligopoly in bus operations.

Once again this suggests a determinate outcome at about three buses per hour each, and again it is at 1.3 times the level of output of the monopolist, if one makes allowances for the indivisible nature of a bus, and would correspondingly be at a lower level of profits. It would thus pay both firms to arrange to reduce output and share the route at a lower level of service.

There are several interesting points to note about this model. Firstly, we will consider why it is that even with one company operating eight buses it would still pay the other operator to put on one bus, whereas the monopolist would not wish to put on more than four; this is particularly relevant to the question of how many operators will want to run buses on a route. Secondly, we will discuss what would happen if one of the operators had lower marginal costs than the other, for example by running midibuses. (Minibuses are normally defined as those with about 8–12 seats; these are only economical for specialist use or thinly-populated rural areas. For urban running, midibuses with 15–35 seats are more appropriate.)

The competitive rationale for reaction curves

At first sight it would appear that these reaction functions are similar to the normal pattern of marginal revenue. This is not really so. The reason the marginal revenue of service declines with increasing numbers of buses run by firm A is that the patronage for each new bus is taken from a mixture of the patrons of firm A and other operators. Thus the larger the proportion of firm A's buses on the route, the more it is competing with itself. Eventually as a monopolist, the company is competing entirely with itself, and, as shown in the previous chapter, it has no incentive to put on more capacity than is required to carry the passengers. (Note that we have not added the effect of potential generation of traffic into the reaction functions.)

The implication of these reaction functions is therefore that if it is as cheap to put on one bus as to put on many, in other words there are no economies of scale on a particular route, it would almost always pay a new operator to enter a route with a bus. We should therefore see lots of different operators all operating single buses on a route. This is not what we observe, however. In general, routes seem to be shared between very few operators. Why? The following are pure conjectures, but it seems likely that:

1. A single bus is liable to predation: the large operators deliberately run late so as to pick up the passengers just before the lone driver arrives. They might even go so far as to run one bus in front and one behind him, just to make sure he does not pull the same trick on the following bus. (This will be discussed more fully in Chapter 12.)
2. It may also be that the passengers avoid the single bus, because they lack information about its fares, route and general reliability; informing them will involve the operator in costs.

3. Contrary to the received wisdom, there may be operational problems that make running one bus on a route more expensive than operating several.

Different costs

If one operator has lower costs than the other, that operator's reaction function would need to be calculated not on the basis of a marginal cost of say 20 times the fare, but on a lower figure. For example, it was widely reported that midibuses cost roughly the same to purchase and run *per seat* as large buses. This would imply that the marginal cost of service per bus would be proportional to the number of seats, in other words in the proportion of approximately 80 for a double decker, 60 for a large single decker, and only 30 for a midibus. Thus for the company running midibuses, Equation 10.12 would need to be set equal not to $20f$ but $(20 \times 30/80)f = 7.5f$. The effect of this would be to increase the number of buses put on by that operator to the point where the share of the route run would be equal to the ratio of the marginal costs. In our example the operator of the cheaper midibuses would run eight for every three double deckers. The effect is illustrated in Figure 10.5.

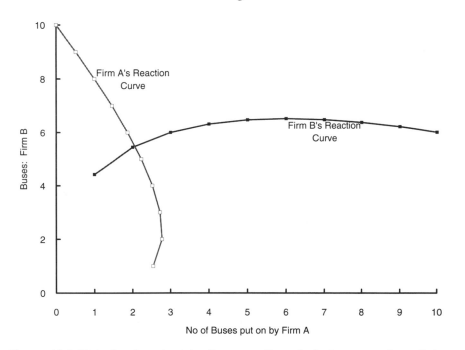

Figure 10.5 Reaction functions in Cournot oligopoly in bus operations; B is a lower cost operator.

In both versions of Cournot oligopoly, some external mechanism has to be found to explain why new firms do not continue to enter, thereby gradually weakening the interaction and increasing competitiveness. This was indeed the hope in both bus and airline operation after deregulation.

However, after a period of reduced industrial concentration, in both US airlines and UK bus and coach operations, there has been retrenchment by small operators, takeovers, and eventually patterns which are often close to monopoly have reasserted themselves. This will be discussed in the concluding section of this chapter. The Cournot and other models are, however, important building blocks in this final discussion, and so we continue with discussion of them, starting with the Bertrand model.

10.2.3 Bertrand: Rivalry on price

In 1883, the French economist Bertrand pointed out that if firms in an oligopoly competed on price rather than on quantity as Cournot had suggested, the results would be very different. Let us for simplicity retain the same scenario as the Cournot model above: two firms producing an identical product, with zero marginal costs, with a market demand curve $P = 100 - Q$. Let the situation start with firm A having a monopoly and therefore charging the monopoly price of 50 francs, and producing 50 cases per week.

Enter firm B, who sees a profit opportunity in A's substantial profits of 2500 francs per week. What demand curve does he face? His product is identical, and thus in the presence of well-informed consumers, his demand is perfectly elastic at the market price; that is to say they will switch products entirely for a mere centime off the rival's price. Let us say he cuts the price to 49 francs. He then captures the whole market, and sells 51 cases.

Firm A now faces no demand, and so cuts its price to 48 francs, and captures the entire market, now 52 cases. Firm B cuts its price to 47 francs, and so on.

Does this tit-for-tat price cutting go on indefinitely, or at least until they are giving away the output? In this case since marginal costs are zero, that is indeed the only logical end. More generally, it would not be expected that a firm would sell at below marginal cost, since then even though marginal revenue equals price, as in this case, selling below marginal cost would involve a loss on each item sold (a loss in the economic sense, of not even making a contribution to overheads). It is not obvious at this stage what share-out there would be between the firms; it is always suggested that if they both offer the same product at the same price they would divide the market equally; there is no basis for this. It should be rephrased as being a random division of demand, with each having equal probabilities of getting any particular proportion. Try selling that to shareholders! This does of course point up a very serious implication: namely, if goods really are homogeneous, prices will almost certainly be approximately equal, and competition will be savage, with market share being decided on potentially very small differences of quality, or sweetener. This is the basis for Sutton's (1991) recent 'discovery' that under these conditions a quasi-monopoly often develops, particularly where there are substantial sunk costs in the form of major investments, as in sugar refining and salt; only with quasi-monopoly does the situation cease to be so precarious.

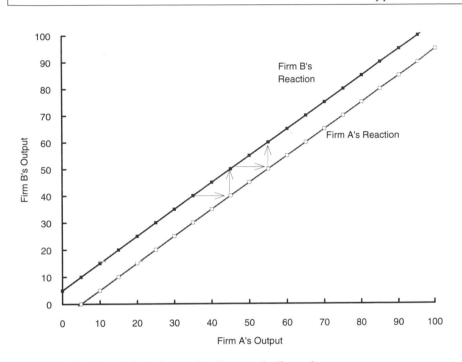

Figure 10.6 Reaction function under Bertrand oligopoly.

Reaction functions under Bertrand oligopoly

Whereas the reaction functions in the Cournot model conveniently lead to a convergence at an industry equilibrium, and this process actually involves adapting to the rival's behaviour by **accommodation**, thus allowing him market room, the Bertrand reaction functions involve each rival going for market domination by cutting price at each stage; there is thus no equilibrium (Figure 10.6).

There is an exact equivalent of this behaviour in the context of capacity, in bus and airline operations etc. It takes the form of at least matching every increase in the rival's capacity, which is what appeared to happen in many places in Britain when urban buses were deregulated, with reports of 'wall-to-wall buses' in Glasgow, Inverness and Hereford. In Edinburgh there was certainly some ludicrous overbussing of some routes. In the airline market, Johnson (1988) noted non-accommodation and some increase in capacity on the Edinburgh and Glasgow routes by the incumbent British Airways, and improvements in their levels of service in the form of breakfast and other meals. In the USA there was a massive increase in the numbers of flights on most routes after deregulation, but this has since fallen back to more moderate levels. Perhaps the most glaring case of this sort of competition was the response by British Airways to the entry of Laker onto the North Atlantic routes. The response to Virgin has been rather similar, with the allegation of dirty tricks suck as hacking into the booking systems to divert passengers already booked with Virgin onto BA flights.

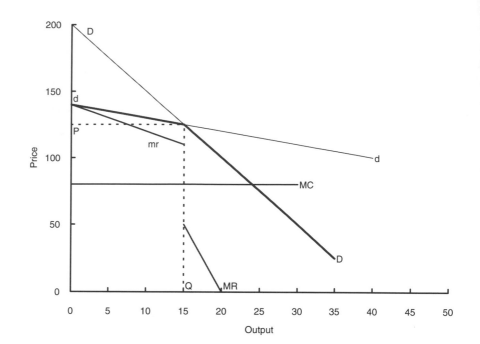

Figure 10.7 The kinked demand curve.

10.3 DETERMINISTIC INTERACTION

10.3.1 The kinked demand curve

The **kinked demand curve** represents the formalization of one view of oligopolistic interaction. Discussions with industrialists in the 1930s suggested that they believed that their rivals were jealous of market share and would therefore respond to any attempts at gaining market share by any individual firm. As implied by the Bertrand approach, one obvious way of doing this is by price cuts, and the obvious response is for the rivals to cut their prices also. If on the other hand one firm wishes to raise prices, it would lose market share, and the rest would correspondingly gain it and so would be content to let the firm raise its price alone. Clearly this implies that the price will stick at whatever the level is in the market, and will only move when all firms feel it necessary.

The fuller analysis is presented in Figure 10.7. We will consider each item in turn:

1. The firm faces the potential demand curve DD, sloping from the top of the graph, which would represent the demand if all firms moved their prices up or down in unison; it therefore represents the firm's share of the market demand. (It is useful to know that such a share of market demand will have the same elasticity as the market demand curve itself, since to keep equal shares, both the change and the base quantity of which that change is a proportion will have to be the same fraction of

the market demand. As the elasticity of market demand is sometimes known to a fair approximation, this is useful information if all are changing prices together and shares are expected to remain constant.)

If the rival firms will not let any single member cut the price on its own, it is this demand curve that will be relevant for cuts in price from the point of equilibrium at the time, where the price P and the quantity Q indicate the existing market situation. Hence the section below this price is shown in bold.

2. This demand curve DD has a marginal revenue curve MR, of which we show only the positive portion which finishes at the output of 20 units, and is shown as starting from below the quantity sold at the market price, denoted by the dotted line at 15 units. This is the relevant section, given that this demand curve is relevant from this point.

3. The firm also faces a potential demand curve dd (starting at a price of 140), which is the demand curve that the firm would face if all other firms kept their prices constant when it changed its price. As established in the introduction, the rival firms will be delighted to let any maverick raise its price, so that they can pick up at least a part of its market share. This demand curve is thus the relevant one for prices above P, and this section is shown in bold.

4. The corresponding marginal revenue curve for that section of the demand curve is shown as mr.

5. As stated previously, the condition for profit maximizing is always that marginal cost should equal marginal revenue; here, however, we have a discontinuous marginal revenue curve, and so any marginal cost that falls within the discontinuity will be the profit maximizing level. As can be seen, this would be true for any marginal cost between 50 and 110 units.

This appears to have all the elements of a good theory: an empirical base in the views of industrialists, a rational exposition of the mechanisms which conforms to the wider implications of the rest of theory about the firm. Unfortunately, it docs not appcar to conform to reality in that studies have shown that oligopolies do not in general have more stable (i.e. rigid) prices than other industries. In periods of inflation, this is not surprising; while marginal cost might be 'sticky', it would by the normal processes of inflation gradually be pushed up to the point at which the more elastic demand curve's marginal revenue (mr in the diagram) would intersect with it. Under these circumstances, it would pay the firm to raise its prices even if its rivals do not. However, since the inflation would presumably be affecting all firms similarly, the price rise might well be followed rapidly by other firms. Furthermore, this is still a 'naive' approach, in that all firms are facing constraints on their prices, due to their interactions, and yet they do nothing to solve the situation. Game theory has given us some suggestion as to how they could be expected to do so, without invalidating the view of each industrialist that they dare not go it alone. Before considering this, it is worth looking at the traditional analysis of cartel operation, since like the Cournot and Bertrand approaches it gives an understanding of some of the mechanisms that operate in the more sophisticated strategic approach embodied in game theory.

10.3.2 Cartels and collusion

Cartels are in general illegal, and so one must add the problem of judicial action to any problems of coordination and enforcement by members. We shall see that there are likely to be problems of both sorts in any cartel. It is clear from the analysis of Cournot and Bertrand oligopoly that the monopoly price would lead to higher profits in the industry as a whole and that it would therefore pay members of an industry to collude in order to obtain that monopoly price. However, this implies that they can agree how to share the proceeds, and this, as we shall see, is not a trivial problem.

From Chapter 9, it is evident that the basis for decisions on the monopoly output and price revolve around the marginal costs and marginal revenues. Let us for the moment assume that the product is homogeneous – like salt or wheat, for example – so that marginal revenues should be common to all firms in the industry. Each firm would then wish to produce at the point where its marginal costs equalled that common marginal revenue. However, this would mean that a firm with high marginal costs would only produce a very small share of the total market, in contrast to one with low marginal costs. If the marginal costs were a small proportion of the total costs, this would leave the low quantity producer severely disadvantaged. The solution normally suggested by economists is that the high quantity producer share its profits with the low quantity producer in order to ensure that overall industry profits are being maximized (production at a higher marginal cost than necessary will clearly be reducing those profits). It therefore follows that unless the lowest marginal cost firm is willing to share its profits in this way, there will be an insuperable problem of division of output between producers. Naturally this can be overcome by agreements, but of course these will not fully maximize profits and may leave the lowest cost producer feeling that it is giving up more than is just.

If the agreement on price and quantity can be reached, this leaves each firm with a very strong incentive to cheat. Depending on the elasticity of demand, each individual firm can sneak extra output onto the market at some price just below the agreed monopoly price while still making a very handsome markup. For example, if the elasticity of market demand were -4 and one of the firms was allocated one-quarter of the market, with a price cut of 1% that firm could increase its output by 16% if it could negotiate a special deal with some bulk purchaser to take that amount at 1% below market price. Knowing the optimal markup will be 25% in this context, this means a 24% markup on the discounted portion and increases profits therefore by a very large amount, provided that the firm did not have to make additional investments to provide this output.

The incentive to cheat means that it is important that the cartel has some way of verifying that its members are behaving 'honestly'. This is obviously difficult unless they have complete inspection powers, which itself implies an amazing degree of trust. The account of the Italian Flat Glass cartel (*Official Journal of the European Communities*, 1989a) provides a readable and amusing example of how such cartels are brought to book. This product is fairly typical of those where cartels are feasible: there should be a relatively homogeneous product and relatively few players in the market both on the supply side and on the demand side. It would thus appear that it might be very difficult to organize them in the service industries; however, this is not so. There are several famous examples of cartels still in operation. IATA, which controls international air traffic and fares, the Shipping Conferences, which meet to agree shipping rates and services for international waters, and the international telecommunications agreements which are all conducted between a few large firms, often with the participation of governments. The other means by which such cartels are established are by trade associations, who may agree prices without necessarily agreeing quantities for each firm. This is still generally illegal under European Community law, and while it has largely been stamped out in Britain, it is a major part of the work of the French Conseil de la Concurrence. There may also be considerable potential in the field of local authority subcontracting. Indeed, there are six large French companies which provide many of the local authority services as franchisees; it is suspected that they do not compete over-vigorously.

10.4 STRATEGIC APPROACHES

10.4.1 Game theory

The development of strategic approaches in economic theory may be traced back to the development of game theory, although elements were present long before that. The initial model, which provides a useful introduction to this, is known as the Prisoner's Dilemma. It can be used to support most of the approaches discussed above, except for collusion, providing that there is only one round of the game. With further rounds, the possibility of punishment for hostile behaviour and reward for accommodating behaviour is introduced, and with it comes a means of developing tacit collusion: that is to say, collusion without any explicit agreements ever being reached. This pattern of behaviour will be shown to vary, depending on the amount of information that is available and on the position from which each player starts, and it therefore introduces the potential for making strategic decisions prior to the start of interaction, which can influence the outcome.

Section 10.4.2 will therefore introduce the basic Prisoner's Dilemma game and its application to economics. It will then consider the implications of repeated rounds of the Prisoner's Dilemma game; thereafter it will look at the question of entry by new firms and the strategic issues surrounding entry deterrence. This will be shown to rely on the credibility of the threats posed by existing firms, and various of these threats will be examined for credibility. In particular, it is not credible that there are such things as contestable markets in which the mere threat of entry is enough to ensure that prices are kept to the minimum sustainable level.

10.4.2 The Prisoner's Dilemma

The **Prisoner's Dilemma** refers to games where the best possible outcome for each individual is one in which he or she takes aggressive action and the other party does not; the next best outcome is for both to be accommodating, and the worst outcome is for a party to be accommodating when the other is aggressive. The original version which gives it its name is the old conundrum relating to the two prisoners, Ricardo and Bentham, who are caught with stolen goods from a recent robbery. They are kept in separate cells and so cannot communicate. Each knows that if he shops the other, he will only get a light sentence for receiving stolen goods (say 1 year). If they both keep their mouths shut and admit to nothing, they will both get a moderate sentence (say 3 years) for being accessories to the robbery. If one squeals, the 'honest' party that does not will get a long sentence (say 10 years). If they try to shop each other, they will get 6 years each. This could be formalized into a payoff matrix, as shown in Table 10.2.

Table 10.2 Payoff matrix for the Prisoner's Dilemma, years in prison for Ricardo/Bentham, respectively

	Ricardo	
Bentham	Squeals	Keeps mum
Squeals	6/6	10/1
Keeps mum	1/10	3/3

Now under these conditions, what does the rational, selfish prisoner do? Let us look at Ricardo's options. If he squeals and so does Bentham, they get 6 years each. If they both keep mum, they get 3 years each. If Bentham is a mug and keeps mum while Ricardo squeals, they get 10 and 1 years, respectively. Thus, whatever Bentham does, it is best for Ricardo to squeal; in either case it reduces his penalty compared with keeping mum. He also knows that Bentham faces the same dilemma, and so will be tempted to squeal. It is thus clearly sensible for him to squeal.

In the economic sphere we can substitute firms for Ricardo and Bentham, and aggressive price and output policies for squealing (accommodating policies being the parallel to keeping mum). Under this scenario, we have a powerful motive for acting competitively, and so we might justify a relatively lax policy on cartels and collusion, because they are so unlikely. A few moments' thought will show that this is not a good parallel either to the prisoners' case or to the economic situation, because it implicitly assumes that there is no further possible contact between the two sides. In reality, of course, life goes on, and there is likely to be either a return match, even if only when the shopped prisoner comes out on parole; one or both may even have taken out a contract on the other to ensure that there is no squealing. Under these circumstances the payoffs with the death contracts might be as shown in Table 10.3.

Table 10.3 Payoff matrix for the Prisoner's Dilemma in the presence of contracts, years in prison for Ricardo/Bentham, respectively

	Ricardo	
Bentham	Squeals	Keeps mum
Squeals	6 + death/ 6 + death	10/ 1 + death
Keeps mum	1 + death/ 10	3/3

This makes the payoff very different, and the worse solution in each case is to squeal. The equivalent in economics would be if the opposition have committed themselves to a market in some way, such that it will always pay them to fight. The question is whether there are any such commitments.

Even without the sort of commitment suggested above, if the game is repeated year after year, this might change it considerably. We saw under Bertrand competition that aggressive behaviour could imply rapid loss of profits, and we showed that Bertrand competition was equivalent to any really aggressive rivalry that implied the upward sloping reaction functions, such as matching the rival's increases in service on a one-for-one basis. Furthermore in economic life, although almost all our models imply instant reactions, the real world does not respond so quickly. Thus if a Bertrand style price war was started, as was done by Tesco in the late 1960s, the opposition, mainly Sainsbury, could respond vigorously, under-cutting the firm that started it, and thus reducing its profits below the level it had hoped to achieve by grabbing market share with low prices. The opposition would be alerted that future steps might be even more damaging; in fact after a period of low prices (or analogous over-servicing of air or bus routes) it seems likely that the aggressor might try to raise prices, in the hope that the signal would be accepted and that the other would follow. In that case, the path towards tacit collusion is begun. The collusion might only extend to price rises, and not to a share of the market; this might be left to competition on other aspects of quality, promotions and advertising, where similar wars could break out.

In this world of strategic play, however, things may not be all they seem. It is *possible* that such price wars might themselves be collusive activities, with the dual objectives of putting the Office of Fair Trading off the scent of an unduly cosy relationship between major players, and/or of pushing minor players into bankruptcy so that the firms starting the war could take over their market share. Akehurst (1984) provides an account of the Tesco–Sainsbury war of the late 1960s.

10.4.3 Threats credible and incredible

The essence of a credible threat is that it should be in the person's interest to carry out the threat when the time comes to implement it. The repeated prisoner's dilemma relies for its effectiveness on some punishment that is likely to occur if a non-cooperative policy is followed. Failure to match the opponent in a price war leads to loss of market and profits; thus a threat to match price cuts is likely to be carried out and is credible. What about the threat of a larger bus or air operator to cut prices across the network, if a smaller rival follows certain policies? Unless it is known to both parties that the smaller rival is near to bankruptcy, such a threat is unlikely to be credible: the larger its market share, the larger the losses that will be made by the bigger firm. Similarly we may ask whether the threat to swamp a route with extra buses is credible; if it goes beyond the point indicated by the Cournot reaction function suggested above, it is generally not. This depends however on the signal such a response would give to the rival. We discuss this next in the context of Entry Deterrence.

10.4.4 Entry deterrence

Section 8.4 dealt with the issues of barriers to entry and their relationship with rates of entry. Monopoly and oligopoly would degenerate into more competitive structures in the presence of entry, and even if this were limited, sharing out a market with more rivals is not a pleasant prospect. Thus the ability to deter new entry would seem to be of interest to any monopolist or oligopolist, and has certainly been a theme in the economics literature. We can now examine this question with the aid of the ideas about credible threats, and using the notion of an entry deterrence game. Before doing that, however, it is worth considering the plausibility of the simple model of entry deterrence which is important in the literature and which, like the kinked demand curve model, seems to reflect an issue mentioned by industrialists.

The 'Sylos postulate' suggested that firms would deter entry by setting output, and hence price, at a level which would not allow sufficient market room for any new entrants, because the incumbent firm would maintain this level of output after entry and this together with the entrant's output would cause the price to fall to a level at which the entrant could not cover average costs. This is now generally discredited, since (i) it implies the willingness of a monopolist to sacrifice profits for an indefinite period in order to forestall entry; (ii) as entry usually takes time, it would seem

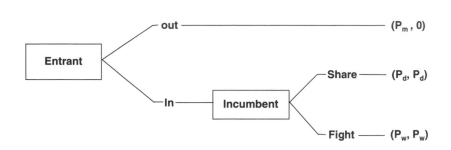

Figure 10.8

much more useful to react as entry is being undertaken to defeat the entrant, or possibly to accommodate him or her; and finally and most devastatingly, (iii) the threat to keep output at the same level after entry is not credible. Indeed, if the entrant wishes to apply the same logic, it could be the incumbent that is forced out, because if the entrant wishes to force the expansion of output, and both firms make losses, the one with the larger market share is liable to make the largest losses. The incumbent would have to rely on the presence of sunk costs, which would give an advantage in the war to the death implied by such a situation. Such sunk costs however, may be a 'strategic commitment', analogous to the contract taken out on each other by the prisoners.

The simplest analysis of entry deterrence is now usually considered as a game of the type illustrated in Figure 10.8, attributable to Dixit (1982).

The symbols in brackets are the profits of the incumbent and entrant, respectively, under different scenarios. They are as follows: Pm is the incumbent's monopoly profit, in the absence of entry; 0 means that the entrant thus has zero profit; Pd is the profits of both firms, if they share the market; and Pw is the profits of both firms if they have a price war.

It is usually assumed that Pm > Pd > 0 > Pw. It is obvious that the threat to make losses to deter entry is not credible when there is the alternative of making a rather more modest profit by accommodating the entrant. It is now considered to be a general requirement that the game should be credible at each stage; an equilibrium reached with threats that are credible at each stage is said to be a **perfect equilibrium**.

The discussion then revolves around the question of whether there are commitments that make it profitable to fight, and thus make entry deterrence credible. Following Dixit again, the game would then have two branches, one the exact replica of the first game, and the second of the first game but with the addition of commitment. This is reproduced in Figure 10.9.

The only new symbol is C, the cost of the commitment. This provides a credible threat, if Pw > Pd − C, i.e. the incumbent would make greater losses in the event of sharing than from a price war. Since in the previous game, the expected outcome was Pd, the commitment is worth entering into if Pm − C > Pd, in other words, if monopoly profits minus the cost of the commitment are still greater than the profits that would remain if a

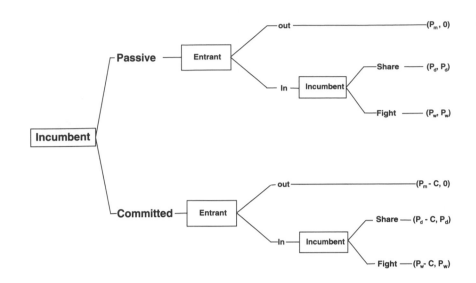

Figure 10.9 The entry deterrence game with commitment.

rival has to be accommodated. Dixit (1982) points out that any such commitment provides a double social loss: the losses from the monopoly power it generates, and the losses from the commitment used to generate the monopoly power. We will discuss this further in the next chapter.

Let us consider some candidates for this commitment:

- Sunk costs: possibly. We have already seen in the discussion of the Sylos postulate that overinvestment in capital would not in itself provide such a commitment; it would merely create redundant spare capacity. However if an investment in capital would so lower marginal costs at large scales of output that accounting losses would be made under accommodation (Pd) because the market was no longer large enough to offset these capital costs, then it might be credible to fight. This would only be convincing if the capital costs were sunk (as opposed to fixed) costs, in other words if the capital could not be resold at a price which would make sharing more profitable than fighting (thus making Pd − (losses on sale of capital) < Pw).

- Investment in goodwill by advertising: not possible as a signal of aggressive response to entry (but probably as a barrier through sunk costs). There are two possible consequences of massive investment in goodwill by heavy advertising and the building up of brand loyalty: firstly, that in spite of success among existing producers and existing products, the goodwill does not persist in the face of the new entrant's offering, in which case any extra advertising incurred merely to act as a deterrent will only have weakened the firm financially; and secondly, the goodwill sticks, customers remain loyal, but then the last thing the big player wants is a price war, with all those profits on the large output to loyal customers being cut by low prices. Under such circumstances, far from being aggressive, the firm should 'welcome' new entrants and indicate that it will not start a price war: 'That would be contrary to the industry's interests', and such statesman-like phrases spring to mind. This is the so-called 'Fat-Cat strategy' (Fudenberg and Tirole, 1984). The same source suggests that underinvestment in advertising, such that every bit of market share must be fought for, would lead to a 'lean and hungry look' and would therefore discourage entrants.

This does not mean that high advertising encourages entry, merely that it does not act as a signal that the incumbent will react aggressively to entry. It may act to deter entry, as we saw in Chapter 8, by making it expensive to enter, because the entrant will have to incur a large cost in order to make itself heard, and it may influence the entrant's view of the likely commercial success of the venture; if there is a 'fat-cat' incumbent, there is a risk that the entrant will not be able to cause a shift in brand loyalties, and as we noted before there are few costs so sunk as a failed advertising campaign. Thus the costs of exit through failing to shift brand loyalties are correspondingly high. There is a lot of evidence pointing to the difficulty of breaking down brand loyalty (Scherer and Ross, 1990). Sutton's (1991) work also implies this since it appears that many of the industries with strong primary brands have persisted with these strong brands for many decades which have remained the dominant brands in their expanding markets.

- Range packing: very probably. Range packing is the process of making sure that there are no niche markets to be exploited by new entrants by filling every known niche. The classic article on this subject is by Schmalensee (1978) in which he makes the very convincing case that the major breakfast cereal producers – Kelloggs, General Mills, General Foods and Quaker Oats – pursued exactly such a policy. The key element is that brand proliferation should take place before entry, since it otherwise implies a price or advertising war after entry, with disagreeable effects on profits. The equivalent in the service industries is particularly evident in air or bus timetabling, allowing no niche for potential new entrants to exploit. This might work to deter entry, but is likely to be a poor policy from the point of view of profitability. Thus it may be better to go for monopoly levels of service, and fight any attempted efforts at entry. The vigorous pursuit of new patients by pre-emptive visits to all new residents by a health practice would provide another example of this – it would of course just be as part of commitment to excellence of service.
- Reputation for aggression might also be a means of deterring entry. The discussion of this question goes back to Selten's (1978) discussion of the Chain Store Paradox, and is very clearly reviewed in Dixit's (1982) article. The situation envisaged is one in which a chain store has to decide whether to fight or accommodate a new entrant in one of the many markets in which it operates. Given that there are many markets, if fighting in one would discourage other would-be entrants it is likely to be

profitable in the long run. The paradox is that if information is perfect, there is only an incentive to try to fight new entrants into sub-markets if there is no 'final market', since it cannot be sensible to fight in that final market for the reasons discussed in the entry deterrence game. It is simply not a credible threat. If it is not credible to fight in the last market, it is also not credible in the previous one either for the same reason, and because you cannot gain a reputation unless you can persuade the entrants that you are irrational. Thus on this basis it is never sensible to fight.

Two other bases are possible: firstly, the reality may be that the market is essentially infinite, because successful entry into one place does not preclude repeated entry there, and the market is thus one equivalent to a statistical procedure 'with replacement'. Thus there is indeed an infinite queue of potential entrants and potential markets for them to fight in. Secondly, and more importantly, the situation changes if there is potential irrationality, or lack of information. If the incumbent *may* fight, then instead of the fully informed basis for a credible threat, there is the possibility that the incumbent might be deluded into fighting (or even not deluded in scenario one: that he assumes a market with replacement). This means that the entrant's decision is based on an assessment of the probability that the incumbent will fight, let us say of q; thus the decision is to go for the profit Pd, but now the equation for expected profit is $q(Pd) + (1 - q)Pw$, where Pw is a loss. This is much less attractive. It relies entirely on the reputation element embodied in q. This reputation element will be severely weakened if the incumbent has accommodated entry anywhere, since this sends the message that the incumbent will accommodate. Thus if the incumbent wishes to follow a strategy of entry deterrence by virtue of reputation as a fighter, he or she has to remember that the decision to fight is almost mandatory, since each decision to accommodate lowers q and hence makes entry and the costly fight more probable.

Consideration of reputation and entry deterrence demolishes the theory of **contestable markets**. This theory was applied in the context of the opening of bus operations to competition in the UK (White Paper on buses, 1984). The theory suggests that even where there is only one firm supplying the market, prices will be at the minimum feasible, if (i) there is equal access to the technology of production, (ii) there are no sunk costs, (iii) incumbents cannot change prices instantly, and (iv) consumers respond instantly to price increases. This is because, if the prices rise above the minimum, the potential entrants will actually enter, and serve the market at lower prices than the incumbent, and then exit costlessly (no sunk costs) if there is retaliation from the incumbent. This, however, relies absolutely on the assumptions that there are no sunk costs and that the incumbent cannot adjust prices faster than the consumers respond to the lower prices. If these assumptions do not hold we have the situation identified by Dixit and exemplified by Sutton (1991), where the competitiveness of the industry leads to low entry and domination by major producers, essentially because it is so competitive that no sensible potential entrant will actually think of entering the market.

10.4.5   Discussion of entry and concentration

Based on the arguments of Sutton (1991):

1. Entry is more probable as profits are seen to be higher (and incumbents softer); thus monopoly pricing by a cartel leads to maximum entry and minimum concentration. This would seem to be particularly likely if the firms are seen to be 'cosy' high-cost producers.
2. If accommodation, along the lines of a Cournot oligopoly, is taking place, profits will be at an intermediate level and hence entry would be moderately enticing.
3. If Bertrand-type price competition takes place, profits may be very low and entry will be unattractive, both because of low profits and because of the aggressive nature of the industry.

Sutton's (1991) great contribution is to marry these considerations with the traditional notions of barriers to entry relating to fixed costs and barriers to exit by virtue of sunk costs. Where these are present, the persistence of high levels of concentration becomes a consequence of the presence of these sunk costs.

Firstly, very high concentration persists where no product differentiation is possible, as in salt and sugar, and where Bertrand competition is likely because of the importance of fixed costs in total costs, which means that overcapacity through uncoordinated investment pushes all firms into deficit and precipitates price wars for survival. The plant which led to overcapacity is not saleable, and is thus a sunk cost.

Secondly, where product differentiation exists, but on stable products whose specifications are not subject to rapid technological change, such as foods, the expansion of markets may be achieved by the increase of advertising to retain (or gain) market share, thus leading to surprising levels of concentration; the dominant firms remain entrenched with high shares of the market and high profits. Entrants come and go at the margin around enterprises such as Coca Cola, Pepsi Cola, Campbells Soups, etc.

10.5   ADVERTISING UNDER OLIGOPOLY

As in all other aspects of pricing and firm policy, the decisions of oligopolists have to allow for an extra dimension, that of the response of their rivals. Thus the nice simple Dorfmann–Steiner formula has to be replaced with one that carries an extra term which reflects (i) the firm's own elasticity of demand in relation to the other firms' advertising, and (ii) the elasticity of response of other firms's advertising to an increase in the firm's own advertising. (Various fuller mathematical formulations will be found in Clarke, 1985 or Hay and Morris, 1991, p. 130.) As the first element must be assumed to be negative, it reduces the firm's own advertising elasticity of demand, and the second provides the multiplier on that decrease. We could add these into the formulation for the

Dorfmann–Steiner result to get an estimate of the benefits of advertising to the firm. Let us illustrate this with an example; assume:

- Firm's own advertising elasticity of demand (α: >0.12)
- Firm's own price elasticity of demand (absolute value) (η: 2.5)
- Firm's elasticity of demand with respect to *other* firm's advertising (A): -0.05
- *Other* firms' elasticity of advertising expenditure, with response to the firm's advertising (E) 0.5

Thus, applying the correction to the Dorfmann–Steiner formula:

$$\frac{\text{Advertising}}{\text{Sales}} = \frac{\alpha + (A \cdot E)}{\eta} = \frac{0.12 + (-0.05 \times 0.5)}{2.5} \tag{10.15}$$

The trouble is that this is a much more complex set of items to estimate. The impact of advertising on demand is always difficult to estimate, but to estimate how much of the change observed is due to one's own advertising and how much to the effectiveness of other firms' advertising is very difficult. The logic of the marginal revenue of service might be expected to apply; the lower one's share of the market, the higher one's expectation of shifting demand in one's own favour by product differentiation activities such as advertising. This must, however, depend on making a sufficient impact to be heard, which may be difficult if one is a small player.

Experience might indicate how other firms respond to increases in one's own advertising budget. This might be by a 'share of voice' mechanism, and this would indicate that if one had a sixth of the total market advertising budget, that they would match the proportional increase exactly so that the industry budget would go up by 6 times one's own increase – an example of Bertrand style reaction functions in advertising. This elasticity would therefore always be equal to one. If so, and all firms are therefore retaining their share of industry advertising, one might expect these effects to cancel out, and the firm's own advertising elasticity to be equal to that of the industry, by analogy with the 'share of the market demand curve'. These are strong assumptions, however, and experience and strategic thinking should be applied to such problems. The equation merely provides the very important conceptual and accounting framework for the play of such experience.

FURTHER READING

Again, almost all economics texts handle the question of oligopoly, but none includes the element of marginal revenue of service except Straszheim (1974). The problem is to find a text that makes the bewildering variety of approaches understandable. An excellent introduction to a vital aspect of oligopoly theory is provided by:

Lyons, B. (1987) Strategic behaviour by firms, in Clarke, R. and McGuinness, T. (eds) *The Economics of the Firm*, Oxford, Basil Blackwell, chapter 4, pp. 62–82.

For those with time, and the ability to handle the mathematics which come in occasionally, a finely worked route through the maze is provided by:

Hay, D.A. and Morris, D.J. (1991) *Industrial Economics and Organization*, 2nd Edn, Oxford, Oxford University Press.

Competition policy and regulation

INTRODUCTION

The control of monopolistic and predatory activities can only be understood in the light of current thinking about competition and monopoly. Although these have been considered from the point of view of the firm in Chapters 9 and 10, and briefly mentioned from the point of view of public policy in Chapter 3, there has been no consideration of the implications of monopoly for the economy as a whole, nor the controls which have to be observed by firms. Previous texts usually consider this under the implicit heading of manufacturing industry; it is however equally – if not more – relevant in the context of services.

You can scarcely get more monopolistic than the public utilities. UK food retailing is dominated by the six large multiple retailers, who are moving more and more into non-food areas, and who have already formed the subject of a major Monopolies and Mergers Commission report (1981) in relation to the discounts they receive. The brewers' monopolistic positions were largely supported by their ownership of the service outlets in the form of pubs. Under monopoly we shall include oligopolistic practices such as cartels and accommodation over prices designed to give advantages akin to monopoly to oligopolists. Section 11.2 therefore considers the issues of losses to society due to monopolistic practices, and the way these losses may be passed to different sectors of the economy as part of 'rent seeking', which might be called a market for privileged positions. In section 11.3, we consider the controls on restrictive practices; section 11.4 deals with controls on the abuse of monopoly power and briefly introduces the control of mergers which might lead to monopoly power or its extension. In section 11.5 we examine very briefly the issue of price and profits regulation which applies to the utilities, and in section 11.6 we conclude with a brief discussion of the regulation of professional standards, notably in the sectors of medicine and accountancy.

There are now two sets of laws on competition policy which apply in the UK and all other EC countries: national law and European Community law. There is thus a potential for conflict in relation to the relevant jurisdiction. The general rule is that Community law prevails when there is a **community dimension**. That is defined as a situation in which trade between EC states might be affected. The boundary is drawn very wide; it is sufficient for the actions of firm(s) in one member state to be discouraging entry, or providing a standard price across a border in spite of transport cost differences (thereby discriminating on price) for it to have a community dimension. This sometimes occurs in unexpected ways, such as the complaint against the UK government for its subsidies to the Rover company when selling it to BAe, which were held to distort competition by giving Rover a cost advantage. Because it was in competition with other EC car manufacturers, this had a community dimension and was declared illegal.

11.2 LOSSES RESULTING FROM MONOPOLY

The losses from monopoly used to be considered as simply those resulting from the restriction of output, which because of the monopoly price was valued at well above its opportunity cost. Thus welfare could have been increased by increasing the output, as would have occurred under more competitive pricing. Subsequent thinking on the subject, however, suggests that the really major losses come from a combination of the loss of stimulus to be efficient, and even more importantly from the activities undertaken in order to retain monopoly, or by others to gain monopoly. To do this we consider first the traditional element of 'deadweight losses' of monopoly, using the diagrams applied in Chapter 9 to monopoly pricing, but now analysing their implications for economic welfare. We shall then discuss the various items that will go to make up the increases in cost we might expect under monopoly, and the cost to the economy of the anti-competitive activities.

11.2.1 Deadweight losses

The deadweight loss of monopoly is the result of the higher prices charged and the consequential reduction in output. The higher price, and hence the profit margin on each item, causes some reduction in the level of output, and of course as a result, fewer inputs go into production of the particular item or service than would otherwise be the case. Although these inputs can be used elsewhere in the economy, they can only be presumed to produce items which are attracting a price that is approximately competitive. This is the same as saying that they go to the production of things that are valued at just more than the cost of production. The monopolist by contrast is producing things valued at considerably more than their costs of production. This area of loss is shown in Figure 11.1 by the triangle abc.

That area represents the loss of **consumers' surplus**. This is the surplus of value to the consumers as measured by their willingness to pay for each individual unit consumed above its price. In most contexts it represents the value to the consumer over and above what they have had to pay for the item; however, since they are not being given the chance to purchase these units, in this case it is the value over and above opportunity costs,

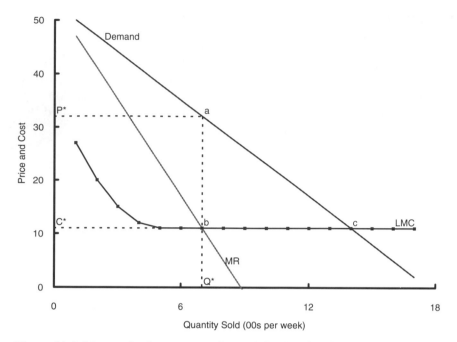

Figure 11.1 Monopoly: long-run profits and dead weight loss.

which would have been the price in a competitive market. Because we are considering the situation in which a monopolist is set up and preventing entry, we need to consider the long run, which includes the opportunity cost of capital, and not the short run; thus, it is not the short-run marginal costs that are the opportunity costs of producing a further unit of output with a given amount of capital invested, but the cost of increasing output taking into account the cost of capital; this is the long-run marginal cost. (Remember that long-run marginal cost is defined as the increase in long-run total costs due to a unit increase in output.)

Under the fictional standard of perfectly competitive markets, the amount produced would have been *c*, where price equals long-run marginal cost. Up to this point it would have been worthwhile for a competitive firm to invest in capital and to use resources to produce that final item. In our context, because the monopolist has some control over output and hence price, this desirable point, where the costs of production just equal the willingness of the consumer to pay, is not reached. Indeed if the world were adequately represented by our straight line demand curve, and constant long-run marginal cost as shown here, the competitive output would have been twice that produced by the monopolist (because MR declines twice as fast as the demand curve). abc is a right-angled triangle, with the height ab equal to the monopolist's markup. Thus the deadweight loss would be half the monopoly profits. It gives an estimate of losses of approximately 4% of gross corporate product – the output of private and government corporations. (See Clarke, 1985, chapter 10 for a more rigorous account of the problems of measurement).

The monopolist's profit, the rectangle P*abC*, is not seen as a social loss at this level of economic thinking. It is a transfer payment from consumers to the monopolist, and as such involves no change in the resources used, and so no economic cost. Even more modern economic approaches do not challenge this view as such. The key problem here is related to income distribution, and this does not seem to be a purely economic problem, but to require both ethical and economic decisions. It is therefore a 'social-democratic problem' as discussed in Chapter 2. Not that this profit is economically insignificant: its economic significance derives from the activities that the monopolist will undertake in order to preserve it, and that potential rivals will engage in to get hold of it. Before considering this aspect, however, we shall consider the factors which might induce higher or lower costs among monopolists as opposed to firms facing competitive markets, since it would alter our negative view of monopoly if it could be shown that it brought lower costs.

11.2.2 Factors raising or lowering costs under monopoly

The most easily appreciated factor is that without competition the monopolist may opt for a 'quiet life'. The managerial aspects of technical progress such as 'rationalization' of jobs, which often leads to conflict, may be avoided, and indeed the desire to avoid expensive redundancies could lead to overmanning. The management itself may opt for the known ways of doing things, and not search for new approaches, which could take work and would inevitably upset those colleagues whose power base might be eroded or who might have to do more work.

Technical advances resulting from new scientific discoveries or the availability of new types of capital goods are also likely to be slowed down by the true monopolist. This follows from the fact that the premature scrapping of capital to make way for the new technology, costs the monopolist money, and there is no competitive advantage from doing it – there are no competitors. This is one way in which 'tight oligopoly' differs markedly from true monopoly; in 'tight oligopoly' we might expect price forbearance to be the norm, but competition by technical progress may be at its most rapid since it would allow the firm to steal a march on its rivals. Under both monopoly and the more profitable varieties of oligopoly, there is the profit which permits research and development; this element is therefore one of the factors that help to reduce costs under monopolistic structures.

It is often stated that the reason for monopoly is the presence of substantial economies of scale. The concept of **natural monopoly** takes this further: it is a situation in which one firm can serve the market more cheaply than two. The examples usually cited are the major public utilities – gas, electricity, water and telephones – where the provision of capital in the network is usually sufficient to serve the whole market and where the duplication of that network would therefore duplicate costs. This is strongly contested by Primeaux (1979, 1985), who found that prices in electricity companies in various places in the USA were lower where there was competition than where there was monopoly, even though the size of market might not be particularly large. Further evidence for this can be found in Millward (1982), who looks at the other utilities as well. Both his work and that of Primeaux show that it is not a question of private or public ownership as such that determines whether prices are lower, but whether there is competition or not. This is an important conclusion for regulation policy, as we shall see in section 11.5.

11.2.3 Expenditures to retain or gain monopoly

Investment is expected to take place where there are profits to be made that are above the cost of capital. If, however, there are barriers to entry, whether in the form of government regulations, brand loyalty or patents, potential competitors will have to find ways around these barriers if they are to have a share of the monopoly profits, and the monopolist will be spending money to defend the monopoly profits already enjoyed. Defensive expenditures will include advertising, which we saw can be used as a barrier to entry, pre-emptive patenting (that is to say, buying up potentially useful patents and patenting alternative technologies from one's own laboratories to ensure that others cannot use them), and lobbying the legislature to try to ensure that any regulations surrounding the industry defend the monopolist's position. They might also include excessive capital expenditures which were designed to reduce the marginal costs of production (as discussed in section 10.4.4).

The excessive expenditures incurred by others trying to get into the market exactly mirror the defensive expenditures – advertising, potentially unprofitable R&D and lobbying. There is no reason why in a world of imperfect information the costs should be limited to the level of profits achievable, although it would obviously not be rational to invest more than the potential returns, and as such the investment should only continue up to the point of exhaustion of those profits. The monopolist might well have the information to carry out investment in this way, but of course would not wish to do so beyond the point at which the threat of entry by others ceased. The potential entrants, however, probably do not know what other potential rivals are investing, and it is therefore possible that the sum of these investments would actually exceed the level of profit. It should be noted that these activities are entirely wasteful, although there might be some unexpected spin-offs from the R&D.

If regulatory barriers, such as licenses for taxis and heavy goods vehicles, or scarcity of landing slots for airlines, are the cause of shortage of supply and hence monopolistically high prices, the battle may be shifted from service and price competition to black market payments (or bribes to officials) for the licenses. Alternatively, this ownership may form the basis for the value of a firm at takeover. The potential for the competition to be shifted to the bribes payable to officials and thence to the bribes to gain official positions is also ever present (Posner, 1975).

Finally, to the costs incurred by the firms should be added such costs as are incurred by the government in controlling monopolistic activities, and by the firms in response to this control. Even these are unquantifiable since only some of the firms' costs will be recorded; others will simply be part of management costs. Some of these costs may be the result of misperceptions by government or special pleading by rivals. The rivals might after all use the competition authorities to protect their own positions rather than to favour competition – to 'protect competitors not competition'. There is an extreme view which holds that all such controls are unnecessary since the competitive process will allow entry, or force monopolists to be efficient because the lure of the profits will encourage other firms to enter the market one way or another, and the higher the profits the stronger the stimulus. The problem is thus self-liquidating; small low profit monopolies do not distort the competitive process significantly, and so are not worth pursuing; large monopoly profits will be a large attraction to competitors, who will enter even though the barriers are very high. The only insuperable barrier is government regulations. This is the so-called 'Austrian' view, or sometimes the 'Chicago' view, which sees the costs of control of monopoly as government-induced costs to solve a government-induced problem!

It should be pointed out that there is an equally plausible contrary argument to the Chicago School, namely that unchecked monopolistic practices would lead to monopoly driving out competition, rather than the other way round. While government is likely to be an imperfect economic agent, the benevolence of monopolistic firms in allowing competition hardly seems plausible. The present social contract is that firms should be free to maximize their profits within the framework of law; the removal of that framework would not guarantee competition.

There have been some estimates, even if extremely tentative, of the total costs of such monopolistic practices to the economy. Advertising has been mentioned as the most evident cost of defending a monopoly position. In the UK in 1968/9, adding the costs of advertising, the existing profits and the deadweight loss, the total potential loss amounted to 7.2% of gross corporate product; in the USA on average from 1963 to 1968, it amounted to 13.14% (Clarke, 1985). These estimates assume full profit maximizing behaviour, whereas such monopolies often appear to charge rather less than the maximum profitable price. The straight line demand curves assumed are likely not to be correct, but we cannot know the relevant alternative. Advertising may have an informative function as well as the emotive one implied here. All of these considerations would suggest an overestimate. However, the estimate of monopoly profit does not allow for the raised costs due to inefficiency and blocked technical progress, and no estimate is made for lobbying, or government policing expenses, or for the defence costs to firms.

The control of monopolistic abuse has two major branches: firstly, that of controlling the sort of practices that restrict or distort competition, called restrictive practices, and secondly, the control of the abuse of monopoly power by charging excessive prices, excessive advertising, pre-emptive patenting or purchase of raw materials and the takeover of rival firms to get into a more strongly monopolistic position.

11.3   THE CONTROL OF RESTRICTIVE PRACTICES

Restrictive practices typically involve price fixing, of which retail price maintenance is the clearest example, restrictions on output or technical development, agreements to share a market, or 'tying contracts' where purchases of one item are conditional upon purchases of another. They also crucially involve more than one firm; they are thus either tacit or formal agreements. The same practices might arise from the operations of a monopolist, but they would in general then be caught under another set of laws relating to monopoly or its abuse. This section discusses the UK restrictive practices legislation, including the Competition Act 1980, and the European Community legislation which follows from Article 85 of the Treaty of Rome.

11.3.1   UK restrictive practices legislation

Restrictive practices are dealt with in UK legislation under two headings: restrictive practices and resale price maintenance. The evolution of the legislation on both aspects represents the evolution of thinking in economics and government from an acceptance of the wisdom of 'orderly markets' and the dangers of destructive competition, to our present position which mistrusts any attempt to reduce competition, and which therefore starts from the position that all such attempts are *a priori* illegal and should probably be banned. Whether the earlier anti-competitive stance stemmed perhaps from the era of the guilds, and national trading monopolies such as the East India Company on which much of our industrial structure was built, or whether it emerged from the experiences of the competition that resulted from the 1930s slump, is now immaterial. It is however worth noting that the slump is now thought to have been at least largely caused by the increase in protectionism in the 1920s and 1930s, and the accompanying cartelization in the UK, France and Germany. This cartelization probably covered about 30% of industry just before and after the Second World War.

The abolition of Resale Price Maintenance is now history, except for pharmaceuticals and the Net Book Agreement. The latter is retained precisely for the reasons that other resale price maintenance has been scrapped. It allows the retention of high prices, which thereby permit more retailers to exist since discounts to bulk sellers are not permitted and hence the latter have no cost advantage. The higher margins permit smaller outlets to survive on the relatively restricted level of sales; hence 'real' bookshops can survive in relatively small market areas. It was felt that unfettered competition and lower prices would drive out such small sellers and thus deprive whole regions of the country of booksellers and the cultural benefits that they bring. Furthermore, by avoiding the competitive pressures at the retail level, the publishers can cross-subsidize low-volume titles with the relatively high-volume ones and so take more risks and publish a wider range of books. These arguments have prevailed against the arguments for greater competition and thus expansion of the market by lower prices, and competitive pressures for efficiency on the retailers. The Net Book Agreement is under heavy attack from the larger and more efficient retailers.

The basis of attacks on restrictive practices is still the 1956 Restrictive Trade Practices Act; restrictive agreements had by law to be registered with the Registrar (now with the Director General of Fair Trading since the 1973 Fair Trading Act), and were deemed illegal unless specifically exempted by the Restrictive Practices Court on one or more of seven 'gateways', providing it was not generally 'against the public interest':

1. To protect the public against injury.
2. That removal would deny the public 'specific and substantial benefits' (the most frequently used defence).
3. To counteract measures used by others to restrict competition.
4. To enable parties to negotiate fair terms with others.
5. Because removal would have serious and persistent effects on unemployment.
6. Because deregulation would cause substantial reduction in exports.
7. To maintain another agreement itself exempt.

A further clause was added in the 1976 Restrictive Practices Act:

8. While not necessary the agreement does not restrict or discourage competition to any material degree.

The protectionist tone of these gateways provides an interesting contrast with the present emphasis on competition at home in order to keep firms competitive in export markets. However, they led to an enormous reduction in the number of agreements, and the Restrictive Trade Practices Court in general took a strongly procompetitive line. (For a more detailed review see Clarke, 1985, chapter 11). It is interesting to note that the cases ruled on by the OFT between 1980 and 1983 listed in Clarke (1985, p. 249) all involve service industries, and this is to be expected since it is at the level of the service delivery that so many anticompetitive practices take place.

Attitudes have changed between the 'corporatist 70s' and the 'Thatcherite 80s', and this can be seen in the wording of the 1980 Competition Act, which shifts the approach to one more closely related to the EC legislation controlling anticompetitive practices. These are defined as:

> a course of conduct which has or is intended to have or is likely to have the effect of restricting, distorting or preventing competition in the United Kingdom.

The Director General of Fair Trading can initiate an investigation into any such suspected activities. Investigations may decide there is no (or no significant) effect on competition, or require undertakings from the firms to desist (these will be monitored for 5 or 10 years), or the practices may be referred to the Monopolies and Mergers Commission for a ruling on whether they are against the public interest and a recommendation to the Secretary of State for Industry whether to ban the abuses by an Order in Council.

11.3.2   EC legislation: 'Concerted practices'

The language used by the European Community legislation is somewhat different from that used traditionally in the UK. In particular, it talks of 'concerted practices' rather than restrictive trade practices. Control of such concerted practices is based upon Article 85 of the Treaty of Rome. Concerted practices are defined as:

> practices which while not contractually binding, indicate the substitution of cooperation for the risks of the market, and competition.

And cartels:

> the contractual cooperation of independent companies in similar activities with the goal to influence the market in a monopolistic way. (Liefmann, quoted in de Jong, 1988)

However in all Community legislation there is a *de minimis* rule, that very small firms will not come under consideration. This is defined as Agreements of Minor Importance: if firms participating have a market share of not more than 5%, and their aggregate turnover does not exceed 50 million ECU, a significant restriction of competition does not exist. Below 15% there is a presumption of 'no distortion'; above 15% individual examination for harmful effects is the rule. Caution should be exercised in assuming that this rule applies, as it depends on the definition of the 'market', which is always problematic in competition cases, national or international.

Treaty of Rome: Article 85

The first clause of Article 85 reads:

> 1.   The following shall be prohibited as incompatible with the common market: all agreements between undertakings, decisions by associations of undertakings and concerted practices which may affect trade between Member States and which have as their object or effect the prevention, restriction or distortion of competition within the common market, and in particular those which:
>
> (a) directly or indirectly fix purchase or selling prices or any other trading conditions;
> (b) limit or control production, markets, technical development, or investment;
> (c) share markets or sources of supply;
> (d) apply dissimilar conditions to equivalent transactions with other trading parties, thereby placing them at a competitive disadvantage;

(e) make the conclusion of contracts subject to acceptance by the other parties of supplementary obligations which, by their nature or according to commercial usage, have no connection with the subject of such contracts. (Butterworths European Information Service, 1989, p. 155)

Clause 2 declares such agreements void at law; this means that they have no legal force, and so any party to the agreement can break it without risk of being found guilty by the courts of breach of contract.

Clause 3 defines four cumulative conditions for exemptions:

1. The agreement must contribute to improving the production, or distribution, of goods or to promoting technical or economic progress.
2. The consumer must be allowed a fair share of the resulting benefit.
3. The agreement, in achieving the improvement and the fair sharing, must not impose restrictions that are not indispensable to the attainment of those objectives.
4. The agreement must not allow the parties to eliminate competition in respect of a substantial part of the products in question.

To qualify for an exemption, the parties to the agreement must notify the Commission before the agreement comes into force. (In the same way, restrictive practices must be notified in the UK.) In the absence of such notification the Commission will declare such agreements illegal, and fines of up to 10% of world turnover for those guilty of practising them can be levied. There are also heavy fines for not supplying information on time if requested by the Commission. Community competition law has teeth.

Application of Article 85

1. Even where agreement in either the contractual sense or informal sense is absent, 'parallelism' of action can be seen as a 'concerted action'. The European Court of Justice decision in the Aniline Dye Case observed that a 'concerted practice' was:

   a form of coordination between undertakings which, without going so far as to amount to an agreement properly so called, knowingly substitutes a practical cooperation between them for the risks of competition.

   Thus the raising of prices in concert by equal proportions by all the major suppliers of dyes in the EC on three separate occasions was seen as a concerted practice.
2. Any suggestion of contact between firms, even if not binding, is seen as indicative of a 'concerted practice'. Thus letting competitors have a price list before the price rises come into force is clearly a 'concerted practice'.
3. The firms do not have to have their headquarters in the European

Community; British (pre-EC entry) and Swiss firms were fined in the Aniline Dye case for their activities in the EC. It is activities on EC territory, not the origin of the firms, that defines the jurisdiction.

4. The phrase in section 1, '*may* affect trade between Member States', should be noted. This empowers the Commission to examine activities in one country that could have the effect of restricting access to that country's market, or conversely that may artificially increase the trade between member states. It was considered illegal when Belgian cement producers charged the domestic Belgian price in the more distant markets in Germany, since it did not reflect the transport costs and thus amounted to discriminatory pricing (the Cimbel case).

5. Sole dealerships are permissible, and have been given block exemptions, but there may be no restriction of the flow of imports of the same product from other EC countries, or elsewhere, in order to protect that dealer's market. This restrictive practice may be attacked on the basis of Article 30 relating to the free movement of goods. The attempts of Grundig and Pioneer to prevent such 'parallel imports' were attacked on this basis, Pioneer being fined 6.95 million ECUs.

6. The same considerations apply to trademarks and patents. In the Sirena-Eda Case, the American company Mark Allen licensed Sirena to use the trademark 'Prep' and also a German import–export house, Novimpex, which bought the German product and sold it in Italy. The European Court of Justice ruled against the plea by Sirena that this was undermining their trademark. For patents, Sterling Pharmaceuticals' Dutch subsidiary obtained a license from Sterling, who granted parallel licenses in the UK and Germany. One of the licensees, Centrafarm, imported the product from Germany into Holland; the plea to stop this was similarly disallowed.

7. 'Block exemptions' for cooperation in marketing and joint product and market research have been granted subject to: (i) firms cooperating not being in control of more than 20% of the market in EC or substantial areas thereof, and (ii) not having aggregate turnover of more than 500 million ECU.

8. Franchising is encouraged as a means of entry and/or expansion of competitive firms, but while the franchiser's knowledge and methods (including the identity, reputation and commercial methods) are protected, and franchisees are not allowed to open further shops in competition with other franchisees without approval, clauses which impose prices or aim to secure market sharing between franchiser and franchisees, or between franchisees, are prohibited. This applies within and between member states.

9. There are no very clear rules relating to joint ventures. The justification of any joint venture is that unique risk should be diversified. Thus R&D in telecommunications or aerospace is often very large in scale and very risky, and so might gain exemption. Such joint ventures will be less acceptable the larger the market share of

participants, the more they aim to fix prices, and the more ancillary behaviour is determined by the agreement.

10. Buying shares in a firm may be a means to influence behaviour of competitors to restrict competition. To come under Article 85, control over another firm must be obtained, and there must be an agreement:

(i) There is such an agreement in the case of public offers.
(ii) There is not when shares are bought on the stock exchange.

Only agreements between competitors come under Article 85. (Note that the structure of cross shareholdings among competitors is particularly prevalent in France. See, for example, Gugenheim and Selosse, 1991.)

11.3.3 Summary: Restrictive practices

It is the European Community legislation that is setting the tone for national legislation throughout Europe. There are however considerable differences in the level of control already practised in the various countries. In France the legislation was much strengthened in 1986 by the *Ordonnance* of the 1st of December, which abolished price controls and set up a much more vigorous competition policy to be operated by the Conseil de la Concurrence. The Conseil de la Concurrence is now vigorously combatting all the little agreements between various trade associations throughout the country, including those professional associations such as surveyors, which fix levels of fees or prices. It also pursues firms which do not publish price lists, as this is seen as a way of price discriminating, as well as attacking more fundamental abuses. A fine of 166 million francs was imposed on a cartel of 70 road construction firms for market sharing agreements in 1989. The German authorities, in the form of the Kartellamt, now have a long history of such competition enforcement, much as in the UK. Many of the Mediterranean countries have almost no competition law or authorities of their own, and rely on the European Community Law. This as we have seen is fundamentally pro-competitive, and follows the assumption that any agreements that restrict the freedom of the market are illegal. It is not absolute in this commitment and allows agreements if it can be shown that they bring real social and economic benefits, i.e. that they do not only benefit the firms involved, but will also result in reduced consumer prices.

11.4 CONTROL OF MONOPOLY

It is often forgotten that one of the basic reasons for nationalization, e.g. in gas, electricity and telephones, was to control monopoly. Perhaps this is forgotten because other reasons for nationalization predominate, notably ideology in the takeover of coal and steel or *ad hoc* decisions by government stepping in to save 'vital industry' as in the cases of Rolls-Royce and British Leyland. This is also forgotten because the vociferous arguments of the Chicago School contend that it is only governments that can create damaging monopolies. The 'corporatist' approach of Britain through the 1960s and 1970s, and of France to this day, nevertheless required the control of monopoly and so this is reflected in both national and European Community legislation.

11.4.1 UK legislation: Control of monopoly

In the UK legislation has covered both monopolies and mergers. The earliest legislation is the 1948 Monopolies and Restrictive Practices (Inquiry and Control) Act. This introduced a case-by-case examination of monopolies to investigate whether a monopoly (then defined as one firm controlling 30% of domestic supply) exists and to evaluate it relative to the public interest. This was supplemented in 1956 with the introduction of the Monopolies Commission. With the 1973 Fair Trading Act, the name was changed to the Monopolies and Mergers Commission, and the Office of Fair Trading was set up to keep monopoly situations in the UK (redefined as having more than 25% of the market or where mergers involve total assets of more than £30 million) under review to 'promote effective competition'. If necessary the merger or monopolistic practice may be referred to the Monopolies and Mergers Commission, who recommend to the Secretary of State for Industry:

1. to ban it by statutory order, or enforce conditions on it;
2. that the firms have entered into voluntary agreements not to engage in the practices in question; or
3. that the practice or merger is not against the public interest, and should be allowed to continue.

11.4.2 EC legislation: Article 86

Article 86 of the Treaty of Rome reads as follows:

> Any abuse by one or more undertakings of a dominant position within the common market or in a substantial part of it shall be prohibited as incompatible with the common market in so far as it may affect trade between Member States. Such abuse may, in particular, consist in:
>
> (a) directly or indirectly imposing unfair purchase or selling prices or other unfair trading conditions;
> (b) limiting production, markets or technical development to the prejudice of consumers;
> (c) applying dissimilar conditions to equivalent transactions with other trading parties, thereby placing them at a competitive disadvantage;
> (d) making the conclusion of contracts subject to acceptance by the other parties of supplementary obligations which, by their nature or according to commercial usage, have no connection with the subject of such contracts. (Butterworths European Information Service, 1989, p. 156.)

Application of Article 86

The key factors in the application of Article 86 have been:

- There must be a 'dominant position'.
- It is not dominance but abuse which is frowned upon.
- There must be a likely effect on interstate trade.

We will consider these in turn.

Dominance is clearly a difficult concept to operationalize in that there is no neat dividing line at some percentage of market sales beyond which a firm can be said to be dominant. It must also depend on the strength of the other firms in the industry. For example if a local bus company held 60% of the market, but was part of a duopoly, one would probably require evidence of dominance. If, however, it faced only very small firms, it might well be seen as having a dominant position, and attempts to monopolize individual routes and so gradually drive out the other companies would probably be seen as predatory. This dilemma is also faced at the larger scale of the European Community. The findings of most importance are shown in Table 11.1.

Table 11.1 Cases defining the concept of dominance under EC law

Case	Finding
Hoffmann La Roche	47% of the market for Vitamin A, but two largest rivals only held 45% of the market between them
United Brands (Chiquita)	40% of market for bananas; remaining firms very small, and substantial barriers to entry
IBM	40% of market for computers (and 39% of data processing) but IBM seven times larger than nearest rival)

This picture is, however, complicated by the precedent established in the Continental Can case; it was found that although Continental Can held a dominant market share of metal cans, the alternatives of glass or plastic provided sufficient potential competition to render that dominance illusory.

In the context of the European Community (as in national competition law) it must be decided what constitutes a 'substantial part' of the market in question. 'In a substantial part' of the EC can be taken as within a member state as shown by the case of Continental Can, which not only established the principle of competition from related markets, but also established that a 'substantial portion' could mean a part of two countries, in this case north-west Germany and the Netherlands. The US company 'Continental Can Inc.' bought the West German company Schmalbach-Lubeca-Werke, makers of light metal cans, transferred it to a holding company, Europemballage Co., then made an offer for a large

Dutch can producer Thomassen & Drijver-Verblifa NV. The latter was seen as infringement of Article 86 by the Commission because of the dominance in metal containers for meat and fish, and in metal caps for preserve jars. The European Court of Justice found against; not because of too small a market share, but because of potential competition from other containers, such as glass jars or normal tins.

Abuses: the Commission has attacked several cases of the first type of abuse mentioned under section (a), 'imposing unfair prices or purchase conditions', particularly any refusal to supply, as in the case of Commercial Solvents who refused to supply a necessary raw material to a drug producer because Commercial Solvents had decided to produce the drug through one of their subsidiaries. These categories are by no means mutually exclusive in many cases and it is both clause (a) and clause (d), 'making contacts subject to acceptance by the other parties of supplementary obligations', that were infringed in the cases where fidelity rebates were offered. These clearly affect the purchasing retailers as well as other industrial concerns. For example both the cases below were deemed abuses of dominant positions:

1. Two West German sugar producers offered fidelity rebates conditional on their being sole suppliers.
2. Hoffmann La Roche offered fidelity rebates; 'Whether to compensate for the exclusivity or to encourage a preferential link, the contracts provided for fidelity rebates based not on the differences in costs related to the quantities supplied by Roche but on the proportion of the customer's requirements covered'. Since rebates were calculated on all products, Roche tied in other products to its supplies of vitamins.

Price discrimination is seen as both evidence of dominance and an abuse. Thus United Brands (Chiquita Bananas) were penalized for charging different prices for the same product, without the justification on grounds of differences in costs. AKZO dominates the market for motor vehicle paints, and have been attacked several times. The first was for predatory pricing to drive rivals out of business. The second was for refusal to supply the technical information needed to use their paints to companies that had bought materials through parallel importers (i.e. importers who had bought in a low cost country and sold in the UK).

Mergers

In both the UK and the EC mergers fall under policies to control monopoly, although merger policy as such is a new aspect of EC legislation being incorporated into Council Regulation (EEC) No. 4064/89 (*Official Journal of the European Communities*, 1989b), which came into force on the 21st September 1990. Prior to that, 'concentrations', Eurospeak for 'mergers', could only be controlled *ex post* by application of Article 86 for abuse of monopoly position. While of considerable interest, it is very similar to present UK law and even the forms of notification required by the EC were incorporated into the UK system as voluntary practices by the 1989 Companies Act. In the EC case this notification is compulsory, as is the furnishing of information on time. In the UK notification to the Director General of Fair Trading of the proposed merger allows him to give the merger clearance, and with that clearance comes the guarantee that the merger will not be referred to the MMC.

Mergers across EC boundaries are feasible, as shown by the various transnational activities of the car firms, including the recent merger of Perrier and Nestlé; takeovers, on the other hand, are often extremely difficult because of the different legal structures of firms in various EC countries. This specialist topic is documented in Coopers and Lybrand's (1989) report on barriers to takeovers in the European Community.

11.5 REGULATION OF PRIVATIZED UTILITIES

Regulation has been applied to many industries which we would no longer consider in need of regulation. However, the problem of regulating natural monopolies (those industries in which it is at least theoretically cheaper for one firm to produce rather than two, see section 11.2.2) still remains. It is to this problem that the theories set out below principally apply. The theory of regulation of utilities is usually divided neatly into rate of return regulation and price regulation. As we shall see, the distinction is not in practice as neat as this. As rate of return regulation has a longer history than price regulation, being the preferred mode for the privately provided utilities in the USA, we will discuss it first. We will then discuss the apparently superior incentive structure of price regulation as practised in the UK for gas, water and telephones. This is followed by the theory relating to franchising as a substitute for regulation. Finally, we will turn to the question of regulation of access to professions or limitations on business activities in the next section, with particular emphasis on the professions.

11.5.1 Rate of return regulation

Rate of return regulation is defined as setting a maximum permissible rate of profit for the industry. The regulator then leaves the industry to decide how best to organize output and prices within that limit. It is easier to understand the basic dilemmas of the approach if the rate of return is expressed as an equation:

$$\text{Rate of return} = \frac{\text{Total revenue} - \text{Total cost}}{\text{Capital invested}} \tag{11.1}$$

Clearly if the rate of return permitted by the regulator is below the cost of capital, there will be no investment. Thus the regulator must permit a higher rate of return than the cost of capital in the market. Assuming this to be the case, it will be desirable for the firm to maximize the amount of profit. Given inelastic prices, which are likely unless the monopolistic utility has pushed prices up to extravagant levels, the total revenue can be made to exceed total cost fairly easily. The amount of profit can therefore be controlled by the firm by the amount of capital invested. The more it invests, the more profit it can make, albeit at the average rate prescribed by the regulator. Thus there is a strong tendency, following this line of argument, to overinvest in capital, and thus to incur excessive costs. This effect is called the Averch–Johnson effect after the economists who first published on the subject. For a more rigorous treatment see Hay and Morris (1991) or Vickers and Yarrow (1988).

It will also be evident that with inelastic demand the firm could allow costs to rise with virtual impunity, since it can increase revenue by raising prices. If the regulator has to permit the firm to make enough profit to remain viable, costs can rise with impunity, and this form of regulation would become equivalent to a cost-plus system, without any incentive to efficiency.

Fortunately, this is not how it actually works in practice (Kahn, 1992a,b). As Kahn reports, the actual practice is for regulators to note the course of prices, and if these are stable or declining a higher rate of return is permitted; conversely if they are thought to be rising excessively the rate of return is depressed. Thus the actual practice is closer to price regulation than to the theoretical model upon which it is supposedly based.

11.5.2 Real price regulation

The system used in the UK for the regulation of gas, electricity and British Telecom is a system based on the regulation of real prices, i.e. prices adjusted to take account of general inflation. It is, in other words, a system based on the retail price index plus or minus a given percentage, known as RPI-X. This allows the firm freedom to set prices for individual services within this ceiling, and to maximize its profits subject to those prices, and hence minimize costs. The level of X should be fixed for several years at a time so that the firm can plan its operations effectively, and reap the rewards for improvements in efficiency. Initially X was set at 3.5% for British Telecom for 5 years; in fact it was raised to 5% after 3 years. This was supposed to last a further 5 years; again it was raised after 3 years, this time to 7%. However, this was planned to last only 2 years. In each of these cases it was raised prematurely to head off the potential political storm due to popular reaction to the enormous profits that were being made.

The duration of each set of prescribed prices is known as the **regulatory lag**, and as stated above, the longer it is, the more the firm is rewarded for efficient operation. However, when one takes account of strategic motivations for the firm, it is obvious that when such a lag is a fixed period there is an incentive for the firm to raise costs in the final year of the period in order to get more favourable treatment for the next regulatory period.

Was this cleverly avoided by BT's regulator, or did his office merely underestimate the potentials for cost reduction?

The phrasing above conceals the fact that there are many variants to this system. For gas, it is the revenue per therm rather than the tariff that is fixed, allowing British Gas to adjust the standing charge and the tariff as it sees fit. Furthermore, there is an additional item in the equation which allowed British Gas to pass on to the consumer the full extra costs of any rises in the price of gas. This has now been modified to provide an incentive for British Gas to be efficient in the purchasing of gas. For BT it is not a single set of tariffs but the weighted average of the major tariffs that falls under regulatory control. BT thus has an incentive to 'Ramsey Price', i.e. to discriminate subject to this limit (see section 9.6, Equation 9.5). In the water supply industry special factors are inserted for the rise in costs due to new purity standards for drinking water and purification standards for the treatment of sewage (Dorken, 1992).

This sort of regulation requires a lot of very detailed information on costs, quantities, prices and quality to be collected by the firm and passed to the regulator. It is therefore correspondingly expensive. One contributor to the discussion at a recent conference said that the amount of information required from the Water Boards had increased tenfold since privatization (Gilland, 1992, p. 91). The huge increase is partly because this approach sets up a strong incentive to reduce costs by reducing quality. Naturally this would not obtain if sales could be increased by more than the cost of the relevant expenditure on quality improvement; this may have been the case for BT, particularly as the quality improvements allowed value added services to be offered which were not regulated and were therefore correspondingly profitable. In the case of British Gas, however, quality has been a bone of contention between British Gas and the regulator throughout. In the case of water, the National Rivers Authority has been pressing for the implementation of EC water quality standards, which imposes very heavy investment costs on the Water Boards. The water regulator, who feels that the rise in prices required to cover these costs is excessive compared with the benefits that will be achieved, has stoutly resisted this pressure.

In addition to being expensive in terms of information gathering, there is a severe problem in all forms of regulation if the regulated firms are also competing in unregulated markets. Under either form of regulation, the regulator has to be careful that costs are not being included in the regulated sector which are in fact part of production for the unregulated one, since this would give the regulated industry a cost advantage compared with its rivals. This requires further vigilance by the regulator and yet more information collected for him.

11.5.3 Regulation by franchising

Demsetz (1968) suggested that the process of regulation could be simplified, and indeed often by-passed, by franchising. Competition for the franchise replaces the complexity and cost of ongoing regulation. This appears to have been accepted successfully, for instance, as a means of introducing incentives into the previously hierarchical cleaning services of local authorities, the NHS and various other government direct labour organizations. This approach will be much more severely tested in the franchising of the railway services; we shall see that the subsequent arguments against the Demsetz view (Vickers and Yarrow, 1988, pp. 110–115) appear to invalidate the Demsetz hypothesis for both public utilities and the railways.

The Demsetz hypothesis (often called the Chadwick–Demsetz hypothesis after an earlier economist whose views Demsetz revived and amplified) is that regulation of natural monopolies, with its continual monitoring and perverse incentives, can be replaced by setting up a competition for the monopoly rights based on predetermined quality standards. The winner is the firm that agrees to fulfil this contract at the lowest price to the consumer. There are two important assumptions (Demsetz, 1968, p. 58):

1. Inputs must be available on the open market, so that there can be a sufficient number of bidders to ensure competition.
2. The cost of collusion among bidders must be high.

The assumptions on which he builds up his example are interesting:

> The criticism made here of the theory of natural monopoly can be understood best by constructing an example that is free from irrelevant complications, such as durability of distributions systems, uncertainty, and irrational behavior.

Unfortunately, it has emerged since that these 'irrelevant complications' are actually the core characteristics of the regulation problem. Thus local authority cleaning services, refuse collection and unremunerative bus services have been very successfully franchised since there is no problem of infrastructure to sell at the end of the franchise and the various inputs are generally widely available on the open market. However, none of these is a natural monopoly. The problem that has been solved is that of empires created within a political organization and it is not surprising that these can be franchised without serious problem. They are no more of a problem in economic terms than setting up a branch of McDonalds.

However, the utilities have almost opposite characteristics. The huge sunk costs of the networks means that there is no possibility of purchasing them on the open market. They have very long lives, as can be appreciated by a country that is still using many of the sewers laid in Victorian times. The indivisibilities of these networks, and their spare capacity, are the characteristics that make these utilities natural monopolies, and the franchising of such natural monopolies could only be tackled by franchising the management contracts, since there are insuperable problems of valuing the capital assets, should the franchisee change. This solution through management contracts was suggested by Demsetz. However, it is likely to infringe Demsetz's second assumption, since there are likely to be the same few expert firms competing against each other repeatedly in many different places and therefore developing means of collusion and market sharing. This is exactly the suspected problem between the major infrastructure managers which operate this sort of system in France at present. Such market sharing, if it exists, cannot be said to be bringing disasters any more than our nationalized industries pre-1980 could be said to be disasters – partly because there are a group of local authority officers who are getting very expert in purchasing and bargaining with these oligopolistic firms.

There is a further major problem, even with the management contract, for such natural monopolies. If the contract is very short, lack of competition is liable to emerge because the chances of winning a change of franchise are small and so the incumbents become entrenched. If, however, this does not happen, the problems of changes of management and consequent disruption are likely to be severe. Thus it would appear that the franchise period should be lengthy. However, with a lengthy period the market situation is likely to change, as is the technology of production and distribution; the original conditions of the contract are therefore likely either to yield heavy windfall gains to the franchisee or to cause rigidities which will cost society dear. For example, you could not expect to run a TGV on old track, but under a long-term contract the TGV might not have been considered.

The management contract type of franchise has another severe problem; the management will know what infrastructure development it thinks is desirable. It has every incentive to try to shift costs from its operation to the infrastructure owner, thus to persuade the owner to overinvest particularly in capital that will save current costs (energy or labour for example). This problem can theoretically be overcome by an efficient contract which sets up the criteria for the payment of rental on such new capital, but only if the contract is also flexible in terms of allowing for new products and processes (such as the TGV and its associated infrastructure). Equally, if the owner is unwilling or, because of government spending restrictions, unable to keep the infrastructure up to standard, the quality standards built in to the contract will become unenforceable. In the presence of shifting expectations, this process will occur even without particular ill-will by the infrastructure owner, and it is to be expected that such wrangles will make the system one in which blame will be passed from one group to the other to the satisfaction of no one, least of all the consumer. The experience of penalty clauses in the building and civil engineering field – that they are usually unenforceable – provides a good analogy for this approach of split responsibilities. One of the major advantages of the market system is its amazing flexibility in the face of change; the rigidity of contract implicit in this approach of operation split from ownership, and operation geared to social as well as purely commercial ends, seems a very weak parallel to a market.

The alternative franchising technique that was under consideration for British Rail was to franchise both track and management. This has been rejected, presumably because of the problem of transferring the assets should there be change of franchisee. Two possibilities exist: the first is that the debts incurred through investment should be passed on with the franchise; this will ensure that the franchisee invests as much as is required to keep the franchise going, since it will automatically pass on the costs to the entrant if it loses the franchise. The trouble is that such an approach is open to the abuse of overinvestment, followed by a very low bid by the incumbent to keep the franchise. It thus passes on the losses consequent on its mismanagement to either the government, who have to subsidize the operation more lavishly, or to a rival firm, thereby weakening them. Alternatively, the capital is valued at its market value, and the original franchiser retains any debts that are not covered by this. This would make a cautious approach to investment mandatory, since the firm must be able to bid full market cost for the assets and still retain viability in the next round of the franchise. This would ensure proper market behaviour, but would certainly mean that the firm would not make heroic investments, in the hope, for example, that improved quality would yield large financial returns. Investments in high speed rail links would thus have to be heavily supported by the government.

11.6 PROFESSIONAL STANDARDS AND ENTRY INTO THE PROFESSIONS

The ambiguity of regulatory devices is well illustrated by the regulations surrounding professional organizations. There is a clear case on the basis of information asymmetry for regulations on professional standards. The reason I engage a doctor, accountant or lawyer is almost always that I do not know enough about the subject in question to do the work myself. That same ignorance provides the reason why it is difficult for me to judge whether the advice is good. Thus professional competence is a serious uncertainty. Particularly when major abuses occur, there is an outcry in favour of greater control. The professions thus have substantial examination and accreditation procedures which attempt to enforce standards. To do this, however, they have to weed out the poor candidates, and this can be used to restrict the numbers entering the profession.

Rigorous standards may also be extended to the crafts; in Germany the Deregulation Commission (1991) did extensive work on the craft system in that country, and suggested that it should be deregulated to a substantial extent. For example, the present system is one in which there is a lengthy apprenticeship system, which involves training on and off the job, followed by a period as a craftsman (*Geselle*), of some 5 years. Only after this can craftsmen proceed to the Master Craftsman certificate, and only master craftsmen can open up businesses on their own account. This of course gives a pool of highly skilled craftsmen who can then be employed by the master craftsmen at relatively low rates, since they must serve this time in order to reach the position to exploit this group in their turn. The government put forward proposals to end this practice, but withdrew it in the face of resistance from the existing craftsmen.

The danger comes not only from the restriction of entry, but once in place, the membership of the association usually carries with it effective 'trade union' membership, in that the professional associations will negotiate pay and conditions as far as possible. This is much less true of the dispersed professions such as lawyers and accountants, and more true of those who form a substantial block of public sector employees such as NHS doctors. Equally, such employees are faced by a monopsonist who is usually keen to keep their pay down as far as possible. The conflicts are thus more evident.

11.7 CONCLUSIONS

Most authorities agree that where possible the introduction of competition is superior to regulation. Thus the first sections of the chapter are devoted to an analysis of the problems of monopoly and the means of controlling monopoly power. The importance of this will be seen in the next chapter, and in its most complex form in the final chapter on the health services. Traditionally, the public utilities have been considered to be so inherently monopolistic that they have either been nationalized, as in most of Europe, or heavily regulated, as in North America. Dissatisfaction with both systems led to a major flowering of the writings on the economics of regulation, and some of the conclusions have been presented here. The great question is whether the present attempts to introduce competition will succeed, or whether regulation will return after a period of improvement, due to competition lasting only long enough for the rival firms to learn how to introduce effective collusion.

The basis for this is experience with the US domestic airlines, where according to Kahn (1992a, p.10), benefits worth $100 billion have accrued to consumers since 1985. This will be discussed further in the next chapter. There seems to be some potential for introducing competition in the fields of energy; British Gas is to be divided into many operating divisions and independent gas producers are to be given access to the delivery systems. The electricity generating industry was sold as a duopoly, which many feel to have been a mistake motivated by the desire of the government to maximize the revenue received from the privatization. The difficulty of these decisions is illustrated by the contrary view that it was not a mistake, and that with many independent generating stations trying to sell to the grid in the presence of fluctuating demand, the volatility of electricity prices would have made the market almost impossible to operate. Furthermore, the structure of costs in the electricity industry would tend to lead to what is called destructive competition – the cycle of high prices created by shortage of capacity, which itself is the result of a previous round of price wars leading to firms exiting from the industry and thereby closing down capacity (see Kahn, 1970, pp. 9–10, and Chapter 12).

FURTHER READING

On UK and US competition policy, a very good introduction is provided by:

Clarke, R. (1985) *Industrial Economics*, Oxford, Basil Blackwell.

The best introduction to EC policy is provided by:

Swann, D. (1992) *The Economics of the Common Market*, 7th Edn, Penguin, Harmondsworth, pp. 124–142.

The best – though difficult – introduction to the regulation of privatized utilities is provided by:

Vickers, J. and Yarrow, G. (1988) *Privatization: An Economic Analysis*, London, MIT Press.

A beautifully fluent discussion, which avoids excessive technicality, is given by:

Kahn, A.E. (1992) The purposes and limitations of economic regulation; The achievements and problems of deregulation (pp. 1–18) and Reflections and conclusions on British and US experience: The future of regulation (pp. 93–104), in Gilland, T. (ed.) *Incentive Regulation: Reviewing RPI-X and Promoting Competition*, London, Public Finance Foundation.

Transport $\boxed{12}$

12.1 INTRODUCTION

There is a huge literature on transport economics but surprisingly little devoted to the managerial economics of the topic. Particular topics closely related to transport have come up in various previous chapters. The gravity model is one of the most frequently used techniques in transport modelling, and some of the allocation models for facility planning or the design of delivery systems use this technique. In Chapters 9 and 10 the question of marginal revenue of service was considered in relation to bus and airline operations. This chapter looks more at the industrial structure of transport with a view to understanding some of the industry-wide developments likely, and the predatory tactics to which the industry is vulnerable.

The first aspect of the transport industry that we consider is the trucking industry; we take a long view, using Kahn (1970, pp. 178–193) to go back to the 1930s, to consider the meaning of 'destructive competition', a concept still bandied about, often with little definition. We shall consider the industry in its deregulated state in Australia and in the UK. This may seem a diversion into history; however, both the French and the German trucking industries are now being deregulated, and so there are new opportunities in those markets.

Bus operation would appear to be like trucking. We shall see that it is not. The key change is that buses have to run to a timetable; this completely alters the possibility of predation. Thus the bus industry is in danger of reverting to a set of local monopolies. If so, deregulation is likely to prove perverse in the long run, or merely a prelude to re-regulation. We shall also consider long-distance coach operation, which appears to parallel the airline industry.

Airlines would appear to run like buses to a timetable; we shall compare the situation in the airline industry in the USA after deregulation with that in the trucking industry after deregulation. Since it is likely that we shall face deregulation of European airlines in the near future, we shall look at the means of restricting competition by the larger airlines, and any inherent characteristics of the industry which would predispose it to monopoly or oligopoly.

Finally, the question of the development of the railways will be examined in the light of the efforts of France, Germany and the UK to improve the performance of their respective statutory monopolies. These represent three different approaches to the problem; the French are adopting a corporatist approach, of the sort that we tried in the 1970s, but with their technical strength and flair for the larger gesture, and lack of hostility to the public services, they may pull it off. The Germans are going for the most radical form of privatization with the retention of a regulated private monopoly for the rail track and the auctioning of slots to run the trains. The UK, as mentioned above, is going for franchising by major route, which seems to be another anticompetitive move by government.

12.2 TRUCKING

12.2.1 Destructive competition

According to Kahn (1970, pp. 173–178), **destructive competition** is that situation where the presence of competition reduces the welfare of not only the firms who may face prolonged periods of losses, but also of the consumers. The worsening of the consumers' welfare comes about through excessive volatility of prices and some problems of smooth supply, and/or through competitive shaving of quality. The circumstances under which such a situation may occur are the following:

1. A high capital requirement, with capital that is long lived and cannot be diverted to other uses. This is classically the situation for the public utilities. The capital involved could also be human capital.
2. The gestation period for an increase in output must be lengthy. Thus major infrastructure works, such as power stations or reservoirs, would require several years to complete, as do increases in livestock.

The potential consequence of these two items is that if demand declines, the industry faces a long period of overcapacity, and since the costs of capacity are an important part of total costs, this will inevitably mean losses for a long period. It may be accompanied by price cutting to below the level of average long-run costs. The bankruptcy of one firm may mean that cheap capital is available for someone else and hence allow entry to an industry with excess capacity already. If there is a revival of demand after long periods of decline, the second assumption will mean that there is substantial undercapacity, and hence high prices. With the high profits that this implies, there will be a tendency for excessive investment, which will once again create overcapacity when it comes on stream. It will be recalled that these conditions can also lead to monopolization of the industry, as shown by Sutton (1991), and this may break this cycle. These conditions are thus necessary but not sufficient conditions for destructive competition.

The result of the excess capacity is reduced earnings both for management and workers, and such permanent states of crisis invite government intervention either in the form of regulations, to control competition and foster a better quality of service in the industry, or in the form of subsidies, such as the Common Agricultural Policy.

12.2.2 Application to trucking

Neither of the two criteria seem to be fulfilled for trucking, where the capital is relatively cheap, and only lasts a relatively short time with normal use. It can also be diverted to other parts of the industry, and even sold in other countries. The human capital is also not very specific, and can be used for many other 'driving' jobs, or retrained.

Why, then, was the 1935 Motor Carriers Act passed in the USA, giving the Interstate Commerce Commission wide powers of regulation? Kahn's account provides interesting parallels for our own relatively high level of recession. The 'excessive' competition was due firstly to some overinvestment in the young industry of the time. This therefore made for an ample stock of vehicles. The supply of labour was not merely inelastic in the face of the fall in demand, but because of the ease of entry and the desperate shortage of other jobs in the depression, the numbers actually increased as demand fell. (There is probably a similar phenomenon occurring today in the UK with the formation of business consultancies by redundant executives. It's the only industry where you fire someone because there is not enough work, and you create a new competitor.) Thus the decline in US trucking profits, inevitable under such a situation, was borne at least in part by the 'compression of earnings' of the owner–manager. With the non-existent welfare system of the time, these earnings were virtually indefinitely compressible, there being no alternative sources of income. The shortage of work also lengthens the life of the capital, and the bankruptcy of one firm leads to the cheap means of entry into the industry of another. With this sort of chaotic decline, it is no surprise that safety and other such qualitative considerations go by the board. With social suffering, and the external effects of loss of safety and loss of quality of service (although good service would no doubt have been available at a price; the relative price might however have been very high), it is no surprise that the call went out for regulation. This would be supported by the US railways, also feeling the pressure of competition. Furthermore in such a spiral of decline, competition is itself no longer a 'good' word. The Interstate Commerce Commission was thus given very extensive powers of regulation, principally of licensing individual carriers. This in turn created huge rigidities in a potentially very flexible industry, with a large number of trucks going about with loads in only one direction because, with the restrictions on types of goods carried, return loads became impossible to find. The burden of regulation, in form filling and policing, as well as the presence of mergers to purchase licenses to transport, and some bribery to get the relevant permissions, are the inevitable outcomes. The cynics living off such a system, the good conscientious servants of the system and the truckers who have paid for their licenses in order to get in on the action will all oppose its demise vigorously. Arguments will be mustered on the experience of the period before regulation that safety will be compromised; quality will disappear, unreliability will be the result of competition; poverty, ruin and disorder will stalk the streets.

On deregulation in Australia in 1957, there were indeed many of the problems identified. However, in three years the industry had settled down, and was working much better than before with higher profits as well as greater flexibility and consumer satisfaction. Even the railways had to improve.

The safety question was also examined in the UK before deregulation; it was found that no difference seemed to exist between regulated and unregulated sectors of the industry. Kahn suggests that such considerations as safety (or implicitly noise or air pollution) can be left to policing either by police or by special bodies; there is no necessity to regulate the economic aspects of entry and price in the industry to achieve such goals.

While there are some very large firms in transport, including the outstandingly successful worker buy-out of British Road Services, now TDG, there is also a host of very small firms, right down to owner–drivers often working on contract to large manufacturing or trading organizations. (A good example of the use of franchising in the service sector; there is no reason why a large firm needs to integrate forward into distribution given the competitive nature of this industry. It merely adds some £100 000 for each truck to the assets of the company, and since it is competitive it is almost impossible to make significant excess profits on it; furthermore in times of recession, it is difficult for the integrated firm to shed either the capital assets or the labour, whereas the owner–driver takes this risk. However, whether it is advisable to franchise an owner–driver, or a larger firm with more flexibility to respond to sudden peaks of demand, and possibly a sophisticated distribution planning system, depends on the individual case. For a large firm, it is naturally possible to have sophisticated distribution systems in house, since these will give monopolistic profits, and to contract out the actual provision of trucks and driving to individuals.)

The deregulation battle is still being fought in Germany. Regulation was introduced there to reduce competition with the railways, themselves a major source of state funds at the time when regulation was introduced (Laaser, 1991, pp. 136–140), and in France, where the motivation was much the same but where the railways own the largest trucking company. The pressure for deregulation is partly under the influence of the EC since all such regulations within countries reduce the freedom of movement and trade across the Community. The first steps were taken with the passing of the cabotage directive, allowing trucks of other nations to pick up return loads, or further loads, within the EC. At present this looks like favouring the Dutch, who have a very long tradition of being transporters to Europe and who have a substantial fleet of vehicles, and firms used to large-scale organization. The Germans are concerned since they only get the insignificant benefit of the purchase of fuel and a few meals etc. from the trucks that cross the country, causing congestion and destruction to the motorways there. Special taxes on foreign vehicles in the form of permits were prohibited by the EC as discriminatory and contrary to the free movement of goods (Article 30 of the Treaty of Rome). The same would not apply to universal road pricing for all vehicles. It was suggested that it would be introduced for goods vehicles from 1994, and for private cars from 1995 (Böhme and Sichelschmidt, 1993, pp. 11–12).

12.3   FARE STAGE BUS AND COACH OPERATION

Bus and coach services remain extremely closely regulated in most of the European Community, with the exception of the UK. After a brief examination of the regulatory rationale of France and Germany and some of its apparent consequences, we will look at the experience of deregulation of the services in the UK. Express coach services will be considered first and then we will consider the experience of local fare stage bus deregulation.

As a hypothesis for the section, you are invited to consider whether the coaching and local bus industry is as near as we can get to a 'contestable market', and as such whether the Dixit critique of such markets may not be appropriate. The critique amounts to saying that the market is so competitive that no one should consider entry unless they have some advantage on the basis of cost or product. Such differences would of course break one of the assumptions of the theory, that both incumbents and entrants have access to the same technology, and therefore costs. You may wish to consider whether the implicit critique of contestable market theory is invalid because of network aspects and product differentiation. Finally, whatever is decided on the question of contestable markets, the potential role of the competition authorities and the questions of justiciability in relation to predatory tactics will clearly be important, and may determine whether deregulation is desirable in the long run. 'Justiciability' refers to the issue of whether it is possible to devise rules on which guilt or innocence can be decided. For example, how can one decide whether a price cut by a strong firm is a competitive response to a rival's price cut, or whether it has the predatory intent of driving the rival to bankruptcy?

12.3.1   The rationale for regulation in France and Germany

In both France and Germany, buses and coaches are regulated largely to protect the railways from 'destructive competition'. Both rail services have a public service obligation, to provide transport to all parts of the country without discrimination. The definition of discrimination is, however, the social and not the economic version; that is to say equal prices are charged to social equals, as opposed to charging prices reflecting the costs of provision. Thus rail fares are set in relation to distance travelled and not costs. This at once prevents, or at least complicates, the adaptation of services to demand. It may be that at a lower cost there would be enough passengers to make the service viable, or more likely, fares might have to be raised in areas that are expensive to serve either because of terrain or more probably because of insufficient density of population. This would conflict with the governments' objectives of support for rural populations, particularly in France. The implicit cross-subsidy in not matching costs makes all such services liable to 'cream skimming' (or 'cherry picking' as it is called in Germany). **Cream skimming** is where the service becomes unviable or more expensive for the majority of users when a group of users is 'abstracted' by a competitor offering lower charges or better service. With indivisibilities in supply, as in the provision of a bus or train, the remaining users have to pay more for the same service if it is to cover its costs. If this makes the service too expensive, it may lose sufficient users and become completely unviable. The potential for such competition has been realized for a long time, and laws have been passed in both countries to prevent it, by giving the state railways complete monopolies over all public transport, with the exception of certain urban environments where a local monopoly is set up, such as the RATP in Paris, which involves both SNCF and the RATP (the Paris Regional Transport Undertaking which runs the buses and the Metro).

This does not mean in either country that all buses are actually run by the railways (or in France by one of the innumerable subsidiaries of the Railways – some 256 in 1991 – but in this context the principal subsidiary of interest is Cariane, which is the major coaching subsidiary). Cariane may run the service itself or may subcontract to small operators, often extracting the monopoly rent resulting from its statutory monopoly and leaving the minimum feasible return for the small operator. In Germany small local operators may be employed on a similar subcontracting basis, but more commonly the Deutsche Post provides a combined postal and bus service, as do the Postbuses in the UK. The organization is, however, different from the UK's in that the German Postbuses are primarily buses which deliver mail to the post offices for local delivery, whereas in the author's experience in the UK the Postbus is part of the delivery system to outlying farms and settlements, and correspondingly extraordinarily slow. In both France and Germany there are some complaints about the lack of sensitivity to market opportunities, and about excessive costs. Because of the railways' monopoly, long-distance coach services are not an alternative to the railways in either country; almost no long-distance coach services exist.

12.3.2 Deregulated coach services in the UK

Coach services were deregulated in the UK by the Transport Act of 1980. This permitted any operator to provide coach services providing they were for distances of more than 30 miles measured in a straight line. The effect of this is chronicled in Kilvington and Cross (1986), and a summary is provided in Vickers and Yarrow (1988, pp. 372–375). The case highlighted by the latter is that of the entry into this market of British Coachways, who attempted to compete on price, and entered with prices half those of National Express. To the author, this indicates a touching but totally misguided faith in contestable markets as a theory, and in its applicability to coach services, or a belief in the inability of the incumbent company, National Express, to respond because of an adverse cost structure. One must also assume that British Coachways cannot have believed that the response of National Express in matching these prices could be judged predatory by the Office of Fair Trading, since this would presumably mean that their own prices on entry were equally predatory. (Vickers and Yarrow (1988, p. 374) suggest that National Express were in fact engaging in predatory pricing, but do not raise the point that the competition authorities could hardly do anything if the entrant was also acting in a predatory manner.) The result was the speedy exit of British Coachways, progressively from about 6 months after entry and almost completely within 2 years.

The circumstances surrounding the demise of British Coachways show how restrictive the assumptions of contestable market are. National Express were able to respond rapidly with low prices to match those of the entrant, and well before the entrant could build up a market presence. The incumbent had an established market and the goodwill that goes with it, even if this was only through the customers' knowledge of their services. The only way the entrant could have overcome this was by heavy advertising, and this of course is a major sunk cost. Secondly, National Express were able to deny British Coachways access to the Victoria Coach terminal, and hence interchange for British Coachways passengers with National Express services elsewhere. The rival terminal was near Kings Cross, and was less accessible. This is the equivalent of denying interconnection facilities for a telecommunications company, as pointed out by Vickers and Yarrow.

More generally, the result of the deregulation was to increase services and cut fares on the more popular routes, and cause considerable retrenchments on other routes. This is exactly what one would expect to see from deregulation, where there is relatively free and vigorous entry, as there was. Cream skimming becomes the norm, and thus the cross-subsidies vanish, and the routes surviving on the basis of cross-subsidy also vanish. Whether this is socially desirable is open to question. Liberal opinion would suggest that the increase in market transparency is worth obtaining, and that such routes as have been cut should be restored on a franchised basis, with the franchise going to the firm demanding the lowest subsidy. It is also possible that after the initial shock, firms will realize that such routes can be served, if they charge higher prices. At present this is pure theory, since the author knows of no examples.

12.3.3 Fare stage bus services

The predominant pattern of development in the fare stage bus sector after deregulation in 1986 has been a rapid entry by smaller firms, which then were either absorbed by takeovers, withdrew or remained small players, with the continued domination of the incumbent operators. The latter have often extended their market areas, usually within the approximate boundaries they used to serve, or by completing routes of which they served a part. In spite of 27.6% of urban areas being affected by competition, the Transport and Road Research Laboratory estimated that only 10% of routes were affected by 1987 (cited in Preston, 1988, p. 13). In some cases, larger competitors have entered and forced out weak incumbents. Experience has been very varied, but competitive markets with lots of operators each manning a route on a small scale have not emerged anywhere.

Typically, fares have been matched to the level of the lower fare of the operators, and any wars have taken the form of service level wars, trying to dominate the route by overbussing. This is clearly more cheaply done by the use of minibuses. In many cases where the rivals are of sufficiently similar size and financial standing, the period of aggression has been followed by more or less gradual accommodation, exactly as suggested by the repeated prisoner's dilemma games. Where one of the rivals has been substantially larger or financially stronger, the overbussing has frequently been associated with various predatory practices; the most common is the running of buses just before the rival's, thus picking up his passengers. In some cases this has even been accompanied by running a second bus behind the smaller rival's to ensure that he can neither turn back and start the route again, or drop back to allow a larger interval in which passengers can arrive. In one case in Fife, the two shadows actually asked the rival's driver when it was his break so that they could go to the lavatory!

The Office of Fair Trading and the Traffic Commissioners come out of this very badly. Clearly any such infringements should be monitored covertly, since they will disappear if any warning is given. In the only two cases known to the author, the Traffic Commissioners sent a letter to both operators telling of the date of a monitoring exercise. Exemplary behaviour ensued. In one case, this resulted in a 40% increase in revenue of the smaller operator; this was not considered evidence! The smaller operator in that case had to withdraw from operation of the route and now restricts itself almost entirely to tendered services. In the light of this one cannot but wonder whether this was the pattern also reported in the Highland Scottish Omnibuses Ltd case before the Office of Fair Trading (1989, p. 41, paragraph 5.23).

The other way in which the Office of Fair Trading comes out badly is the delay in processing complaints. Clearly in the context of oligopolistic rivalry, particularly in cases involving entry by a smaller operator, a quick response is vital if the funds of the smaller operator are not to be exhausted by the predatory tactics of the larger incumbent. In the Highland Scottish Omnibuses Case (Office of Fair Trading, 1989), the entrant, Inverness Traction, started complaining about predatory tactics such as the running of unscheduled duplicates just before Traction's scheduled departures in July 1988; notices of an investigation were only served in March 1989, by which time Traction had debts of £150 000 and was negotiating to be taken over by Alexander's, a coach company based in Aberdeen. Traction was taken over before the judgment was given. Traction's failure was partly due to the almost predatory entry that had been practised by starting with fares about 40% below those of Highland

Scottish Omnibuses and at a service frequency which matched Highland's existing service, thus doubling the service level; Highland matched the fares on most routes and undercut on one, and increased its frequency in response to Traction's entry: both of these actions were considered predatory by the Office of Fair Trading.

Inverness Traction seems to have been as guilty of predatory tactics as Highland's, which seems an exceptionally stupid approach for a financially weak entrant. Presumably they should have relied on gradual entry such that predatory tactics would at least not be profitable for the larger incumbent, or would be very obvious and thus possible to combat at law. Entry even under these conditions would always seem dangerous if one considers the following: the static Cournot model suggested in section 10.2.2 suggests that it will pay an entrant to come into almost any market at a low level of operation. But following the accommodating behaviour implied by Cournot, this process would lead to a competitive market as the result of continued entry and thus zero economic profits. To avoid this one might expect any monopolistic incumbent to wish to have an entry-deterring stance, which as we saw could only be credibly maintained by vigorous defensive action at each stage. This appears to have happened in most cases according to Preston (1988).

(A point of interest: discussions with some of the participants in the Highland case suggest that much of the problem was deep antipathy between one of the founders of Traction and the management of Highland. This was not, however, confined to the management, and workers joined in the mutual predation with apparent relish.)

Highland's response to Rapson's Coaches, who had put on a rival service on one of the other routes in Inverness, had been to double its frequency from three to six buses an hour, which added to Rapson's extra two buses amounts to an enormous increase in service. When this was joined by Inverness Traction, albeit on a very slightly more roundabout route, and with the lower fares that were matched by Highland, Rapson's had to withdraw from the service. The report (Office of Fair Trading, 1989) makes no further mention of this, presumably because it is unclear whether it was Highland's or Inverness Traction's activities which killed off the competition from Rapson's. Other competitors seem to have weathered the storm and remained in contention at the time of the report, although the actions of Highland Scottish Omnibuses in expanding its output seem to this author to be at very least questionable, and certainly designed to signal that accommodation, if not withdrawal, by the entrant had better be the next step.

The failure or inability of the Office of Fair Trading to prevent the elimination of smaller companies stems from the problems of justiciability of competitive as opposed to predatory behaviour. The reports make quite clear that the present judgements are based on the criterion that services must run at a point where average revenue on the service is greater than or equal to avoidable (alias variable) costs; this is an adaptation of the Areeda–Turner condition, which states that prices below marginal costs are clearly predatory, and that these can be approximated by average variable costs in industries with constant marginal costs. This is based on the notion that under competition this is the short-run minimum to which prices could fall before the firm would cease production. However no one has to my knowledge suggested rising marginal costs in the bus industry, and so these variable costs will always be below total costs. This position is therefore essentially also a predatory one, if the firm moves into it voluntarily. We could therefore define as predatory, entry at a level of either price or quantity which would force average costs to be below average revenue on the route as a whole, using the entrant's total costs as the yardstick; in the presence of such entry, the incumbent could appeal for protection. Equally, if the monopolistic incumbent expanded output on entry, or cut fares such that in spite of a non-predatory entry, average costs on the route would fall below average revenue judged by the incumbent's costs, this would also be judged predatory and the entrant could obtain protection.

This might be criticized as protecting competitors and not competition, but seems the only way of protecting competition if one follows the Dixit rejection of contestable markets. That is, unless one wishes to ensure that competition can only occur between large firms, whose financial backing allows them to make predatory entries in this sense, with the goal either of enforcing accommodation or forcing out the weaker incumbent in pursuit of monopoly. The criterion suggested above would enforce 'cost contestability' since if lower cost enterprises entered and the incumbent could not reduce costs to match, the incumbent would have to withdraw.

While such a criterion would protect competitors and arguably competition, it would appear to force such a level of competition if rigidly (and speedily) enforced that there might be some unexpected side effects.

1. Contrary to popular opinion, peak hour services tend to be the most expensive to put on, since they are usually only full in one direction, and neither crew nor bus may be needed for the rest of the day. This can be mitigated by the use of large buses, such that they are full at the peak, and have substantial spare capacity at other times of the day. However these are still more expensive to run than midibuses for the off-peak period, unless fares are so low that only a large bus at approximately capacity loading can cover its costs. Thus an entrant running midibuses at a constant rate (and accepting lack of capacity at the peak) could undercut and drive out the incumbent or force him to imitate this approach (an example of cream skimming). The local authority would then have to arrange for tendered services to be put on in the peak hours.

2. It would also have the potential effect of causing certain services to operate only on the parts of routes with most passengers; thus the ends of routes might be poorly served. This is exactly analogous to the problems of peak hour service, but transposed into the spatial context. The need for an even loading would ensure a good match between the number of passengers on the various parts of the route and the service levels.

3. This approach also leaves the question of redistributing buses from routes that have a particularly high flow in the peak to those that have relatively higher flows in the off-peak. Such buses are arguably operating at marginal and not average cost, since they would be 'paid for' by the peak hour passengers. This argument is in fact easily resolved by combining the two routes for revenue and cost purposes. As pointed out by Kahn in relation to trucking, this sort of imbalance between supply and demand is either a product of regulation that forces trucks to return empty, so that the established cost structure is for one-way operation, or more generally, is a sign that capacity has not adapted to the level of output, and the trucks are not being used appropriately by carrying loads in both directions – or in our context, buses shifted to equalize marginal revenue across all routes.

4. This rigorously procompetitive stance would face some problems in the presence of secular decline in the numbers of passengers. The question of which operator cuts and by how much, or how far fares should rise, becomes a strategic game; since if the policy were successful it would be played out among firms that were not equals, continual judgements would be needed to police this structure, or it would develop into a collusive oligopoly as market sharing and pricing agreements developed. This would seem to defeat the object of the exercise.

It should be noted that the above possible results all implicitly assume that reactions to entry will be 'fully rational', i.e. that consumers will be indifferent as to which bus company they use, and will choose entirely on quality. They also assume that it does not take time to develop a market because of the slow growth in public knowledge about the new routes, fares and service. In general there are thought to be at least some of the public who will try out almost any new thing – a large group who will gradually convert as reputation grows, and a smaller group who will not change unless they have to. If this is the case, assuming equal qualities of service, it is only if the first group switch and remain with the new (remaining seems unlikely if they are natural switchers), and offset the stayers in terms of numbers, and the slow shifters shift in roughly equal proportions, that the market will in fact be shared. Furthermore, the lower the scale of entry, the less likely information is to be spread by word of mouth and the longer it will take to build the market. Thus there will be a sunk cost in the period of market build-up for the entrant. This can be shortened by heavy advertising, but at a cost. The apparently neutral policy outlined above is still therefore to the advantage of the incumbent and gives some protection.

Predatory practices in this industry have also consisted in denying access to bus terminals, or, after the Office of Fair Trading ruled that denying access was anticompetitive in the Southern Vectis Case (Office of Fair Trading, 1988), only giving the entrant peripheral stands, and very often deliberately obscuring them with one or more of the incumbent's buses. In some cases, inspectors have been employed to redirect passengers from the entrant to the incumbent's buses. Furthermore, the information kiosks or offices have been manned only by the incumbent's staff, who have practised a policy of no information or disinformation about the entrant's services. The entrant's staff have been excluded from rest-room, cafeteria or other facilities at the station.

A further favourite anticompetitive device is the use of season tickets which give access only to one operator's buses. This is clearly much to the advantage of the larger company, since access to a wider range of services is likely to be valuable. The convenience of season tickets and their considerable advantages in saving boarding time and hence speeding the operation of the bus are benefits that make the trade-off between legislation against this practice and the benefits in terms of improving competition of dubious social benefit. This type of tying contract is a recurring problem in the transport field, in relation to these season tickets, frequent flyer programmes on airlines, and inter-line ticketing in the railways, if they are indeed privatized and franchised in separate lots. It is compounded by the bias from the ownership of booking offices, or computerized reservation systems in the context of airlines.

A major purpose of the 1985 Transport Act, which deregulated fare stage bus services, was to stem the increasing flow of subsidies to buses. This had risen from £71 million in 1972 to £897 million by 1982 in current prices; that is a rise from £31 million to £435 million in 1980 prices. The deregulation was accompanied by two measures to ensure this reduction: firstly, local authorities, most significantly the major conurbations, were no longer allowed to provide blanket revenue support subsidies and this resulted in very large rises in fares in the metropolitan areas – a mere 15% in Manchester but 250% in south Yorkshire. Secondly, as all the services were to be privatized, or treated as if they were even if ownership remained with the local authority, the local authorities could no longer rely on cross-subsidy to keep unremunerative services going. Firms were to submit tenders for each service; the local authority had to accept the firm willing to do so at the lowest subsidy. This process has in general been regarded as a success, at least in terms of controlling local authority expenditure under this head. The total expenditure on revenue support in 1990/91 was £223 million, of which £84 million was in London.

In summary, it looks as though in spite of some entry at the start of deregulation, and continued competition, there has been surprisingly little deconcentration of the industry. There have been several takeovers, so that many of the operators are now part of substantial groups. Whether the benefits of competition will therefore be lasting remains to be seen. It should however be remembered that most bus services are in a difficult position because of competition from the private car. What will now happen to any attempts by planning controls to shift passengers from cars to public transport, and hence for most of the UK to buses, is anyone's guess. It can no longer be planned by the local authority, but it should in theory be perfectly simple: expansion of demand due to restrictions on the car would lead to expansions of capacity by the bus operators and naturally, as we saw, if a more rigorous competitive structure is enforced, this would lead to a perfect match between capacity and passengers. This, however, ignores problems of peaking, and of through ticketing, both of which might pose real obstacles in this context. Traffic congestion is considered to cost £15 billion per year, and so its solution by integrated traffic management may once again become an issue; we will perhaps see whether supply will respond appropriately.

12.4   RAILWAYS

Railways throughout the world tend to be nationalized industries, and in most of Europe they have also had the benefit of substantial state subsidy as well as protection by regulation. This section will consider the situation in France, Germany and the UK as the problems are in many ways similar, but the solution being proposed in each case is very different. The French are hoping to gain greater market sensitivity by devolving authority to the regions and emphasizing comprehensive transport planning and the integration of different modes of transport. The Germans and the British, on the other hand, are aiming to retain an authority to look after the track; this will remain in government ownership in the UK, whereas in Germany it will be a private company, with a government regulator. In both countries the operational activities will be privatized but the proposed method of privatization is different in each. In Germany they are planning to franchise time slots, whereas the British plan to franchise whole routes. All three claim to be meeting the requirements of the European Community policy on railways, which calls for separation of track and operational finances in order to be able to charge for the use of the tracks by rail services offered by the railways of other countries as well as domestic ones. This section aims to look at the implications of these different strategies, and whether they can all fulfil the European policy requirements.

Before proceeding further we will define the term 'slots', which will be used frequently both in this context and in relation to landing rights at airports. Slots are periods of time for which a particular user has the right of access to the infrastructure. A slot in the context of railways might be the period from 09.00 to 09.10 using a certain platform at Waverley Station, Edinburgh, and then depending on the operational definition it might include the use of the rails on the London line for a certain period. In this context, as in the context of airlines, the mix of types of train or plane is crucial, since one of the major determinants of their frequency is the gap required for safety. If a fast train is following a slow one, there will initially have to be a large gap so that by the time it comes to a stretch on which it can pass the slower train, there is still the required distance between the two. In the context of airlines, the turbulence created by a Boeing 747 can literally turn a light aircraft upside down if it is following within two miles. A smaller commercial airliner still requires a substantial distance to avoid dangerous turbulence. It follows that the capacity of a facility can be increased by scheduling large planes or fast trains in a block rather than interspersing them with smaller or slower ones.

12.4.1 France

The railways in France benefit both from huge state subsidies and the complete protection of a regulatory environment in which they determine whether bus lines can operate in competition with them; this they very rarely allow. Nevertheless they require ever larger amounts of subsidy, and the amount of freight carried is declining year on year. A recent major report, the *Rapport Haenel* (1993) has carried out an in-depth investigation into the various problems. It found no good solution to the loss of freight traffic, although it was of the opinion that the railways had been inflexible and insensitive to the needs of their users. On the passenger side, although the spectacular *Trains à Grande Vitesse* (TGV) have been successful in attracting increasing numbers of passengers, they have failed to offset the losses on the regional and national express network. Haenel (1993) traces part of the problem to the insensitivity of the railways to passenger needs, and to their failure to adapt to new market situations. The suggested remedy is to split the running of the railways into major supporting directorates at headquarters, such as Finance, Engineering, Ordering and Supplies, and Personnel, but to entrust the operational aspects to the local regional railway authorities. These regional authorities have been outposts of the central departments and have tended to report to their departmental seniors in Paris rather than to provide solutions for the customers in the regions. Thus a *région* wishing to organize more frequent services within its jurisdiction had to deal with the representatives of the different directorates of the SNCF, which slowed and complicated negotiations. With the new arrangement, the regional office of the SNCF will put forward the solutions and will buy in advice from the headquarters departments as required. The emphasis of the regional solutions is to be the integration of the railways into a multi-modal transport plan. This sounds conceptually very similar to the plans produced in Britain in the 1970s for the conurbations. One can recognize the purchaser–provider split beloved of the British government in the proposed relations between the regions and the central offices. It will be interesting to see how this mix of socialist planning and near-market organization works; the organizational structure certainly looks very complicated.

12.4.2 Germany

The German situation is considerably more serious than the French. The debts and annual deficits are enormous; there is huge overstaffing on the state-run West German railways; many of the surplus staff are *Beamte*, state officials who have jobs for life according to Federal law. The accounting system is typical of that of a regulated industry that is out of control; it is designed to conceal performance as far as possible, so that no one can be held responsible. The old East German railways have even worse overstaffing and have suffered from gross underinvestment, and hence very poor equipment. Naturally the two organizational structures are incompatible. They are therefore forced to change, and this change comes at a time when there is a strong trend towards deregulation in Germany. It is therefore no surprise that they are aiming for the most complete privatization of any of the three countries being considered. The following section is taken from the author's paper on the reforms in France and Germany (Bowers, 1994, section 2.3).

These major reforms are to be achieved in several stages, as shown in Figure 12.1, which is translated from the editorial in *Internationales Verkehrswesen* (Anonymous, 1992, p. 305). There appear to be no changes in the planned timetable of reform on its passage through cabinet, according to Thimm (1993). The first stage, starting 1st January 1994, is to transfer the running of the railways to an authority called the *Bundeseisenbahnvermögen* (literally Federal Railway Assets, known henceforth by its acronym BEV). Its main function is to set up two separate branches, one for operations and one for government activities. The functions of the divisions of the operational branch are clear from their titles. The government branch is, however, more opaque; three divisions will be set up, the first to operate the necessary inspection and control services – effectively the railway regulator; the second will take over the entire personnel of the present railways and hire them out to the various other branches as needed. (They will be paid the rate for the job that is established under the new companies. If that means taking a pay cut, the difference will be made up by the BEV.) The third branch will act as a treasury and will pay the debts incurred by the two railway companies and arrange the finance for any planned investments. (These debts amount to some 149 billion Deutschmarks, which includes DM 24 bn for underestimation of payments to personnel, and DM 80.5 bn owing to reserves for pensions. Both reflect the creative accounting applied in the past to mask the poor performance of the Deutsche Bahn (*Regierungs-kommission Bundesbahn*, 1991, p. 55). They are being taken over by the government in order to give the new companies some chance of viability.)

The second stage will be the creation of a new company, the DBAG (*Deutsche Bahn Aktien Gesellschaft*, German Railway private limited company). This will take over the operational aspects of the BEV. Local authorities (*Länder*) will buy unremunerative services from either this company or any other that will operate them. Some of the local railway companies may have an advantage here as they operate more cheaply than the existing DB (Laaser, 1991, p. 37, table 14). The present level of subsidies is however guaranteed. The treasury and personnel aspects will remain with the BEV. The regulatory aspects and any other public sector operations will be taken over by the Federal Railway Office (*Bundeseisenbahnamt*).

Stage three consists of the further separation of the three operating divisions into individual limited companies within the DBAG, which will act as a holding company. Thus there would be a Passenger company, a

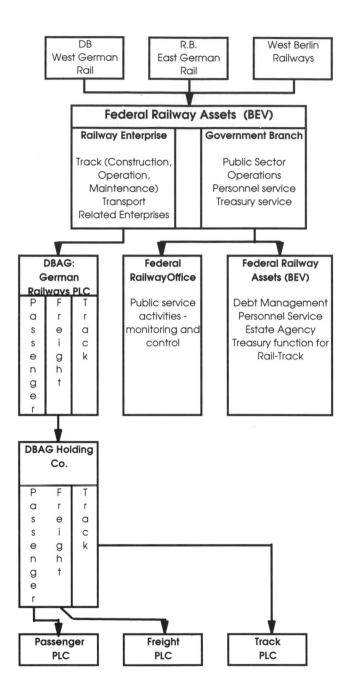

Figure 12.1 Stages towards privatisation on the German railways.

Source: Translated and adapted from Internationales Verkehrwesen 1992, p. 305

Goods company and a Track company. The passenger and goods companies will compete in an open market for slots franchised by the rail company. This market will also be open to railway companies from abroad, or the independent companies operating within Germany now. This would take place within three years after the founding of the DBAG. The final version of the Act (Thimm, 1993, p. 200) seems to insist on the split of the company into three divisions whereas the original figure in Anonymous (1992) suggested a transport company and a rail lines company. The figure has been modified to fit with the act.

The fourth and final stage is the complete privatization of the three companies and the winding up of the DBAG. This would therefore leave three companies, the one a monopolistic owner of the rails and infrastructure, presumably under close control of the Federal Railway Office, and two transport companies, working in competition with other railway companies. The law emphasizes the need to retain the entrepreneurial and free market nature of the rail company, and to ensure that it does not take on altruistic or other activities. As was seen above, the slate will be wiped clean by the shifting of the 'old debts' to the BEV; however, the Act is clear that the company will be responsible for the repayment of all future loans to the government. It seems that the government will be responsible for the interest payments (Thimm, 1993, p. 201).

This system should produce a truly competitive outcome; it is made plausible partly by the number of railway authorities next to Germany's borders, who might well bid for slots on the German system, possibly in order to integrate it with their own long-distance trains.

12.4.3 Great Britain

The proposal for the privatization of British Rail is to set up a rail track authority under government ownership, a regulator to allocate franchises and to arbitrate on disputes between the track authority and the franchisees, and to franchise routes to private companies. At present, the proposal is that these franchises should run for seven years; as the capital stock required to run a train has a very much longer life, there is a vigorous debate about the length of franchise. Under the present proposal it is expected that there will be very difficult problems at the point where assets have to be handed over at the end of franchises.

This proposal is an extreme test of the Chadwick–Demsetz hypothesis. It would appear to allow for competition only at the level of purchase of the franchise, whereas the German proposal encourages continuous competition on each route. It will cause a maximum of problems in relation to boundaries, since many trips will inevitably involve using the lines of several different franchisees. It is not clear whether through trains will operate. There will have to be some form of through ticketing, and credit transfers; this is apparently already operated between the different regions of British Rail. It therefore poses no insuperable problems; indeed the banks have an enormous system of inter-bank transfers on which to model it. However, it could pose some unpleasant problems in terms of consumer perception, since the prices could appear quite anomalous if one franchisee is charging on a very different basis from another. In theory, it should pay the franchisees to coordinate their train timetables to gain a maximum amount of interconnection, since this should encourage more people to travel. This will however imply a good deal of communication between franchisees, and one wonders how competitive the market will remain, or whether communication will be followed by collusion.

The reason for selling the railways off in this manner is presumably the same as operated in other privatizations: they will get a better price for a monopoly.

12.4.4 European Rail Directive 91/440

This directive is the result of much hard bargaining in which there were apparently two distinct camps: a predominantly north European group including Britain, Denmark, the Benelux countries and Germany, and a southern group including France and the Mediterranean countries. The northern group favoured the separation of rail track and operations, and the independent franchising of operations, so that trains operated by British railway companies could buy slots which would allow them to run trains from Inverness to Vienna or Madrid in competition with companies from any of the other EC nations, or indeed Japanese companies operating within the EC. The southern group, however, wished to retain strong national control over all the aspects of railway operations in their countries, and therefore vetoed the Commission's ideal of an open railway throughout Europe. The result is the retention of the split between track and operations, at least in accounting terms, and the requirement that any charges to international groupings be non-discriminatory. However, the international groupings would be set up on the basis of bilateral agreements, thus retaining national controls.

Clearly none of the arrangements outlined above infringes the European Directive. However, the French system, with its emphasis on the primacy of regional requirements within France, will tend to pose considerable problems for the organization of through trains if there are busy routes involved. Indeed, one might doubt whether it will be any easier to organize an international grouping to do this than it is to organize through trains under the present Berne Convention arrangements. The UK franchising system at first looks more open, but is in fact at least as problematic since the franchises are let for whole lines and the franchisees could therefore be as uncooperative as they liked, as in the French case. Indeed, there will be the additional complication that each franchisee on the route will have blocking powers over the route as a whole; this gives very considerable monopoly power, akin to the owner of the last plot in a major building project. Indeed in theory, that final owner can extract the complete monopoly profit from the whole route. It is really only the German system that would lend itself to a pan-European railway system. However, the German system is unlikely to become operational for at least five years, and who knows what changes may take place by then?

12.5 AIRLINES

This section considers the parallels between the developments in US airlines since deregulation in 1978 and those observed in bus deregulation in the UK. Airlines were completely regulated, along with trucking, in the USA. The Civil Aeronautics Board prevented duplication of services and entry, such that the airlines were sufficiently protected to allow costs to escalate and fares to rise correspondingly. In general, load factors were low. After deregulation, as was observed in trucking in the USA, and in buses in the UK, the number of firms multiplied and competition in various forms flourished. Thereafter there was a period of consolidation during which the number of firms fell back approximately to its pre-deregulation level, but prices and costs have remained relatively low and the number of passengers has increased very considerably.

As in the case of buses, the cost of staff decreased. (Preston (1989) considered that in the UK some large bus companies permitted new entry in order to put competitive pressure on their own bus crews to accept lower wages and greater flexibility of working conditions.)

With the entry of competitors, and the fall in the cost of aircrew, the frequencies of services increased markedly. In the initial period airline profitability fell, and this was one of the pressures which led to consolidation. These pressures were sufficient to generate destructive competition; the number of aircraft available, combined with the adverse economic conditions in the period 1979–1982, meant that the predicted flexibility of use of aeroplanes was not possible to realize. The surplus aircraft therefore enabled small operators to enter the market, and further increase competition at a time when there was no possibility of generating a sufficient revenue to cover costs. This is exactly parallel to the situation in trucking in the 1930s, although very clearly the 1970s/1980s situation was not nearly as grave.

With this intense competition, average fares fell by 30% in the period from 1978 to 1984. The pattern of fall illustrates the difficulty of estimating the price being charged for a service. The full-price fares increased, in some cases by large amounts (up to 250%); however, the discount fares fell on average by 10% and there was a very significant increase in the proportion of travellers on discount fares – from 45% in 1978 to 80% in 1984 (McGowan and Seabright, 1990, p. 289). This fall in average fare was accompanied by a 50% increase in passenger miles between 1978 and 1985.

Large companies put pressure on their smaller rivals by several means, some of which we have come across before.

1. Predatory pricing was used in some cases; the most famous is probably that of Laker on the North Atlantic route. The price response of British Airways to Virgin's transatlantic services was vigorous but not apparently predatory in the technical sense.
2. Computerized registration systems were used to good effect by lines large enough to develop them. They allowed the airline providing the

system to favour its flights in the presentation of the package, and most flights are apparently booked on the basis of the first screen that appears on the computer. The worst abuses were prevented by regulations, but bias cannot be entirely eliminated. Secondly, the systems gave their owners an enormous amount of information about the market on each particular route, since they recorded all reservations and enquiries and were programmed to optimize the proportion of full-price and cut-price seats on the owner's airline. In the BA–Virgin case, it was alleged that they were also used to actually divert passengers, although this appears to have been on the basis of hacking into Virgin's computers.

3. Frequent fliers programmes, which reward the frequent traveller with free air miles, naturally benefit the largest airlines in much the same way as season tickets benefit large bus operators in any city. They are in a sense a form of tying contract, which are normally illegal under competition law. It will however be difficult to outlaw them, since they are very popular with travellers and their parent companies, who use them as a tax-free bonus to their employees. If the threat from smaller airlines declines, frequent flier programmes are likely to disappear. Lower fares will be a better means of differentiating the product if all lines are offering air miles.

4. In the USA there are relatively few airports where congestion is a serious problem; however, not surprisingly these are the most important. The allocation of landing slots in these airports has had several perverse effects from the point of view of the preservation of competition. Firstly, they are allocated on the basis of 'grandfather rights', that is to say the established airlines who already had slots retain them unless they fail to use them; they can also trade them with other airlines. Secondly, a tradition had grown up that the price of a slot was related to the size of the plane, smaller planes paying less. This is clearly not appropriate, since the congestion is related to spaces at terminals and to actual runway time. Small planes use the same space and take more runway time than larger ones, particularly when one allows for the fact that they require to keep greater distances from large planes on landing or takeoff. The appropriate way of charging for slots would be by auction, so that the more profitable the route, the more an airline would be willing to pay; this would both encourage the use of larger planes and would discourage the use of congested airports as hubs in a hub-and-spoke system if there was an alternative direct route. These considerations are going to be particularly important in the European context, since many of our airports are congested. It is notable that under Bermuda II, the international agreement on airline operation, the auctioning of slots would not be permitted; the USA in particular is extremely concerned about the possibility of charging in this way for slots at Heathrow, since the North Atlantic routes would be severely affected.

The ownership of slots also favours the scheduling of flights as a spoiling tactic. It is possible that a route could actually support two

flights, and thereby provide full satisfaction of consumer requirements. However, if a dominant airline can timetable its flight so that it
spans the periods in which demand is most acute and schedules a large
aircraft, this may leave insufficient customers for even a smaller
aircraft. The price of tickets can be correspondingly raised: this is
known as the Crowded Bus problem (see McGowan and Seabright,
1990, pp. 341–343).

Once a reasonable degree of consolidation was achieved, the market
followed a pattern of price leadership based around Texas Air.

The pattern of competition provides no support for contestable market
theory, although this theory was put forward as being applicable to
airlines in the USA, just as it was suggested for buses in the UK. There
has been almost no hit-and-run entry, and the pricing has depended on
actual competition on the routes with potential competition in the sense of
other airlines being established at one of the airports along the route also
contributing to lower costs (Hurdle *et al.*, 1989). Competition on a route
may be limited by the potential of the route, and for routes with few
travellers the size of plane that can be used economically has important
implications since the costs per seat mile of a 500-seat Boeing 747 are
approximately one-third of those of a BAC 111, which has only 91 seats
(McGowan and Seabright, 1990, p. 323).

Although the market is by no means contestable in the sense that profits
will induce immediate entry, McGowan and Seabright (1990, p. 331)
suggest that competition is sufficient to enforce what they call **cost
contestability**. This is the situation where there is strong downward pressure on costs, since a high-cost airline is vulnerable to entry as it will take
time to reduce those costs in the presence of competition. They point out
that the lower costs and correspondingly lower fares are quite likely to
imply higher profits, and this appears to have been the result in the USA
once consolidation had taken place.

12.6 SUMMARY

It has become clear throughout this chapter that all of the transport
industries which rely on timetables and networks are subject to predatory
practices which may stifle competition. This only exempts trucking, which
may well be a naturally competitive industry. Equally it has been shown
that competition following deregulation has tended to contain costs and
ensure that services are appropriate for the market; a free market therefore provides a better environment than the regulated structures that
preceded it. It cannot, however, be emphasized too strongly that a slack
competition policy in these industries could lead to private monopoly and
hence all the evils of the regulated environment without any of its social
benefits, in particular the ability to protect the interests of minority groups
and control of externalities through cross-subsidization. The free market
still allows for these social goals to be achieved using tendered services to

provide transport for groups who are not well served by private transport, and to control pollution and other external effects using taxation – such as road pricing or fuel taxes – and/or direct regulation by pollution controls.

(Trucking may therefore provide an example of monopolistic competition. The range of different 'addresses' in terms of types of provision on both supply and demand sides may preclude oligopoly, particularly as entry from neighbouring addresses would seem to be very free, whether those addresses are defined by size of organization or type of service offered.)

FURTHER READING

A marvellous mix of theory and empirical example is given by:

Kahn, A.E. (1970) *The Economics of Regulation: Principles and Institutions*, 2 vols, New York, Wiley.

A good review of the effects of deregulation on the coach industry is given by:

Vickers, J. and Yarrow, G. (1988) *Privatization: An Economic Analysis*, London, MIT Press.

The changes in airline behaviour are reviewed by:

McGowan, F. and Seabright, P. (1990) Deregulating European airlines. *Economic Policy*, October, 284–344.

Health services and the market for health

13.1 INTRODUCTION

This chapter looks at the managerial economics relating to the largest single service industry, which in the UK used 6.6% of GDP in 1992: the health services. We will examine it in four sections:

1. A brief outline of the previous and present structure of the NHS will be given. Since the latter is based on setting up markets within the NHS, we will then examine the potential effects of market signals on medical practices.
2. Markets in health care almost inevitably involve problems of insurance, and the associated issues of moral hazard and adverse selection. It will be shown that these affect not only the relationship between the patient and the insurer but also the relationships of health service professionals with both their paymasters and their patients, although the relevance of moral hazard as opposed to economic motivation is questioned.
3. Competitive markets are supposed to equate costs and benefits. The problems of estimating costs in health care will then be suggested in relation to joint costs and the required pricing mechanisms. We will show that the present policy of requiring trusts and other providers to price on the basis of average costs gives solutions which are almost bound to lead to deficits and certainly do not provide a good mechanism for allocating health care.
4. In section 13.4 we will examine the types of market structure that we would expect to result from the reforms in the expected interactions of district health authorities, their own providers, in the form of both hospitals and general practitioners, the independent hospital trusts and the GP fundholders. It is anticipated that there will be considerable monopoly power in the system, and hence that it will not make an efficient market. Indeed, we could anticipate that this new system will create a public relations and marketing sector in the industry.

13.2 THE NHS PAST AND PRESENT

The NHS was set up after much initial protest from the medical profession in 1946, and to discuss so large an organization for the complete period from then until 1989 seems cavalier. However, throughout that period the NHS was a unitary structure funded entirely by central government. It therefore represented one of the largest single hierarchies in the world; the author is unable to confirm that it was the third largest after the Soviet army and the Indian railways, but the myth points up its very large size. Since it also was designed to remove health care from the market, there are no unambiguous measures of demand by which to ration the supply of health care. It is therefore an exceptionally political environment, and as such is subject to all the problems of 'government failure'. These include the unprovable accusations of excessive size, as suggested by Niskanen (1971), regulatory capture by groups within or outside the organization since focused groups can have a disproportionate influence in any such organization, and finally the usual complaints about bureaucracies or monopolies, that they prefer to serve themselves than to serve the public.

One version of the causes of the 'crisis in the NHS' in 1989 was that the human resource policies of the NHS were inadequate, and this was reflected both in poor pay and in poor industrial relations (Duncan *et al.*, 1992). This was not however the view of the crisis taken by the Social Services Select Committee, who came to the view that the problems in the NHS were largely those of ineffective management due to lack of control of expenditure. This manifested itself in very large differences in length of stay for similar operations and in the resources apparently used, suggesting a lack of efficiency within the service. The focus of the reforms was therefore to find a way of using the resources actually devoted to health care in more effective ways.

Prior to the reforms, the structure of the NHS may be seen as comprising two sets of agencies: the Family Practitioner Committees, paying general practitioners, dentists, pharmacists and ophthalmologists as independent contractors to the NHS and serving as the gatekeepers to the second group, the more specialist services provided by the hospitals, who were run by the District Health Authorities along with the Community Health Services. In England in 1983, the Family Practitioner Committees were responsible for the disbursement of 23% of NHS expenditures, and the District Health Authorities for 68%. Throughout the 1980s, various schemes were introduced in providing fees for individual services to general practitioners, to encourage provision of birth control, cervical smear tests and vaccinations, for example. The principal source of GP funding was still the direct payment of their salaries. It will be noticed that apart from the relatively small operations covered by fee for service contracts, there are few direct incentives linking payment to quality or quantity of service.

Discussion about the lack of incentives and the consequent inefficiency of the service focused on two sets of 'perverse incentives' in the system as it then was. The first of these perverse incentives manifested itself in the problems of organizing payments for 'cross-border flows' under the RAWP. The system in force in 1989 allocated hospitals that had received patients from other Health Boards a sum based on the average costs of care in that diagnostic group. This was subject to two problems: firstly, that the patients crossing borders contained a substantial number of difficult cases requiring particularly specialist treatment at greater than average expense; and, secondly, that the system was so slow and complicated that payments were made two years in arrears. In a period of rapid inflation the lack of incentive such an uncertain system provides is clear. A further perverse incentive derived from the fact that day patients were not paid for at all; to get payment the hospitals would have had to force the patients to stay overnight. There is however doubt about the importance of these perverse incentives, since incentives apparently hardly had any impact on the staff in charge of admissions, whose medical orientation was unaffected by such long-range financial considerations for the organization as a whole. There must, however, have been perverse incentives set up at the level of investment and expansion, though again the inter-relationships may have been weak.

The final assertions of the last paragraph, that the medical orientation of the staff who actually took decisions neutralized the impact of the perverse financial incentives operating at the level of the organization as a whole, provides the key to one of the other main planks in the support for the 'purchaser/provider split': the idea that the NHS was being run by and for medical staff with an ancillary aim of providing a service to the patients. This is an aspect of the set of factors coming under the rubric of 'producer led demand'. Where decisions are being taken by an elite group with little managerial constraint, there is an obvious possibility of such abuses occurring. These may take various forms. Doctors may fail to match services to the requirements of the patients by not giving them sufficient information to take decisions on the alternatives for treatment, or by failing to give enough information to reassure patients that the discomfort is a normal part of the healing process. They may fail to organize appointment systems appropriately, thus causing unnecessary waste of patients' time, in the name of efficient use of doctors' time of course. At a more abstract level, it might take the form of the conservatism of continuing to prescribe expensive branded drugs when generics of equal effectiveness have become available, or prescribing expensive placebos such as cough medicines, vitamins, or – more sinisterly – tranquillizers, to get troublesome patients out of the surgery, failing to keep up with developments in treatment, or failing to monitor colleagues who for reasons of overwork or negligence are endangering patients or providing poor value for money. All these will be recognized as typical complaints of consumers against the monopolistic supplier, and it was therefore hoped that by providing competition these problems would be reduced. However since the purchaser has to be well informed if competition is to work, the appropriate purchaser seemed to be the general practitioners, spurred on by their competition for patients.

There is an alternative explanation to the whole process of reform which would revolve around the theory of regulation outlined in Chapter 3 in the critique of Anderson's view of social-democratic relationships. The breaking down of the service into rival units, each of which has an interest in retaining secrecy for commercial reasons, breaks down the large blocks of staff and unions which can provide a rival source of information and a countervailing power to the government. In terms of Stigler's (1971) theory it reduces the concentration of the interest group and increases any costs they might have in seeking regulation. The government can also shift any problems of shortage of resources to assertions that it is mismanagement that causes them rather than the shortage of resources. This is likely to be a watertight case, since, as will be shown, it is impossible to establish the costs of a particular procedure because of joint costs, and the 'perfect' management system (i.e. one that is perfectly informed) is undesirable, since it would require more than optimal resources. Hostile parties can therefore always point to 'abuses' and waste. In this view, the hidden agenda is to weaken the bargaining power of the NHS and thus be able to introduce cuts in service levels without taking the blame for doing so. This is a particularly shrewd approach with producers of 'reputation goods' since they cannot afford to allow their reputation to be tarnished if their rivals can use this to pick up business at their expense. We would therefore expect to see the NHS Trusts defending their levels of service, and in so doing, defending the government, even if the funds are in fact inadequate.

13.2.1 The purchaser/provider split

The merits of splitting the purchasing decision from the decisions about the actual supply of treatment were pressed initially by Enthoven (1985). The idea was that the GP is the expert agent of his or her patients and that he or she would therefore be able to purchase the specialist care from hospitals in a normal market transaction between well-informed participants. Thus in the early stages we were promised a computer system which would be on each GP's desk and which would show the prices of operations being offered and their availability at hospitals in the neighbourhood. Furthermore, since GPs would be budget limited, they would have a strong incentive to provide care cost-effectively, and in particular to carry out procedures in their own surgeries where this was safe and practical, rather than sending the patient for expensive hospital treatment at the patient's inconvenience (since an extra trip, and often a longer trip would be required), and the government's expense (since such treatment swells the requirement for hospital services, and these are apparently more expensive than GP services due to the overheads and infrastructure required).

The purchaser/provider split has been implemented to give two main sets of purchasers and three sets of providers. All money comes from the Department of Health, but it is channelled either to the District Health Authority via the Regional Health Authorities, or directly to fundholding General Practitioners. The DHAs as purchasers are enjoined to seek the best value for money in health care with the budgets available to them. These budgets are based on the resident population in their areas and go to purchase both General Practitioner services and hospital and other specialist services. The fundholding practices are large practices with lists of more than 9000 patients, although that limit may be removed, who are responsible for purchasing all forms of health care provided that any one episode does not cost more than £5000. If a patient suffers a heart condition requiring by-pass surgery, which costs considerably more than £5000, the payment for this episode will be made by the NHS directly to the provider of by-pass surgery. There is an experiment in progress which gives the GPs control over the complete budget, including such expensive episodes (Giles, 1993). The extent of switching between providers by these fundholding GPs is likely to provide the competitive aspects of the market, since they are not bound to go to any particular provider and may indeed go to providers outside the region. Thus they buy from whatever purchaser provides the best value for money in terms of timely delivery of services within reasonable reach; they may set up bulk contracts in which they agree to buy all their services of a particular type from one particular provider, or they may hunt around for the best deal at the time. The Glennerster Report (1992) showed that even in the very early stages, where the hospitals were often ill-equipped to provide price quotations for individual operations, these practices were having considerable influence on the levels of service provided for their patients.

The providers may be divided into the following groups: District Health Authorities' hospitals and general practices, NHS Trusts and private sector providers. The District Health Authorities now fund general practitioners who do not wish to take up fundholding status in order to avoid the managerial responsibilities inherent in controlling their own budgets, and these GPs are expected to send their patients to the specialists with whom the District Health Authority has taken out contracts. It may take out contracts with its own hospitals, with local NHS Trusts or with private sector providers. The District Health Authority hospitals and specialist providers differ from Trusts only in that they operate as units within the overall District Health Authority budget. The NHS Trusts, however, operate their own budgets on the basis of revenues received from the two sets of purchasers for services provided. At present both District Health Authority and NHS Trust hospitals rely principally on bulk contracts to provide amounts of any particular service, usually similar to those provided in previous years, at agreed prices. While this makes the bulk of the market less competitive, it allows both providers and purchasers to plan expenditures more effectively. Any of the purchasers may take out similar contracts, or contracts for individual items of service, with private sector providers.

Since the District Health Authority would have to fund any losses made by its own hospitals, there is an obvious tendency for DHAs to purchase from their own providers; however, fundholding GPs now service more than 25% of patients in England and Wales and there is therefore considerable flexibility in the system. This affords a strong incentive to the various providers to improve their services. Since GPs are budget-constrained, there must be some question as to whether cost minimization is the dominant incentive in the system. There is however no question that the split between DHA GPs and fundholders provides the basis for a 'two-tier system'. This follows from the overall budget limitations on the DHA hospitals, who have a captive market in the patients of DHA General Practices, but they have to compete for the extra funds provided by the fundholding general practitioners when they purchase services from the hospital. The incentive to provide timely treatment for the patients who bring in extra resources is thus stronger than the incentive to treat patients who are locked into the DHA as provider. This finds its starkest expression if the DHA budget runs out before the end of the year; wards are then closed, and only those with access to external funding can still be treated. Furthermore, fundholders' budgets were initially fixed at relatively generous levels in order to facilitate transition to independent management.

It is clear that one effect of the new system will be to increase management costs. These will be manifest in two major ways; it will be necessary to collect more detailed material internally on costs, and if payment is by individual patient on a cost-plus basis, this level of detail will extend to the costs associated with each patient. The collection may become an end in itself. It should however involve management time in its analysis and in the development of improved practice on the basis of the findings. Such a learning organization might well recoup the resources used by the improvements in efficiency, but this is not a certainty. The savings in a manufacturing context are often spread over thousands of units of output; while this would be true of such procedures as receiving patients and collecting their basic data, it would not be true of such things as individual operations, which are only performed in much smaller numbers. The savings thus have to be larger since they will affect fewer units of output, and the product of savings times the number of units is likely to be smaller. Secondly, management resources will be expended on marketing – finding new clients and retaining old ones. As management costs have increased from 6% in 1989 to 12% in 1993, we may wish to consider that they were approximately 22% in the USA in 1980 and 1985 (Donaldson and Gerard, 1993, p. 30).

13.3 MARKET INCENTIVES IN HEALTH CARE

Although health care is a private good in the sense that it is both 'rival' and 'exclusive', it is a most unusual one in that the consumer faces the potential for disaster of two types: firstly, a disaster in the sense that one's whole life can be altered for the worse by poor health; and, secondly, a disaster in the sense that the financial costs of treatment may exceed one's ability to pay. Thus it is a classic case of a service for which one might wish to take out insurance. However, as we noted in Chapter 3, such markets lead to severe problems of motivation, and even provision in the sense of suffering from 'missing markets', due to the combined effects of moral hazard and adverse selection. These turn out to be all-pervasive, and an examination of them shows that it will be impossible to have 'perfect motivational signals' in the health care market. Following Donaldson and

Gerard (1993) we shall examine these in relation to patients' consumption of health care, doctors' provision of it, and insurance companies' willingness to insure.

Not only is the market in health care subject to perverse incentives, but it is fraught with ethical problems. The most all-pervasive is the question of who should pay for health care and whether it should be available to all, and hence whether it should be linked to the person's ability to pay. Since the normal allocation mechanisms of the market rely on this to restrict demand which might otherwise be infinite (though this is highly contestable), abandonment of this principle raises questions of rationing, and takes us back to the issues of 'social solidarity' discussed in Chapter 3. We will therefore discuss the questions of rationing by price in relation to the question of access, and give some prominence to the discussion of the basis for assessing 'moral hazard' in the context of health care.

It might be thought that these are issues of public policy, and that managers will simply carry out orders received from the legislature; this author would doubt the ability of any legislature to provide such full guidance that managers would be able to carry out its intentions without an understanding of the principles. Furthermore, the legislature may well provide contradictory guidance, and at least part of the manager's role will be to provide advice on the appropriate resolution of the contradictions and the future development of policy. This is no different from the need for the Managing Director of a firm to provide suggestions to his or her Board of Directors on the future strategy of the firm.

Ideally, we might consider the relevance of various issues of medical ethics, in relation to which treatments to provide. While the well-educated medical manager needs to be well-versed in them, we shall *not* get involved here, even though they involve both consumer choice and allocation of resources, and hence should be considered within the realms of economics.

13.3.1 Moral hazard and the consumer

Diagnosis and treatment require both theoretical and experiential knowledge by the practitioner. This implies that the 'patient' cannot know the full extent of required treatment; indeed he or she will often not know even the diagnosis. With this information asymmetry comes the possibility that the more knowledgeable party may deceive the other, to its advantage. Supplier-led demand with professionals prescribing overtreatment is an obvious possibility, and is discussed in the next section. This section, however, deals with the potential that desire for attention, discomfort, worry about health or the desire for a sick-note may cause people to demand more health care than is good for them, and certainly more than they would if they had to pay the full costs of care. The view is sometimes expressed that the demand for health care is unlimited and that care given freely at the point of service is likely to be grossly overused, and to drain national resources in unsustainable ways. This then leads either to arguments in favour of treating health as a truly private good, and requiring payment for it on a fee-for-service basis so that market forces may prevail, or to the arguments about the rationing of health care which will be taken up in the final section.

This section considers the impact of various payment systems on demand by patients. Firstly, we consider the ways in which consumers may be dissuaded from overconsuming by the charging of fees for service, or insurance premiums. We shall also consider evidence that these charges may deter people from consuming health care even though they would benefit from it. These issues may all be regarded as examples of 'moral hazard'. We shall also consider the related problem of 'adverse selection', which affects all insurance based systems.

The material cited in this section is drawn from Donaldson and Gerard (1993); readers who wish to take these arguments further are warmly recommended to this source, which is commendably short, very clearly written and very widely researched.

13.3.2   Health care and moral hazard: An attack on the concept

Moral hazard was defined in Chapter 3 as occurring when 'the terms of a contract cause an opportunistic alteration in the behaviour of one of the parties'. Thus, in relation to the actions of patients, the two elements are, firstly, that the membership of some health care scheme should alter that behaviour; and, secondly, that this change of behaviour is taking advantage of the clauses of the contract by using information available only to the patient to turn the deal to the patient's advantage. There is nothing opportunistic in the take-up of the insurance to cover the expenses of full health care in cases of accident or severe disease, even though the patient might literally not otherwise be able to raise the money. It becomes 'opportunistic' when behaviour is changed by, for example, failing to take the care of one's health that is implied in the contract, or going to the doctor for trivial complaints that do not really require treatment and thus raising the insurance company's costs without real justification. Such changes are unobservable since they rely on information on the level of demand in the absence of a contract and opportunism held only by the insured party. This makes it impossible to judge whether the increase in demand that results is opportunistic or simply the appropriate result of the insurance contract. The contract was after all taken out with the specific aim of making health care affordable at the time of consumption.

It is tempting to assume that all increase in demand by the patient for low cost health care can be equated with moral hazard. Only the patient can know what would have been consumed without the insurance policy, and thus any changes can be equated with opportunistic behaviour, since this knowledge is not available to the insurer to judge whether a particular visit was justifiable. This seems approximately equivalent to saying that the contract is based on a 'need' for health care, and that there should therefore be no change of behaviour whatever the prices or absence of them. That this is not a meaningful notion can be derived from the debates about the removal of birthmarks, and other cosmetic surgery. It is clear that in some cases the improvement in well-being is every bit as great from these 'optional' operations as from orthopaedic surgery for the reconstruction of ligaments or other 'essential' items. Nor can we define need by the saving of life, since there will be significant cases where the quality of the life to which the person is returned may be such that there is doubt about the value of saving it. For example the saving of a dear friend of the author's from pneumonia, only to face continuation of the pain of collapsed vertebrae and senile dementia in an unfamiliar environment of hospital, was at best questionable.

The definition provided by Donaldson and Gerard (1993, p. 31) is different from ours, and avoids the question of opportunism. For them moral hazard is defined as an increase in demand for health care due to a lowering of price compared with that which would have been consumed if the consumer had been fully informed and had faced the 'proper' market price, in the form of the opportunity cost of the treatment. This implicitly defines the contract of insurance to cover only such treatment as would have been consumed in the perfect market. But given ignorance on health matters by the patient, there is no unambiguous rational basis for a decision about visiting a doctor. Thus the fully informed rational decision is not necessarily a useful theoretical fiction in this context, but such fully informed rational decisions are the foundation of the perfect market. Their absence precludes the perfect market. The information problems are exacerbated by the presence of risk, and our discussion of risk in Chapter 7 suggested that it was likely to be a hazy concept for many people even in the context of investment decisions where information was relatively good. In the medical context, as an individual cannot know the full implications of the range of risks and costs of treatment, a perfect contract is impossible to specify even theoretically. In lay terms, what we are trying to identify is whether behaviour is being changed in accordance with the contract or not, but as we cannot know how the individual would behave without the contract, this is not a meaningful concept.

With this level of doubt about the validity of the term 'moral hazard' in this context, we will concentrate on the perfectly valid information about changes in behaviour in relation to market signals. The information about such changes, even if we cannot specify optimal behaviour or hence optimal signals, may allow us to take informed decisions as to the type of payment structure that will be desirable in health care. The next subsection thus deals with the changes in consumer behaviour in response to different pricing structures.

13.3.3 Changes in consumer behaviour in response to payment structures

The types of payment systems as outlined by Donaldson and Gerard (1993, p. 88) might be divided according to the influence of payment on consumer demand, as shown in Table 13.1. This table excludes both the insurance scheme with a maximum payout clause and the pure free market fee for service, which represents a situation that is much more extreme than the cell in the top-right of the table. It aims to divide the methods of charging according to their impact on the consumer. The impacts on the behaviour of the providers are discussed in section 13.3.4. The columns represent the absence or presence of price based disincentives to consume health care; the rows the absence of or potential disincentive to, being insured. Taking each cell in turn:

Table 13.1 The influence of payment on consumer demand

Effects of increases in costs in the long run	No fee payable for service	Fee payable
No impact	National Health Service: General Practitioner/ hospital treatment	National Health Service; prescription charges; dental treatment
	Insurance schemes paid by employers	Employer's insurance schemes with co-payments
Increased membership premiums	Health Maintenance Organizations	Private insurance with co-payments

- The first cell indicates that for the purposes of demand moderation, the NHS-style free service should be identical to the insurance schemes paid by the employer providing for full payment of the fees and other costs. In neither of these methods is the consumer faced with any consequence of the costs of his or her demands. This is treating the topic in a purely economistic mode; it may be that the NHS commands a sense of loyalty and hence responsibility in use by consumers, whereas the commercial nature of insurance-based schemes encourages the consumer to 'get full value for money from the firm's contributions' and hence to overconsume.
- The second cell shows the situation where, because there is no price mechanism operating at all, the idea of gross overutilization of such schemes has encouraged many of them to incorporate some form of 'co-payment', where a fee is charged, which may or may not relate to costs. While in the case of the NHS prescription or dental charges there is no such relationship, in other schemes in the USA, for example, a 25%, 50% or 95% co-payment has been incorporated. These fees are designed to, and empirically do, reduce the demand for services, though they appear to affect the poor, with little change in behaviour by the rich.
- The third cell includes schemes where there is no fee for treatment, but where the costs of the premiums will go up to reflect the increases in costs for treatment. This provides only a very weak, and possibly perverse, incentive to reduce demand. It will be weak because any holding back by one customer will have only a tiny effect on the total

bill, and that customer has no leverage on the others and so no control. It is a classic free-rider problem. Such free-rider problems often seem to engender a frame of mind which says, 'If I don't someone else will, and then I shall have to pay; I had better get my money's worth'. Private schemes of this sort with restrictions of access to certain forms of treatment seem likely to engender a particularly strong reaction, and very possibly legal action to try to get one's money's worth.

- The fourth cell includes both sets of motivations; the co-payment to restrict demand, and the rising premiums to reflect overall rises in costs.

It may be helpful to think of the two issues in the two rows of the table as affecting the decision to purchase the insurance, and the relative performance of the scheme representing relatively good or poor value for money. It would be at this point that the difference in costs and service for schemes with restrictions on the maximum payouts would enter the consumer's decision. The decision whether to use the insured service can be seen as more probably related to the columns of the table.

The most substantial experiment reported by Donaldson and Gerard (1993, p. 89) comes from the Health Insurance Experiment conducted by the Rand Corporation:

> Families participating in the experiment were randomly assigned to 14 different fee-for-service (FFS) insurance plans, or to a pre-paid group practice. The FFS plans had different levels of cost sharing which varied in two dimensions: first the coinsurance rates were zero (viz. free care), 25, 50 or 95 per cent; and second, each plan had a maximum dollar expenditure (or MDE) limit on annual out of pocket expenses of 5, 10 or 15 per cent of family income up to a maximum of $1,000, beyond which the insurance plan reimbursed all covered expenses in full.

The number of people involved was 5809 for the free plan and cost sharing, and 1982 were allocated to the prepaid group practice.

Those who paid no fee incurred total expenditures 67% greater than those who paid 95% of the costs, and visited doctors in surgery 63% more often. Those who paid no fee incurred expenses 25% greater than those who paid a quarter of the fees. Expressing these as price elasticities for health care indicated a price elasticity of between −0.1 and −0.2 (Donaldson and Gerard, 1993, p. 90), and these differences were related to the difference in the number of times they went to the doctor rather than the expense of the treatment once there. This suggests that few patients resist doctors' suggestions.

It further points up the danger that if doctors' fees declined through economic competition, the effect would be, under a fee-for-service regime, to encourage a greater level of overprescribing in order for doctors to gain a target level of income.

The reduction in demand was, as one might expect, greater for lower income than for higher income groups. In poor income groups (the lowest third of the income distribution), people who were paying for health care were 46% less likely to present themselves to the doctor with a case of acute pharyngitis (sore throat) than those receiving free care. This difference was even greater among children, where poor children were 32–67% less likely to go to the doctor. The probabilities for the higher income group with sore throats were approximately equal, whether they were paying or not; the richer children were between 35% less likely and 119% more likely to go: in other words, it either made no difference whether they were paying or not, or some perverse effect of paying for service was present.

It might be thought that the differences in demand were due to people cutting out trivial trips to the doctor. However, this does not appear to be the case, since an examination of the likelihood of getting what was judged by doctors as 'highly effective ambulatory care' was much less among poor children as opposed to rich children. The poor children in cost sharing plans were 44% less likely to go to the doctors for such care than those in free service plans; the difference for richer children was only 15%. Donaldson and Gerard also quote the results of Foxman et al., who demonstrated that cost sharing reduced appropriate as well as inappropriate antibiotic use to similar degrees (p. 91).

These results are similar to those reported for other co-payment experiments, such as the charge levied in Saskatchewan in 1968 of $1.50 (Canadian) per office visit and $2.00 per house call. The effect was to reduce use by between 6% and 7% for the whole population, but by 18% for the poor. Such experiments can have perverse effects, which are equally predictable in economic terms. The introduction of Medicaid charges of US $1.00 per visit and $0.50 per prescription reduced doctor visits by 8% but hospital demand, which was not charged for, went up by 17% and thus raised the programme costs considerably (Donaldson and Gerard, 1993, p. 91). This offers a clear example of the general proposition that one should expect high cross-elasticities between close substitutes – and that in the presence of easy substitution price differences will lead to diversion of demand.

The study by Birch on UK prescription and dental charges (Donaldson and Gerard, 1993, pp. 92–93) showed that consumption of prescriptions fell by 7.5% in the non-exempt groups whereas they increased for the exempt group by 1% between 1979 and 1982. In a later study he also showed that 'elderly consumers of dental care who are not exempt from payment of charges are four times more likely to receive emergency care only, than elderly people who are exempt from such charges. The former group is also 340 times more likely to receive a check-up only, and, when receiving treatment, receive 40 per cent less treatment than exempt patients'. Donaldson and Gerard point out that some of the latter effects could be the result of producer induced demand, in that dentists might be inducing demand from the exempt groups to raise their incomes at no cost to their patients.

The difficulties of interpretation of demand changes are well illustrated by two problematic items mentioned in this section of Donaldson and

Gerard. Firstly, although the expenditure on medical care by poorer people was clearly lower when they were cost-sharing, this did not seem to affect their health status. This, however, may be taken more as an illustration of the difficulties of judging health status, particularly if one has to allow for some illness that is 'created' by doctors – either in the form of medicaments which disagree with the patient and aggravate their condition or in the form of minor illnesses which clear up with or without treatment but which are only registered if a visit to the doctor is made. Thus people who go to the doctor more appear in worse health. Secondly, it appeared from some of the studies (Donaldson and Gerard, 1993, pp. 94–96) that people receiving free health care from a health maintenance organization actually demanded much less since overall expenditure was considerably lower. However, it would appear that this follows from two effects which cast doubt on the reality of lower demand: firstly, there is evidence that the health maintenance organizations only accepted healthy people as members. This is therefore an example of adverse selection by the provider rather than a change in demand by the consumer. Secondly, the health maintenance organizations tended to discharge patients much more rapidly, and cause costs to rise in nursing homes and the like. The difference in costs is thus partially illusory and is due more to provider actions than consumer behaviour. It is to the effect of economic incentives on providers of health care that we now turn.

13.3.4 Changes in provider behaviour in response to economic incentives

The traditional image fostered by the professional associations is of doctors, or other health care workers, as the perfectly disinterested agents, who put their knowledge at the disposal of the patient, never stinting on effort or expense. Such rosy views naturally belie a reality in which the decisions of even the most dedicated doctor have to balance his or her own survival and effectiveness with the amount of work required to satisfy the patient's needs. This conflict over resources has been largely masked by the weakness of management control, and the willingness of staff to adapt to shortage of resources constraining service delivery by a mixture of personal commitment, rationing by waiting and conservative decisions about care for those who might not benefit. There was also enormous potential for passing expenses to other agencies, or indeed accepting expenses which were in fact consequent on poor social provision in housing or care. (The excessive length of stay in hospitals of people who had unsuitable homes or lack of required assistance for recuperation provides a well known example; this practice is likely to be threatened by the present clarification of budgetary responsibilities and tightness of funding.) On the negative side, information asymmetry allows doctors to get away with poor care as the result of the ignorance of the patient, coupled with the well-known ability of the human organism to heal, particularly if undertreatment is balanced with a judicious over-referral to specialist services for any suspected life-threatening conditions. Like most non-doctors, I am happy to believe that the former explanation, of carefully rationed care which avoids real risk to the patient, is much more appropriate than the latter.

Such global characterizations are not helpful for analysis. If we accept self-interest by both doctor and patient, we find a substantial area of overlap since it is in the doctor's interest to retain the respect of his peers and his potential and actual clients, and thus to cure the patient. Furthermore, there is that fascinating conditioning which we call conscience, and which once inculcated forms a strong part of our self-image and hence, in economese, our utility function. However, while it is in the patient's interest to be cured and the doctor's to do the curing, there are substantial grey areas in any decisions by the doctor, in the form of the extent of tests to be prescribed, or whether to favour the aim (suggested in the French system) to get the patient back to full fitness for work as quickly as possible no matter what the expenditure on medicines, or the equally laudable aim of minimizing possible drug side effects by minimizing the range of drugs prescribed. The benefits may be very ambiguous, particularly if the doctor is also having to consider basic shortages of resources, and hence the opportunity cost of treating one patient more lavishly being the non-treatment of another patient. Thus the differences in funding methods, and hence the differences in self-interest, may have very considerable impacts on practice. This is certainly 'moral hazard' in the sense of changing behaviour as the result of the contractual conditions, but one might bring forward the same arguments about opportunism being absent. In this case it is more difficult, since the doctor has the knowledge and the patient has not. Thus a moral purist might say that opportunism, 'self-interest with guile', might be said to be probable.

The tendencies we would expect are in general obvious. Where there is a fee for each unit of service, there will be a tendency to increase the number of units; where the fee varies according to the condition (the Diagnostic Related Group or DRG), there will be a tendency to record any diagnoses where more than one condition prevails as being predominantly the more lucrative condition. These sorts of bias are likely to exist wherever payment or results are measured by a particular item; if number of bed-nights is the measure of the moment, hospital stays will be extended unless no beds are free. If it is the number of cases treated, creative accounting may be applied to the definition of a case, people being called in once for diagnosis and once for treatment being treated as separate cases, etc. (This is no different from the production engineer's measures of 'efficiency' in terms of machine utilization – the percentage of time a machine is being used – which encourage useless production for which there is no market, or British Coal's useless pursuit of greater output of coal in order to reduce the cost per tonne even though it could not be sold.)

The effects of shifting from a cost-plus system (retrospective reimbursement), where all costs are met by the insurance company, to a Prospective Payment System (PPS) based on either some standardized fee per day as in the SHARE programme for a type of case or fees based on DRGs paid per episode, are documented by Donaldson and Gerard (1993, pp. 125–128):

> Both PPSs reduced cost per day and costs per admission relative to the comparison group. The SHARE programme reduced costs per day by 9.1 per cent. The DRG programme reduced costs per day by 9.8 per cent and costs per admission by 14.1 per cent. However both programmes increased admissions, the SHARE programme by 8.8 per cent and the DRG programme by 11.7 per cent, thus supporting the hypothesis that these particular types of PPS encourage more episodes of care despite reducing the cost of each episode. Hospital lengths of stay were shortened by 6.5 per cent under the DRG programme, but were unaffected by the SHARE programme.

There is also evidence for DRG creep, that is to say for the gradual shift from low paying DRGs to high paying DRGs (Donaldson and Gerard, 1993, p. 128). The types of treatment also change; no changes were recorded in intensive care but there were reductions in non-surgical procedures such as CAT scans and physiotherapy. A particularly disturbing report comes from Fitzgerald *et al.* (quoted in Donaldson and Gerard, 1993, p. 129) on the treatment of fractured hips:

> Although mean length of hospitalization fell (from 16.6 to 10.3 days) after the introduction of PPS, the number of physical therapy sessions received also decreased (from 9.7 to 4.9) and the proportion of patients discharged to nursing home care increased (from 21 per cent to 48 per cent). More revealing about effects on patient well-being is that, after six months, 39 per cent of patients remained in nursing homes under PPS as opposed to 13 per cent pre-PPS. According to the authors these results suggest deteriorating care and an overall cost increase.

These results show very clearly the direct results in terms of differences in the types of care, and the indirect results in terms of shifting costs to the nursing home sector as a result of the stimuli provided by the payment system. However, the numbers dying within 30 days declined and within 180 days remained unchanged under PPS, and as further reading of Donaldson and Gerard shows, the results are by no means borne out in every study.

Similarly, there is evidence of adverse selection: the use of information held by one party to select into a scheme favourably. Firstly, it is clear that health insurance is about sharing risks, and that in theory, if the band of risks covered is too wide, the lower risk individuals will not feel it worthwhile to join insurance schemes, and the costs will increase because of the adverse selection of higher risk groups. This increase in costs in turn makes the scheme less attractive to lower risk persons. In the end the costs may be so high that even the high risk persons do not find it worthwhile to contribute. Considerable evidence for this process is found in Donaldson and Gerard, chapter 9.

The results of the appropriate commercial response by insurance companies to this problem is to narrow the range of risks covered in any premium group, so that as far as possible persons of equal risk are pooling their resources as implied by insurance. The closer match between risk and cost is the only way missing markets can be avoided – missing markets being the condition where both parties would be willing to trade, in this case take out insurance and insure, but are prevented from doing so by the particular pattern of organization of the market, often the lack of information available to both parties. The result of reducing the range of risk in each band is of course that poor risks, whether they are poor risks as the result of self-induced or natural causes, find it impossibly expensive to get insurance. Direct tests of this are difficult, since the reasons for non-insurance and the interaction with the costs of insurance would need to be fully known. It is, however, clear that lack of insurance in the USA correlates with poverty *per se* and with being non-white (Donaldson and Gerard, 1993, pp. 36, 153–157).

The second form of adverse selection occurs where the provider has knowledge of the probable costs of care for a person wishing to join a scheme (Health Maintenance Organizations or fundholding General Practices for example, as well as insurance schemes), and uses that knowledge to refuse or discourage that person from joining, often in spite of a contract to provide universal care. Thus the chronically sick, such as diabetics and drug or alcohol abusers, may find it difficult to gain access to systems of care that are appropriate for them. From the doctor's point of view one can sympathize; who would deliberately expose themselves to a lot of extra work, for which the pay would be inadequate by any standard since it is based on average costs for normal patients, and where there is a risk that the presence of that expensive patient will force uncomfortable choices to be made about the treatment of less expensive ones? The evidence from the USA (Donaldson and Gerard, 1993, pp. 155–156) seems to confirm the presence of such 'favourable selection' from the point of view of the Health Maintenance Organization, and it is clear that the increasingly tight capitation allowances in GP practices working within the District Health Authority and the limits on funding implied by fundholding practices will encourage 'favourable selection' in the UK.

The extent to which this refusal to supply is further encouraged by the moral climate created by the commercialization implied by 'internal markets' and the change of attitudes this implies is yet to be documented. Williamson (1975) provides almost the only serious attempt to incorporate such psychological factors into the economic working of organizations, and unfortunately this was dropped from the agenda of his later work. From personal experience of school teachers' strikes at various removes, and the present commercialization of the university system in the UK, as well as the cogent analysis of the 'NHS Crisis' by Duncan *et al.* (1992), it seems likely to this author that these changes in attitude will be very costly in terms of refusal to supply, and that they are extremely difficult to reverse.

The argument being put forward by Donaldson and Gerard would in this author's estimation be summed up by the following propositions:

1. It is impossible to establish allocative efficiency criteria, because of the failures in information which preclude the development of a 'perfect market'.
2. Thus we are in a situation of the 'second best', where partial moves to greater allocative efficiency will have unpredictable and very possibly perverse systemic results.
3. Greater efficiency is thus more likely to be achieved by managerial intervention, in particular by two sorts of monitoring and evaluation: (i) assessment of simple efficiency criteria of amount of unit labour and consumables used per procedure, and more importantly (ii) health gain measurements to ensure that best practice is followed and that useless or low usefulness activities are eliminated. This might involve the further development of such measures as QUALY – quality adjusted life years – as a measure of outcome, but these would certainly need a considerable amount of development.

Within either the return to hierarchy or the pursuit of internal markets, the understanding of costs is important. We therefore consider this in the next section, before using it in section 13.5 to discuss the implications of the purchaser/provider split and the types of market this seems likely to develop.

13.4 COST ESTIMATES FOR THE HEALTH CARE ORGANIZATION

This section deals specifically with the cost estimates required for pricing and the implications of costs for market structure in market or quasi-market situations. It does *not* discuss the overall social costs of different policy approaches.

The discussion in this section will focus on the case of pathology laboratories, which seems to the author to incorporate many of the principles of costing and control applicable to the even more difficult field of hospital and other facility cost management. The issues we shall be considering will cover questions of the presence of X-inefficiency and the extent to which this is likely to be solved by the introduction of competition and economies of scale, and hence whether there is reason to think that there is natural monopoly, or the potential for destructive competition. Secondly, the presence of joint costs and their implications for pricing will be considered. In the final subsection we shall discuss the implications of these cost structures for personnel and the dynamic aspects of management of quality and cost control, and the product mix, in the sense of the cost effectiveness of different pathology tests.

This section relies on the paper by John Stilwell (1993), to which readers are referred. The discussion of it is placed in the context of the earlier chapters of the book.

13.4.1 The pathology laboratory

According to Stilwell, pathology laboratories provide four major types of service: biochemistry; haematology, which is concerned with diseases of the blood including HIV; histopathology, which looks at cell structures; and microbiology, which identifies organisms which may produce disease and tests their sensitivity to drugs. Each branch has been subject to different levels of technical progress. The improvements in process control by the use of microprocessors, and the development of reagents which simplify tests and essentially shift the costs from the laboratory to the centre of production of reagents, have had particularly marked effects. The impact of these changes on productivity has often been uneven because of the lack of management processes which would ensure that the necessary adaptation of manpower and organization followed the introduction of the new technology. This is discussed in section 13.4.2. There is thus at least some apparent scope for improving efficiency by improving management. These unrealized efficiency gains are called X-inefficiency and are considered further below, before we examine how the costs may be expected to vary according to the number of samples processed by the laboratory – in other words the presence of economies of scale and their implications – in section 13.4.3.

13.4.2 X-inefficiency: Presence and causes

In any industry where there is little consumer pressure, and in health care because of the level of information asymmetry, we would expect there to be inefficiency due to slack practices and the lack of stimulus to improve. This effect would be stronger where this lack of stimulus is backed by organized monopoly in the form of a national health service, or in the USA, by virtue of limited choice and some element of professional ethics preventing publicity of the defects of other practices or clinics. This may be exacerbated by the bureaucratic structure of the industry; for example Stilwell cites the lack of clear investment decision criteria, and the lack of integration of investment in new machinery with staff training or staffing complements. In the wider health field, X-inefficiency is widespread; it is clear from the very wide disparity in practice between different nations and even different parts of a nation in the amount of surgery and the level of drug prescription that there is a lack of agreement about best practice (see Andersen and Mooney, 1990; Vayda *et al.*, 1984). The interesting issue is whether this disparity is predominantly the consequence of unethical practice following economic stimuli, or simply variations in views about appropriate treatment unrelated to the self-interest of the profession. In either case, since it has very different cost implications, it is certainly not the efficient outcome of a competitive market.

13.4.3 Economies of scale, natural monopoly and destructive competition

Economies of scale were shown to be due, among other things, to indivisibilities in the available sizes of machine, such that the capacity of the machine would remain underutilized until large-scale production was achieved, and potentially to greater specialization at larger scales. While both of these almost certainly operate in this field, the most evident would appear to be the first, and we shall consider the impact of this on costs in the laboratory. Table 13.2 shows the results of surveys on the staff required to process different numbers of samples. As can be seen, this gives a difference in labour productivity of approximately 800%. While some of the difference in labour productivity may be due to increased reagent and equipment costs which may not be viable for small laboratories, it looks as though there are substantial real cost differences, with advantages lying with the largest laboratories.

Table 13.2 Numbers of staff required to process samples

Source	Laboratory throughput (number of samples)	Number of staff
Audit Commission (1990), average laboratory	70 000	5
Stilwell (1991)	100 000	5
Stilwell (1992)	300 000	2.75

The process for haematology samples in particular is roughly as follows: a sample is received from the doctor; it is then placed in racks for testing. The automatic machinery and relevant reagents then take over and provide a series of approximately six tests per sample. There is thus a direct labour input in the placing of samples, and in the communication of results to the doctors. This labour input is roughly constant per sample, whatever the scale of operation. The reagent costs vary considerably according to the type of test, but again are independent of numbers of samples treated. (This of course could change if the NHS no longer has centralized purchasing arrangements as the result of the introduction of quasi-markets and independent organizations within the NHS such as the Trusts.)

The capital costs of the test machinery are again independent of sample size, since the machines can handle many more samples than any but the largest laboratories have to deal with in a year. Thus the smaller the laboratory, the larger the amount of spare capacity. The effect of this on costs is shown in Table 13.3; it assumes an analyser cost of £150 000, which gives an annual cost in the first year of £39 000 and which is then constant for the next nine years at £30 000 according to the example in Stilwell (1983, p. 95).

Since all of the other costs are constant per unit of output, assuming that the labour requirements are accurately adapted to the level of throughput, the scale effects would seem to be entirely related to the change in the level of fixed costs per unit. Thus the average total costs for different scales might be as shown in Table 13.4.

Table 13.3 Average fixed costs, the effect of scale

Annual throughput (number of samples)	Average fixed cost in pence (total fixed cost per annum: £30,000)	Average fixed cost per test in pence
50,000	60	10
100,000	30	5
200,000	15	2.5
400,000	7.5	1.25
500,000	6	1

Table 13.4 Average total costs for blood samples at different scales of operation

Item	Cost per test in pence Throughput: 000s samples				
	50	100	200	400	500
Labour	2.5	2.5	2.5	2.5	2.5
Consumables	2.5	2.5	2.5	2.5	2.5
Equipment	10	5	2.5	1.25	1
Overheads and phlebotomy costs	25	25	25	25	25
Average total cost	40	35	32.5	31.25	31

As Primeaux (1979) showed, the fact that there are economies of scale over the whole range of the market should not force us into rejecting a solution which involves competition, even though that competition means that the economies of scale will not be fully utilized by the firms in the market. He showed clearly that the competitive pressure produced by rival firms forced them to be more efficient than monopolists working in the same size market. We might therefore encourage in the brave new world of quasi-markets a variety of pathology laboratories in any particular area, so that the purchasers could shop around and hence exert the competitive pressure required.

There is, however, another reason why one might be suspicious of attempting to develop very large-scale laboratories serving a whole region. As well as routine tests which can be processed within a day or sometimes a week, there is a need for very rapid results from so-called 'hot labs', processing samples taken during operations, to reveal, for example, whether malignancy is present before completing an operation. These laboratories need the same equipment as the very large laboratories. Although the per-unit cost from the large laboratory would be very low for routine samples, the capacity invested in that laboratory is entirely surplus to requirements since the local laboratories could cope with all the required work. Taking work from them and giving it to the 'mega-lab' would merely push up their costs, since they would then be working even further below capacity.

We are thus left with contradictory indications; on the one hand it would be desirable to introduce competition in order to reduce X-inefficiency, but if we consider the requirements of the doctors for rapid results, we cannot allow competition to operate since this would make the smaller laboratories more and more costly. Three solutions suggest themselves:

1. We might opt for a management solution based on monitoring, which would accept the need for the localized laboratories, and the desirability of sharing out the work so that they are as efficiently utilized as possible, but would monitor their efficiency by developing a management accounting framework, and a knowledge of good practice so that 'yardstick competition' was being applied, but with managerial rather than market controls.
2. The second solution would be based on letting the market work, and encouraging mega-labs to compete with smaller labs by allowing all of them to price discriminate, so that the urgent 'hot-lab' work would pay the equipment costs, and the rest would be charged at marginal cost. This would give the well-run small laboratory an advantage over the mega-lab, since the latter would not have the option of doing 'hot-lab' work, unless it were located in the largest local hospital. The effect on rapid result test costs would be to raise them considerably, and as the hot-lab would be in a monopolistic position, some very careful controls would need to be instituted to prevent overcharging for rapid results, and cross-subsidy (which amounts to predatory pricing) on the work for which there was competition. We will return to this question in section 13.4.4. This solution is potentially unstable since the laboratory with the highest volume of rapid result work would have cost advantages both in terms of the costs of such work and its ability to cross-subsidize routine tests.
3. The third solution would be to press for the development of hot-lab technology which would permit true micro-labs for almost all the really urgent tests, and allow the market to operate for the routine tests. The second solution would tend to favour this result, since the high costs of rapid testing would prompt a search for alternative solutions of this sort – provided that some incentive to search remained under the monopoly.

Particularly if one considers the possibility that with smaller levels of output the difficulty of matching staffing to levels of demand increases, there is an obvious risk of destructive competition (as discussed in Chapter 12). The conditions for this are that the presence of spare capacity makes it optimal for each individual firm to charge a price below average costs, and potentially as low as marginal costs. This could clearly be the case if several existing laboratories were to be thrown into competition. This would lead to a period in which equipment could not be replaced, and potentially therefore a situation in which there would be a considerable backlog of obsolete physical capital to be replaced at some later date. Since at least some of the reason for replacing material is technical progress, this might have undesirable effects on the quality of care and it would certainly pose some problems for future budgeting since there would be a discontinuity in capital requirements, if these were still being rationed in the normal government style. There would also be a discontinuity in pricing since prices would suddenly increase when the destructive competition had run its course and one of the competitors had withdrawn from the fray.

13.4.4   Joint costs: Implications for pricing

The problems identified in pricing for pathology services are an example of the extremely widespread problem of joint costs in the health service. Joint costs occur wherever an input is used for more than one output, and where its use cannot be allocated to the different outputs. In general such joint costs mean that relative prices for the items produced jointly are set in relation more to demand than to cost. Great care has to be taken not to cut items which have joint costs allocated to them on an arbitrary basis, and which on that basis are 'not covering costs'. The example of the airline flight cited in section 7.3.2 provides a good paradigm for this problem.

A classic example of joint costs is the production of pineapple juice from canning pineapples; the process of peeling and slicing the pineapples produces a considerable amount of juice, and the proportions of pineapple and juice are approximately constant given the technology in use. Market demand for the two may however not be in the same proportions, and there is no way of allocating costs to allocate the relevant shares of costs to the two processes. Pricing is therefore entirely based on maximizing joint profits. In this case the relevant approach is to add the marginal revenues from each product at each quantity of output, provided that the marginal revenues are both positive; negative marginal revenues are ignored. This joint marginal revenue is equated with marginal cost, and the relevant quantity is produced; the relevant price is the maximum that can be obtained for that output in the market. If one of the marginal revenues would be negative at that output, revenue from that item is maximized (a price is charged such that the quantity sold would be at the point of zero marginal revenue). The surplus output is destroyed. Naturally this assumes that the necessary advertising to maximize profits at this price has been undertaken. The process where outputs are not produced in fixed proportions, which must be normal in the health services, is much more complicated in that the only solution is to model it mathematically, since it involves both the choice of total quantity and price and the relative quantities and prices. The formal calculations are given in Reekie and Crook (1987, pp. 391–398).

This solution does not seem feasible in health care contexts even in a free market. The production function that links numbers of different types of cases to costs would be very complex and is certainly not known at present. Even in the USA, where insurance claims should give hospitals a strong stimulus to get appropriate costing methods in place, and insurance companies should have a strong incentive to check costs, the costs would seem to be largely market based (Harrison, 1993, p. 6). The explanation for this complexity may be attributed to several factors, some of which are closely related to the theme of the costs of service industries:

1. In common with other service industries, the matching of demand to previously provided supply may be difficult; this will be particularly so in the accident and emergency sector and those which deal with infectious diseases. Thus, any estimate of cost based on the actual time used by a particular type of treatment needs to be grossed up by the amount of time that the staff have to be idle in order to provide such treatment in a timely manner. If there is no 'idle time', higher than normal demand cannot be served.

2. The need for facilities to be located close to the people they are to serve means that the problems of indivisibilities are likely to be numerous. Any large-scale facility, CAT scanners, lithotripters (machines for breaking up gall and kidney stones by ultrasound), kidney dialysis, and others are likely to be underutilized if widely available, but to be largely unavailable to those in whose areas they are not present. The same may be true of specialist teams for micro-surgery, bone marrow transplantation etc. For this reason, a method of reducing spare capacity by importing patients for such teams will have beneficial impacts on costs, and must therefore be accompanied by an appropriate pricing structure. If average costs are charged, there is every incentive for the other districts to obtain their own machines, and overcapacity is ensured everywhere; thus some price below average cost needs to be charged which recognizes that any extra revenue is helping to pay off the cost of the machine. A more distant facility puts extra transport costs on patients and/or the district health authority and should thus attract a lower price.

3. In general the minimum cost of procedures is probably predictable; the error in any estimate of the average time taken comes from the wide range of possible complications. This will make an average useful only for the crudest of budgetary plans. The effect of the high cost, long-stay exception is to make mechanistic planning difficult since each occurrence of an exceptional stay will displace other pro-grammed activities if the organization is working to capacity. In any sequential production process, errors in terms of losses of production time are not self cancelling; the delay in one area has knock-on effects in others, and disrupts their schedules. Since average costs depend on throughput, they are forced up by decline in throughput caused by delays. Thus planning on the basis of average cost for each procedure will underestimate the required capacity by ignoring its interactions with other procedures. For an excellent and accessible introduction to these problems written in the form of a novel, see Goldratt and Cox (1984).

The two key factors in solving this sort of problem are firstly not to plan only on the basis of smooth operation, and secondly, therefore, to have emergency procedures for coping with the exceptional situation. 'Exceptional' situations are of course only just outside the normal situation, because of the interlinked effects of delays at any part of the service delivery process. Thus the more efficient the organization is at matching supply capacity to demand, the more crises of this type it can expect. Unless it has good techniques for coping with such crises it will face unpleasant consequences in terms of cost overruns and in terms of staff morale. One might question whether it is this sort of error in planning that causes the reported problems of finding a bed in so many cases, or whether the problem comes from the staff's efforts at providing an optimal service, neglecting the managers' strictures about capacity. For logical completeness we should also include the possibility that the situation is one of evolving chaos, because none of the government authorities, the local managers or the operational staff understand these processes.

Note that the method used for pricing of joint costs in Reekie and Crook assumes away these problems of error-prone costs and is thus in a very real sense misleading. Marginal costs may only be identifiable *ex post* – and thus by definition cannot be used for planning.

4. The theoretical approach for the pricing of joint products suggested above involves the use of marginal cost and marginal revenue to set the levels of output and hence price. This conflicts with much of the work on health care pricing, which is based on average costs; this includes PPS (the prospective payment system based on average costs for each diagnostic related group) and the recent pronouncements of the NHS Management Executive that prices should: 'be based on full (net) costs so that for a provider's annual assumed volume of service, income from contracts will recover the quantum of cost with no planned cross-subsidisation between contracts' quoted in Harrison (1993, p. 6) from the NHS Management Executive's *Costing for Contracting – 1993/4 Contracts*. Any attempt at using average costs has several perverse results. Firstly, it is impossible to allocate overhead costs other than arbitrarily, and this will inevitably mean that some contracts are favoured. That is just another word for cross-subsidization. The devastating effects of this point are amplified below. Secondly, it prevents the use of marginal cost pricing for the situations in which a facility is working at below capacity. Thus a facility working below capacity will under average cost pricing be higher cost than a facility working near, at, or over capacity and so will lose customers who could attend at only marginal costs. Thirdly, it provides incentives for each area to duplicate investments in expensive facilities, since if it could charge average costs, it could recover the costs of investment in much the same way as the earlier investors could. The costs it would impose by the use of the machinery would, however, not affect the investment costs and would therefore lower

average costs. The pricing should therefore reflect this. Fourthly, it provides incentives for adverse selection; if only average costs are paid, it pays the provider to take only below average cost cases.

The first point mentioned above, the potential for cross-subsidization, needs further amplification. If purchasers are as cost-sensitive as they should be, they will purchase procedures from the lowest cost provider. In some cases this will reflect genuine efficiency advantages of one hospital rather than another; in others it will simply reflect the different accounting conventions used. In the latter case, if all procedures multiplied by their unit accounting costs add up to the total costs of the hospital, choosing those that are cheapest in each hospital and avoiding those that are more expensive will cause losses for *all* the hospitals concerned. Thus, the market will cause the relevant hospitals to lose money. A numerical example may help to clarify the argument.

In Table 13.5 we set out a simple example of the distribution of time required in different areas of the hospital for two operations. These operations are at present performed in two rival hospitals. Each is equally efficient and so the times and staffing required are identical, but because of different methods of charging overheads, they each price the two operations involved differently, as shown in Table 13.6.

Table 13.5 Distribution of time required in different areas of the hospital

Operation	Hours in surgery	Days in intensive care	Days in hospital
1	2	1	10
2	3	1	8

Table 13.6 Pricing of the two operations

Hospital	Surgery hourly charge (£)	Intensive care daily charge (£)	Residual days in hospital daily charge (£)
1	250	230	230
2	350	350	185

The resulting cost allocation is shown in Table 13.7, with the very similar total revenues achieved.

However, even though the hospitals are equally efficient, and have set their prices according to recommendations at average costs, the prices have come out differently, and so if we assume a ruthlessly efficient

Health Authority, wishing to get best value for money for its area, it will presumably choose to buy the operation from the cheaper hospital. The results in terms of revenue are shown in Table 13.8; both hospitals make losses of some £15 000.

Table 13.7 Cost allocation

Hospital	Cost of procedures		Number of operation 1	Number of operation 2	Total cost
	Operation 1	Operation 2			
1	3030	2820	98	100	578 940
2	2900	2880	98	100	572 200

Table 13.8 Revenues, assuming complete switching

Hospital	Number of operation 1	Number of operation 2	Total revenue
1	0	200	564 000
2	196	0	568 400

However, the resulting complete reorganization required, as shown by the changes in surgery hours and hospital bed days, might be impossible in the short run, and might push up costs – it might fortuitously increase efficiency as the result of specialization, but this could not be relied upon. Depending on the organization and the way in which the operations were distributed it might do the exact opposite (Table 13.9).

Table 13.9 Requirements before and after

Hospital	Surgery time		Bed nights	
	Before	After	Before	After
1	496	600	1978	1800
2	496	392	1978	2156

13.5 MARKET STRUCTURES IN THE NEW NHS

The proposed quasi-markets in the NHS are still evolving, and it is the intention of this section to show some of the problems associated with this structure. This should not be taken to indicate either that there were no problems with the apparently monolithic structure of the 'old NHS', or that the problems suggested will automatically prove fatal. It would be the contention of this author that there is no ideal structure in a situation of such information asymmetry. It is however possible to make any structure much less effective than it could be by failing to understand the stimuli it sets up and the rules under which it is likely to operate – for example, by suggesting the use of average costs as discussed above.

As a caveat before embarking on this discussion, one should also bear in mind that the economist's bias is to see everything in terms of self-interest, and with further bias towards seeing self-interest in the sense of financial interest. The Hippocratic oath under such a perspective becomes a means of inducing confidence in the purchasers of health care; a doctor's or nurse's efforts to make a person as comfortable as possible in the certainty that there is nevertheless no outcome likely but the patient's death, and to look after the whole person, not just the dying body, is no more than the creation of goodwill, to encourage further patients to come to that doctor or organization; within the organization it is the clinician's desire for promotion that ensures more than 'perfunctory performance'. The author would view this as a gross oversimplification, particularly because man is a social animal and social conditioning, and the sense of guilt that goes with it, will cause a substantial amount of altruistic behaviour, as will the pleasure to be had from social interaction. Furthermore, as outlined in Chapter 4, man is a learning animal, and stimulation in the sense of new things to do, particularly when they involve extending the range of competence in some coherent way, provide not only the material for promotion but also an intrinsic satisfaction which again ensures much more than 'perfunctory performance'. For a social animal, however, many of these valuable attributes can be negated by the sense that they are not valued by society. Thus the attitude of economists, that all altruistic behaviour is really mere self-interest in the sense of base financial advantage, or the denigration of professional ethics and competence by politicians, is potentially grossly harmful, and makes the cynic's view self-fulfilling.

The cynical view is, however, of value in indicating the direction in which the organizational stimuli are pointing: stimuli such as financial self-interest, or the even stronger stimuli of losing professional standing by being made redundant – the very term indicates much of the human import. If they point in directions opposite to those perceived by the professional as valuable, they will almost always result in stress, through dissonant values, and may result in a retreat into cynicism and the following of financial motives over professional and 'altruistic' motivations. As there is strong evidence that our clinical staff are paid less for a given job than they would be in many other countries, notably the USA, it seems very unwise to push them towards cynical financial manipulation of their jobs. (See Parkin et al., 1987, for evidence that much of the lower expenditure in the UK on health care is the result of the lower relative pay of health care professionals, and Donaldson and Gerard, 1993, p. 169, table 10.1).

The question is what sort of market structures do we expect such arrangements to produce, and on balance do we expect them to have favourable or unfavourable results compared to other market structures? The first division we must come to is that between areas dominated by Health Authority provision, with only a very small proportion of independent fundholding GPs as contrasted with those areas where fundholding is the dominant pattern, or at least a very significant pattern of provision. We consider the first under the title 'Health Authority Hierarchies' and the second under 'Fundholders and Quasi-Markets'. The second division might be between areas where specialist provision is by one dominant hospital, whether it is of Independent Trust status or run by the District Health Authority, and areas where there is potential competition between several hospitals. These are discussed under 'Local Monopolies' and 'Strategies for Trusts Facing Rivalry'.

13.5.1 Health Authority hierarchies

The Health Authority-dominated area represents in economic terms a continuation of hierarchical control with greater encouragement to the purchasing side to shop around for the best bargains. It is thus exactly akin to a conglomerate firm, with internal divisions, but for whom it is always open to go to the market rather than its own divisions for supplies. In this case, however, there is no external market for the final product which will act as a control on value for money of the service. It therefore represents a shift in the internal balance of power within the 'monolithic' NHS in favour of managers and away from the medical staff *per se*. The only unambiguously positive economic element that can be cited is the avoidance of any unnecessary transactions costs in this relatively rigid system, since the search for lower prices and better quality will be within the discretion of the management. However, if they try to behave as if it were a market situation, they may still incur these costs by decree; it should be remembered that these administration costs can reach more than 20% of total costs (experience from the USA cited in Donaldson and Gerard, 1993, p. 30). It is perhaps worth quoting Quam's view on the subject:

> The sheer number of independent agencies for financing medical care each with different eligibility requirements and benefits adds considerably to costs. The aggregation of federal programmes, separate state programmes for the poor, mentally ill, disabled, pregnant women and young children, tax subsidies, veterans' programmes, military programmes, patient out-of-pocket payments, and over 1000 private insurance companies is the financial mechanism for American health care. Every programme duplicates the costs of premium collection, billing, actuarial rate-setting, and financial management. Every health care facility must administer a billing and cost accounting apparatus to link each charge and service incurred to an individual patient. Every workplace must administer a benefits department to evaluate insurers' bids, forecast costs, and collect the premium. (Quam, 1989, pp. 115–116)

The items listed will not differ significantly in the UK where fundholding arrangements predominate. It is thus no surprise that the percentage of costs devoted to administration has already risen from 6% in 1989 to 11% in 1993. Given the twelvefold differences in price quoted by Glennerster (1992, p. 22) this may be money well spent or not.

13.5.2 Fundholders and quasi-markets

Where the GP fundholders dominate, or provide such a significant part of the market that the local specialist providers such as hospitals rely on the fundholders for their viability, there is the semblance of a market. Dissatisfaction with quality of service, delay in treatment or cost may lead to switching of demand to other providers; at the very least there is a threat of such behaviour. This, according to the Glennerster report (Glennerster *et al.*, 1992) was having an effect on improving the notice surgeons took of the GP and of their patients in the areas surveyed. Thus there is strong reason to believe that patients of fundholding GPs will get treatment at both favourable rates and with timely service within the limits of the hospital's capabilities.

Indeed, there is considerable worry about the possibility of a 'two-tier' service developing, with the Health Authority patients receiving routine care, or indeed being caught up in delays when the budgets for each hospital are exhausted, whereas the patients of fundholders will be served well and immediately because they bring in extra revenue to the hospitals. In an environment where budgets are the limiting factor on a hospital's ability to treat, it seems impossible that this should not be so. In the longer run, this should increase the numbers of patients enrolling with fundholding GPs and decrease those with District Health Authority GPs, thereby forcing the whole system towards greater dependence on the internal market.

The second major problem of a fundholding based system, along with the problem of the ethically dubious two-tier service, is the potential it raises for cream skimming. The evidence pointing to the emergence of this problem with Health Maintenance Organizations in the USA has already been mentioned. It is clear that with budget limitations, the long-term expense of patients will become a serious issue. In areas with a high proportion of old people and other risk groups, some effort will have to be made to make the capitation fee sensitive to their probable costs of treatment so that there is at least a reasonable probability that the less healthy members of the population will not be a net drain on the practice's finances.

The other major impacts that fundholding might have are at least likely to be favourable. The pressure to keep costs down, and the shift in the responsibility for such costs to those who generate them should cause ingenuity to be used to find good but cheaper means of treatment. Thus there is likely to be an impact on the distribution of activities between agencies within the health service. For example, the practice might find it cheaper to hire its own chiropodists, physiotherapists or even surgeons to do minor operations within the surgery rather than within the hospital. Such savings could represent the impact of truly lower costs, because of:

1. Underemployed resources in the GP surgery, providing a sort of economy of scope.
2. Lower transactions costs, both because of the lack of need for communication with the hospital or other external agency, and the consequent need for appointments, diagnosis and records within that agency, and indeed the need to sort out which agencies can provide the service and their terms of trade.
3. Lower overhead costs within the practice, due to the lower use of nursing or other staff. For example it may be perfectly safe and practical to operate for removal of skin blemishes simply with the assistance of a practice nurse whereas in hospital a larger team would be used, because it is required for other operations.
4. Surgeons or other practitioners charging lower fees per operation than their gross costs to the hospital.

Alternatively, it may be an accounting problem, whereby the hospital is 'overloading' the overhead costs onto the operation, thus charging too much. This, as shown above, would produce only spurious gains.

It is interesting to consider whether the information flows between patients will be sufficiently good to ensure that fundholders providing better service will gain more patients and hence higher budgets. At present it is illegal for the doctors to make money directly from the surplus they create by good luck or good management; such surpluses have to be put into the practice in the form of investment in equipment and the like. Thus the incentive to attract more patients is only present if the shortage of patients causes problems of availability and scheduling of doctors. Thus if this constraint is not present it is difficult to see how excellence is rewarded – unless by the ability to skim the cream of patients, which seems a socially perverse motivation. It would also have the vice of being self-perpetuating; the practices with the best reputations would get the least costly patients, they would thus be able to lavish more attention on those that required care, and they would thus confirm and increase their reputations for excellence, and their ability to skim off the cream of the patients.

This prediction might be vitiated if the model by Satterthwaite (1979) discussed in section 9.7 is valid. Here the number of doctors and the information is so broadly diffused between members of the public that no consistent picture emerges as to the quality of different practices, and choice therefore becomes more random as the number of practices increases. In the Austrian tradition, any such lack of information would be overcome by market based provision of information; that this might be highly unreliable and taken over by the producer interests can easily be verified by reading a review of a computer product that you know at all well in one of the independent magazines. The author would wager that you would find that the review fails to tell the reader of any of the distinguishing failings of the product, and is likely to be so imprecise about its virtues that no knowledge could be gained. It is furthermore unlikely that this information would emerge in such media, since the interest is strictly local. It therefore has a small market; the information would be expensive to collect, since most people only see their doctors for trivial reasons, and so can only judge whether they are 'nice' or not; thus to get significant information would require large samples. Furthermore, quality is largely a matter of judgement and can only be assessed in a meaningful way by comparison with other similar services; very few people have any basis for making this comparison. It was hoped that 'medical audit' would solve such problems. However, this is most unlikely unless the doctors are grossly unfit to practise, since the inherent variability of severity of disease and hence of outcomes requires large samples of each disease to establish significant differences. Furthermore if results are to be published, and hence to provide a basis for consumer choice, 'games' will be played with the data to influence the results. It therefore implies some sort of government inspectorate, but the risk of causing a loss of confidence by adverse reports would push the agency to produce bland reports which would therefore not inform the consumers. If such a model predicting the randomness of choice is valid, it implies that the rewards for good service are entirely internal to the practice. This implies that behaviour will be rewarded that 'makes the patient feel good' and minimizes the work done and the expense borne by the practice.

13.5.3 Local monopolies

On the second issue of the degree of monopoly among specialist providers seems to hang much of the success of the reforms. Hospital and specialist services account for approximately 63% of the total NHS bill, and we would not generally expect large benefits to flow from creating semi-autonomous monopolies.

In the USA the places that benefited from cost reductions as the results of various cost-containment exercises were those where there was competition between providers (Donaldson and Gerard, 1993, pp. 134–136). This is what we would expect from a market system, in the absence of changes of power between monopolistic purchasers and monopolistic sellers. However, reference to the original work of Robinson et al. (1988) and Robinson and Luft (1988) shows the situation to be more complex than this and once again fits well with what we might expect from the theory of oligopolistic rivalry. In the period before 1983 when the prospective payment systems (PPS) were introduced as a control on prices in hospitals, hospitals faced varying degrees of rivalry depending on the number of hospitals within reach of the patients and their GPs, in other words within their market area. They faced almost no price constraint, however, since payment was by reimbursement of costs and the only challenges permissible under this system were on grounds of being charged for costs not incurred in treatment of the patient. Thus, since every patient was profitable whatever the costs, providing they were insured, the problem was to attract as many patients as possible. To do this the hospitals opted for a full range of services and the relevant high-technology equipment. The incentive to do this was strongest where competition was most vigorous, and so costs were found to increase as the number of competitors within a radius of 24 kilometres increased. Two factors are thought to contribute to the extra length of stay, i.e. to the cost variable measured in the Robinson *et al.* (1988) article. The first is the preference for physicians and surgeons for longer lengths of stay in order to ensure that the patient is on the road to recovery before discharge, and the second is the availability of spare bed capacity in the hospital. The latter is an important attractor since the ability to get patients admitted quickly to the hospital has a major influence on choice. The average length of stay was 17% longer in hospitals with more than 11 'neighbours' than for those with no neighbours, and this ranged from only 7% extra for hysterectomies to 23% for cardiac catheterization. They point out that this scramble to do everything for everyone probably has adverse consequences for the quality of medical care since there is a lot of evidence that particularly for cardiac surgery the success rate is considerably increased if surgeons with practice and experience of the treatment are involved. Thus, general surgeons performing the operations infrequently will generally have lower success rates.

Robinson and Luft (1988, pp. 2678–2679) show these cost effects in terms of cost rather than length of stay, and reveal that the overall movement towards PPS reduced the differences in costs between the 'high competition' (better called 'high rivalry' areas with more than 11 neighbouring hospitals) and zero competition areas, but by no means eliminated them except in California. This is due to the different regulations introduced in California in 1982; purchasers were allowed to select preferred provider organizations (PPOs) on the basis of costs as well as other facilities. This enabled them to bargain with the hospitals where there was competition, but self evidently not where there was no alternative but to using the local hospital. The effect was to reduce the cost difference between monopolistic hospitals and those rivalous hospitals with more than 11 neighbours from 13% in 1982 to a small but statistically insignificant difference in favour of the rivalous hospitals (−1.3%). For the USA as a whole, the difference in costs declined from 27.5% to a difference of 23%. In other areas with particularly strong regulatory regimes – New Jersey, Maryland, New York and Massachussetts – the effects in rivalous areas were also stronger than the overall effect. These areas also contained cost inflation more effectively than other States.

For the UK, we might expect conditions favourable to the reduction or at least containment of costs to be better in the areas with rivalry between providers, since purchasers are allowed, and encouraged, to take out contracts with preferred providers, and hence they can bargain to get a reduction in costs. There is a risk that the shift of power may be too great in favour of the purchasers, since their individual interest is entirely towards true cost containment ('true' because they have no incentive to accept shifting of costs from the hospital directly to their own budgets by, for example, inadequate hospital stays, with consequent problems of treating the patients themselves). However, this cost containment could reduce the amount of money available to carry on research or to purchase new equipment and hence provide more up to date medical care.

A possible solution to the monopolies that will be created in areas where there is a dominant Hospital Trust could perhaps be found for this in terms of 'yardstick competition' (for a fuller explanation of yardstick competition, see Vickers and Yarrow, 1988, pp. 115–119). This involves paying only the national average cost of a service, in this case presumably a procedure of a particular type. This puts pressure downwards on those places which charge higher than average costs, by not meeting these higher costs, and gives a small (?) windfall gain to those charging below the national average cost. Assuming the pressure results in change, the following year, the national average cost has fallen, and the price goes down accordingly, bringing further places under pressure. This therefore has a strong downward pressure on costs. A crucial assumption is, however, that conditions are homogeneous. If London hospitals are indeed situated on very expensive sites, but otherwise are equally efficient, this would cause their costs to be higher, without there being potential efficiency gains to be achieved. Rigid application of the cost formula would however cause a steady drain on the cash available to London hospitals. Furthermore, care would have to be taken that the differences in costs were not due to the problems of allocation of overheads, since the problem of average costs noted above would otherwise be occurring. Finally, we would expect a rapid onset of DRG creep, with the diagnoses being weighted towards the more profitable options, and their severity exaggerated; in fact, the nation's health might take a spurious turn for the worse.

A further area of concern with the development of quasi-markets, particularly where there are both substantial proportions of fundholding GPs combined with a lack of monopoly among hospitals and specialist providers, lies in the potential for the development of a new industry within the health service, of marketing, and particularly of marketing in the sense of negating the effects of adverse publicity. This has been widely reported in the USA and is clearly a source of pure cost increases. Its effects will be cosmetic at best, and may be dangerous even beyond the present desire of the service to conceal its mistakes. The reports of staff contracts with the Trusts in which staff are not permitted to reveal any internal information to the press or outside agencies can be seen as part of this trend. Again, the USA experience is worth considering. Quam (1989, p. 116) states:

> The process of competition itself has increased costs. Hospital spending on advertising increased fivefold from 1984 to 1987. Expenditures by HMOs in Minneapolis, the most competitive HMO market in the nation, on radio, television, and direct mail advertising increased by 50 per cent, to $15 million, between 1984 and 1985 at the height of

market competition. To a British audience, advertising health care like fast food seems absurd. In the US, hospitals advertise on motorway billboards, television and radio. The American College of Surgeons advertises in weekly news magazines such as *Newsweek*, on the value of surgery.

Local monopoly is clearly a more comfortable and potentially more profitable position for a hospital or other provider. It will be interesting to see whether such local monopolies take stringent steps to prevent entry by potential rivals. This might occur by ensuring that all private care was catered for by the hospital rather than by private agencies; this would have a further benefit of ensuring a maximum flow of patients in any given specialty and thereby giving surgeons as much experience as possible in their special areas. It is difficult to see any alternative approach to creating barriers to entry than the simple use of such economies of scale and facilities as are available to the hospital. Should entry occur, it will be a fine judgment as to whether quasi-predatory pricing to eliminate the entrant would be worthwhile. This would almost certainly depend on whether the hospital had existing spare resources and sufficient revenues to keep those resources in use in spite of predatory pricing. Clearly prevention of entry when the hospital is at capacity would depend critically on the ability of the hospital to persuade its health authorities or the Department of Health that it needed the extra capacity – in other words we have once again a situation in which lobbying for favourable regulation would be crucial to the success of the organization.

13.5.4 Strategies for Trusts facing rivalry

A key factor in deciding on strategy for trusts with the misfortune to have rivals within their natural catchment areas is the presence of potential 'product' differentiation. This could be a source of tacit collusion in the form of sharing the market according to different specialties; this would satisfy the health requirement of ensuring adequate specialization and provide each of the participating hospitals with an effective local monopoly. If such arrangements cannot be made, there is a risk of Bertrand-type rivalry occurring, with price-cutting resulting potentially in losses to all hospitals involved. Under such conditions, one of the keys to success will be the ability of the management to use price discrimination by loading as much of the overheads as possible onto those areas of work in which they have relative monopoly, thereby giving themselves more leeway to undercut their rivals in areas in which they wish to develop that monopoly. Intelligent use of the optimal markup formula should help in this aim; the elasticity of demand is likely to be high in those areas where rivalry is intense and may be very low in areas where there is no alternative supply. Care would have to be taken not to charge such high prices that rivals would wish to enter the area concerned; many of these specialisms are geared more to personnel than to equipment, and as such the rival may be able to buy in personnel that will allow rapid entry into a particularly profitable field. Equally, the monopolistic trust should be aware that any such purchase implies the substitution of that specialty for another unless its rival is in a particularly favourable economic position.

If rivalry is intense and prices are likely to be very close, the role of marketing will become paramount. Close prices imply that there is little basis for choice, and therefore that elements of product differentiation are likely to determine that choice; thus creating a good image by favourable articles in local papers and favourable reviews in local radio and television news items, as well as achieving publication in the medical press, are all important policy goals. Countering any adverse publicity is clearly also vital. Maintaining favourable relationships with local GPs, particularly the fundholding practices, and any GPs known to be influential in the health authority's contracting decisions, will be equally if not more important. Techniques might include the provision of enjoyable and useful training courses, particularly those which favour the use of that hospital's proprietary software or medical practices, and careful structuring of decision criteria to favour the hospital's approaches. Under these circumstances, the risk of the development of the marketing officer (aka development officer?) and a complete section of staff devoted to this activity is clear; for the hospital it is going to be vital that the function is adequately fulfilled – whether it is done by a designated group, or by infusing all the relevant personnel with a 'market orientated approach' will depend on the particular circumstances. Furthermore, it represents such a pervasive change of approach that it is almost impossible to isolate the costs and benefits involved.

Human resource policies are also part of this process of product differentiation, involving more than those aspects of training and development which are required under a monolithic structure such as the NHS. Staff may be poached from rivals in order to weaken their ability to provide specialisms, though this is clearly a very dangerous strategy in that it implies providing more lavish remuneration and/or facilities, both of which are liable to push up costs, and the most dangerous situation to get into under oligopolistic rivalry is to become the high-cost producer. Thus the other aspects of human resource policies which may be extremely important are the development of flexible working practices so that the costs of downturns or delays in demand are passed on to the workforce rather than the hospital. Any such strategies have to strike a balance between the requirements of the organization and the requirements of the individuals serving it, to prevent defections by all the best staff to rival providers. The likely outcome of such policies has already been seen under 'contracting out'; the lowest paid are usually those with least economic muscle, and their wages and conditions are very often further depressed. Equally the use of part-time staff has been shown by the supermarket chains to provide people with useful extra income as well as providing a flexible workforce and avoiding various overhead payments for the supermarket. Whether health service workers can properly be used in this way must be open to question, since one would assume that most health service workers have a greater requirement for skill than checkout operators. At the other end of the scale, consultants who by their reputation provide the basis for monopoly power are put in a very powerful position; they could put in claims to appropriate all the 'profits' from that monopoly power. This would, however, then leave the hospital with no leeway on other prices. The human resource manager will therefore be fulfilling a vital role in both controlling these claims to contain costs while at the same time giving the relevant personnel that sense of satisfaction which will keep them in the service of the hospital.

The requirement to use labour efficiently should be of national benefit insofar as it reduces cost and allows skilled labour to be used in more profitable ways.

The pressure to keep costs down and revenues up should ensure that investment is undertaken with a view to developing monopolistic markets of large size; monopolistic markets because the lack of rivalry should lead to relatively favourable prices, and large size because the capital investment will then be more fully utilized. Good purchasing policies by the DHA and fundholders may cause specialist care to be purchased from a much wider area, and care would therefore have to be taken by the providers that they were not assuming monopoly on the strength of transport costs which might now be rather low. This motivation to search for the gaps in provision and the rewards for filling them effectively is one of the benefits of the internal market. Again, with the potential to improve utilization by gaining patients from outside the area, the market development officer will be important.

13.6 SUMMARY

The change in the National Health Service from pure hierarchy to a quasi-market brings with it a different set of motivations. The changes brought about involve the splitting of District Health Authorities into purchasing and providing branches; the purchasing branch is supposed to buy health care in the internal market from whatever sources are most effective in providing it. This includes purchasing general practitioner services from those GPs who do not wish to become fundholders. These GPs have to purchase from the providers of further care with whom the District Health Authority has a contract. The District Health Authorities may also act as providers of specialist care in the form of hospitals and clinics. The DHA provision may be seen as a continuation of the NHS hierarchical forms of organization; it has however the possibility of purchasing from independent sources, which was not effectively the case in the 'old NHS'. Competition for health care comes in two forms:

1. The Fundholding General Practitioners get their budgets directly from the Department of Health, and with them can purchase health care from any accessible provider, or expand the services they provide themselves;
2. There may be competition between the DHA hospitals and the NHS Trusts, which are independent charitable trusts set up within the NHS

to provide health care, usually but not exclusively hospital care, or indeed between different NHS trusts.

At present the difference in the structure of finance between DHA GPs and Fundholders seems to give the fundholders much greater leverage, and hence to promise a two-tier system. This may push more and more GPs into fundholding, and hence increase the number of different purchasers of health care, and thus the numbers who may switch from less satisfactory to more satisfactory providers. It is hoped that this power of fundholding GPs and District Health Authorities will make the whole system more efficient.

In theory none of this affects the patient's right to free care at the point of provision. Experience in the USA with HMOs suggests that fundholding GPs, and indeed DHA funded GPs who do not wish to do more work than is necessary, may skim the cream of the patients. That is to say, they may spare their own budgets by refusing to accept onto their lists the chronically sick or those who represent a considerable risk. If this is allowed to happen, it will tend to be a self-reinforcing cycle, with the GPs with the fittest patients being able to purchase the best care, because of the relatively low demands on their budgets, and hence gaining the best reputations, and hence being able to choose between patients. This is one of the many economic incentives provided by markets in health care. It represents a good example of the workings of such a market with the vital elements being the asymmetrical information. This makes any suggestion that markets will work in an ideal way very suspect. The way such markets work in the USA was given considerable prominence; it gives little confidence in the market system as practised there, but is very useful as an indication of the forms market behaviour might take in the UK.

In section 4 on costs in the NHS, considerable prominence was given to the problem of allocating overhead costs. It was stressed that there is no unambiguous way to do this, unless there is a competitive market which gives market prices, which would force the allocation of overheads within whatever structure is given by those prices. In an imperfect market such as health care, this forces each supplier to operate a system of price discrimination, recovering overheads from the surplus over marginal cost for each procedure. We stressed the dangers of causing accidental bankruptcies or mad reorganizations by using average cost pricing under the conditions prevailing in the new NHS.

Section 5 considers the types of market likely to be created by the new NHS. These are likely to be either monopolies or local oligopolies among the providers of specialist care. Local monopolies will, in the view of this author, need to be controlled by yardstick competition, which implies the development of the National Audit Office or some such auditing department to provide national price figures for different procedures. Charging the national average prices should gradually reduce costs, but with a market such as health care the information asymmetries will potentially allow some evasion of the intentions of the policy makers in even the best designed quasi-market. In local oligopolies, the likelihood is that there will be attempts to monopolize the market, otherwise known as sharing it. Insofar as rivalry breaks out, it should lead to some interesting strategic moves, including the application of price discrimination (which is inevitable if our account of joint costs is correct, but which will here be strategically motivated to enable the monopolization of the market). The vulnerability of the higher cost producer will probably lead to further developments of the 'flexible workforce', with its exploitation of the most vulnerable, and potential high rewards for the consultants and others who help to gain the monopoly power needed to defend each provider's position. It will also lead to the development of marketing in the service; whether the social cost or benefits of this development will prevail will probably never be known since to be successful it seems likely to have to change the whole ethos of the service. Certainly, appreciation of monopoly and oligopoly theory should be of considerable use to the new NHS managers.

FURTHER READING

An excellent introduction to the problems of changes of behaviour under different pricing regimes, including the 'no price' provision of the NHS, is provided by:

Donaldson, C. and Gerard, K. (1993) *Economics of Health Care Financing*, Basingstoke, Macmillan.

Other approaches can be followed up from the references.

References

Akehurst, G. (1984) 'Checkout': The analysis of oligopolistic behaviour in the U.K. grocery retail market. *Services Industries Journal*, **4**(2), 189–242.

Akerlof, G. (1970) The market for lemons: Qualitative uncertainty and the market mechanism. *American Economic Review: Papers and Proceedings*, **51**, 236–244.

Allen, J. (1988) Towards a post-industrial economy? in Allen, J. and Massey, D. (eds) *The Economy in Question*, London, Sage, chapter 3, pp. 92–135.

Andersen, T.F. and Mooney, G.H. (1990) *The Challenges of Medical Practice Variations*, Basingstoke, Macmillan.

Anderson, E. (1990) The ethical limitations of the market. *Economics and Philosophy*, **6**, 179–205.

Andrews, P.W.S. (1949) *Manufacturing Business*, London, Macmillan.

Anonymous (1992) Erster Schritt auf dem Weg zur Privatisierung – Bahnstrukturreform im Bundeskabinett bescholssen. *Internationales Verkehrswesen*, **44**, Heft 7/8 Juli/August, 304–306.

Archibald, G.C., Eaton, B.C. and Lipsey, R.G. (1986) Address models of value theory, in Stiglitz J.E. and Mathewson G.F. (eds) *New Developments in the Analysis of Market Structure*, London, Macmillan, pp. 3–52.

Bacon, R. and Eltis, W.A. (1976) *Britain's Economic Problem: Too Few Producers*, London, Macmillan.

Baumol, W.J. (1977) Macroeconomics of unbalanced growth: The anatomy of urban crisis. *American Economic Review*, **57** (June), 413–426.

Becker, G.S. (1965) A theory of the allocation of time. *Economic Journal*, **LXXV**, 493–517.

Beesley, M.E. (1965) The value of time spent travelling. *Economica*, **32**, 174–185.

Biggadike, E.R. (1979) *Corporate Diversification: Entry, Strategy, and Performance*, Boston, MA, Harvard University Press.

Bishop, M. and Thompson, D. (1992) Regulatory reform and productivity growth in the UK's public utilities. *Applied Economics*, **24**, 1181–1190.

Bliss, C. (1988) A theory of retail pricing. *Journal of Industrial Economics*, **xxxvi**(4) (June), 375–391.

Böhme, H. and Sichelschmidt, H. (1993) *Deutsche Verkehrspolitik: Von der Lenkung zum Markt*, Kiel Discussion Papers no. 210, May, Kiel, Institut für Weltwirtschaft.

Bowbrick, P. (1992) *The Economics of Quality, Grades and Brands*, London, Routledge.

Bowers, P. (1994) Railway reform in France and Germany, Working Paper Series No. 94.4, University of Edinburgh, Management School.

Brealy, R.A. and Myers, S.C. (1991) *Principles of Corporate Finance*, 4th Edn, New York, McGraw-Hill.

Brooks, M. (1992) An investigation into the relationships between time constraints, income and consumption of consumer services. BComm Dissertation, Department of Business Studies, University of Edinburgh.

Butterworths European Information Service (1989) *Butterworths Guide to the European Communities*, London, Butterworths.

Cable, J.R. (1988) Organisational form and economic performance, in Thompson, S. and Wright, M. (eds) *Internal Organisation, Efficiency and Profit*, Oxford, Philip Allan, pp. 12–37.

Cable, J.R. and Schwalbach, J. (1991) International comparisons of entry and exit, in Geroski, P.A. and Schwalbach, J. (eds) *Entry and Market Contestability: An International Comparison*, Oxford, Basil Blackwell, pp. 257–281.

Caves, D.W. and Christensen, L.R. (1980) The relative efficiency of public and private firms in a competitive environment: The case of Canadian Railroads. *Journal of Political Economy*, **88**(5), 958–976.

Central Statistical Office (1992) *The Pink Book 1992: United Kingdom Balance of Payments*, London, HMSO.

Chenery, H.B. (1979) *Structural Change and Development Policy*, New York, Oxford University Press.

Cheung, S.N.S. (1983) The contractual nature of the firm. *Journal of Law and Economics*, **26**, 1–21.

Clarke, R. (1985) *Industrial Economics*, Oxford, Basil Blackwell.

Clarke, R. and McGuinness, T. (eds) (1987) *The Economics of the Firm*, Oxford, Basil Blackwell.

Coase, R.H. (1937) The nature of the firm. *Economica*, **4**, 386–405.

Coopers and Lybrand (1989) *Barriers to Takeovers in the European Community*, London, Coopers and Lybrand. (The Department of Trade and Industry report of the same name and year based on this is much less informative.)

Dean, J. (1976) *Statistical Cost Estimation, Study 4, Department Store*, Bloomington, Indiana University Press, pp. 271–295.

de Jong, H.W. (1988) *The Structure of European Industry*, Dordrecht, Kluwer.

Demsetz, H. (1968) Why regulate utilities? *Journal of Law and Economics*, **11**, 55–65.

Department of Employment (1993) *Employment Gazette, February*, London, HMSO.

Deregulation Commission (1991) *Opening of Markets and Competition*, A report presented to the Federal Government in March 1991 (translated from the German).

Dixit, A. (1982) Recent developments in oligopoly theory. *American Economic Review: Papers and Proceedings*, **72**(2), 12–17.

Dixit, A. and Stiglitz, J.E. (1977) Monopolistic competition and optimum product diversity. *American Economic Review*, **69**, 961–963.

Donaldson, C. and Gerard, K. (1993) *Economics of Health Care Financing*, Basingstoke, Macmillan.

Dorken, J. (1992) RPI-X: Then and now, in Gilland, T. (ed.) *Incentive Regulation: Reviewing RPI-X & Promoting Competition*, London, Public Finance Foundation, pp. 19–48.

Duncan, C., Sams, I.K. and White, P.J. (1992) Part three case study: NHS in crisis, in Duncan, C. (ed.) *The Evolution of Public Management*, Basingstoke, Macmillan, pp. 263–323.

Earl, P. (1983) The consumer in his/her social setting – A subjectivist view, in Wiseman, J. (ed.) *Beyond Positive Economics?* Macmillan, Basingstoke, chapter 10, pp. 176–191.

Earl, P. (1984) *The Corporate Imagination*, Brighton, Wheatsheaf Books.

Earl, P. (1986) *Lifestyle Economics*, Brighton, Wheatsheaf Books.

Elfring, T. (1988) *Service Sector Employment in Advanced Economies*, Aldershot, Avebury (Gower Publishing).

Enthoven, A.C. (1985) *Reflections on the Management of the National Health Service*, Nuffield Provincial Hospitals Trust Occasional Paper No. 5, London, Nuffield Provincial Hospitals Trust.

Fama, E.F. (1980) Agency problems and the theory of the firm. *Journal of Political Economy*, **88**(2), 288–307.

Foot, D. (1981) *Operational Urban Models*, London, Methuen.

French, S. (1986) *Decision Theory*, Chichester, Ellis Horwood.

French, S. (1989) *Readings in Decision Analysis*, London, Chapman & Hall.

Fudenberg, D. and Tirole, J. (1984) The fat-cat effect, the puppy-dog ploy, and the lean and hungry look. *American Economic Review: Papers and Proceedings*, **74**, 361–366.

Geroski, P.A. (1991a) *Market Dynamics and Entry*, Oxford, Basil Blackwell.

Gersoski, P.A. (1991b) Domestic and foreign entry in the United Kingdom 1983–1984, in Geroski, P.A. and Schwalbach, J. (eds) *Entry and Market Contestability: An International Comparison*, Oxford, Basil Blackwell, pp. 63–88.

Geroski, P.A and Schwalbach, J. (eds) (1991) *Entry and Market Contestability: An International Comparison*, Oxford, Basil Blackwell.

Giles, S. (1993) G.P.s get control of total health budget in pilot project. *Health Services Journal*, 11 November, p. 8.

Gilland, T. (ed.) (1992) *Incentive Regulation: Reviewing RPI-X and Promoting Competition*, London, Public Finance Foundation.

Glennerster, H., Matsaganis, M. and Owens, P. (1992) A foothold for fundholding: A preliminary report on the introduction of GP fundholding, London School of Economics Research Report.

Goldratt, E. and Cox, J. (1984) *The Goal: Excellence in Manufacturing*, London, Croom Helm.

Goodwin *et al.* (1984) *Public Transport Demand Elasticities: Background Papers 246*, Oxford, Transport Studies Unit, 11 Bevington Road, Oxford.

Gugenheim, J.-M. and Selosse, P. (1991) *Stratégie des Grands Groupes Français de Transport de Voyageurs*, OEST/DTT/TER. Arche de la Defense, Paris la Défense.

Haenel, H. (1993) *Rapport de la Commission d'enquête chargé d'examiner l'évolution de la situation financière de la SNCF.* Sénat seconde session ordinaire de 1992–1993, No. 335, Juin.

Harrison, A.H. (1993) Health policy review 1992/3, *Health Care UK 1992/93.*

Hay, D.A. and Morris, D.J. (1991) *Industrial Economics and Organization*, 2nd Edn, Oxford, Oxford University Press.

HMSO (1992) *New Opportunities for the Railways: The Privatisation of British Rail*, cm 2012, July.

Hotelling, H. (1929) Stability in competition. *Economic Journal*, **39**, 41–57.

Hughes, C.G. (1980) Estimating employment in hotels and guest houses: a case study of Pitlochry, Tourism Planning Study Occasional Paper 1, Department of Urban Design and Regional Planning, University of Edinburgh.

Hurdle, G.J., Johnson, R.L., Joskow A.S., Werden G.J. and Williams, M.A. (1989) Concentration, potential entry, and performance in the airline industry. *Journal of Industrial Economics*, **XXXVIII**, December, 119–139.

Janelle, D.G. (1969) Spatial reorganisation: A model and a concept. *Annals of the Association of American Geographers*, **59**, 348–364.

Jensen, M.C. and Meckling, W.H. (1976) Theory of the firm: Managerial behavior, agency costs and ownership structure. *Journal of Financial Economics*, **3**, 305–360.

Johnson, P. (1988) The impact of new entry on domestic air transport: A case study of the London–Glasgow route. *Services Industries Journal*, **4**(2), 299–316.

Johnson, P. and Thomas, B. (1990) Measuring the local employment impact of a tourist attraction: An empirical study. *Regional Studies* **24**(5), 395–403.

Johnston, J. (1960) *Statistical Cost Analysis*, Chichester, Wiley.

Kahn, A.E. (1970) *The Economics of Regulation: Principles and Institutions*, 2 vols, New York, Wiley.

Kahn, A.E. (1992a) The purposes and limitations of economic regulation; The achievements and problems of deregulation, in Gilland, T. (ed.) *Incentive Regulation: Reviewing RPI-X and Promoting Competition*, London, Public Finance Foundation, pp. 1–18.

Kahn, A.E. (1992b) Reflections and conclusions on British and US experience: The future of regulation, in Gilland, T. (ed.) *Incentive Regulation: Reviewing RPI-X and Promoting Competition*, London, Public Finance Foundation, pp. 93–104.

Katz, M.L. and Shapiro, C. (1985) Network externalities, competition, and compatibility. *American Economic Review*, **75**(3), 424–440.

Kessides, I.N. (1991) Entry and market contestability: The evidence from the United States, in Geroski, P.A and Schwalbach, J. (eds) *Entry and Market Contestability: An International Comparison*, Oxford, Basil Blackwell, chapter 2, pp. 23–48.

Kester, W.C. (1984) Today's options for tomorrow's growth. *Harvard Business Review*, **62**, 153–160.

Kilvington, R.P. and Cross, A.K. (1986) *Deregulation of Express Coach Services in Britain*, Aldershot, Gower.

Kim, J.-C. (1985) The market for lemons reconsidered: A model of the used car market with asymmetric information. *American Economic Review*, **75**(4), 836–843.

Kuznets, S. (1966) *Modern Economic Growth: Rate, Structure, and Spread*, New Haven, Yale University Press.

Laaser, C.-F. (1991) *Wettbewerb im Verkehrswesen: Chancen für eine Deregulierung in der Bundesrepublik*, Tübingen, JCB Mohr.

Law, C.M. (1980) *British Regional Development Since World War I*, Newton Abbot, David & Charles.

Layard, P.R.G. and Walters, A.A. (1978) *Micro-Economic Theory*, Maidenhead, McGraw-Hill, pp. 304–313.

Leech, D. and Cubbin, J. (1978) Import penetration in the UK passenger car market. *Applied Economics*, **10**, 289–304.

MacDonald, R.L. and Swales, J.K. (1991) The local employment impact of a hypermarket: A modified multiplier analysis incorporating the effect of lower retail prices. *Regional Studies*, **25**(2), 155–162.

Markowitz, H. (1952) The utility of wealth. *Journal of Political Economy*, **60**, 151–158.

Marsh, P. (1990) *Short Termism on Trial*, London, Institutional Fund Managers Association.

Martin, S. (1988) *Industrial Economics*, London, Collier/Macmillan.

Mata, J. (1991) Sunk costs and entry by small and large plants, in Geroski, P.A and Schwalbach, J. (eds) *Entry and Market Contestability: An International Comparison*, Oxford, Basil Blackwell, chapter 3, pp. 49–62.

Mayes, D.G. (1987) Does manufacturing matter? *National Institute Economic Review*, November, 47–58.

McGowan, F. and Seabright, P. (1990) Deregulating European airlines. *Economic Policy*, October, 284–344.

McNicoll, I.H. (1992) Small area input–output analysis: A case study of Shetland for 1987/88. ESU Research Paper No. 25, Scottish Office Industry Department, Edinburgh.

Millward, R. (1982) The comparative performance of public and private enterprise, in Lord Roll (ed.) *The Mixed Economy*, London, Macmillan. (Reprinted in Kay, J., Mayer, C. and Thompson, D. (eds) (1986) *Privatisation and Regulation: The U.K. Experience*, Oxford, Clarendon Press.)

Monopolies and Mergers Commission (1981) *Discounts to Retailers*, House of Commons Papers HC311, London, HMSO.

Niskanen, W.A. (1971) *Bureaucracy and Representative Government*, Chicago, Aldine–Atherton.

Office of Fair Trading (1985) *Competition and Retailing: A Study to Update the 1981 Report of the MMC 'Discounts to Retailers' (HC311)*, London, Office of Fair Trading.

Office of Fair Trading (1988) *The Southern Vectis Omnibus Company Limited: Refusal to Allow Access to Newport Bus Station, Isle of Wight*, A report by the Director General of Fair Trading of an Investigation under Section 3 of the Competition Act 1980, 17th February, London, Office of Fair Trading.

Office of Fair Trading (1989) *Highland Scottish Omnibuses Limited: Local Bus Services in Inverness*, A report by the Director General of Fair Trading of an Investigation under Section 3 of the Competition Act 1980, 17th February, London, Office of Fair Trading.

Official Journal of the European Communities (1989a) No. L33/44 of 4-2-1989, Commission decision of 7 December 1988 relating to a proceeding under Articles 85 and 86 of the EEC Treaty (N/31.906, Flat Glass) (89/93/EEC).

Official Journal of the European Communities (1989b) No. L395/1 of 30–12–1989, Council Regulation (EEC) No. 4064/89 of 21 December 1989 on the control of concentrations between undertakings.

Pappas, J.L. and Hirschey, M. (1987) *Managerial Economics*, 5th Edn, Chicago, Dryden Press/Holt Reinhart & Winston.

Parkin, D., McGuire, A. and Yule, B. (1987) Aggregate health care expenditures and national income: Is health care a luxury good? *Journal of Health Economics*, **6**, 109–127.

Posner, R.A. (1971) Taxation by regulation. *Bell Journal of Economics*, **2**, 22–50.

Posner, R.A. (1975) The social costs of monopoly and regulation. *Journal of Political Economy*, **84**(3), 807–828.

Preston, J. (1988) *Regulation, Competition and Market Structure: A Literature Survey of the Fare Stage Bus Industry*, Leeds, Institute of Transport Studies, Working Paper 267.

Primeaux, W.J. (1979) Some problems with natural monopoly. *Antitrust Bulletin*, **24**, 63–85.

Primeaux, W.J. (1985) An end to natural monopoly. *Economic Affairs*, Jan/March, 14–15.

Quam, L. (1989) Post-war American health care: The many costs of market failure. *Oxford Review of Economic Policy*, **5**(1), 113–123.

Rajan, A. (1987) *Services: The Second Industrial Revolution?* London, Butterworths.

Reekie, W.D. and Crook, J.N. (1987) *Managerial Economics*, Oxford, Philip Allan.

Regierungskommission Bundesbahn (1991) Bericht der Regierungs-kommission Bundesbahn Dezember 1991, unpublished report, Bundes-ministerium für Verkehr, Bonn.

Ricketts, M. (1987) *The Economics of Business Enterprise*, Hemel Hempstead, Harvester Wheatsheaf.

Robinson, J.C. and Luft, H.S. (1988) Competition, regulation, and hospital costs, 1982 to 1986. *Journal of the American Medical Association*, **260**(18), 2676–2681.

Robinson, J.C., Luft, H.S., McPhee, S.J. and Hunt, S.S. (1988) Hospital competition and surgical length of stay. *Journal of the American Medical Association*, **259**(5), 696–700.

Robinson, R. (1988) *Efficiency and the NHS: A Case for Internal Markets*, IEA Health Unit Paper No. 2, London.

Rosen, S. (1974) Hedonic prices and implicit markets: Product differentiation in pure competition. *Journal of Political Economy*, **82**(1), 34–55.

Rosenbaum, D.I. and Lamort, F. (1992) Entry barriers, exit and sunk costs: an analysis. *Applied Economics*, **24**, 297–304.

Sahlins, M. (1974) *Stone Age Economics*, London, Tavistock Publications.

Satterthwaite, M.A. (1979) Consumer information, equilibrium industry price, and the number of sellers. *Bell Journal of Economics*, **10**, Autumn, 483–502.

Scherer, F.M. and Ross D. (1990) *Industrial Market Structure and Economic Performance*, Boston, MA, Houghton Mifflin.

Schoemaker, P.J.H. (1982) The expected utility model: Its variants, purposes, evidence and limitations. *Journal of Economic Literature*, **20**, 529–563.

Schwalbach, J. (1991) Entry, exit, concentration and market contestability, in Geroski, P.A and Schwalbach, J. (eds) *Entry and Market Contestability: An International Comparison*, Oxford, Basil Blackwell, pp. 121–142.

Schmalensee, R. (1978) Entry deterrence in the ready-to-eat breakfast cereal industry. *Bell Journal of Economics*, **9**(2), 305–327.

Scitovski, T. (1976) *The Joyless Economy*, New York, Oxford University Press.

Seale, S.S. (1977) *The Impact of Large Retail Outlets on Patterns of Retailing*, Scottish Office Central Research Unit Paper, Edinburgh, Scottish Office.

Selten, R. (1978) The chain-store paradox. *Theory and Decision*, **9**, 127–159.

Shavell, S. (1979) Risk sharing and incentives in the principal and agent relationship. *Bell Journal of Economics*, **10**, 55–73.

Silver, H. (1987) Only so many hours in the day: Time constraints, labour pools and demand for consumer services. *Services Industries Journal*, **7**(4), 26–45.

Starkie, D. (1984) BR privatisation without tears. *Economic Affairs*, Oct/Dec, 16–19.

Statistisches Bundesamt (1992) *Statistisches Jahrbuch 1992 für die Bundesrepublik Deutschland*, Wiesbaden.

Stigler, G.J. (1971) The theory of economic regulation. *Bell Journal of Economics and Management*, **2**, 3–21.

Stiglitz, J.E. (1979) Equilibrium in product markets with imperfect information. *American Economic Review*, **69**, 339–345.

Stiglitz, J.E. (1986) *Economics of the Public Sector*, New York, WW Norton & Co.

Stilwell, J. (1993) Pathology services. *Health Care UK 1992/93*, 88–96.

Straszheim, M.R. (1974) The determination of airline fares and load factors: Some oligopoly models. *Journal of Transport Economics and Policy*, September, 261–273.

Strong, N. and Waterson, M. (1987) Principals, agents and information, in Clarke, R. and McGuinness, T. (eds) *The Economics of the Firm*, Oxford, Basil Blackwell, chapter 2, pp. 18–41.

Sutton, J. (1991) *Sunk Costs and Market Structure: Price Competition, Advertising and the Evolution of Concentration*, Cambridge, MA, MIT Press.

Thimm, R. (1993) Bonner Bericht: Bahngesetzentwürfe zur Beratung im Bundesrat. *Die Deutsche Bahn*, **3**, 199–204.

Titmuss, R.M. (1970) *The Gift Relationship*, London, Allen and Unwin.

Vayda, E., Barnsley, J.M., Mindell, W.R. and Cardillo, B. (1984) Five year study of surgical rates in Ontario's counties. *Canadian Medical Association Journal*, **131**, 111–115.

Vickers, J. and Yarrow, G. (1988) *Privatization: An Economic Analysis*, London, MIT Press.

Wilde, L.L. and Schwartz, A. (1979) Equilibrium comparison shopping. *Review of Economic Studies*, **46**, July, 543–553.

Williamson, O.E. (1967) Hierarchical control and optimum firm size. *Journal of Political Economy*, **75**, 123–138.

Williamson, O.E. (1975) *Markets and Hierarchies: Analysis and Antitrust Implications*, New York, Free Press/Collier Macmillan.

Wilson, A. (1974) *Urban and Regional Models in Geography and Planning*, London, Wiley.

Wiseman, J. (ed.) (1983) *Beyond Positive Economics?* Basingstoke, Macmillan.

Yamawaki, H. (1991) The effects of business conditions on net entry: Evidence from Japan, in Geroski, P.A and Schwalbach, J. (eds) *Entry and Market Contestability: An International Comparison*, Oxford, Basil Blackwell, pp. 168–186.

Index

Note: Figures are indicated by **bold page numbers**, tables by *italic numbers*